bs has a PhD from the Courtauld Institute of Art. A full-
and occasional translator of Spanish and Latin American
as been obsessed with all things Hispanic since childhood.
Honorary Research Fellow at Glasgow University, and the
n knight of 'The Very Noble and Illustrious Order of the
poon', he divides his time between Britain and Spain. His
t book, *The Factory of Light*, was shortlisted for the Thomas
avel Book Award.

Ghost Train Through the Andes

On My Grandfather's Trail in Chile and Bolivia

MICHAEL JACOBS

JOHN MURRAY

© Michael Jacobs 2006

First published in Great Britain in 2006 by John Murray (Publishers)
A division of Hodder Headline

Paperback edition 2007

The right of Michael Jacobs to be identified as the Author of the Work has been asserted by him
in accordance with the Copyright, Designs and Patents Act 1988.

3

A CIP catalogue record for this title is available from the British Library

ISBN 978-0-7195-6181-8

Typeset in Monotype Bembo by Servis Filmsetting Ltd, Manchester

Printed and bound by Clays Ltd, St Ives plc

Hodder Headline policy is to use papers that are natural, renewable and recyclable products and
made from wood grown in sustainable forests. The logging and manufacturing processes are
expected to conform to the environmental regulations of the country of origin.

John Murray (Publishers)
338 Euston Road
London NW1 3BH

In memory of my grandparents Bethel Jacobs
(1881–1955) and Sophie *née* Solomons (1886–1971), and
for my niece Sophie

Contents

Illustrations

Preface
The Letters in the Attic

My first memory of life is of my grandfather on his deathbed. I had stumbled by accident into a room with heavy drawn curtains, a turquoise Chinese carpet, and a faint smell of joss sticks and French polish. I had just turned three.

The little I remember from this time seems to involve unsupervised wanderings through my grandparents' ivy-covered house in London's Hampstead Garden Suburb. There was my discovery of a red wooden sewing spool in which I got a finger stuck; and there was a more painful encounter with a still hot iron, for which my nanny Woodsie was blamed. As always she had been paying less attention to me than to my elder, and in her view more beautiful and intelligent brother.

But my one and only memory of my grandfather has such a sharpness and wealth of detail that I like to think of it as preceding all other memories of my distant past. I can recall exactly my hesitant pushing open of an upstairs bedroom door; the unexpected sight beyond of an old man hidden beneath a dark olive eiderdown; and the way his kind frail face turned around to encourage me to come closer. In the meeting of our eyes something of his spirit seems to have attached itself to mine. In that transcendental moment it was perhaps determined that I would eventually follow him to a world far removed from the one of security and privilege in which I had first known him.

I returned frequently to that room after his death, in the course of a broader and ever more absorbed exploration of the house at 30 Meadway. Every Sunday afternoon without fail my brother and I would be taken to my grandmother's for the ritual of five o'clock tea, over which she would preside, seated behind a mahogany trolley covered in a gold-embroidered yellow cloth. The tea, invariably Earl Grey or Lapsang Souchong, was accompanied by a plate of cucumber and Marmite sandwiches, a home-made Victoria sponge cake, and muffins kept hot under a silver cover. My grandmother, pausing to ask each guest in turn whether they wanted milk or lemon, poured out the tea into peacock-patterned cups of Spode bone china. A kettle of hot water resting on a gilded bronze trivet ensured that the teapot was constantly full, thus interminably protracting the ensuing polite conversation. Terrified that I was going to be asked to speak, and incapable in any case of getting a word past my talkative brother, I waited in impatient silence for the two of us to be dismissed from our social duties. A nod in our direction indicated that this longed-for moment had finally come.

Sometimes we would rush off to watch *Doctor Who* or *Captain Pugwash* on a pioneering television set bought by my grandfather at the height of his long illness. More often than not, though, the crackling and fizzling of the machine forced us instead to play whatever old-fashioned games we could find tucked away under a coffee table supporting photo albums, and a canvas folder beautifully embroidered with the words 'Radio Times'. Very often I would end up holding an inlaid rosewood box containing the exquisite ivory and bamboo pieces of mah-jong, an ancient Chinese game made popular in the West by British expatriates in Shanghai. Its rules remained incomprehensible to me; but the very act of opening the box, and the subsequent contemplation of the enigmatic characters and symbols that lay within, gave me the sensation of embarking on some mysterious treasure hunt.

Soon the playing of the games under the coffee table gave way to the more compelling activity of scouring each of the house's crammed rooms in search of the enticingly unknown. We came across such strange objects as a somersaulting Chinese acrobat, a nineteenth-century barometer, a bearded old man squatting behind the doors of a miniature pagoda, a case of geometrical instruments of unfathomable use, and the worn wooden model of a sailing ship in which I half-expected to uncover a secret parchment rolled up inside the central mast. But it was only after my grandmother had made us aware of what she called the 'box room' that we realized that our hunt had only just begun.

A confusion of boxes, chests, broken furniture, and gilt-framed pictures lay stacked up to the rafters of an attic reached by a wooden ladder. The boxes were so full that the contents of some of them had spilt out, revealing at our first wonder-struck visit a pre-First World War stamp album with franked images of Queen Victoria and Kaiser Wilhelm II, and pages devoted to long-lost places from French Sudan to Tristan da Cunha. From that moment onwards permission to visit the box room became a regular feature of the Sunday visits, and would remain so after the teas had extended into suppers, and adults and adolescents alike had united to watch – on a newly acquired television set – *The Forsyte Saga* and Kenneth Clark's *Civilisation*.

As I entered my mid-teens, the accumulating discoveries in the box room contributed to my increasingly exotic vision of the family's past. The engravings of Masonic symbols; the invitation to a grand dinner in Hull at which Queen Victoria had been present; suffragette posters drawn by my great-aunt Louise; photos of my grandparents surrounded by Chinese servants; an erotic drawing dedicated to my grandmother by the Catalan artist Galí; a snapshot of her with Samuel Beckett in a Parisian cafe – these and other tantalizing fragments were viewed by me through an imagination that by now was over-steeped in the classics of world literature.

I was in love for the first time, unhappily, and was trying to sublimate this condition by reading Stendhal's *Scarlet and Black*, Alain Fournier's *Le Grand Meaulnes,* and any other French novel I could find with young, impassioned protagonists, when my searches in the attic uncovered a romance worthy of the fictional world I largely inhabited. Attempting to dislodge a box wedged beneath three others, I released an avalanche of crumbling pale blue envelopes addressed to my grandmother under her maiden name of Sophie Solomons. The postmarks were from different parts of the globe, but the handwriting was unmistakably that of my grandfather Bethel. I picked out a letter at random. '*Ma chérie,*' it began, 'I desire you more than ever . . .'

Feeling like an unwanted intruder, I soon put the letter down, but was left wondering how far back this correspondence went, and whether I would be able to trace the love affair to its inception. So I continued rummaging until I came to a letter sent from London on 8 March 1910. It had a slightly formal tone that made me feel less guilty about glancing through its contents, which mentioned 'a delightful tête-à-tête' Bethel had just had with Sophie, his first cousin, who would have been twenty-three at this time. They had apparently not seen each other since they were children. Bethel, who was five years Sophie's senior, was a civil engineer on a brief visit from Paris, while Sophie had recently come to London to train for what she hoped would be a career as a singer. The reunion had taken place at a tearoom on Baker Street, and seemed to have involved much discussion about 'music and literature'.

There were a number of other letters written from Paris and Hull later that year, but, before I could read them, and unravel the process whereby 'Dear Sophie' became 'Ma Chérie', the sound of my name being called from downstairs brusquely curtailed my researches into the budding affair between the two cousins. Hurriedly I collected together all the letters and returned them to their box. Frightened of being thought a voyeur, I would never mention this find, nor even open the box again in my grandmother's lifetime. But somehow my knowledge of the letters' existence, a knowledge which I am sure Sophie suspected, contributed to a growing closeness between my grandmother and myself.

I had reached an age when you feel that sensibilities within a family have skipped a generation, and that you have more in common with your grandparents than with their children. Sophie was someone whose adventurous life epitomized for me the bohemianism to which I had come to aspire. Large-featured and with a commanding, aristocratic presence, she had been a celebrated former beauty whose sophisticated cosmopolitanism went hand in hand with an endearing naivety, earning her during her Paris days the nickname of 'l'innocente d'Irlande'.

Sophie's proverbial innocence had enhanced her reputation as a muse to artists and writers, often leading her into situations that were far from innocent. Even though one of her large, intensely blue eyes had in old age been lost to cancer, to be replaced with a glass one, the remaining eye still had a flirtatious spark to it which must once have given encouragement to numerous famous admirers. Galí, a well-known painter in his native Catalonia, had tried to persuade her to abandon Bethel and run off with him to Spain; James Joyce, inviting her for a weekend to his country property outside Paris, had made a pass at her that had reputedly led to her shocked and abrupt departure.

As she advanced into her eighties, I rebelled against the tradition of going to see her only on Sundays, and started dropping in on my own on my way back from school. Slowly she took me into her confidence, telling me stories about her past that sometimes not even my parents had heard. Speaking with a slight trace of accent from her native Dublin where, she insisted, the best English was spoken, she enunciated each word like an actress speaking a monologue. She talked to me about everything, from her childhood pet goat which had drowned in a vat of boiling tar, to intimate revelations about the pleasures of nude swimming off the French Riviera. And inevitably she talked about my grandfather.

The Bethel who was slowly forming in my mind seemed to be a person totally different from the woman he had married. Essentially cerebral and aesthetic in his pleasures, his principal distraction during the last, illness-dominated years of his life was to lie in bed while my mother, or some other member of the household, read out to him a book on pure mathematics. I found it hard to envisage such a person at ease in the glamorous social world enjoyed by Sophie. Throughout his lengthy retirement, which had begun in his mid-forties, he appeared to me as a quietly apologetic figure overshadowed by a wife who, famously, had shone in the Irish literary circles of Paris and London. Only in his earlier existence as a railway engineer and an infantryman in the First World War did he emerge into the limelight in my perception, and come irresistibly to hold my attention.

What struck me especially was the story of the immense hardships, frustrations and setbacks suffered in the course of his eight-year courtship of my grandmother. In her telling of it, this story took on the quality of an epic quest set against a historical and geographical background of the most compellingly dramatic character. Most vivid of all were the scenes that had taken place in South America, amidst landscapes of the greatest possible extremes. From the interminable, desiccated expanses of Chile's Atacama desert up to the sublime heights of the Bolivian Andes, he had travelled back and forth for nearly four years, dreaming all the time of the woman he had left behind in England. With Sophie as the narrator, I joined Bethel on these journeys, lingering as he did in mountain encampments, desert mining stations, and places with such mythical-sounding names as Anto-fagasta, Cochambamba, and Potosí.

So detailed were my grandmother's South American descriptions that I had difficulty in believing that she herself had never been there. 'I felt almost as if I had,' she explained. 'All through our life together he spoke to me about his experiences in Chile and Bolivia. And, when he was out there, he used to write to me almost every week.' With a feigned innocence comparable to her own, I asked if his letters had survived. 'He was such a wonderful writer,' she replied, 'that I never threw anything he wrote away. I thought one day his letters could be published.' And her replies? 'Oh they were far too personal,' she said in a shocked tone. 'I destroyed them ages ago.'

The moment I had dreaded for so long finally arrived: my grand-mother died during my first year at university. With her death I experienced for the first time the sense of disbelief that someone who had played such an important part in my life would no longer be around, at least not in person. There came also the worry about what would happen to the stored-up memorabilia of her life. My father and uncle, Sophie's two children, were faced with the task of clearing up, in just a few days, a house where, as I knew only too well, countless unsuspected marvels lay hidden among even greater quantities of worthless objects and papers. In the end there was little choice but to throw boxfuls of presumed junk onto a bonfire, to call in a dealer to buy books by the yard, and even to pay someone to remove what was still left after everything else had been disposed of. For years afterwards I shuddered at the thought of what had been unquestionably lost, from a limited edition of engravings by Max Ernst to the stamp album I had so treasured.

I feared that Bethel's letters to Sophie had met a similar fate; and it was not until almost two decades later, well into my father's own, early, retirement, that I heard they had apparently survived in their entirety. My father, who had rigorously written down his daily thoughts and activities since at least his early teens, had maintained a lifelong fascination with the journals and correspondence of other people. Liberated from almost thirty years of work as a company lawyer, he had set himself a series of literary tasks that would somehow bring together the fruits of all his readings and reflections. After publishers had rejected, first a volume of his Pooter-like musings on everyday matters, and then an account of his experiences as an intelligence officer in Sicily where he had fallen in love with the woman who would become his wife, he had edited and typed out his father's letters as a final attempt to fulfil a now desperate desire to have a book published.

I hoped against hope that this time he would be successful. But when he showed me the completed manuscript, with its respectful but misjudged omission of the personal, passionate element that I imagined gave life to the letters, I knew that the literary ambitions which had sustained him throughout his latterly frustrating career would never be realized. Already he was showing the first symptoms of Alzheimer's. Within a few years he would die in a nursing home in the London suburb of Finchley, reduced to a baffled figure in an arm-chair, blankly watching some television chat show, remembering nothing about his past or his family, or at least – I preferred sometimes to think – not having the words any more to articulate what had remained in his once intellectually curious mind.

Bethel's letters, in their complete, original state, came finally into my possession. They joined the two other mementoes I already had of my grandfather: a black hard-cover notebook in which he had fas-tidiously noted down the declension of irregular Spanish verbs; and a chipped plaster life mask of his face which had accompanied me through a succession of student lodgings before finding a safer and more permanent home above a bookcase in my East London study. The notebook had been given to me by my grandmother after I had enthusiastically taken up learning Spanish at school. The mask, dating from the later part of Bethel's life, had ended up after the sale of 30 Meadway lying ignominiously in my parents' attic until I rescued it some years later. I had always been fascinated by my grand-mother's tale of how Bethel had had his face covered in plaster, through which two straws had been placed to allow him to breathe through his nose.

Despite decades of grime which had embedded itself into all the pores and wrinkles, this mask was so extraordinarily lifelike that I could understand why my grandmother had displayed it in the very room where he had died. For her, something of the real person was present in this likeness; and I almost believed that she had wanted it to come into my possession so that Bethel and all she had told me about him would stay alive in my memory. Perhaps too she had intended that this ghostly object would one day be the trigger that would set me off on a journey of discovery into my family's past.

That day came soon after my fiftieth birthday. In the pensive aftermath of the celebrations, I looked up from my desk to stare into the mask's enigmatic eyes, and thought for the first time in ages about Bethel's letters. I had yet to read them in their entirety; and felt a sudden compulsion to do so there and then. Immediately I brought down from its shelf the dusty box in which the letters were kept. The task of going through them had now been made easier by my father, who, with his characteristic businesslike efficiency, had sorted them out into neat chronological bundles held together with rubber bands. Within minutes I was able to find my way back to March 1910, and from there to follow undisturbed the story of my grandfather's rapidly developing relationship with Sophie, and of his solitary departure to South America nine months later.

The story captivated me more profoundly than it ever would have done when I was younger. It was not just the wealth of extra detail that turned it for me now into something more than a romantic and exotically located tale of enduring love. There was also my new perspective as a middle-aged, early twenty-first-century observer, for whom Bethel's unwavering belief in Western notions of civilization and progress seemed as quaintly innocent as his passionate faith in the redemptive power of a single great love.

Drawn ever more deeply into this story, I was soon formulating ambitious schemes of placing it within the context of Western aspirations in South America, and of exploring its possibilities as a poignant metaphor of the hopes and ideals of a world soon to be shattered by the First World War. But it was not just my historical instincts that had been awakened by the letters. Something more basic and also more mysterious had been stirred inside me, something connected with my present circumstances, and the stage of life I had reached. I had begun to think again about my roots.

The strong sense of family connection and duty which shone through the letters touched me greatly. It made me aware of how much

I had confounded the expectations of my upbringing, and of how my own existence lacked clarity of purpose in comparison with Bethel's. I had never had children or a stable job; and I had spent much of my life trying to get as far away as possible from Hampstead Garden Suburb where I had been brought up. A passion for Spain, nurtured since my early teens, had always symbolized for me my longing for independence, and this had recently led to my spending ever longer periods in a remote Spanish village whose inhabitants I had come almost to think of as an alternative family. These letters seemed now to be guiding me back to my real family which I had so long neglected.

The first sign of this was my desire to learn more about my father's ancestors. I realized now how little I knew about them. My brother and I had generally described ourselves as half-Irish and half-Italian. We often boasted about the illustrious role my grandmother's family had played in the Irish Renaissance, and about my mother's distinguished and ancient lineage, which included a notorious medieval count, a pope who had come into conflict with Louis XIV, and Beethoven's great love Luisa Guiccardi (of *Fur Élise* fame). We played down our connection with Bethel's native Yorkshire town of Hull, which did not fit in at all with the glamorous image we had of our ancestry. Yet Hull was where our roots were strongest, for it was Sophie's ancestral home as much as it was her husband Bethel's. The two of them were products of a family that had dominated Hull's history in a way of which I was still unaware.

In looking now into this Hull connection, I only intended to uncover enough of the background to try and understand what had shaped Bethel's personality and those inflexible attitudes of his which he would take with him to South America. I had no wish to get bogged down in the dreary ramifications of genealogy, a discipline often made banally simple today by the use of 'internet research tools'. For a long while I even hesitated before entering a website called 'Jewish genealogy'. My misgivings were not unfounded, for no sooner had I typed into the search box the words 'Bethel Jacobs, Kingston-upon-Hull' than I too would succumb to that same mania for genealogy that had claimed so many of my age.

The instant appearance on the screen of a family tree dating back to the late eighteenth century set in motion a process of discovery as addictive as the searches in my grandparents' attic. One website led to another, bibliographical references mounted, unsuspected new relatives started getting in touch with me, until eventually, one damp December morning, I caught the train to Hull.

It was then that I became conscious of a force other than genealogy that was giving momentum to my quest. As I sat hypnotized by the accumulation of grey and featureless scenes speeding past the train window, a memory, as vivid as my first and only memory of Bethel, resurfaced in my mind and made me wonder whether the journey on which I had embarked would take me not just into the past but into the supernatural.

That memory was of Sophie, and it reminded me that I was travelling to Hull in fulfilment of her last great wish. At the very end of her life, when she had turned for spiritual advice to a rabbi, she started to talk of going back one day to the town she had not seen since her youth. She wanted in particular to hunt down the tomb of a mysterious 'Gentleman Jacobs of Hull', whose name, like that of the district where the family business had been, 'the Land of Green Ginger', became forever lodged in my consciousness.

'When I get better.' she told me as she lay dying in my uncle's house in Nottingham, 'we'll go on a journey together.'

Once she might have suggested Antofagasta, or Cochabamba, or Potosí. But even she, who could scarcely accept her age, was sufficiently realistic to have a less ambitious trip in mind. I waited for her to articulate the word 'Hull', but the extrasensory perception that she had started to acquire in this, her last day, interrupted her train of thought. 'You'd better go downstairs,' she said, overhearing noises imperceptible to anyone else, 'your father has just entered the house.'

The next time I saw her she too had become a spirit. It was 2.37 a.m., the exact hour at which her grandfather clock in London inexplicably stopped. Young, beautiful and smiling, she came into my bedroom at the moment of her death, and left me feeling so calm and happy that I would only be distantly aware a few minutes later of the sounds of my father crying on the landing

As the train went past Doncaster and Loughborough and Wolverhampton, I thought of that night in Nottingham, and of the dying Bethel, and of all the other ghosts which lurked at 30 Meadway. And, as I did so, I murmured as in a litany a series of phrases from the sentence Sophie never completed:

'And we'll go together to Hull. And we'll look for the tomb of Gentleman Jacobs. And we'll go to the Land of Green Ginger.'

ANTOFAGASTA AND BOLIVIA RAILWAY: ANTOFAGASTA TO OLLAGUE SECTION

CHILE

Ollagüe
Ascotán
Conchi
Calama
Pampa Unión
San Pedro de Atacama
Chuquicamata
Oficina Araucana
Oficina Prat
Chacabuco
Mejillones
Baquedano
Arturo Prat
Antofagasta

0 miles 50
0 kilometres 80

BOLIVIA RAILWAY: ORURO TO COCHABAMBA SECTION

BOLIVIA

Cochabamba
Vinto
Parotani
Buen Retiro
Talcapayo
Orcoma
Arque
Changolla
Aguas Calientes
Coma Coma
Banderani
Oruro
La Paz
Río Mulat-

0 miles 50
0 kilometres 80

BRAZIL
URUGUAY
Montevideo
Buenos Aires

BOLIVIA
Lake Titicaca
La Paz
Viacha
Oruro
Cochabamba
Pass of Sucre
El Condor
Potosí
Río Mulato
Salar de Uyuni
Uyuni
Averoa
Ollagüe
Ascotán
Calama
Chuquicamata
San Pedro de Atacama
Mejillones
Baquedano
Antofagasta
Arica
Iquique

Caldera
Copiapó
La Calera
La Ligua
Valparaíso
Santiago de Chile

PERU

ARGENTINA

CHILE

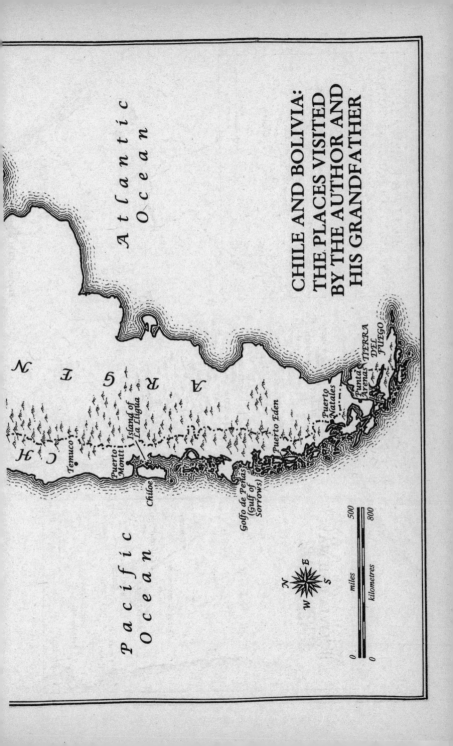

CHILE AND BOLIVIA:
THE PLACES VISITED
BY THE AUTHOR AND
HIS GRANDFATHER

I

To the Land of Green Ginger

———◆———

THE TRAIN ENTERED Hull's Paragon Station under a dreary, unyielding sky. Droplets of rain, as if wrung from a giant, sodden cloth, began moistening the carriage windows in a half-hearted gesture of welcome. 'Thank you for travelling today with GNER', announced a cheery voice as I took my place alongside the morning commuters, waiting impatiently for the doors to open and release us all into the greyness.

My grandfather Bethel had devoted much of his life to the construction of railways. He came from a family which would have considered the railway as an eloquent symbol of progress. But those were straight-thinking days when the train traveller had little choice other than to purchase either a single or return ticket. They were days that seemed to me now as remote as the prospect of limitless sunshine.

An unwise decision to combine my sentimental pilgrimage to Hull with family visits to Nottingham and York had plunged me into the midst of a labyrinth where vast amounts of mental energy had to be spent working out the optimum combination of routes managed by entirely separate private companies. All of these offered a no less bewildering number of 'fare types', including 'apex returns', 'super saver returns', 'weekend returns', and a rogue category known as 'special offers', which offered the perplexing news that it would be cheaper to get from London to Edinburgh than from London to Hull.

The city to which I had finally come, carrying a wad of tickets costing more than a week's holiday in the Mediterranean, seemed to reflect this muddy confusion. Though Bethel's Hull had been an exemplary modern city, with 'model' neighbourhoods and a port that ranked with that of London as Britain's main point of arrival from mainland Europe, extensive Second World War bombing, followed by massive unemployment and a haemorrhaging of its population, had helped to change all that. The tourist brochure I picked up in the station referred to Hull as a 'vibrant riverside city'; but this was not how it was seen by its most famous resident of modern times, Philip Larkin, who had difficulty in thinking of 'just one nice thing' to say about it. 'Oh yes,' he eventually blurted out, 'it's very nice and flat for cycling'.

Walking out of the station in search of the Hull of my ancestors, I briefly recalled a more positive era in the city's history at the sight of the former Station Hotel, where Queen Victoria had been lavishly received on her visit to Hull in 1854. But a look inside the blandly revamped lobby was insufficient to bring back the past, so I went back on to the street and caught a bus heading eastwards, towards the docks and ferries and the thoroughfare of the Hedon Road. The rain had turned by now into a steady drizzle as I sat behind the driver, straining hard to catch a distant glimpse of Hull's latest attraction, a jagged glass and steel bulk known as the Deep ('the world's only submarium'). In the process I almost missed the prettified remaining buildings of the old riverside town, which came suddenly and momentarily into view, pathetically anachronistic in the context of the encroaching concrete and suburbia. Then the clouds descended lower still, obscuring everything.

My first obligation was to find the tomb of Gentleman Jacobs of Hull. But though my library researches had convinced me that the man in question must be my great-great-grandfather, the original Bethel Jacobs, I had no idea whether his tomb had survived, or where it would be if it had. To make matters worse, there was no proper Jewish community left in Hull to help me. The Jews who remained in the city had moved into outlying districts, leaving not a single functioning synagogue in the centre. A local historian with whom I had corresponded suggested I should take a look at the Jewish tombs located off the Hedon Road. He warned me, though, that the road had recently been widened into a dual carriageway, and that notices had been posted beforehand advising the descendants of those buried there to come forward.

The bus driver left me in the rain next to what turned out to be the muddy, bull-dozered wasteland marking the site of the former Hedon Road cemetery. I was about to retrace my steps back to the city centre when I noticed further down the road a fenced-off patch of green between the dual carriageway and a street of late nineteenth-century suburban houses.

'That's the Delhi cemetery,' a solitary passerby informed me, 'but it's never open these days.'

Through the barbed wire and thick, overgrown hedge I thought I could make out a Star of David and some Hebrew lettering. I encircled the perimeter, looking in vain for an easy way in. I had started to climb a metal fence topped by a roll of barbed wire when a young man with cropped hair and a pierced lip nonchalantly appeared. He was wearing overalls and carrying a key and a bag of gardening implements. Oblivious of my presence, he opened the gate and went straight in. I asked if I could follow him. He shrugged his shoulders in a gesture I took to mean yes. Putting down his bag next to a modern tomb, he began clipping the grass around it.

'I'm looking for the tomb of one of my ancestors,' I volunteered.

'Feel free,' he muttered without looking up from the ground.

Awkwardly I decided to try one final question on him:

'You wouldn't know of the tomb of Gentleman Jacobs of Hull?.'

He made a noise that could have been variously interpreted as a snort or a chortle, and carried on clipping.

My grandmother Sophie had led me to believe that the tomb I was now looking for was a monument locally cherished, impressive in its proportions, and bearing the name by which its subject was popularly remembered, 'Gentleman Jacobs of Hull', inscribed between quotation marks. I had somehow got it into my head that the man had acquired this title for being an extravagant dandy, and I had accordingly invented for him a colourful and irreverent personality at odds with the staidness of his background. However, my recent research into Jewish genealogy had failed to uncover such a person among the Jews of Hull. What I had discovered instead were Jacobses who had been prominent Hull citizens, driven by an overriding sense of civic pride, and anxious to be thought of as gentlemen as their way of becoming accepted into Christian society.

In 1290, over 200 years before Spain undertook a similar course of action, England expelled its Jews. In 1655 Oliver Cromwell successfully pressed for their re-admittance. Though my grandmother, as an

Irish patriot, could never forgive Cromwell for having annexed Ireland to England (and indeed she often disparagingly referred to the English as the 'Cromwellians'), as a Jew she at least had to acknowledge him as probably the first national leader to champion her race.

Thanks to Cromwell, a growing number of Jews started to arrive at the port of Hull, a few of whom decided to look no further in search of a permanent English residence. By the end of the eighteenth century, a small but prosperous Jewish community had been formed at Hull, among whose forty or so members was the first known ancestor on my father's side, Israel Jacobs, whose origins I could trace no further back than to Scarborough. Though he was the only Jacobs I had come across to be officially recorded as a 'gentleman', there were two reasons that had persuaded me that it was not him but his son Bethel whom my grandmother had known as 'Gentleman Jacobs of Hull'. Not only did Bethel become one of the Hull's grandest nineteenth-century residents; but also it was in honour of him that two of the most important men in Sophie's life had been named: the cousin whom she would later marry, and a brother who would achieve celebrity both as a gynaecologist and as the one Jewish player in the Irish Rugby team.

The original Bethel was the sort of larger than life patriarch whom every family would be proud to have as a progenitor. He was a model of civic virtue, as outwardly perfect as some ancient Greek hero. And it is easy to imagine how my grandfather, when overcome in his travels by an occasional despair and feeling of futility, would find sustenance in the fact that he shared a name with someone who had epitomized unswerving ideals and a limitless faith in the future.

The life of Bethel, son of Israel, had coincided significantly with the dramatically rising fortunes of a city which, from having a population of 29,500 in 1805, had more than doubled in size by the middle of the century. From an early age Bethel must have had instilled in him the idea of civilization as a continuous pattern of improvement, with each generation making a significant advance over the preceding one. In Bethel's case he would have been faced with the challenge of following and superseding the example of a much-respected father. He would achieve this aim effortlessly. Taking over from his father Israel as a jeweller, clockmaker and silversmith, he built upon the firm's rep-

utation to such an extent that he received a royal patent after designing the gold plate displayed in the Station Hotel on the occasion of
Queen Victoria's stay there in 1854. At the same time he ensured that
the family's already high standing within Hull's burgeoning Jewish
community became unchallenged. Marrying into the family of the
Jacobs's main Jewish rivals in Hull, the Lyonses, Bethel laid the foundation stone of a new synagogue, campaigned for the creation of a
Jewish school, was warden for many years of the Hull Hebrew
Congregation, and brought a greater respect than ever to his community through his promotion of religious tolerance and his remarkable
influence on Hull generally. As a result of the overwhelming number
of committees he headed, the societies of which he was president, and
the exalted positions he held, ranging from town councillor to Master
of the Humber Lodge of Freemasons, Bethel Sr did perhaps more than
anyone to make the city's Jews become thought of as gentlemen.

However, mere social and professional status was not enough for
Bethel. His vision was of a world where material advancement had to
be accompanied by physical and spiritual well-being, as well as a keen
social and patriotic consciousness. Actively concerned with the lot of
the poor, a governor of the Hull workhouse, a passionate education-
ist, a benefactor of limitless charities, president of the Hull Mechanics'
Institute, and a founding member of the city's public library, he was
also a fervent patriot who responded to the threat of invasion from
France's Napoleon III by becoming a lieutenant in the local battalion
of the Rifle Volunteers. As a sportsman, he excelled in archery, and
was a treasurer and prizewinning member of the Hull Archers, at one
of whose meetings he was called upon to sing a song to the sport
written by himself. Above all, he found fulfilment in the cultivation
of the arts and sciences.

Educated in Leipzig, Bethel developed as an intellectual all-rounder
of a kind almost impossible to conceive of today. Talented both as an
artist and as a musician, he was a founder and first president of the
Hull College of Art, and participated as a flautist, cellist and singer in
numerous charity concerts. His interest in the latest scientific developments was reflected in the 'electrical time ball for the benefit of sea
captains' which he set up outside his shop; and it led to Hull's successful bid to hold the twenty-third annual meeting of the British

Association for the Advancement of Science. When the Great Exhibition was being organized in 1851 at London's Crystal Palace, the man put in charge of the Hull area committee was, unsurprisingly, Bethel, whose astonishingly versatile background made him also an ideal president of the Hull Literary and Philosophical Society, where he would address crammed halls on subjects such as 'the Nature and Characteristic of Animals mentioned in the Old Testament'.

Sadly, not a single likeness has come down to us of this near unimaginable human paragon, the one bust of him, presented to Hull's Royal Institution, having suffered the fate of the building itself when it was destroyed by bombing during the Blitz. To find a description of the man under the daunting list of titles and credentials, one has to turn to the vague and lofty words of praise penned at his death in 1869 by the obituarist of the *Jewish Chronicle*:

> He was a man of intense earnestness, and although he was true to his faith, he was most tolerant in religious matters and full of strong sympathy for all that was true, noble and good. He was admired for the high consistency of his life. He took great interest in local subjects, yet intensely enjoyed his own family circle; possessing a large fund of animal spirits, he was, in return, beloved . . . He possessed a fine physique, and a powerful frame.

Many hundreds of spectators, according to this same article, turned out for his funeral. The hearse was followed by a guard of honour formed of officers of the Hull Volunteer Rifle Corps, behind whom came sixteen mourning carriages, thirty cabs, and several private carriages. I tried to imagine this procession making its way down the Hedon Road towards the half-forgotten cemetery I was now scouring in the hope of encountering a Gentleman Jacobs. While the enigmatic gardener silently pursued his task, I headed towards an obelisk which stood out on the horizon, separated only by a hedge from the dual carriageway beyond. After a hundred yards or so, it became depressingly obvious I had reached a part of the cemetery reserved for the Jews.

The jagged, swastika-daubed remains of smashed headstones lay piled up as in an expressionist composition. Curiously, the white marble obelisk that had caught my attention rose up in dignified isolation behind all this, damaged not by vandalism apparently but by years of neglect. The long inscription was so worn as be largely inde-cipherable, except for a handful of fragmentary words such as 'fellow townspeople' and 'sincerely lamented', and a phrase in bolder letter-ing which sent a sudden tingle through my body: 'Sacred to the memory of Bethel Jacobs, Died 26th December, 1869, Aged 57.'

I paused for several minutes before this, as if waiting for some post-humous blessing from the man whom I had come to think of as the founder of a dynasty now long into its decline. The monument itself, with its great presence, was undoubtedly the one my grandmother had been so eager for us to find. But now that I was here, I was anxious to scrutinize the surrounding tombs to see if the remains of any other Jacobs had managed also to survive demolition, desecration and abandon.

All that I came across were the tombs of two of Bethel's eleven chil-dren. A simple rounded slab commemorated the short-lived Edward Lewis Jacobs, who inherited the family business and had apparently showed a gift for music. In contrast, a plinth in shiny Cararra marble, unworn by time but thrust dramatically askew by erosion, had been erected for Joseph Lyon Jacobs, the eldest of the children, and the one destined to be his father's true successor. Though Joseph had chosen the path of law, he had assumed many of Bethel's titles, and had been similarly assiduous in his charity work and intellectual pursuits.

'True to the tradition of his father's House,' read his epitaph, 'He led a life inspired by the loftiest principles of Honor and humanity. He employed his rare gifts and attainments for the benefit of the Townsmen irrespective of race or creed.' But Joseph too had died young. 'His virtues had endeared him to many a heart, and his demise at the age of 45 was mourned as a widespread calamity.'

I remembered that Joseph's death had not been quite in the spirit of his life. Mysteriously, he had fallen from an upstairs window while playing a game of billiards.

Trying to recall what else I knew about Bethel's children as I waited for a bus to take me away from the Hedon Road, I was struck by one salient feature common to them all: they were extraordinarily high achievers. I had always assumed when younger that talent in Sophie's family had largely resided in her uncle Charles Mattathias Jacobs (the third eldest of Bethel's children), an early mentor of my grandfather who had made his name and fortune by creating the world's first underwater tunnel under New York's Hudson River. But the more I found out about Charles's brothers and sisters, the more remarkable they appeared.

There was, for instance, Sophie's mother Rosa, whose dark portrait had hung in the stairwell of 30 Meadway, and had made me feel I was in the presence of an empress with little tolerance for human failings. Known in the words of one of her contemporaries for her 'high culture and powerful intellect', Rosa was an excellent linguist who wrote poetry, played the piano very well, and had a passion for the theatre. After an extended education in France and Germany, she had forged my family's Irish link by marrying in 1876 an Irish optician celebrated in Joyce's *Ulysses* as Dublin's honorary Austro-Hungarian consul. Their grand Regency house at 26 Waterloo Road, where Sophie and her three siblings were brought up in an atmosphere of lively intellectual activity, was a place I had made a point of seeing on my last visit to Dublin: a strange twist of fate had turned this former nest of Hapsburg sympathies into the Romanian embassy.

And then there was my grandfather's father, Benjamin Septimus Jacobs, the only one of Bethel's children after Joseph to have made any mark on his native Hull, where he had perpetuated the family tradition of undertaking good works and holding impressive titles. I had some idea of his talents from the countless charming illustrations and cartoons that had filled the boxroom at 30 Meadway; but I had no inkling of his work as an architect, his true profession. Before looking for the address I knew so well from my grandfather's letterheads, I was keen to see Benjamin's proudest architectural achievement, the former synagogue on Linnaeus Street. If, of course, I ever managed to be rescued from the no man's land in which I now seemed to be stranded.

For over half an hour I had been waiting alone at the bus stop. The rain had fortunately stopped, but the weather was turning colder, and the sky had assumed a chilling, leaden glow. I continued pacing up and down for a while, trying to keep warm as midday approached, and the few hours of daylight became fewer still. Then I gave up on the bus and hailed a passing taxi.

The driver, a burly, talkative man with yellow hair, looked briefly puzzled when I asked to be taken to 'Linnaeus Street'. 'Here,' he said, correcting my over-classical pronunciation, 'we call it 'Linnie's Street.' He knew of the synagogue, and indeed fondly remembered the place when it was still functioning, a memory that gave him the excuse to start lamenting the decline of Hull in recent years. I murmured sympathetically, while casting my mind back to the changing Jewish Hull of Benjamin's time.

The city's Jewish population had by then begun to swell alarmingly. Vast numbers of Jews were escaping from Eastern Europe with the aim of reaching America; and the cheapest way of doing so was by way of England. In 1881, the year of my grandfather's birth, no less than 50,000 Jews had arrived at Hull. Between 1892 and 1894 this number would rise to 126,645. To the jeers and taunts of children shouting, 'Ruskies, Ruskies!' most of the immigrants would be conducted by horse-drawn buses to the Paragon station, from where they would travel by train to the port at Liverpool. However, many of the Jews had turned up at Hull with nothing more than the clothes they were wearing. Unable to travel on any further, they ended up living in Hull, often under circumstances of the utmost misery.

The streets off the Hessle Road, along which we were now battling against the pre-Christmas traffic, were compared by one late nineteenth-century journalist to 'the foulest slums in Constantinople'. In 1880, in an attempt to alleviate such poverty, and to provide assistance to those Jews who wished to continue their journey to America, the Hull Hebrew Board of Guardians was founded. Joseph Jacobs, its first president, was succeeded in 1883 by his brother Benjamin who, nearly twenty years later, became involved in a scheme to build a new synagogue and Hebrew school to serve the poorer elements of the city's Jewish community. Tellingly, when in 1902 his design for the synagogue had been presented and accepted, it had almost immediately to be modified to accommodate the still rapidly growing congregation.

We turned off the Hessle Road into a street dominated by the concrete blocks and towers of 1950s council estates. 'Linnie's Street,' muttered the driver as we pulled up next to the only two buildings in the street of an obviously earlier period. In darkened red brick, and joined together by a closed ironwork gate, they looked like the entrance to a collegiate courtyard. A round blue plaque with the words. 'Built in 1902 to a design by Benjamin Septimus Jacobs,' indicated that I had come to the right place. The buildings must have been those of the Hebrew school that had formed part of the synagogue complex. I spoke into an entryphone and was answered by a suspicious voice reluctant to let me in. I said I was the great-grandson of Benjamin Jacobs. The gate opened automatically, and I walked through a shaded courtyard towards the former Western Synagogue.

It was an eclectic building of vaguely Byzantine inspiration, with stained-glass front doors, an upper row of narrow rounded windows, and corner towers with steeply pitched slate roofs. Attached to the façade was a foundation slab recording that the building had been opened on 25 September 1902 by 'Osmond Elim d'Avigdor Goldsmid Esq'. I knew him as the son of Benjamin's sister Henrietta, who had married into the family of the first English Jew to be elevated to the nobility. But the slab described him simply as 'grandson of the late Bethel Jacobs'.

I went inside, to be confronted not by the grand gilded hall I had imagined but by the modern low-ceilinged reception area of an organization calling itself 'the Judaeo-Christian Society'. The man at the desk showed me some information explaining the society's admirable intention of fostering better relations between Jews and Christians. More worrying were the various Zionist quotations. I wanted to leave quickly. My taxi was waiting at the gate, and, in any case, there seemed nothing to be gained from seeing more of the modernized interior. I turned round to the door; and as I did so a tall man with a broad-rimmed hat and a ponytail strolled in from the courtyard. He looked like a cross between an art school teacher trying to appear Bohemian, and an ageing rock star confined to playing to expatriates on the Costa del Sol.

'Doug,' the receptionist said to him, 'This is Michael Jacobs, the great-grandson of Benjamin.'

'You don't say!' exclaimed Doug in a tone of excitement which must once have greeted those claiming direct parentage from the late Bethel Jacobs. As he held my hand hard for a few seconds, I could not help wondering what such a person was doing in the apparently strait-laced Judaeo-Christian Society.

'I'm the society's archivist,' he announced, 'You must come upstairs to see the exhibition I've put on about your great-grandfather.'

The portrait of a heavily mustachioed man whom I had seen before without knowing him to be Benjamin, and the many photos of important public buildings he had erected in Hull, were not the only surprises awaiting me upstairs. 'A relative of yours was here the other day,' Doug told me. 'He was the grandchild of Benjamin's brother Charles.'

The idea that some person unknown to me was on the same trail that I was following was slightly unnerving, and my first thought was that my journey had already begun taking an esoteric turn. What made it so eerie was that I was absolutely sure that no such relative of mine existed. According to the family tree, and to what I had always been told, Charles Jacobs had married but had died childless.

Thinking more carefully about this, I decided that either Doug had made a mistake, or else my outwardly perfect ancestors harboured some dark family secret. Doug, noting my pensive, slightly perplexed expression, riffled through a filing cabinet and scribbled down 'the telephone number of your relative'. I politely put this away in my pocket but without any immediate intention of using it. It was probably just another of those multiple diversions laid out to entrap addicts of genealogy.

Now I needed to get going. The taxi meter was running outside, and I was anxious to hunt down my grandfather's family home while it was still light. I asked Doug if the place was still standing, but he did not know, though he did comment when he saw the address: 'Very posh, very posh.'

The taxi driver thought differently. Two Westbourne Avenue had been one of the city's most fashionable addresses when the street had been built in the late 1890s. And the neighbourhood had remained what he called a 'good' one until very recently. But in the last few years it had gone 'seriously downhill', with large Victorian family homes, once big enough for servants, being divided up into flats 'filled with Kosovans, Iraqis and other flotsam and jetsam'.

We entered a district of imposing residential houses leisurely arranged along wide green avenues. The red brick house to which Benjamin, his wife Isabel, and their three children had moved in 1898 was still there. It might have outwardly lacked the grandeur of my grandmother's Dublin residence; but it conveyed a mixture of prosperity and good taste. A hint of ostentatiousness in the ornamentation was mitigated by the rectangular simplicity of black and white bay windows imbued with something of the spirit of Charles Rennie Mackintosh. I got out of the taxi and walked through a gap in the holly hedge where a garden gate had obviously once stood. Further changes became apparent on reaching the glazed front door. A broken panel of glass had been replaced by a piece of off-white board, next to which was a scattering of doorbells inscribed in marker pen with different apartment numbers. I rang each of them in turn, but no one was at home. Through a gap in one of the lace curtains, I noticed a sitting room covered in toys, and a partition panel crudely interrupting the egg-and-dart moulding on the ceiling.

The improvised, impermanent look of the interior seemed ironic when I reflected that the house had been the one stable feature in my grandfather's life during the long period when he had struggled to establish his career. The youngest of Benjamin's children, and the only boy, he had been seventeen at the time of the move here, and on the point of starting training as an engineer. Soon afterwards he became apprenticed to his uncle Charles in New York, and then followed him to Paris, where he would stay on in the forlorn hope of a job. For nearly a decade he would flit between Paris, London and Hull, barely furthering his career, but nurturing a love of French culture that he shared with Louise the sister of his to whom he was closest in age and sympathies.

Louise was a painter of outstanding promise; and it was thanks to a sketchbook of hers which I had found at 30 Meadway that I could now fill out the sad interior in front of me with images from its former existence: Isabel seated at the 'boudoir' grand piano my grandparents would inherit; the maid in her apron carrying in a tray of teacups; her elder and similarly unmarried sister Ethel, immersed in a book; the portly Benjamin peering over his lorgnette to draw the beloved family dog Pips, whom Louise, later a victim of dementia, would end up thinking she had become.

Throughout Bethel's years of travelling backwards and forwards from Westbourne Avenue, Louise would often be with him, inspiring in him the constant hope that the creative talents of the Jacobses would find through her their finest fulfillment. She had begun painting landscapes and still lifes which had an uncanny, magical luminosity. When, early in 1910, Louise exhibited at the Paris Salon and was favourably compared in the *Figaro* to the once highly regarded French artists Léandre and Belleroche, Bethel confidently predicted that he would soon be 'basking in her reflected glory'. He would never have imagined that fame would always elude her; and that what little recognition she gained would be eclipsed by the success of Sophie's elder sister Estella Solomons, Louise's inseparable painting companion. Bethel, I suspect, far preferred Louise's calm and measured manner of painting to Estella's turbulently romantic and uneven style, which he probably saw as symptomatic of the latter's gregarious, rebellious, and – for him – corrupting personality. But, as he was also aware, if it had not been for the friendship between the two women he might never have been encouraged to go to that rendezvous on Baker Street whose consequences would transform his life.

Tearing myself away from the window of the house, and from all the multiplying memories evoked by Louise's sketches of its interior, I told the taxi driver to take me back to the city centre, where I still had a number of other sentimental errands to carry out. He left me on the edge of a square named after Queen Victoria. There, among a sorry scattering of eclectic structures expressive of the civic confidence of another age, I spotted an impressive, Dutch-inspired red stone building I was now able to identify as the work of Benjamin Septimus Jacobs. I experienced a sudden surge of pride.

I strode across the square and into the pedestrianized Whitefriargate, a street lined with branches of those ubiquitous chain establishments that give to modern British towns a disorienting sameness. I was almost surprised when, halfway down the street, I came across a café that was neither a Starbucks nor a Seattle Coffee Company. A glance at the street number made me more astonished still: I had reached the clock and jewellery business of the original Bethel Jacobs, the family patriarch.

While sipping a coffee inside, I thought again about my grandfather's years in Hull. My coming today to the city had made me appreciate more than ever just how oppressive the weight of family precedent must have been for him. How could he possibly live up to his forebears, let alone surpass them? This was a dilemma that could only have intensified after he had fallen in love with someone who shared the same dominating ancestry. The pressure on him now to succeed must have become unbearable.

He might once have thought that the prestige of his family name, and the wealth of his important contacts, would have helped him in this, and given him a head start over so many of his contemporaries. However, one of his recent bitter realizations was that all this counted for little when it came to finding a job as an engineer. This was a time when Western-trained engineers were more in demand than ever; but the competition for jobs was similarly intense. In comparison with his uncle Charles, Bethel was not someone who was good at self-publicity. Nor could he have been helped by the unworldly attitude that he appeared at times to have towards his profession.

'My ambition,' as he claimed to Sophie in one of his first letters to her, 'does not run very high these days. Some quiet good work and no one to bother me and life in the open air and I will be more than satisfied.'

But the simplicity of these professed wishes was at variance with the complexity of the situation he was now landed in. He needed to prove himself professionally before being able to fulfil his dream of marrying Sophie; and yet to achieve this aim he would almost certainly have to be posted for a good three years to a distant country. In his letters to Sophie he mentioned the possibility of there being work for him in Russia, India, Brazil, Argentina, and even Canada. However, the rejections accumulated; and though this gave him time to make firmer his still very tentative relationship with the woman he loved, it also made him fearful of ever being in a position to marry. By the summer of 1910, he was telling Sophie that she was the only person in whom he could confide, his sister Louise having tired of his mood of acute self-pity. Luckily, just as despair seemed imminent, the perfect solution to his problems presented itself in the unexpected availability of a job on the Isle of Man, a place ideally situated for him since it was halfway between England and Ireland. Bethel placed most of his remaining hopes on trying to obtain this post.

As always, his main chance of success lay in the intercession of his hugely influential uncle Charles. Ever since his time as Charles's apprentice, Bethel had been understandably convinced that his uncle would land him an excellent job. Indeed, he had gone to Paris in the expectation of being eventually offered one by a French firm with whom Charles had collaborated. He felt terribly let down when Charles told him that his French contact had refused to employ Bethel on the grounds that he was English ('Thanks to Charles,' he would later write, 'I absolutely lost 20 months of my life').

Yet Bethel was still at the stage when misgivings about Charles alternated with feelings of having 'misjudged him a bit'. Charles was clearly a persuasive talker; and, after a long 'yarn' with him one night, Bethel was able to write to Sophie that 'I really believe he is going to do what he can for me as soon as anything suitable turns up.'

Bethel's ambivalent relationship with Charles was a subject that was beginning to dominate my thoughts as I stayed on at the café to take sporadic bites at a disappointingly stodgy chocolate brownie. And every time I thought about Charles, I found myself thinking of Doug's tantalizing reference to the recent visit to Hull of Charles's 'grandchild'. I remembered the telephone number Doug had given me. Perhaps this was the right moment to use it. On managing to retrieve from my pocket the crumpled paper on which it was written, I pondered again the wisdom of potentially uncovering family skeletons. Then I rang the number on my mobile.

'We had almost got round to tracking you down,' said the friendly voice on the other end, instantly arousing my suspicions that I was about to enter a genealogical labyrinth greater even than that opened up by the internet. 'Do you mind if my wife listens in on the other line?'

The listening would in fact be done almost exclusively by me. Arthur Walker, the man whom I had rung, leisurely started to tell me of an episode of family history so extraordinarily involved that its opening line might best have been, 'Are you sitting comfortably?' His wife Ruth, unable to contain herself any longer, broke into the conversation almost immediately, and soon took over completely the exposition of her husband's origins, which she herself had uncovered, bringing to bear on them investigative skills that had made her children dub her 'Ruth the Sleuth'. Frequently going off at a tangent, and with an inexplicable urgency, she revealed within minutes that there were ties linking the Jacobs family to the Rothschilds, the late magnate Jimmy Goldsmith, and the makers of Teacher's whisky.

However, all this was irrelevant to the main story, which concerned Arthur's mysterious past. Arthur's mother, Carolyn, had died long before her son had reached 'the age when people start becoming interested in their origins'; and it had been left to Carolyn's younger and only sibling Dorothy ('whom everyone in the family calls Aunt Bell') to tell him that he was descended on his mother's side from a long line of crofters from the Hebrides. His maternal grandmother was called Fiona MacGibbon. But Aunt Bell had never said anything to Alastair about his grandfather, other than that he had been killed in the First World War, and was known as 'Charles Matthias Jackson'.

'We know from Aunt Bell,' continued Ruth, 'that Fiona had sailed to New York in her twenties to work as a stenographer. She told us too that her mother had ended up as a secretary to a British engineer. Then we found among her surviving possessions a silver cigarette case inscribed 'For Charles M. Jacobs, New York, August, 1910'. After that we were able to identify him as the elderly gentleman in a kilt who appears next to Fiona in a photograph of the two of them dated that same month and year. It seems that for Charles's sixtieth birthday, on 8 August 1910, Fiona presented him not only with the case but also the kilt of the MacGibbon clan.'

'At first,' continued Ruth, 'we believed that Charles Jacobs, like many Jews, later decided to Anglicize his name. But the idea of a sixty–year-old going off to fight in the First World War was patently absurd; and, in any case, we know that the engineer Charles Jacobs died much later than 1914. Finally we had to conclude that Jackson was a complete fiction, and that the real father of Carolyn and Aunt Bell was the man whom the two children had always thought of as their grandfather.'

The thoroughness of Ruth's research was so relentlessly impressive that I was soon learning that Charles, on his frequent visits to New York, stayed in the celebrated Dakota of John Lennon fame, and that it was there that he kept Fiona and their two illegitimate daughters.

'And he obviously became very fond of the place,' Ruth went on, for when Charles and his official gentile wife moved in 1911 from Paris to London, he gave the name 'Dakota' to the house they bought in Wimbledon, 'which, by the way, is still standing. It's the oldest house in Wimbledon, it dates back to 1500. We managed to find it only the other day.'

The angry looks of a sedate, tea-drinking couple, and the beeps on my offending mobile to indicate that the battery was running low, finally forced me to bring Ruth's speech to an abrupt end. We promised to stay in touch. My ears were now ringing, and I had been reduced to such a numbed state that I had to order another double espresso.

It took several minutes of vacant staring at my finally abandoned brownie before I could take in the news that Uncle Charles, son of one of Hull's most respected Jewish families, and the man after whom I had received my own middle name, had had a secret life with a Hebridean crofter's daughter, and had even started wearing the MacGibbon tartan. Only after finally accepting all this did I reflect on its significance to my grandfather's story. The reasons for Charles's casual, cavalier treatment of Bethel in 1910 had become strikingly obvious. Charles, newly embarked on a complex double life, and about to be a first-time father at the age of sixty, had more pressing concerns than his nephew's future.

Bethel, needless to say, would have been appalled at Charles's behaviour. The comments on love, which occupied a growing amount of space in his letters to Sophie, only admitted the possibility of a single, all-encompassing and lifelong passion. His was an ardour and idealism that could not as yet conceive of cynicism and compromise in personal relationships. The idea that the materialistic Charles was dividing his time between two women might have confirmed the unreservedly negative opinion of his uncle that Bethel would end up with. Charles would become almost an ogre to Bethel, a person whom he could characterize as 'an anomaly in the Jacobs family', a money-grabbing playboy with an 'amazing ignorance of the theoretical side of engineering', and no knowledge whatsoever of literature, art and science.

The Isle of Man job inevitably did not come through. However, unaided by Charles, Bethel was offered in mid-November a job as an assistant engineer to the Antofagasta (Chili) and Bolivia Railway Company. The starting annual salary was 300 pounds, and he was given until December 27 to prepare himself for a stay of at least three years in what was the remotest destination of any of the ones for which he had applied.

Little more than six weeks remained for him to make sure as best he could that Sophie would keep faithful to him throughout this long period abroad. Their opportunities to be together had so far been relatively few and short; and though latterly they had taken to kissing and embracing during these sporadic, brief encounters, their relationship had been largely an epistolary one. In these letters he had attempted to convey the extent of his passion for her, but, as he confessed, 'When one lets one's emotions free play in passionate words, they seem either devoid of sense, or sentimental.' Not even his increasing resort to French to give vent to his most intimate thoughts and memories could resolve this problem.

Now that the full expression of his feelings had become a matter of the greatest urgency, the only solution seemed to lie in his being able to talk directly to her. But the moment for doing so was being endlessly postponed. Bethel felt obliged to spend the weeks prior to departure with his family in Hull, to which Sophie appeared at first reluctant to go. I could fully understand her hesitation.

The need to make a quick decision now about their future together had probably unnerved her. Marriage to a first cousin, though relatively common among Jewish families of the time, was not something to be entered into lightly; and I knew that both her parents and Bethel's were greatly worried about the medical consequences of such a match (and not without justification, perhaps, in the light of my father's Alzheimer's). Then there was the prospect of having to commit herself in her mid-twenties to a period of three years of waiting for Bethel, which would mean that she would be almost twenty-eight when he returned, a late age for a woman of her generation to start a family.

But worse than all of this was the great and possibly irreconcilable difference between their personalities. Sophie was overwhelmed by Bethel's intellect; and greatly touched by his unfailing support of her singing career, which had received recent setbacks in the form of failed exams and growing parental opposition. Nonetheless, Bethel's letters reveal a certain priggishness and stuffiness that must have been anathema to the jollier and more open-minded Solomons. The politically active Estella, who was soon to win over both Sophie and Louise to suffragette and Irish causes, seems in fact barely to have concealed her lack of respect for Bethel. Many years later, when he came over to Dublin in a British Army uniform, she notoriously stole his overcoat so that it could be used in an undercover IRA operation.

The situation between Bethel and Sophie was in any case still unresolved by the end of November, reinforcing the latter's morbid suspicions that she did not love him in the way he had been led to hope.

'Why,' he wrote on 29 November, 'have you left us in suspense, *chérie*?' Going to Hull, as he pointed out, was 'not like going away to a more or less uncivilized country nine thousand miles away for three years at least . . . I do so want to see you again before I go. And to carry an echo of that glorious voice of yours with me across to the other side of the world.'

But another week went by, and Sophie had yet to make any promise about coming to see him in Hull. 'Why do you make it so hard for me?' he asked her on 7 December. Convinced by now that she did not really love him, in despair Bethel played his last card, putting in a letter what he had intended to say in person. He proposed to her.

'Dearest,' he pleaded, 'you will not let me go away with the memory of your clinging caresses and whispered *je t'aime* on lips that proved it still fresh and feel that it will be but a hopeless fancy that conjures up a vision of the happiness that all this seemed to me to promise.'

I drank the last cold drops of the coffee and went outside to resume my soon to be completed tour of Hull. The last school day before Christmas was coming to an end, and the mid-afternoon sky was already being fast enveloped by the night. Dutifully I visited two of the city's museums to admire a handful of objects designed by Bethel's great namesake: several clocks, and a golden arrow made for the Hull Archers. Then I joined the growing crowds of shoppers parading under broad streets illuminated by desultory lights in the shape of bells and holly.

Inside the city's main bookshop, a branch of Waterstone's, I looked through the 'top-selling titles' and picked out *The Idler Book of Crap Towns: The 50 Worst Places to Live in the UK*. Browsing though its pages I discovered that my London home district of Hackney had been nominated the fifth worst of these places, and Hull the worst of all.

'Hull did teach me one valuable lesson,' wrote one of the book's authors. 'No matter what happens to me in later life, no matter where I live, or how bad things are, I know that it can never, ever be as bad as living in Hull.'

Outside, under the orange glow of light pollution, office workers were scampering off to pubs and Christmas parties. As if in macho defiance of the freezing damp air, young men and women confronted the elements wearing T-shirts, short sleeves, mini-skirts, and skimpy, body-clinging tops. The night became darker and the revellers fewer as I came to a quiet part of the city centre, a place that revealed another side to the Britain of hooligans and urban decline. I could have been in a heritage centre. What had once been the lively commercial hub of maritime Hull was now a tidy and intimate group of museums, listed buildings, sedate restaurants, and solicitors' offices. Around the corner from a near-empty Pizza Express, and down the narrow Bowlalley Lane, where Benjamin Jacobs had had his practice, was the tiny street that had given its name to the area. It was the name that had been at the back of my mind since I was a child: the Land of Green Ginger.

Dimly visible in the subtle light given out by pseudo-Victorian lamp-posts I spotted a blue plaque, which I hoped might explain why this ordinary street of red brick buildings had been thus named. I was puckering my eyes to read the words when, as in a miracle, they were suddenly and brilliantly illuminated. I looked behind me to find a couple of young men holding a spotlight. 'I won't ask you why you've got one of those,' I remarked as they went off laughing and half-drunk into the dark streets beyond. They had held the spotlight for the time it took me to write down the plaque's inscription.

'One of the oddest street names in the country,' it read, 'the Land of Green Ginger was the title of a Winifred Holtby novel. The name's origin remains a mystery.'

There was another mystery that absorbed me as I started walking back to the Paragon station. What was it that made Sophie suddenly overcome her doubts, and eventually go up to Hull to give an answer to Bethel's desperate question? She had left it as late as 16 December to do so, less than two weeks before he was due to sail for South America. By that stage even Bethel must have stood disbelievingly as she had answered him with a resounding 'Yes'. Yes, she had repeated, turning his anxious mood into one of euphoria. Yes, she would wait Penelope-like for his return, and then they would be together for always.

Sophie was a woman who made impetuous decisions to which she resolutely stuck; but that still did not explain why she finally agreed to marry someone she scarcely knew. As I reached the railway station, to await the last train out of Hull that night, I tried thinking of her waving from the window to the man she would not see again for at least three years. I could not decide whether, beneath all the joy of being loved, and the sadness of separation, she had a faint sense of having made a terrible mistake.

What I would find out many months later, in circumstances so unexpected as to reinforce my consciousness of some guiding hand from the other world, was what Bethel himself had felt after Sophie's train had gone. I was writing this book and unsure as to how to end the present chapter when an Irish woman of my age turned up on the doorstep of my isolated Andalucían home. She said she had been given my address by Arthur Walker, and that she was the grand-daughter of Sophie's charismatic brother, Bethel Solomons. Without further ado, she opened the small rucksack she was carrying and presented me with a yellowing letter written in the same hand and on the same Westbourne Avenue-embossed stationery that I now knew so well. It had been sent, she explained, from 'your Bethel to my Bethel'. She thought I should have it.

Written on 19 December 1910, 'having just returned here alone from the station,' it was a long letter from my grandfather thanking his cousin for his congratulations on the engagement ('There is no one whose approval and good wishes I could more appreciate than yours, old man, knowing what you and my Sophie are to each other.'). The optimism and elation of a man happily in love and on the point of a great adventure shine through its pages; but they are offset by an emotion which he prefers to 'leave unsaid', but that comes to him the moment Sophie has left. The suddenness of her not being there has shocked him more than he can ever have expected.

Burdened with guilt and saddened by the thought of 'how much time must elapse before Sophie and I see each other again' ('Three years is not such a long time,' he has always been telling her), he tries to persuade himself that he has made the right decision by implying that the job he has accepted is his first real chance to prove himself and be a worthy member of his family:

'I feel it terribly hard but somehow wrong to go away for three long years, perhaps, and leave her. But if ever a man had an incentive to fight for success; well, I have now, and, as you say, I am sure things will turn out all right, and we'll all live happy ever after.'

The shutters of the station's W.H.Smith had been pulled down; and a bucket and pail indicated that Burger King was on the point of closing. Less than a handful of travellers remained in this coldly remodelled late-Victorian building, waiting, as I was, for the last train of the day. An announcement warned us that it would be arriving thirty-five minutes late. I went to sit down on the edge of a bench littered with empty food containers and crumpled cardboard cups.

Here I took the opportunity quietly to assimilate the day's events and finds, but was soon disturbed by an abrupt realization: in little more than a fortnight I too would be heading off to the other side of the world. Though I had often vaguely thought about tracing my grandfather's footsteps in South America, the reasons for doing so had become clearer once I had begun to be more seriously interested in Bethel's story. The historian in me needed to establish a firmer context for this story, to find out what places such as Antofagasta, Cochabamba and Potosí had really been like in his time, to know more about the legacy of Western engineers in Chile and Bolivia, to see what had become of the railway line on which so many of his mental and physical energies had been spent.

Several weeks ago, when my interest in my family's history was already gathering its alarming momentum, I went ahead to buy a return air ticket to Santiago de Chile. But, even when the ticket was in my hand, my journey to South America had still seemed a distant and almost abstract undertaking. Now, all of a sudden, it did not.

And it was not just the reality and imminence of the journey that had finally sunk in; it was also the absolute necessity of doing it. As I began shifting restlessly on the station bench, I thought about how unsatisfactory it would be to leave the tale of my grandparents' unfolding relationship suspended in mid-air at Paragon station, or even to follow its sequel simply through the letters. Coming to Hull had brought out aspects of my family's past which all the reading I had done beforehand had not fully prepared me for. It had convinced me that only by going myself to South America would I be able properly to grasp the continent's overwhelming affect on my grandfather's mind and emotions.

I now felt my own heart beating faster as I gave in to thoughts that I had managed over the past weeks largely to avoid. South America had an almost visceral appeal for me; and I had been drawn since childhood to the idea of some long and picaresque journey through a continent I still saw as having many of the features and qualities I loved about Spain, but in a yet more exaggerated form: the vast empty spaces, the bizarre landscapes, the fantastical literature, the architecture of glorious excess that the riches of Potosí and other fabled mines had financed.

At the time when I had first heard Sophie's tales of my grandfather's wanderings, the prospect of emulating them one day had been encouraged by the discovery at 30 Meadway of the first travel book to have made any lasting impact on me, *Tschiffely's Ride*. Written in 1933 by a Swiss horse lover whom my grandparents later met, this was an account of '10,000 miles in the saddle through the Americas from Argentina to Washington'. With its dramatically captioned photos ('Majestic, mysterious, their origin lost in the dim, forgotten centuries, these giant stone pillars challenge the imagination of modern man'), and its childlike sketch map illustrating the author's route with inscriptions such as 'Primitive Indians', 'Stone idol', and 'Desert, many skeletons', the book captured what I had imagined my grandfather's South America to have been like – a land of endless romantic adventures and exotic encounters.

But now my yearnings for an ambitious South American journey had found a rather different source of inspiration: the early travel diaries of Che Guevara. Shortly before these were turned into a 'major motion picture' (*The Motorcycle Diaries*), I dipped into them almost as a nostalgic tribute to the days, during my late teens, when I had fallen under the spell of post-revolutionary Cuba. Guevara's diaries provided me with a view of South America which was totally antithetical to my grandfather's. They were imbued with a sensibility to all that had gone tragically wrong with the continent which Bethel and all the other hopeful Westerners of his generation had persisted in calling 'the Land of the Future'.

'The train arriving at Platform One is the delayed 23.07 service to York Central,' blared out an indifferent voice at 23.58. The additional delay had allowed time for my feelings of excitement to be tainted with growing unease. The prospect of shortly joining Bethel on the other side of the Atlantic had come to seem infinitely more daunting than before. It was ages since I had had any fears about travelling; but now I was getting as nervous as I had been the first time I had set off alone to Spain from London's Victoria station.

I had hardly travelled before in South America; and I had never been to the Andes. As I slumped onto a seat on the last and nearly empty train of the night, I wondered what other memories I would uncover and what spirits awaken as I left the security of Hull and followed my grandfather to places I would soon hear described as ones where the 'rivers arrive thirsty' and 'the winds become exhausted'.

2

The Other Side of the World

THE CHRISTMAS SEASON was over, and I was rushing in heavy rain through the City of London. Battling ineffectually against the downpour with a broken folding umbrella, I sped on foot past the impatient traffic clogging up Liverpool Street, and veered off into what seemed like an oasis of dignity in the midst of all this noisy confusion. Finsbury Circus appeared to me as a lush garden encircled by a stately, harmonious ring of early twentieth-century buildings. Entering the columned lobby at No. 3, I wiped my clouded, rain-spattered glasses, taking in an environment redolent of empire and bygone aspirations.

Having accepted that I really was going to South America, I had set out in a panic to get ready, and was now coming to the end of a period of hectic preparation. The most urgent task had been to contact my grandfather's old employers, the former Antofagasta (Chili) and Bolivia Railway Company. Though known today by the snappier name of Antofagasta PLC, and owned by a Chilean industrialist of Croatian extraction, the company's directorship had remained British and based in London since its foundation in 1888. It was an example of the strong Anglo-Chilean links that famously made Chile the 'England of South America'.

Barely a few hours before the Christmas break I had been lucky enough to catch the company's present director Philip Adeane, an old Etonian whose bulldoggish appearance and rapid-fire exclamations of 'What? What?' belied an intellectually alert manner. He talked a little about the company's history, and how its interests had switched mainly into mining since my grandfather's day, when it had existed primarily to manage the railway line in between the northern Chilean port of Antofagasta and the Bolivian capital of La Paz.

When I told him of my plan to travel the whole surviving length of this line, he reminded me that its traffic today was almost entirely freight, though the company was obliged by a treaty of 1889 to maintain a token passenger service part of the way to the Bolivian border. He said he could not help me with rail travel on the Bolivian side (which was now the responsibility of Bolivia's national railways), but that he would put in a word for me with 'our man in Antofagasta' to see if there was any chance of my travelling on a freight train or in an inspection cab. Antofagasta, he added, was not the sort of place where I would want to spend any length of time.

'And if it's archival material you're after, you won't find any there,' he said. 'The company's archives are now all here in London. If you're quick you might be able to see them while they're still in our old premises in Finsbury Circus.'

Which was why, on the rainy eve of my departure to South America, I was standing wet and imtimidated in a building with the pukka Englishness and musty grandeur of an old-fashioned gentleman's club. Regaining my composure, I strode past offices belonging to the Bank of India, and then up a sombrely lit flight of marble steps leading to corridors heavy with wooden panelling. On the lintels of all the doors were the inlaid flags of African and Latin American countries, with those of Chile and Bolivia optimistically entwined above faded gold letters spelling out the original name of my grandfather's company. I rang the bell and was greeted by Andrew Bernard, a portly and shyly affable figure who proved to be the sole occupant of an office now in an advanced stage of being dismantled. He was the company's archivist.

'We've moved almost everything to South Kensington now,' he explained, leading me through a suite of empty rooms to a wall of bookshelves at the back of the office. 'The archives will stay here for a few more weeks, before they decide what to do with them.'

Andrew, a self-effacing man with an air of cheery resignation, had evidently enjoyed reading through the thousands of typed leather-bound reports sent from Antofagasta to London. He had meticulously combed the five volumes covering the years 1910–14 in search of references to my grandfather and to those colleagues of his mentioned in his letters. 'There's not much, I'm afraid,' he said, taking me into what had once been the boardroom.

I sat down at an oval table to read through the pages Andrew had marked. But I could not get out of my head snatches from a conversation I had had the night before with a member of Bolivia's political elite, Susana Sánchez de Lozada. An English friend of mine, knowing that I was going to Bolivia, had suggested I got together with her to hear a first-hand account of the country's recent and alarming political developments. For whereas Chile had settled after Pinochet into a period of prosperous and worthy stability, Bolivia had been disintegrating in such a way that a few weeks ago a violent series of events had led to the flight of the twice-elected president Gonzálo Sánchez de Lozada ('Goni') to Miami. 'Goni' was Susana's cousin, and 'a great friend of Antofagasta PLC'.

Within half an hour of being in a London restaurant with the glamorous but edgy Susana, I had been convinced of the imminence of an uprising far bloodier than the one which had recently ousted her cousin. Bolivia's indigenous majority, perceived by my grandfather mainly in terms of picturesque potential, was becoming increasingly frustrated at living in a place where power had always been in the hands of a tiny elite of European descent. Indignation had been intensifying since 1996, when 'Goni' had given foreign companies the control of the country's recently revealed reserves of natural gas. Anti-European feeling was growing, and what was more, 'the Incas believed in cycles of revenge,' Susana told me, side-tracking into the esoteric, and revealing perhaps something of the terror felt occasionally by her class.

Pausing to light a cigarette, she had then expanded on this. 'The predicted amount of time since Tupac Katari's revolt against the Spaniards of 1780 has now elapsed. Something terrible can soon be expected.' My expression must have veered between complete scepticism and mounting anxiety. 'But don't worry,' she had added, seeing perhaps a pallor in my face, 'nothing is likely to happen until the carnival season is over.'

In the hour or so I had left in the archives I made a renewed effort to put disturbing thoughts to the back of my mind, and to focus more on my grandfather's story. This time I succeeded. The tedious reports about gauge sizes, adverse weather conditions, petty quarrels between British and American engineers, proposed financial cutbacks, suggestions for a billiards table for the Antofagasta club, and so on, even came to have a calming effect, and to make me forget that within twenty-four hours I would be flying into the unknown. Yet, as Andrew the archivist had warned me, a search through all this trivia also brought with it the revelation of how disappointingly few references there were to my grandfather. His appointment as 'assistant engineer' was recorded, as were his arrival at Antofagasta and his eventual resignation; and that virtually was it. Unlike his forebears in Hull, he seemed a person destined to be forgotten by history.

With the rain still pouring outside I packed away my scant notes and went to say goodbye to Andrew. '*Pisco* sour,' he muttered enigmatically. 'It's a wonderful drink. You really must try it when you're out there.' Promising to toast him with the drink as soon as I arrived, I left to catch a passing bus; I had just one other obligation before returning home to finish my hasty packing.

The bus took me to the other side of London, to an area known in my grandparents' youth as 'Westbournia'. It had come into existence with the arrival of the railway at nearby Paddington, and had grown into a smart shopping and residential district before being threatened by encroaching overpopulation and the eventual arrival of transient communities. By 1910, when the young Sophie had taken lodgings here, it was still an oasis of respectability, but only just.

I stood with my umbrella in the darkness outside 9 Aldridge Road Villas, one of a row of tall 1880s houses verging precariously on chaotically redeveloped surroundings. This was the address to which nearly all of Bethel's letters to Sophie had been sent. She had stayed in the house as the paying guest of two unmarried sisters, the 'Misses Isaacson', whom Bethel had thought of as being 'so awfully jolly'. I felt as if I had been to this house before as I directed my glance towards the solitary light from an upstairs window that I was sure had been that of Sophie's bedroom. Bethel in South America would often try to picture her in this room, peacefully asleep in bed, or else seated at her writing desk penning words that made him 'almost feel your arms round me and hear your whisper'.

I had always wished she had not destroyed these letters; and I was now more frustrated than ever at knowing so little about what had been on her mind or in her heart during these interminable years of waiting. I stayed looking up at her old window, thinking of her as she started reading the first of Bethel's long descriptions of his slow outward journey. She had been so envious of that journey, she had once told me. 'The places where he was going to had seemed so distant and exotic to us then.'

I hung around like a stalker for a few more minutes, trying to fix her house in my memory, anxious like Bethel to carry it with me overseas as a talisman. Then the bedroom curtains were closed, the light went out, and all that was left was rain washing against the grey bricks.

On 28 December 1910 Bethel said goodbye to his parents, his sister Ethel, and their beloved dog Pips. Accompanied only by Louise he set off from Hull by the same route that had been used not so long before to transport thousands of Jewish refugees on their way to a new life in America. Early the next morning, a Thursday, he boarded at Liverpool the HRS *Oronsa*, a Glasgow-built ship that would be destroyed by a German torpedo less than four years later.

The ship was part of the Pacific Steam Navigation Company, which had been established in the mid-nineteenth century by William Wheelwright, an American engineer and entrepreneur who soon afterwards achieved fame as the creator of Chile's first railway. Thanks to Wheelright, the sea crossing to Chile, once the longest in the Spanish empire, was reduced to a mere forty days, less than half of what it had been at the end of the previous century.

In 1910 the journey to Antofagasta took a little under five weeks; but this must have seemed an eternity to someone such as Bethel waving farewell from the deck to a slowly vanishing Louise. Overcome by a terrible and unexpected sadness at this moment of departure, he noticed that she was suffering as much as he was, and yet neither of them, as he wrote to Sophie only seven hours out at sea,'could say a word to each other of what we felt . . . If ever I go away again by myself, I don't think I should care to have anyone I loved see me off, unless I was coming back very soon.'

There were several consolations, however. His uncle Charles, with whom he had briefly resolved his differences, had shown signs of what Bethel took at first to be guilt and had arranged for him to travel first class (a gesture Bethel would later discover to be only part of his uncle's scheme to get him to befriend another of the first-class passengers, a potentially lucrative patron for Charles). And no sooner had he settled into his comfortable cabin than he received a letter and bunch of flowers from Sophie, much to the envy of his handsome Irish cabin mate, William Burke. Soon afterwards he had the further pleasant surprise of discovering that Burke knew Sophie's gregarious brother Bethel Solomons, and had even played 'footer' against him on several occasions. My grandfather immediately became 'pally' with Burke, whose presence on board, aided by a voice apparently very similar to that of Sophie's brother, was like a permanent reminder of the world he had left behind.

By the Friday, a rather more relaxed Bethel was up early enough to see 'the last of England'. After ordering his 'hot tub' for 7.15, as became his custom, he went on board deck to watch the ship pass the lighthouse at Land's End and then continue on towards the Scillies. The weather was 'grand' and he found himself warm enough to sit around without an overcoat. The good mood that would accompany him for much of the journey was enhanced by the discovery that the ship had a 'decent' library on board, and was fitted with the 'latest Marconi apparatus'. He was also 'tremendously pleased' with himself for having purchased beforehand an excellent pair of 'Goerz glasses' that, in 'this clear atmosphere, show up an amazing amount of detail quite indistinguishable to the naked eye'.

Over the coming weeks at sea he rapidly adjusted to a way of life that would serve him in good stead during his years in Chile and Bolivia. For someone as accustomed as he was to occupying his leisure hours with reading, it was strange to be in a place where the constant noise of the sea, the boat and the passengers made it nearly impossible for him to concentrate on anything serious. He ended up spending his daylight hours observing the almost hallucinatory swell of the waves, scanning the unchanging horizon with his Goerz glasses, or else taking enthusiastic part in deck games ranging from cricket (at which Burke badly sprained an ankle) to the now inconceivable 'cigarette race' ('where the men run up to their partners with a cigarette in their mouths and the ladies have to light it for them when they run back'). At night he amused himself by endlessly playing bridge in the saloon, and listening to a band specializing in 'sweet music of a popular kind'.

As well as subjecting Bethel to the type of music and entertainment that in other circumstances might have appalled him, the boat journey forced him to live at close quarters with a great cross-section of humanity. In his now almost daily letters to Sophie, he devoted much space to the vivid descriptions of his fellow passengers, several of whom brought out the more snobbish side of his character. Up to Vigo he found himself being driven mad by 'an awful ass of a young Spaniard' who 'ran about and played antics exactly like a monkey, and made himself generally objectionable.' But no one irritated him as much as a passenger whom he characterized as 'the most perfect specimen of the parvenu I have ever seen, horribly fat with about three yards of gold chain, half an inch thick diamond ring, etc., and absolutely incapable of aspirating an H.' This person was for Bethel 'the very quintessence of vulgarity'.

In contrast, those passengers with whom he got on well were labelled 'interesting', a word he seems to have applied mainly to people from a similar background to his own, or to those who shared his interests. Burke was one of these, as were the ship's nature-loving, scientifically curious doctor ('Dr Sturdy') and a naval lieutenant whose Portsmouth-based boat had, coincidentally, been repaired by Bethel. Regrettably unworthy of this category was the one passenger who would be with Bethel all the way to Antofagasta – an 'elderly spinster' referred to in the passenger list as Miss Oldham. The purser had put the two of them together on the first night in the dining room, and they had discovered that they were learning Spanish from exactly the same textbooks. However, this did not prove a sufficient basis for a close friendship. By the next day, Bethel was able to report that she was a Catholic, on her way to Chile to be a private tutor, and 'not interesting at all'. Later, he probably avoided her as best as he could, for he found her conversation 'childish and trivial in the extreme'.

But if the people he was with sometimes failed to excite, the journey itself had the quality of a grand unfolding drama which held him ever more surely in its grip. After La Rochelle, where he had been frustrated in his plans to disembark and post a letter to Sophie, he said goodbye to the Europe that had been familiar to him and entered a world progressively more exotic than anywhere he had known before. The Spanish ports of La Coruña and Vigo, viewed through his Goerz glasses (now more in demand than ever), had seemed 'very pic-turesque' places; but it was not until the Portuguese fishing town of Leixoes that he and Burke managed at last to get ashore.

The town itself was 'not very interesting', and the 'horribly dirty streets' were the 'most malodorous' he had ever walked down. However, the sight in the local fish market of some 'gaily bedecked natives', and of a primitive stone-wheeled cart drawn by oxen ('altogether a most interesting vehicle'), gave Bethel a foretaste of the quaintly ethnographic scenes he imagined in abundance in the Bolivian Andes. The following day, on shore at Lisbon, he experi-enced for the first time what he also might have expected from Bolivia: a town in the throes of revolution. King Manuel II had just fled the country, and republican flags hung over trees and lamp posts riddled with bullet holes. 'Everything seemed quiet and tranquil, though I believe there is a considerable amount of discontent brewing.'

Slowly the HRS *Oronsa* headed south towards the equator. As the tropics approached, the sea gradually lost its North Atlantic muddiness, and became phosphorescent and a glorious blue. Cabin temperatures soared at night to seventy-nine degrees Fahrenheit, white clothes became the norm, and there were ever more diversions to prevent people from falling into lethargy. The passengers took on the swarthy crew in a tug-of-war, and, to Bethel's surprise, won. Inhibitions were lost with the growing heat and stickiness; and yet, as if to compensate for this increased informality, everyone started turn-ing up for dinner in evening dress.

With the arrival at Cape Saint Vincent, just south of Tenerife, Bethel's Western sensibilities, lulled into a sense of security by the privileged, protected life on board, were confronted by a strange and disturbing environment. As he took in a landscape of the most terrible barrenness and desolation, he suddenly saw the water around the ship becoming an agitated mass of screaming local boys who refused to go away. While the passengers amused themselves by throwing coins into the sea and watching the boys skillfully dive for them, Bethel pondered the fate of those ninety or so men, mainly Englishmen, who were employed on the island by the local cable company. 'They say that they like the life and that the climate is tip-top, but I don't think I would care to live there under any consideration.'

The morbid impressions left by Cape Saint Vincent were happily soon dispelled under the influence of further games and high jinks on board. More fun than ever was had three days later as everyone prepared themelves for the momentous occasion of crossing the equator. Timber and sailcloth were used to create a huge tank, some fifteen feet long, ten wide, and five deep. Then, to the fearsome sounds of the ship's bells and the whistle siren, the Chief Officer appeared disguised as Neptune, accompanied by other old equatorial hands in wigs and fancy dress. Those who had never crossed the equatorial line before were lathered in paste, shaved with a 'Brobdingnagian razor of wood', and finally hurled unceremoniously into the water. One of the victims was of course Bethel himself. As he splashed around merrily in the tank, he only wished, as he did during all these more treasured moments of the journey, that Sophie was with him.

The further the ship moved away from England the more conscious he was of the distance separating him from his beloved. Not even in that brief moment after leaving her at Hull had he been as affected as he was now by a depressingly vivid sense of how much time remained 'before we can meet again'. Was it possible, he asked, 'to long for anyone at that future date any more keenly than I long for you already?' He gave in more and more to fantasies. One moment he imagined her sitting on the deck chair besides him; the next he was staring at the photograph of her on his cabin wall and pleading for it to speak. On another occasion, watching the moon's reflection on the sea, he imagined her as the one missing element in a scene of otherwise perfect beauty.

As a way of making her share more closely the extraordinary experiences he was having, Bethel was fast becoming a fanatical amateur photographer. He took snaps of virtually everything, and then rushed off to his cabin to develop them. The rocking of the ship, not to mention the sweltering heat, rather hindered the printing process; and the quality of the prints was not helped either by a fault in his camera that left a white streak across them. Nonetheless, he gathered together the best of the photos, as he would continue to do throughout his years abroad, and enclosed them in letters that recounted diary-like his every doing. He posted these at any opportunity, dreaming all the while of the day when he would receive his first letter from Sophie since Liverpool. But he knew he could not expect this until the ship's arrival at the Chilean port of Valparaíso.

On finally reaching the shores of South America, by the middle of January, he calculated that he was still only half way to Valparaíso, a place whose very name, the 'Valley of Paradise', gave it a mythical elusiveness. In the meantime he would have to endure many more crises of longing for Sophie. One of the worst of these came at the north Brazilian town of Recife, where he had his first glimpse of the continent that would be his home for the next few years.

The landing at Recife was known to be a particularly rough one, even on the so-called calmest of days. Departing passengers had to be lowered in baskets onto rowing boats that were violently jostled by a nearly permanent swell. Burke, 'poor old chap', was one of those who were leaving: he was reluctantly taking up an appointment at a Recife bank. While Burke waited to be rowed to the shore, Bethel offered his precious Goerz glasses to a young Brazilian woman who was returning to Recife with her father and sister after eighteen months in London, and who used the glasses to scour the approaching boats in search of the man she had come back to marry. Up to this point of the journey she had apparently been 'a quiet and retiring person', barely speaking to anyone. But when she eventually spotted her fiancé she became so excited that Bethel feared for everyone's safety as the time came for her to be transferred to the man's boat.

This display of emotion, coinciding with the sadness caused by Burke's departure, had a profound effect on Bethel. He envied the ecstatic happiness of the reunited lovers, and he was left reflecting on the loneliness of the solitary European male in faraway corners of the world. Burke, he imagined, would probably end up engaged to the Brazilian woman's younger sister. To be alone in such a place as Recife without any form of sentimental tie was something Bethel could simply not conceive.

As for Bethel himself, a seductive distraction would soon come along in the form of Rio de Janeiro. 'Of all beautiful places on this little planet,' he expounded deliriously, 'I think Rio de Janeiro must be very hard to beat.'

The initial impact of sailing into its enormous bay, with its ring of forest-covered mountains, 'some of them of the most fantastic forms', was disarming enough for someone raised in the greyness of Hull. Later, after going to stay in a hotel 1,000 feet up the Corcovado mountain, it would seem that a part of his sensual being, dormant since birth, had been awakened. Getting up in time to see the sunrise over the bay, he had sat rapt at his window sill as the mountains were slowly bathed in orange and gold light. 'It was the most beautiful sight I have ever seen.'

Afterwards, having gorged on a typically sensual Brazilian breakfast of tropical fruits, he walked along a winding forest path towards the peak of Corcovado. All was lush abundance. The air was heavy with the scent of tropical flowers; lizards scurried for shelter at every turn; and 'gorgeous butterflies of enormous size flew out and nearly hit one in the eye'. He carried on walking as if in ecstasy, pausing every so often to peer through openings in the forest towards the ever-broadening and increasingly spectacular panorama.

Bethel had not entirely lost his critical senses. Down in the centre of Río, already a city of 1,000,000 inhabitants and, according to him, one of the most expensive in the world, he battled with a currency so subdivided into near worthless units that he had to go around carrying huge wads of notes and spending 'money by the million': it was 'enough to turn one's hair grey'. He seems also to have been shocked and surprised by the dependence of the Brazilians on Westerners. Spotting in Río's harbour a British-built Brazilian dreadnought he had actually seen launched at Newcastle, he suspected that the 'native crew have let it get into a pretty bad shape already'.

'The Brazilians,' he elaborated, 'seem incapable of doing anything for themselves. All their electric tramways and improvement schemes of every description are constructed by British and American companies and generally run by them, and many big hotels are run by foreigners, often German' (including, he could have added, the one at Corcovado).

Lifting anchor on the afternoon of 18 January, the HRS *Oronsa* continued its journey south. At Santos, the next stop, Bethel and a fellow passenger went ashore to take a ride on a 'electric car' − 'an excellent service run by an English company, and with cars that were made at Motherwell, near Glasgow.' The following morning, at the Uruguayan capital of Montevideo, there was a general exodus of passengers that would have left the ship largely empty had it not been for the arrival of what Bethel instantly summed up as an 'Italian third-rate travelling opera company'. Then the weather changed, and the memory of calm seas and tropical heat began to seem an illusion. Overcoats came to be worn on deck, and a squall after leaving the River Plate developed into a terrible storm that put most people 'hors de combat'. Bethel was pleased to report that he was one of the very few passengers wholly unaffected by the boat's violent rocking.

These excellent sea legs would stand him in good stead over the coming week when the boat negotiated the Straits of Magellan and then the notorious Gulf of Sorrows. Although it was now the height of the southern summer, freezing winds and dark billowing clouds exposed and concealed in rapid concession a landscape which for Bethel was 'like the Caledonian locks on an immense scale'. Sharp and irregular peaks ran right down to the water, interspersed with the not so Caledonian sight of glaciers which turned 'a gorgeous blue colour whenever the sun caught them'.

Bethel was finally in Chile, and his exultant impressions of the landscape were in sharp contrast to his first impressions of Chilean towns. He was particularly depressed by Talcahuano, where he had been looking forward to see an old friend from Hull, Tom Somerscales, who had a job there as chief assistant at the dockyards. The place was 'a wretched hole and indescribably filthy'. Bethel felt special sympathy for Tom's wife, 'a Hull girl also', who had lived after her marriage in one of Hull's 'model estates' and had previously been studying music for four years in Berlin. 'You can imagine her feelings now,' commented Bethel. Something of the world she greatly missed, and which was also the world Bethel strongly associated with Sophie, was briefly conjured up on the evening of the ship's departure from Talcahuano. The 'third-rate' Italian opera company treated the passengers to a rendition of parts of *Rigoletto* and *La Bohème*, and proved to be not so third-rate after all. 'The tenor in fact was remarkably good.'

Bethel was now in the heartland of Chile. The symbolic frontier had been crossed at the estuary of the Bío-Bío, the river which for centuries had separated territory stubbornly held by the courageous Mapuches from the Chile colonized by Spain. The narrow strip of fertile countryside between the Andes and the interminable coast along which Bethel was sailing must have been enormously inviting to potential settlers in comparison to what came before. The conquistador Pedro de Valdivia, the first Spaniard to set eyes on Chile, arrived there in 1540 from the terrifying expanse of desert to the north. Before being gruesomely killed by the Mapuches (some say by having molten gold poured down his throat), he said of the Chilean heartland that 'there was no better land in the world for living in, and for settling'. Charles Darwin would be similarly impressed.

'After Tierra del Fuego,' he wrote in his account of his momentous journey on *The Beagle*, 'the climate felt quite delirious – the atmosphere so dry, and the heavens so clear and blue, with the sun shining brightly, that all nature seemed sparkling with life.'

As Bethel sailed north in Darwin's wake, he too was rapidly won over by the 'wonderful climate of this part of Chile – these cloudless skies day after day with unfailing regularity but always tempered with a cool breeze in the afternoon, and the evenings delightful.' As Valparaíso approached, and memories of ugly Talcahuano faded under the brilliant skies and the prospect of Sophie's longed-for letter, he might well have recalled lines from a famous poem by Sophie's Irish contemporary Oliver St John Gogarty:

'A ship from Valparaíso came,/ . . . She brought the wonder of her name/And tidings from a sunnier world.'

Bethel arrived there at last on 1 February. The sky that day was so exceptionally clear that the faraway conical peak of Aconcagua could be made out as a gleaming apparition in white.

My own first sighting of Aconcagua was from the plane from Europe. 'If you look to your right you'll see the highest mountain in South America,' dryly intoned the voice of the pilot, waking me from the fitful sleep I had fallen into at around five in the morning. The now ring-bound copies of my grandfather's letters had slipped off my lap, together with a small pile of guidebooks. Breakfast trays were already being handed around, and vaguely human forms were stirring from beneath blankets. Tentatively opening the shade of my window I was blinded by unexpected sunshine. Below me was a crumpled brown landscape, illuminated by a light so sharp and intense that every path, every fault almost, every rock stood out with a miniature-like precision. I let my eyes roam across this treeless expanse until the russet browns were streaked with ever broader areas of porcelain white, and I found myself humbly staring at a dazzling peak almost horizontal with my line of vision. In that instant I felt my grandfather's thrill as he identified this mountain from Valparaíso.

Then the plane slowly began its descent. The barrenness of the Andes was replaced by a rolling mosaic of ochres, greens and yellows, which in turn was abruptly curtailed to the north by a dense bank of coastal fog, extending like limbo to a distant blue horizon. Towards the south, where we were heading, the details of the landscape became blurred under an air thick with dust and pollution.

'We shall be landing at Santiago de Chile in approximately ten minutes,' announced the pilot. 'The temperature outside is twenty degrees centigrade, and the weather is sunny.'

It was ten o'clock in the morning, and I was starting off my travels in South America in a city that my grandfather had been unable to visit. 'I would like to go up to Santiago,' he wrote to Sophie from Valparaíso (then a four-and-a-half-hour journey by train), 'but the state of the exchequer will not permit.'

I was intending to stay in the Chilean capital only for the time it would take to start acclimatizing to Chile, and to understand better the world my grandfather was entering. Then I would join him at Valparaíso, and from there continue north into the desert wastes of Antofagasta, where I saw my real journey as beginning.

Santiago by all accounts had lost much of the appeal it had had for Bethel, now being generally known as the 'dusty city'; and the prospect of my staying there had become even less attractive when I heard that the only person I knew there (coincidentally another grandson of a European railway engineer) was going to be away on holiday. The Chilean summer was at its height, and those who could had left Santiago for the coast or the mountains. I had resigned myself to spending some solitary days in a hotel of a kind permitted by the exchequer when an unexpected email came, just as I was leaving London. This seemed to furnish further evidence that some ulterior force was looking after me.

The sender had introduced himself as Gonzalo Donoso. He was the friend of a friend of mine who had told him about me and what I was planning to do. He wondered if he could help me by putting me up at his house, if I 'didn't mind children'.

I knew that Gonzalo was an architect, and that he had been very close to his late uncle José Donoso, a celebrated writer whose last work, appropriately enough, was entitled *Speculations on my Family's Past*.

A car driven by one of Gonzalo's employees was sent to meet me at the airport. We drove down a multi-lane highway towards steep dusty mountains obscured by a shimmering haze. Industrial warehouses, scorched patches of wasteland, palm groves, golf courses, shopping malls, and fields planted with maize and tobacco passed in rapid succession, contributing to my feeling of cultural disorientation. Here I was in the 'England of South America', though at times I was trying to decide whether I was approaching Los Angeles, or driving through my adopted Andalucía. The dilapidated farm buildings, and the vendors selling produce by the side of the road, lessened somewhat the Californian look, while the resemblance to Spain was confused by the use of a bizarre Spanish full of Americanisms, words of obvious indigenous origin, and such phrases, so baffling to Spanish ears as 'beneficent Chilean prick'. In the end the driver had to explain to me that the sign reading '*polla de benifencia Chilena*' was in fact an advertisement for Chile's National Lottery.

We finally reached the leafy, luxurious suburb where Gonzalo lived. Andalucía had now been left far behind, and elements from California now merged with others unmistakably from northern Europe – English-style gabling, mansard windows, steeply pitched roofs with grey slate tiles. I had the sudden feeling of being in a Parisian garden suburb on a hot summer's day. The driver parked the car under chestnut trees, and pressed a bell half-hidden under an ivy-covered gate. We entered the house through French windows that opened out on to a narrow, shaded lawn. Geraldine, Gonzalo's French wife, walked down the staircase to welcome me. Tall, young and beautiful, she had straight, long blonde hair, a friendly, open face healthily tanned, and a general manner and physique of someone who took rigorous care of herself. From her I received my first lesson in Chilean etiquette. In greeting a woman in Chile you do not do so with a kiss on each cheek, as in Spain, or with three simulated kisses in the air, as in pretentious French society. 'In Chile,' she said emphatically, 'it's only one kiss.'

Geraldine introduced me to her three blonde children (a soulful-looking boy and two perpetually prankish daughters), and then to

Gonzalo himself, a shy and distracted man very unlike the outward-going person I had been led to expect from the confident tone of his email invitation. The family was completed by a rare, and asthmatic, oriental pug, and – an apparently statutory feature of any middle-class Chilean household – a Peruvian maid. The latter's initial appearance, dressed in an apron and carrying a tray of teacups, intensified my sense of being in an exotic recreation of 2 Westbourne Avenue, Hull.

Having flown over the sublimely wild Andes merely a couple of hours before, it was certainly strange suddenly to find myself in a house that immediately conveyed the sophisticated European environment my grandfather had so often dreamt of. A Bechstein piano formed the centrepiece of the elegantly tasteful interior where eclectic *objets d'art* and numerous items of scientific and ethnographic interest revealed the cosmopolitan lives and wide-ranging intellectual interests of the illustrious Donosos. As I was shown up to my bedroom, I paused for a time to study the many ancestral representations that covered in profusion the walls of the staircase. These old photos and paintings had been the starting-point of *Speculations on my Family's Past*, and their dominant presence in Gonzalo's house was like a stern reminder of my reason for being in Chile.

As soon as I politely could I went off to the centre of Santiago to make what I considered as the first soundings of my South American searches. Away from Gonzalo's house and pleasant suburb, the city was the untidy urban sprawl I had imagined, a mixture of brash American and staid nineteenth century, but without the dynamism, or hints of secret corners, that had so immediately excited me in Buenos Aires during a short stay there a few years back. The one feature that might have redeemed the place's initially dull impression was its spectacular Andean backcloth; but even this I would only get to appreciate from photos: pollution levels were now such that the high peaks could apparently be seen just for a few days in the year. For the rest of the year the sole sign of their presence was a sinister brown mountain torrent which gushed manically through the very centre of the city like the effluence from a burst sewage pipe. This was a sight that made me strangely fearful of the eventual moment when I would have to confront the mountains at close quarters.

I tried calming myself afterwards with a visit to the National Historical Museum, which stood in Santiago's large and unwelcoming main square, and drew attention to itself by occupying one of the city's few surviving buildings from the colonial period. A notice forbidding visitors 'to enter the museum in a state of inebriation' seemed indicative of the seriousness with which the Chileans took their fatherland and its history. And the displays inside emphasized how this history had been dominated by mines and the railways that had been built originally to serve them. Pride of place was given to the pioneering railway line built in 1851 by William Wheelwright to transport minerals from the mining town of Copiapó to the port of Caldera: the actual locomotive designed by Wheelwright gained iconic resonance by being situated at the very centre of the entrance courtyard.

Hardly any time at all was needed in Santiago to grasp that my grandfather had arrived in a country where the engineer was god, and where trains were deeply embedded in the national consciousness. The theme of trains was like a thread uniting my disparate experiences in the city, confronting me in numerous paintings and sculptures in the Museum of Fine Arts, in scale models decorating the metro stations, in the title of a key chapter in José Donoso's ancestral memoir (thoughtfully placed by my bedside by Gonzalo), and even in the sitting room of the much-visited house built by Chile's revered national poet Pablo Neruda. 'And that,' said the informative guide pointing to a large lamp hanging behind Neruda's sofa, 'is a relic from the poet's childhood in Temuco, in the south of Chile. It's from an old steam train such as the one his father used to drive. Neruda, in his memoirs, describes how he first began to appreciate the lushness and sensuality of nature while riding in his father's train.'

The train from Santiago to Temuco was the one important passenger train service still functioning in Chile; and I intended treating myself to the journey in the event of my safe return from Antofagasta and Bolivia. For the moment I made do with a cursory glance inside Santiago's ironwork central station before walking off to the nearby National Railway Museum, where I intended to end my brief tour of the city.

The museum was situated in a large public park laid out in 1830. While looking for this, I was sidetracked at the park's entrance by the sight of an old train carriage situated in front of a large neoclassical building. The building itself turned out to have nothing to do with trains, but was instead Latin America's oldest natural history museum. Then I remembered Gonzalo telling me some intriguing stories about a former director of this institution who had been an English engineer. I decided to investigate this further, and was directed across a junk-filled courtyard to the museum's library. Bizarrely, the librarian was expecting me.

'I'd almost given up on you,' he said. 'When you wrote to me three months ago I put aside all the articles I could find on Ricardo Latcham. They're still here on my desk.'

I had never heard of Latcham until the evening before; and I had certainly never written any letter. But none of this seemed to matter to the librarian, who handed me the articles all the same, and pointed me to a table in a library as deserted as the museum itself. As in Hull's Linnaeus Street synagogue, I began to have disquieting thoughts that some elusive being was pursuing the same lines of enquiry as myself, a doppelgänger perhaps. Then I read the documents in front of me.

Within a quarter of an hour I had assimilated the life story of an older English contemporary of my grandfather's who had gone out to South America with a great openness of spirit and no Sophie to keep him tied to Europe. He too had qualified in England as a civil engineer, but he had set off to Chile in 1881 with no specific work awaiting him. He had vague hopes of colonizing the age-old frontier marked by the Bío-Bío river. He did not speak a word of Spanish, and survived at first as an English teacher at Talcahuano. Then he acquired a heavily accented Spanish, learnt the Mapuche language, gave up teaching, spent time in a futile search for mines, and began pursuing the studies that would make him a pioneer not just in Chilean archaeology but also in its ethnography and anthropology. For a long while he financed his studies by working as an engineer on Chile's railways.

I resumed my walk towards the train museum, almost feeling by now that I was being drawn into some deepening mystery. It was a midweek morning, and the park was silent and almost empty. For a few moments there was a flurry of activity as a group of young children emerged from behind the abundant trees, fooled around with wooden swords and cardboard shields, then disappeared. No one else was left except for a man sitting in a distant kiosk selling sandwiches and drinks. The loneliness of the endless long alleys had left me disoriented. I headed towards him to ask directions.

'You look as if you've travelled a very long distance,' he observed before I had barely opened my mouth. The man was tall and gaunt, with strands of dyed hair swept over his forehead, and only two remaining teeth.

'I used to travel once,' he continued, looking at me with a smile that was both friendly and predatory. 'I went all over the world, I did. I was young of course, like you are.'

He was wearing a crumpled purple floral shirt, faded at the collar.

'I know what you're thinking. What am I doing in this kiosk? Well I can tell you this hasn't always been my job. I'm just standing in today for an old friend, she's had to go into hospital.'

His voice seemed to be getting camper by the minute. 'There was this Jew who employed me for twenty-seven years. He had an export business selling jewellery and ceramics. For twenty-seven years my life was one long holiday. I loved travelling, I went everywhere.'

'I like talking to you,' he said, as his speech trailed into a by now unstoppable monologue. 'Now let me tell you about San Marino, that's my sort of place. I almost preferred it to the Vatican. Andorra was nice too. But the country I adored above all others was Mongolia. I just adored Mongolia . . .'

I tried to get away at the point when his rambling, improbable list of places became tinged with a no less fantastical-sounding homoerotic element involving a 'well-armed' Irish friend called Sean ('we travelled to so many places together, we even shared the same bed, but we were never lovers'). But then, as seemed so often to be the way in Chile, the subject of trains made an unexpected appearance.

'What I really loved when travelling, and I haven't been anywhere now in fifteen years, ever since the accident –' he paused to indicate a couple of crutches tucked away behind the counter,' – a van went out of control and crushed my legs . . . But to get back to what I was saying, what I really loved was travelling by train. I've done all the great journeys, the Trans-Siberian, the Orient Express, all of them. Once I went overnight with Sean from Moscow to St Petersburg, and we slept naked in the same tiny couch, and still didn't do anything . . . I loved trains, and that's why I like helping out in this kiosk, it's good being so near the train museum . . . Oh, I've quite forgotten, you were asking me how to get there.'

Still shaky from listening to his monologue I followed the path he indicated and came to what must once have been the railway stop for those coming to the park by train. I paid my ticket and wandered into a well-kept grassy area where examples of almost every type of train ever used on Chile's national railways were as lovingly arranged as if they had been flower beds. With notebook in hand, I methodically went to every one of them, entering the carriages that were open, walking down steps to inspect the undercarriages of the engines, copying down data such as the number of English-built Kitson-Meyer locomotives in operation on the Transandino line between 1911 and 1971, or the passenger capacity of the apparently revolutionary trains in use on the Santiago–Temuco line. After half an hour or so, I came to the same conclusion I had reached after conscientiously ploughing through the main books on South America's railways: I had absolutely no technical interest in the subject. All I could offer, like the man in the kiosk, was an enormous sentimental attachment to trains. They seemed to feature in all my most vivid early memories of travelling.

I was drifting far away from Chile and into memories of past train journeys: going all the way from London to Moscow; sitting on a wooden seat across Portugal next to a baby pig in 1975; turning black with soot during the nights I slept upright on the remaining steam trains of Franco's Spain. Then all of a sudden I became aware of having been in the museum almost an hour without having seen any train used on the Antofagasta line. I wanted to talk about the railway on which my grandfather had worked with one of the museum's staff. I approached a hurried-looking young man who happened to be the director.

'I'm very busy today,' he told me, 'and I'm afraid I can't talk to you.' During his three seconds of hesitation before heading off to do his mysteriously urgent work, I managed to squeeze in a question about the Antofagasta railway. 'Oh, that doesn't concern us,' he said, 'We only deal with State railways. The railway you're referring to has always been privately owned.'

At the point of entering the door to his office, he turned round to supply me with one final and surprising piece of information. 'It's the most profitable railway line in the world.'

There was little need now for me to remain in Santiago. I was anxious to get going to Valparaíso and Antofagasta, and from there to head off as soon as I could into Bolivia, before the carnival season was over and the revolution broke out. The situation in Bolivia appeared to be getting worse every day, and the president who had succeeded the recently deposed 'Goni', a certain Carlos Mesa, had been given until the end of February to begin putting into motion his promised reforms. Already he was resorting to desperate means: he was seeking to boost his popularity by fanning the widespread hatred that had existed towards Chile ever since the latter's annexation of Bolivia's coast after 1879. Bolivians had begun symbolically destroying Chilean goods; and there was a very real danger that the overland borders between the two countries would imminently be closed.

But there was a problem about my leaving Santiago. The more I settled in to life at the Donoso household, the more pleasantly cocooned I felt from the realities I would soon have to face. I was rapidly losing my original discomfort at having a maid tidying up my belongings every morning, making my bed, and washing and ironing my clothes. I was also enjoying the glamorous daily socializing into which I was being drawn by Geraldine and Gonzalo. Much later during my stay in South America, when I had begun feeling like a Gulliver moving from one idiosyncratic land to the next, I would characterize my time with the Donosos as a foray into a world populated by a super-race. Their friends were all like them: handsome, successful, immaculately dressed, international in their background, and fluent in at least three languages; and the women were uniformly tall and blonde. They met up regularly in smart restaurants, or in parties given in well-guarded modern urbanizations on the outskirts of the city.

Gonzalo alone did not always seem entirely part of this world. He was always there, smiling in the background, enjoying his food and wine, and that typically Chilean drink to which I became instantly addicted, the *pisco* sour. However, I had the impression that in another life he would have liked to have broken free from the shackles of too much perfection. I could imagine him in two very different reincarnations: as a wild hedonist, or else as a scholarly recluse, tired of the superficialities of life. The complexity of his personality became more explicable to me after I met his larger-than-life father and namesake, who turned up one evening like some apparition from the English past.

Gonzalo Sr had not an ounce of English blood, but he had the courteous manner of some English aristocrat of old, with a cravat and sports jacket to match. As with many Chileans of his generation, he had had an English nanny and an education at an English college in Chile. This appearance and upbringing, allied with a perfect old-fashioned English, made him the ideal link figure between my grand-father's world and my own; and I was only too pleased when, in the course of our first evening together, he offered to take me to Valparaíso, a town he loved and knew well. But on the way there he proposed furthering my 'Chilean education' by having me stay for a few days at the remote country property where he had chosen to live on his own, 'botanizing, reading, making the time pass'. The name of this place had an almost fairy tale ring to it – La Retama de Catapilco.

Gonzalo Sr collected me early in the morning, and gave me the sort of advice my grandfather must often have been in need of: he told me how much I should tip the maid. I had not thought of giving her anything, not out of meanness but out of ignorance: to an Englishman of my generation it seemed curious if not insulting to leave money to someone employed by your friends. But Gonzalo was a man of traditional courtesies who heightened my fear of social blun-ders by stating that the informal use of '*tu*' might make a woman 'of her class' uncomfortable.

As we drove out of Santiago and towards Catapilco, I quickly learnt more about this man, who would definitely have fitted into my grand-father's 'interesting' category. A doctor by training, he was one of thousands of Chilean intellectuals whose lives had been brutally inter-rupted in 1973 when Augusto Pinochet ousted and executed the liberal reformer Salvador Allende. After going into exile for many years, Gonzalo came back to Chile at the age of fifty-three with the intention of retiring, buying a place in the country, and putting into practice his philosophy of life: to be free, to have no ties. While this might have made him by his own reckoning less than perfect as a father and husband, it had turned him into the sort of mentor I would have loved to have had when younger. A man of contrary opinions with an encyclopedic knowledge about everything, he also had an impish and perverse sense of humour, and a Rousseau-like passion for solitary wanderings in nature.

His relief on getting away from the 'dusty city' was palpable. He had become, he told me, a country person, nervous and irritable if he spent too long in Santiago, and uncomprehending of high-living urbanites like his son.

'Look how the sky is changing,' he remarked, as we passed through what could have been an invisible filter trapping the contaminated air. Further on, emerging from a tunnel, we were back in a Chile as bright and freshly coloured as when Darwin or my grandfather had seen it.

We were now on the world's longest road, the Pan-American Highway. To the south this trailed off into the fjords of Patagonia; to the north it ran almost uninterruptedly to Alaska. For the whole long length of central Chile the road went through scenery apparently almost identical to what we were seeing now – an endlessly expanding and contracting lush green valley, hemmed in by Andean foothills. Before the nineteenth century, when mining became the nation's principle export industry, Chile had been an essentially agricultural country, divided into large tracts of land which had been awarded originally to those who had accompanied the colonizer Pedro de Valdivia. The main focal points of rural Chile were the country estates or haciendas, such as the one at what is now the town of La Ligua, where we left the motorway.

'This was the home in the seventeeth century of La Quintrala,' Gonzalo told me. 'You might have heard of her, she was one of the most notorious figures in our history. She did away with her first husband with a poisoned chicken, and later she seduced and killed a knight of the Order of St John. Then she put the blame for the knight's murder on a servant who was subsequently hanged. Afterwards there was no stopping her.'

La Retama de Catapilco seemed at first sufficiently isolated for La Quintrala's shadow not to intrude. Set in a small valley of its own, off a track bordered by cacti, exotic plants, russet red scrubland, and eucalyptus groves, Gonzalo's house was a pleasingly modern construction in wood, filled with inherited old furniture, and with panoramic windows that made the most of superb sweeping views down to a distant coastal plain.

But behind all this undeniable beauty I began soon to be conscious of an element of menace. Plants of seductively exotic appearance were explained to me as 'insect-eating', or liable to produce extreme allergic reactions in humans; and then I was told that this was the part of Chile with the highest concentration not only of earthquakes, but also of the dreaded Chagas beetle, whose bite caused AIDS-like symptoms that were not often apparent until twenty years later. Trying not to think of all these dangers I jumped into the swimming pool only to land on a giant, decomposing rat.

These were surroundings where I felt I would never be entirely at home; and this feeling of being out of place was reinforced when I tried horse-riding for the first time, doing so in the company of two leather-clad young *huasos* or gauchos. Told off for holding the reins in both hands ('a true *huaso* would never do that'), and unable to keep any control whatsoever over the remarkably tame horse chosen for me, I soon concluded that I would never fulfil my childhood dream of emulating Tschiffely, or even master the equestrian skills my grandfather had needed in South America.

More disconcerting still was the occasion when Gonzalo drove me up into the high Andes which, seen from nearby, had an even more terrifying aspect than I had anticipated. Leaving a green valley, abundant in vineyards and grand haciendas, we ascended in violent hairpins up a bare chasm bordered by giant dark-grey slopes. Sensations of vertigo and claustrophobia merged with feelings of pathos inspired by glimpses of the abandoned Transandino line, a once celebrated railway link between Chile and Argentina which now survived only as fragments of twisted rail, conveying a sense of the futility of human endeavour.

It was more of a relief than ever to return that day to what had became my favourite feature of life at La Retama de Catapilco – the five o'clock tea. Gonzalo Sr was no lover of routine, and liked the freedom of being able to eat whenever he felt like it. However, when it came to afternoon tea, he had an attitude as unbending as my grandmother's had been. Tea had to be served unfailingly at five o'clock, and according to a ritual that began with the placing on the kitchen table of the cracked remnants of a porcelain set dating back probably to Edwardian England. No ordinary cups or plates would do, nor could the tea be anything other than Lapsang Souchong or Earl Grey, accompanied by toast and his own home-made marmalade. The memories all this brought back of Sundays at 30 Meadway reinforced my view of Gonzalo's house as an enclave of security in the midst of deceptively calm surroundings.

The threat that lurked outside seemed to be getting closer. On the night before we were due to drive to Valparaíso, we stayed up as always talking until it was so dark we could barely see each other. Gonzalo spoke that night of near-death experiences in which he had became convinced that his cellar was packed full of corpses in need of being cut up into smaller and more manageable pieces. I went to sleep soon afterwards, and woke up trembling and in a sweat two hours later. I was absolutely sure that a giant bird had flown into the room, and that the flap of its wings on departing had been so strong that my ears had been deafened and the house left shaking.

'That was a very strong tremor last night,' said a nonchalant Gonzalo over breakfast the next morning. 'We tend to have two or three a month. We're due soon for a major catastrophe.'

The coastal fog was slow to lift that morning. We left Catapilco in dense fog and were still in it when we reached the first of a string of coastal villages, places that were laden with romantic youthful memories for Gonzalo. Papudo, with its fish market on the beach, resembled, under these cold grey conditions, a fashionable fishing village on the north-ern Spanish coast. Zapallar was a cross between an old-fashioned resort in Brittany and the bosky, villa-filled peninsula outside California's Monterrey. We went up and down its steep, winding drives, pausing for a moment outside what had been the Donosos' grand summer home, and then again outside a more modest stone villa that had once served as a writing retreat for Gonzalo's brother José, now buried, together with his parents, in an outlying cemetery jutting out into the Pacific.

Cachagua, further south, and more up-market still, was remem-bered by Gonzalo as a left-wing Bohemian haven. This is how it was during the heady, pre-Pinochet days currently being made respectable by a popular Chilean soap opera called *Hippy*. His great friend then in the village was someone with the appropriate name of Casanova, whose house looked down towards an enormously long stretch of sandy beach backed by gentle hills. We made a special detour to see it.

'This was the centre of Casanova's amorous operations,' confided Gonzalo, 'and it almost became mine. I was going to buy it for a song, but then the deal fell through at the last minute. I could have been a millionaire by now.'

Yet he had no regrets. He could have spent his retirement surrounded by Santiago socialites, but he needed his isolation. He was like one of those ancient men I had heard about in Africa's Dogon Valley: they go off on their own to die in caves high up on the cliff face, so at the moment of their deaths their spirits pass directly into nature. Except that Gonzalo did not believe in spirits or the after-life.

The coastal road widened and became noisy with traffic, and soon we were skirting towering holiday homes like those of Spain's Costa del Sol. Under a fast-brightening sky we sped past the bustling resort of Viña del Mar, then at the height of its season. The beaches ended, the warehouses began, and within minutes of leaving Chile's Marbella, we had gone back 100 years or so and entered the port of Valparaíso. Everything was dusty, dirty and decayed. Faded letters over crumbling ornamented plasterwork indicated old customs offices, shops once owned by Croatian and Jewish traders, hotels that had been grand in their time but looked today like brothels.

The road passed the abandoned railway station, then opened up into a broad square fronted on one side by the port and on another by an ostentatious nineteenth-century building with the words '*ARMADA DE CHILE*' spelt out in capitals on the façade. Gonzalo brazenly parked the car in the very middle of the square, allowing me to look more closely at this demented example of neo-French baroque. It seemed very familiar. I took out from my bag a handful of my grandfather's tiny photos of Chile, until I came to one of the building I had been staring at. The photo must have been taken almost on the spot where I was standing. On the back my grandfather had written, 'The Intendencia (City Hall) Valparaíso at the time of the funeral of the late president Montt.' The date was 3 February 1911.

Bethel had woken up that day in a state of nervous anticipation. A grand state occasion was about to take place; but all he could think about was getting to the post office as soon as possible to pick up the letter he was hoping to receive from Sophie. Much could have happened in the five weeks since he had last heard from her. Nothing now seemed as certain as before. She might have concluded that marriage to a first cousin was not such a good idea after all. She might have realized the full implications of losing three of the most formative years of her life waiting for him. She might have written to call the whole engagement off; or she might have postponed writing while deciding what to do. Or her letter might have been lost or delayed, whereupon Bethel would not have known what to think.

The central post office was almost opposite the Intendencia, so I persuaded Gonzalo to walk over there, allowing me to imagine more clearly the sequence of emotions, from my grandfather's anxious arrival at the building to his excitement at discovering that there was indeed a letter awaiting him, and then to his impatient search for a quiet place in which to read it. In the film I would later see based on *The Motorcycle Diaries* by the young Che Guevara, the future revolutionary also receives at Valparaíso a letter from his fiancée. He chooses to read it in one of the stations of the famously rickety funicular lifts that were built between 1883 and 1916 as a link between the narrow lower town and the rapidly spreading residential quarters on the hillsides above. Alberto Granado, Che's companion on his journey across South America, is with him at the time, and shows concern at his friend's sullenness on putting down the letter. Nothing is said; but it is clear from Che's expression that the beautiful young woman whom he has left behind in Argentina has ended their relationship.

Happily, Bethel's letter from Sophie only confirmed her love for him. 'At last!' he penned almost immediately in reply. 'Once more have I feasted my eyes on your own special and most precious calligraphy on an envelope before enjoying the contents, which in the twinkling of an eye reduced eleven thousand miles to a mere nothing.' Yet he still wished for more. 'I wished that your letters could as efficiently annihilate time, for I wanted to know how everything goes with you at this moment, one whole month since you wrote these letters.'

On shore with him at the time he received Sophie's letter was Dr Sturdy, his inseparable companion now that Burke had left the ship. Relieved and delighted to have heard from Sophie, Bethel went happily with his friend to witness the solemn transfer of Pedro Montt's body from the battleship *Blanco Encalado* to the railway station. Montt had actually died five months before, in Bremen, where he had gone to try and improve his ailing health. The grand ceremonies attendant on his posthumous return to Chile were wholly disproportionate to the man's significance as a president; but they were typical of the triumphant, patriotic mood that had been fanned by the previous September's lavish celebrations marking 100 years of Chile's independence from Spain.

Montt's funeral, following on so shortly from the centenary cele-brations, gave Bethel plenty of opportunity to reflect on Chilean politics, and on the way the country had been ruled since 1810 by a feudal-minded conservative oligarchy. Pedro Montt's rather more dis-tinguished father Manuel had been one of Chile's more promising and brilliant presidents, who had began his rule in 1851 by trumpeting the theme of material progress, and emphasizing the role of the telegraph and the railway as the prime instruments of civilization. However, his authoritarian, unbending style provoked almost as much dissent as the proposed reforms of the first truly liberal Chilean president, José Balmaceda, were to do later. Balmaceda, often thought of simplisti-cally as a precursor to Salvador Allende, was a man from a wealthy landowning family who tried to bring about reforms that would have damaged the interests of his class. His rule ended in 1891 with his suicide and a civil war which would be graphically described to Bethel by one of its eyewitnesses in Valparaíso.

Persistent political infighting and a series of brutally suppressed workers' strikes (including, in 1903, that of the stevedores of the Pacific Steam Navigation Company) characterized Chile's emergence into the twentieth century. Little changed under the rule of the hard-working but unimaginative Pedro Montt, and little change was prom-ised during the first months of his seventy-five-year old successor Ramón Barros Luco, a man best remembered today for purportedly remarking that there were 'two types of problem: those that solve themselves and those that have no solution.'

Bethel, to whom Chile's reputation as the 'England of South America' had seemed genuinely an indication of a place where justice and fairness ruled, was already finding the country wanting in what he perceived as English qualities. Though he could admire the Chileans for their 'fearlessness, discipline and organization' in battle, he found that 'politically they are hopelessly corrupt'. For someone raised on ideals of civic virtue it must have been particularly galling to encounter 'utterly venial' local governments who pocketed the taxes and rates, and 'never had any work done to show for it'. The 'wretched' appearance of Chile's towns was for Bethel a direct consequence of such corruption; and though money was being borrowed to finance ambitious improvement schemes, the country was 'getting so wretchedly impoverished' that he saw no way of paying back the loans. To make matters worse, the Chilean national pride was such that they 'prefer to keep things in their hands and muddle along somehow'. Having previously criticized the Brazilians for their dependence on the West, he now recognized 'the benefits that Brazil and the Argentine have gained by giving up most of the public works to foreign enterprise and capital.'

Given Bethel's and Dr Sturdy's as yet very limited grasp of Spanish (which would lead later on their first day in Valparaíso to 'an amusing time trying to explain everything we wanted' to the waiters in the Hotel Royal), the attitudes of the two men towards Chile were of course heavily dependent on those of the country's large and burgeoning English community.

If there was anything specifically English about Chile it was the legacy of the large numbers of English people drawn to the country from the early nineteenth century onwards. Attracted initially by its mines and a reputation for relative stability compared with its neighbours, Chile's English population already numbered 4,000 by 1861, nearly half of whom lived in Valparaíso. As with Spain's sherry capital of Jerez de la Frontera, marriages between the English residents and members of the local upper class were comparatively frequent, so much so that W. H. Koebbel, an Englishman visiting Chile at the same time as Bethel, could note in his book *Modern Chile* (1913), that 'the general appearance of the better class Chilian resembles that of the English to a remarkable degree.' Koebbel was clearly delighted by this, especially as Chilean Englishness came with a sense of humour he thought lacking in other South American peoples.

'That which cannot fail to endear the inhabitants of the long and narrow land to the average Britisher is the fact that so many of their number are not only able to understand and appreciate "chaff", but to render it back, occasionally with interest, in the same spirit in which it is given.'

On reaching Valparaíso, the 'Chilian Liverpool', Koebbel's admiration for the country's inhabitants knew almost no boundaries. This was the Chilean town where English influence was strongest, and where Lord Cochrane had once lived, an English admiral and mercenary, whose help in Chile's war of independence against Spain had made of him a national hero.

'Valparaíso,' wrote Koebbel, 'is perhaps the most Anglicized of all the towns in the South American Republics. Indeed, there are not a few streets whose names ring with a homely sound to British ears – with that of Admiral Cochrane well in the forefront.'

It was from his experiences in Valaparaíso that Koebbel was able definitively to state that an Englishman in Chile 'is, from the social point of view, a far greater success than in many other places in South America'. The average Chilean, in Koebbel's view, was by no means perfect, and, 'for all his alertness and physical advantages, retains many of those Spanish characteristics which we of the North are wont to look upon as defects' (unpunctuality, for example). But he could forgive Chileans everything for their sympathy towards the English. 'As a nation we are popular in Chile!' he jubilantly concluded. 'If for nothing beyond this sense of discrimination we must yield the Chilian [*sic*] profound respect!'

Perhaps it was the Englishness of Valparaíso that gave English visitors to the town a false sense of security. Bethel had arrived here only four years after a devastating earthquake which had greatly exacerbated the decline of its port (to be compounded by the opening of the Panama Canal in 1914). The poverty of the town's back streets had certainly not escaped him; but neither his nor any other English traveller's account properly conveyed the extent of Valparaíso's dangers. A Chilean journalist, writing in the newspaper *El Mercurio* in 1905, described the town not only as 'infected, fetid, pestilent, with its streets covered with a thin layer of fermenting filth', but also as 'a port from which any man who values his life should flee'. Quite apart from lacking a proper sanitation system, Valparaíso was the crime capital of a country that was reckoned in 1902 to have the highest homicide rate in the world. The town's hospitals admitted so many patients with knife wounds that there was not enough room to accommodate the diseased.

The three days that Bethel spent in Valparaíso with Dr Sturdy involved escaping this squalid reality, whether by undertaking long walks in the beautiful surroundings or else by socializing with the more privileged members of the town's English community. Their entry into this world came through an introduction from Bethel's Hull friend Tom Somerscales to his uncle, a 'Mr Sutherland', who ran the local English College.

Bethel and Dr Sturdy set off after their first day's lunch at the Hotel Royal, and a brief rest there to glance through 'some English and French illustrated newspapers', to try and find Mr Sutherland's house. They discovered it was situated in the town's most fashionable residential district, the hill of the Cerro Alegre; and now the pleasantness of life for Valparaíso's better-off English inhabitants was revealed in all its splendour. Mr Sutherland had 'a grand big house with an immense and gorgeous garden, with a perfectly glorious view over the city and bay.'

After being shown around the property, with its two 'very interesting' earthquake-proof houses that were being built for the owner's married daughters, they accompanied Mr Sutherland to a tournament match at the nearby tennis club. Later they accepted his 'very pressing invitation to dinner', and ended the day sitting out on the verandah listening to his recollections of recent episodes in Chile's history. The 'old man' had a way of talking that 'rather betrayed the schoolmaster', but no matter. Bethel, buoyed by the morning's news from Sophie, and doubtless relieved at encountering a way of life in Chile with which he could identify, was in the highest of spirits.

I went with Gonzalo up the Cerro Alegre in search of the Sutherland mansion. We took a funicular lift from a dark and empty station hidden down an alley behind the main square. At the top of the hill I made Gonzalo pose for a photo against the London-built wheel mechanism of 1887: 'In Chile,' he told me just as I was on the point of pressing the shutter, 'we don't say 'Cheese', we say 'Pi-no-chet.'

For a quarter of an hour we strolled leisurely around this near deserted district of gabled red-roofed houses in painted wood, but were unable to find a building with a garden 'immense' enough to match Bethel's description. I speculated that the Sutherlands' property was the one where a fantastical, ramshackle art nouveau house stood now, built in 1916 by the Croatian nitrate magnate Pascual Barburizza. The house, now Valparaíso's Museum of Fine Arts, was closed for renovation; but a shirtless, bearded caretaker gave us a tour of the stripped whitewashed rooms. I absorbed the nostalgic smell of old polished floorboards before walking to a window to take in the coastal panorama of cranes and distant mountains that Bethel had observed from the Sutherlands' verandah.

Though Mr Sutherland himself proved elusive, the legacy of his compatriots became almost overwhelming as we continued our stroll into the adjoining Cerro Alegre, entering the sturdy Anglican church of St Paul's, admiring the huge organ donated by Queen Victoria, walking onto the funicular lift named after her, and beholding what I almost thought was an English-induced mirage when we reached the esplanade of the Paseo Atkinson, with its tiny front gardens, net curtains, dormer windows, a 'bed and breakfast' sign, and overall look of a slice of Southern England as recreated by a German expressionist.

'Do you still use the phrase "little blue room?"' suddenly asked Gonzalo, anxious now in his own words to 'take a leak', and hoping perhaps to come across one of Valparaíso's surviving Twyford's urinals. The impact of so many visions of old England had made him delve deeper into his child-learnt English vocabulary, and he had begun testing me with phrases that had largely died out with my grandfather. 'Sit ye down,' he said after we had walked inside the wood-panelled Café Turri, to 'murder a coffee', 'see a man about a dog', and to enter a conversation about the local football team, which was the oldest in Chile and still bore its original English name, 'the Wanderers'.

Back in the lower town, Gonzalo inquired what else I wanted to see in Valparaíso. Sheepishly I proposed the Neruda museum, having had almost as much as I could take of the town's English past.

'Not on your nelly!' he exclaimed, 'I wouldn't touch the place with a barge pole.' I was keen to know why, but all I got for an answer was the assertion that I had already been to the Neruda museum in Santiago. 'One Neruda museum is one too many if you ask me,' he pronounced as we approached our car on the main square. Two policemen were waiting for us.

Gonzalo now baffled me by speaking Spanish to them with a joke upper-class English accent. They did not look like the sort of people who would appreciate being made fun of. But it became clear almost right away that they thought he was genuinely English; they smiled and were courteous, and even apologized for having bothered us. Parking in the square was illegal and liable to large fines, but they told us not to worry as we calmly got into the car and drove away. A few moments later Gonzalo put on the same accent to ask directions from two Navy police guarding the former Intendencia. Once again, we were treated as if we were the most distinguished of visitors. 'If you pretend you are English,' explained Gonzalo, swerving off into a near vertically-ascending narrow street, 'you are always so much better looked after here.'

The one-storeyed columned house which might or might not have belonged to Lord Cochrane briefly claimed my now wandering attention, which was soon drawn away from the building and into surrounding streets lined by a very un-English jumble of brightly painted corrugated-iron walls. I began thinking again of the young Che Guevara, and remembered how little interest he had shown in the town's remnants of an aristocratic England, and how much instead he had loved 'the madhouse museum beauty of its strange corrugated-iron architecture . . . blending with the leaden blue of the bay.'

When the evening started to set in, and a fog bank could be seen advancing from the sea, Valparaíso became the seedy, menacing place that had seduced Che completely. We were driving, it seemed, in circles, returning repeatedly to the dingy Plaza Wheelwright, the shuttered market place, the former customs house where Pinochet's father had worked, the same old stairs and alleys that trailed off into the darkness. To Che, the pampered son of Argentina's bourgeoisie, but with a developing social conscience, all this was as exotic and bizarrely beautiful as anywhere that he had known before. Others of his kind had been lured in the 1950s down into the port of Marseilles, into the pungent medina of Tangier, or into Barcelona's notorious, absinthe-fuelled Barrio Chino. But Che satisfied his *nostalgie de la boue* (literally, 'longing for mud') down in the backstreets of Valparaíso.

'As if patiently dissecting,' he wrote, 'we pry into dirty stairways and dark recesses, talking to the swarms of beggars; we plumb the city's depths, the miasmas that draw us in. Our distended nostrils inhale the poverty with sadistic intensity.' His companion Alberto Granado, evoking their nocturnal wanderings through the haunts of prostitutes and drunken sailors, put it more succinctly: 'We thought we were in the Casbah in Algiers.'

It was nearly midnight, and Valparaíso belonged now to the past. We had stayed long enough to have a club sandwich in a large and once fashionable cafeteria from the 1950s, with lugubrious bow-tied waiters, an abundance of Formica, an absence of clients, and a former reputation, according to Gonzalo, as a place once frequented by liberated and available young women. Now we were in what seemed like the middle of nowhere – a bus station on the outskirts of the small industrial town of La Calera. The town, like so many in Chile, had been damaged so frequently by earthquakes that there only remained a grid of low nondescript buildings whose age could best be determined by the layers of grime. Late at night the main signs of life had come from the place's disproportionately large number of internet cafes. There was certainly little going on at the bus station, where the refreshment kiosks had closed for the day, and the ticket booths had lights on but there was no one behind the windows. A grumpy young man nodded his head to confirm that the bus north was due shortly.

I told Gonzalo not to wait. We gave each other the hurried, physically awkward hug that Englishmen attempt when trying to look Latin. He walked off quickly, leaving me with the disquieting feeling of being suddenly alone in an immense country.

At this stage of his journey to Antofagasta my grandfather had felt the same. The HRS *Oronsa*, as he wrote to Sophie after the boat had left Valparaíso, 'had become almost home-like and it is of course the last tie with the old country.' There were still forty-eight hours before he was due to arrive at his final destination, but already he had begun thinking of his time on the boat as already over. The atmosphere on board was not the same as before. At Valparaíso a 'huge crowd, mostly Americans of a rather objectionable type' had joined the ship.

Sadder still, almost all those who had been with him since Europe had now gone, bar the dull and unfortunate Miss Oldham. The great-est loss for Bethel was the departure of Dr Sturdy, who had been with him almost every moment at Valparaíso. Together they had returned several times to the Sutherlands, been on an outing to the races at Viña del Mar, and tramped in the nearby mountains, culminating in a fifteen-hour trek to catch an unforgettable last view of Aconcagua. 'I was sorry to say farewell to Dr Sturdy,' wrote Bethel in words almost certainly inadequate to his emotion, 'we had become quite chummy.'

My night bus came, full of tired, pasty faces from Santiago. It was hot and stuffy, and the seat in front of me was reclined almost into my chest. There were luxury buses in Chile with bed-like seats and even cabins; but the abstemious Gonzalo had infected me with his philos-ophy that to travel in any degree of comfort was not to travel at all. I restlessly moved my legs to find a better position, and got into a fitful conversation with a friendly student who told me, as Gonzalo had done before, that the word 'leg' is Chilean slang for 'woman'. I smiled as best as I could at his pun about not getting 'legs crossed'. The next moment he was asleep, with his head slumping occasionally against my shoulder. I prepared myself for a night of unease.

I had wanted ideally to travel north by boat; but there was not even the option of following the example of Che Guevara – bluffing my way at night into Valparaíso's port and then hiding away in a 'shit-filled toilet' on the first boat headed for Antofagasta. Regular cargo boats between the two places were as much a thing of the past as the train service with its name like the title of a Hitchcock film, 'Northern Longitudinal'. Functioning until 1986, when Pinochet had a large section of the track removed, it had linked the Santiago–Valparaíso line with Chile's northernmost town of Iquique. Its starting point was La Calera, which many Chileans only recall as a place to change trains. At Gonzalo's house I had read a book chronicling the real-life mystery of a man, Enrique Riquelme, who had done precisely that. A bank clerk in the southern Chilean town of Chillán, he had been travelling to Iquique to attend the baptism of a grandchild. On the afternoon of 2 February 1956 he embarked at La Calera on the last stage of a three-and-a-half-day journey. He never reached his destination.

The isolated desert location where Riquelme's untouched body was found forty-three years later was many hours away from where I now found myself; but the attack of madness that alone explains his abrupt departure from the train was one I was beginning to understand as I thought of the vast emptiness into which I was heading. Finally I fell into a welcome deep sleep, aware occasionally only of the snore of the man behind, the cramp in my leg, the huge distances covered without even a light to be seen outside, or a passing vehicle. I woke up to the dawn and to a rocky landscape apparently devoid of vegetation.

The regions of Chile are numbered as if in a scale broadly reflecting the diminishing rainfall, as you travel north from the perpetually damp Patagonia (the Twelfth Region) up to the arid wastes of the First Region, where in places it has never rained at all. I was no further than the Third Region; but already the view from my timidly parted curtain was of a bare, corrugated expanse of rocks, stones and sandy slopes. I had reached the notorious Atacama Desert, and I was sobered by the thought that a good 1,000 more kilometres of this bleak void stretched north to the Peruvian frontier. And that it would get worse.

Much of the Third Region was technically only a 'semi-desert', a place where rains were not infrequent during the winter months, and where springtime was famous for the thousands of different flowers that brightly carpeted the inhospitable ground. Moreover, as the bus persevered deeper into the region, and the chilling greyish blue of the early morning light was dispelled by a growing band of ochre orange, unexpected pockets of intense green cultivation began appearing on either side of the road.

It was 7.30 in the morning, and we were entering the long, oasis-like valley where the regional capital of Copiapó was situated. 'The smell of the fresh clover,' Darwin had noted on arriving at the town in June 1835, 'was quite delightful, after the scentless air of the dry sterile Despoblado.' At the town's bus station I extended my stiff, cramped legs, and collected my luggage from the hold. I needed to break my journey briefly, to replenish the mind and body before venturing into the greater wilderness beyond.

I reckoned it would be a long time before I saw a town with such a cheerful, open and well-preserved aspect. The place had a lushly planted, palm-shaded central square, a wonderful array of old wooden buildings, and a history that went back far earlier than the late nineteenth century: Pedro de Valvidia, marching into the valley from the Peruvian Andes in 1540, had embarked here on his campaign to claim Chile for the Spanish crown.

But, as with almost everywhere in northern Chile, it was mining that brought fame to Copiapó. The town, founded officially in the late eighteenth century, when gold and copper were being mined in the area, experienced a dramatic change of fortunes in 1832 with the discovery at nearby Chañarcillo of the third-largest silver mine in South America. For once the main beneficiaries of the mine were not foreigners but Chileans who, until the exhaustion of the seams by 1870, made Copiapó a magnet for financiers, industrialists, politicians and intellectuals. A testimony to the sophistication of these years were the soberly elegant neoclassical structures built from imported Californian pine by British and North American artisans. And a further testimony to the town's progressive nature was Wheelwright's railway.

Two old engines rested in the tidily maintained forecourt of a railway station that could have been a horizontally proportioned church of the Regency period: a small wooden belfry crowned the pediment of a façade whose architectural elements were highlighted in bare, beautifully crafted pine. The building, reputedly now a railway museum, but unmarked and presumably unvisited, was firmly closed; and railings outside prevented me from getting onto an abandoned platform that stood, protected by an ironwork canopy, in front of a scorched slope like the backdrop of an American Western.

The station was on the edge of town, off the road to the port of Caldera, the final destination for the trains which no longer existed. Waiting for the next bus there I debated whether to phone Gonzalo's son from Santiago. He and his family were now on holiday at a small beach resort near Caldera. I had been told to give them a ring should I be 'passing through the area'; but I felt guilty at intruding once again on their privacy; and it seemed almost cowardly to return so quickly to the Donoso fold. I decided to call Gonzalo Jr all the same, but just out of politeness, to find out how they were, to say what a wonderful time I had had at Catapilco.

'Where are you?' he asked before I could say anything. He was almost disbelieving when I told him; he too was in Copiapó, on a shopping trip with his son. He instructed me to wait where I was.

We left Copiapó on the Caldera road, and drove towards Bahía Inglesa, 'the English Bay', where the Donosos were staying. It was comforting to be again with people I knew as the last patches of green, possibly the last in the whole of Chile, died away shortly beyond the town. Semi-desert became desert proper as the great Pan-American Highway, now reduced to a single empty lane, crossed a flat stony plateau bordered by distant, desiccated ranges, microscopically clear under the sharp sunlight.

I asked Gonzalo about the tiny shrines that had now begun to flank the road at what seemed like rapidly decreasing intervals, as if in inverse proportion to the growing monotony of the landscape.

'They're the tombs of people who died there in crashes,' he told me, 'before a priest could reach them.'

The shrines took a fascinating variety of forms, from sizeable huts containing what looked like miniature cathedrals to glass-fronted assemblages rather like the surrealist boxes of the American artist Joseph Cornell. They were called 'animitas' or 'little souls', and were to be found all over Chile; but it was only in this desert landscape that I first become conscious of their existence. Perhaps they claimed the attention more in an environment so redolent of death.

The line of the defunct railway followed the Pan-American for a while before branching off towards the coastal range. We went with it, taking what Gonzalo called the 'long route' to Bahía Inglesa. Our road, a dust track etched into the desert and stabilized by salt, ran for long stretches next to the railway which, as it neared the sea, hugged the contours of giant, wind-carved rocks. We were on a ghost train, I pretended to Gonzalo's son, just before turning a corner and having the very real shock of seeing below us the down-market resort of Puerto Viejo. Improvised cubical houses with painted boards and corrugated-iron roofs spread outwards from the beach into the sur-rounding grey rubble like a slum that had been swept ashore. The summer season was supposedly in full swing; but the atmosphere was as mournful as that of a cemetery.

Bahía Inglesa was for a wealthier kind of tourist, and even its name, though derived from an English shipwreck, had a ring about it of a fashionable resort. Superficially it was reminiscent of one of the wilder stretches of Spain's Almería coast, but hugely magnified and with a character that Almería must have had fifty years ago, before the invasion of northern Europeans in search of a wild and exotic paradise. The tourists who were here, mainly Chileans from the south, appeared almost entirely swallowed up by the grand sweep of the bay.

Gonzalo Jr and Geraldine had isolated themselves from the rest of the resort by hiring one of a handful of Polynesian-style chalets huddled together on a side of the bay exclusively their own. Gonzalo was worried that I would get bored relaxing with them for a few hours on the beach. But, after the night I had been through, I could think of nothing more comforting than being with this young family, building sandcastles with the children, and enjoying a sea so limpid and blue that I felt almost purified on entering it. I only wished I could have stayed longer; but January was passing by quickly, the Bolivian carnival was approaching, and I had acquired some of my grandfather's eventual impatience to reach Antofagasta. So I resolved to stick to my plan to travel there that day on another overnight bus, after what would now be the shortest of visits to Caldera. Gonzalo promised to accompany me in the late afternoon to what I thought of as 'Wheelwright's town'.

'Whenever I go to a new town in Chile,' confessed Gonzalo, after ten minutes of driving me around Caldera, 'I always go straight to the cemetery.'

In the case of Caldera, a surprisingly small community of scattered, modest houses, there was not much else to see. Nothing appeared adequately to reflect the importance the town had enjoyed after the creation of its pioneering railway. The steepled parish church, oddly and erroneously attributed to Gustave Eiffel, was like that of a typical English village, and overlooked a suitably quiet square whose other main point of interest was a strikingly anachronistic coloured cut-out of Father Christmas riding on a sleigh. We did not stop the car there, and only did so for a moment down by the port where, after spotting a bar with the American engineer's name misspelt as 'Weelright', we found that the warehouse-like structure housing Chile's oldest surviving railway station was predictably shut.

'It's not worth seeing,' we were assured by an old man sitting on a bench outside. 'It was wonderful until a few years ago, then they turned it into a cultural centre.'

The monument which said most about Caldera's history was indeed the cemetery. Dating from 1876, when Chile became one of the earliest countries in the hemisphere to separate church from state, it was properly known as the *Cementerio Laico*, and was the national equivalent of Spain's Protestant Cemetery in Málaga, the first non-Catholic burial site in the country. The presence of such a cemetery here in Caldera indicated the extent of the foreign labour force beginning to come to northern Chile then. There were a few mausoleums built for Chinese immigrants and Orthodox Slavs; but the majority of those buried here were British subjects. The oldest tombs had ironwork railings made with scrap material from the railway yard, and were by the same English craftsmen responsible for the parish church. We probably stepped over their corpses as we walked past headstones on which the ubiquitous words 'Forsaken Homeland' were inscribed below the names of British places that seemed even to me now a universe away.

We went on to down several *pisco* sours before Gonzalo left me in the capacious outlying bar that became Caldera's bus station after 10.00 p.m. I was in higher spirits than when his father had said goodbye to me the night before; and I celebrated this by sitting down in front of a row of broken pinball machines to order another drink. The only other person waiting for the bus, a chubby, fresh-faced young man called Yenko, soon came to join to me. He was studying engineering, he informed me, at Antofagasta University.

I told him about my grandfather. I also asked what Antofagasta was like, a question that had troubled Bethel ever since being offered the job there. Enquiries on the HRS *Oronsa* had left him none the wiser.

'I have heard various things about Antofagasta,' he eventually reported to Sophie, 'good, bad and indifferent, but I will refrain from saying anything until I can verify these statements for myself.'

I had yet to hear or read anything good or indifferent about Antofagasta: everyone seemed unanimous in describing it as singularly depressing. So I was surprised and partially reassured to hear Yenko describing it as 'a lovely town to live in, very quiet and friendly, very safe'.

The bus pulled in at midnight, and I took my seat next to a giggling young woman travelling with two others. They were on their way to take up a job at Calama, a place where my grandfather would also be stationed. The name of their destination would later have alerted to me to the probability that they were prostitutes. But I was still as innocent as Sophie had been; and I was quite happy to respond to my neighbour's questions about where I was from, where I was going, and whether I was single. Then the bus left, the lights dimmed, and we drifted off into our separate worlds, under our separate blankets.

I had no difficulty that night in falling asleep, but before I did so, I went over in my mind the last letter Bethel had written to Sophie before arriving at Antofagasta. 'Sophie dearest,' he had begun, 'at this moment you are very much present in my thoughts, for this is my last night on board. Fourteen hours hence will see me landing at Antofagasta, and shortly after I expect I shall know my fate, where I am to go, and what I am to do. It is then that my venture really begins, God send it such success that I may soon be with you again, and for always.'

As I lay hunched up in the bus, with 400 near-uninterrupted miles of desert in front of me, I could almost hear myself mutter the words with which he had signed off this letter of 9 February 1911. 'Come to me,' he had urged, 'Come to me in my dreams tonight to wish me luck.'

3

Through the Great North

———∞———

A T 2.04 A.M., as I slept through the moonlit desert, an earth tremor registering Six on the Richter scale struck at the heart of the town I was travelling towards. The whole of Antofagasta was plunged into darkness, causing late-night revellers to run out panicking into the streets, abandoning bars, the floodlit marina, and parties such as the one given for the 'fourteen hopeful young ladies' competing to be queen in the town's 125th anniversary celebrations. The lights had only just come back on again when my bus entered the station, shortly before dawn. I woke up disorientated by exhaustion and the effects of too many *pisco* sours. For the past five hours I had been in a deep, drugged sleep, unvisited by my grandmother's spirit, undisturbed by thoughts of apocalypse, unaware of crossing from the Third Region into a part of Chile whose name alone hinted at its bleak vastness: the Great North.

My grandfather had reached Antofagasta soon after nightfall. An obscure local writer of the middle years of the last century, Daniel de la Vega, has conveyed the sadness of seeing the lights of his native town from the sea; but he was leaving, and they were symbols of a homeland that was vanishing. For Bethel, arriving, they had had exactly the opposite significance: if the ship was his last link with home, then the lights were emblematic of the insecurity that lay beyond.

I handed over the receipt for my luggage and walked out half asleep into the empty early-morning streets. Yenko, the student with whom I had talked earlier in the night, was still with me. He had taken on the role as my guide to Antofagasta, and was showing me to a nearby hotel I would find 'reasonable and good value'. The street was filthy and slightly menacing; and I would discover the next night that it was the haunt of transvestite prostitutes. But all I wanted now was to get to bed; and so I profusely thanked the obliging Yenko for leaving me inside the small lobby of a hotel not quite as sordid as its approach had suggested. The place had a slightly uncared-for, early 1960s look, and an elderly receptionist with a threadbare suit and matching yellowish hair. A room was available, and I collapsed straight into the bed that occupied most of it.

After little more than half an hour I was roused from sleep by the awakening street and the light filtering through thin unwashed curtains which could not be closed properly. I lay enclosed for a while within the synthetic sheets and blanket, until finally I could bear the room no longer. By eight o'clock I was outside the building, and walking towards the Plaza Colón, the main square in whose former Grand Hotel my grandfather had spent the night of 10 February 1911, his first in the city.

Bethel had been assured in England that his stays in Antofagasta would purely be passing ones. Though he still awaited his specific assignments, he was promised that these would be connected with the construction of a new branch line in Bolivia. With any luck, he thought, he would be able to set off there in the next day or so, and to begin work as soon as possible. He was restless to display his talents as an engineer.

I was hoping for a similarly brief and businesslike first stay in Antofagasta. Half-formed ideas that I had once entertained about spending a month or so in this town, which had assumed a perhaps exaggerated importance in my mind, had been rightly questioned in London by Philip Adeane ('I'm sure you writer chaps know what you're doing, but I can't help feeling that a month in Antofagasta would be a complete waste of your time'). And now that I was here, a few days seemed more than enough to get an initial feel for the place and its immediate surroundings. The impatience with which I had been infected was showing no sign of abating; and I was keener than ever to get started on the principal task I had set myself in South America: to follow as much as I could of the old Antofagasta–La Paz railway.

The token passenger service mentioned by Philip Adeane ran only to the town of Calama, about 200 kilometres east of Antofagasta, on the eastern edge of the Atacama Desert. To cross the Atacama by train there appeared to be no other choice but to sit in the driver's cab of a freight train or to travel with an engineer; and to do so I needed the permission of 'our man in Antofagasta', Miguel Sepúlveda, the Chilean director of the Ferrocarril del Antofagasta y Bolivia (the F.C.A.B.) as it was known in Spanish. Philip, as promised, had sent him the twenty-first-century equivalent of a letter of introduction – an email outlining who I was and what I intended doing. But the man was proving elusive. I had tried contacting him several times from Santiago, but was unable to find out whether or not he would be in Antofagasta to receive me. His secretary thought he might be back in his office by the Friday morning, the morning of my arrival. I was now waiting until it was a reasonable time to ring him.

The temperature, chilly in the early hours, warmed up rapidly as I wove my way through the blackened grid of streets sloping towards the sea from the arid coastal range behind. Much of Bethel's Antofagasta could still be glimpsed amidst the recent blight of crude concrete structures with flaking paint. Brash and shiny modern signs partially obscured the elaborately moulded façades of shops whose dark interiors contained untouched-looking goods stacked in square compartments right up to the ceiling. There were bars which the young Che Guevara would have happily entered, and internet cafés still recognizable as the former premises of English tailors. It did not need much imagination to recreate the Antofagasta that Bethel had photographed – a place with the desperate appearance of a Mexican frontier town, with horses and carriages throwing up dust along wide streets lined with wooden arcades, and low, flimsy-looking buildings partially clad with corrugated iron.

As I neared the Plaza Colón the architecture became more osten-tatious, and imposing functionalist blocks rose up incongruously alongside old pastel-coloured façades with wooden balconies and a profusion of angels, capitals and pilasters of stone or plasterwork. The square itself, an untidy miscellany of twentieth-century buildings overlooking a palm-shaded garden, still retained as its centrepiece what I had seen referred to as an 'imitation of London's Bing Ben'. This squat grey stone clock tower bore no visual relation to its English counterpart; but as I read the ceramic plaque commemorating the local British community's contribution towards Chile's 1910 centen-ary, the distorted chimes of the real Big Ben took me completely by surprise. Sadly the tower had been erected several months too late for its nostalgic sounds to be appreciated by my homesick grandfather during his anxious first night at the Grand Hotel.

This had been badly damaged by fire only a month after his first stay there, and had then been burnt down completely by striking workers in 1917. I had to make do with the pompous 1920s reconstruction, now the headquarters of a bank, as I tried recreating my grandfather's thoughts and movements on the morning of 11 February.

Bethel's first impressions of Antofagasta were unlikely to have been favourable. Though the letter in which he recorded these was lost in the post, he described the town soon afterwards as a 'semi-civilization' where 'everything is dirty and sordid', and 'rather trying to anyone who has the misfortune to be as fastidious as myself'. Opening the curtains of his hotel window for the first time in daylight, he would have taken in the 'hostile and uninspiring surroundings', and almost certainly concluded that the sooner he left the place the better. His fate would be known later that morning, after he had reported to the main offices of the Antofagasta (Chili) and Bolivia Railway Company.

From my vantage point in the Plaza Colón, from which these offices were also visible, I could visualize Bethel leaving the hotel, carrying with him the black leather attaché case in which he had placed the postal order for two shillings and sixpence advanced to him in England to pay for excess baggage. He was in a nervous state, and too early for his appointment, so he bided his time by stopping off at the kiosk on the square to purchase, as I had done, a copy of the *Mercurio de Antofagasta*. Scanning the edition of 11 February 1911, he would have come to a brief notice announcing the arrival of the HRS *Oronsa* the night before. The only two passengers listed as having come all the way from Liverpool were B. L. Jacobs and the perennially initial-less 'Miss Oldham'.

'Bing Ben' struck nine o'clock while I was immersed in these speculations. It seemed a good time to phone Miguel Sepúlveda. Anxiously I dialled his number only be told by the voice at the other end of the phone that he was 'not here'. This was not the news I was hoping for. Not even the prospect of a weekend in Antofagasta was appealing in my present restless mood. 'He's back in Antofagasta,' the voice continued, 'but we don't know if he'll be coming into the office today. He's flying off to Santiago after lunch. Try ringing again in an hour or so.'

I wandered crestfallen down to the harbour, where I passed the time studying the information panels in a regional history museum installed within the wooden former customs house. As I registered the coldly related facts, I paused occasionally to stare out of the window towards the point where the town disintegrated into a crowded cubist composition of tin-roofed prefabricated boxes abruptly terminated by stony mountain walls. Then finally I spotted it. Painted on one of the slopes was the white anchor my grandfather had mistaken for an advertisement, but which, I had just learnt, was a relic from the town's earliest days. A Cornishman, George Hicks, had had the idea of putting it there in 1868, to guide ships to a place then barely dignified with a name, almost impossible to single out in a coastline relentlessly the same for hundreds of miles to the south, for hundreds of miles to the north. Two years earlier no one would possibly have imagined that anyone would one day come and live here, in this most desolate of sites, totally unsuited for human habitation, almost without water, without even a natural harbour. But greed would make anything possible.

The whole history of Chile's Great North, as the museum confirmed for me, was the story of manically determined humans trying to survive against the greatest of natural odds. The Spaniards of the sixteenth century had suspected the vast mineral wealth that lay hidden beneath the surface of this terrifyingly large '*Despoblado*'; but even they, who had created at remote and dangerously high Potosí one of the world's largest cities, baulked at the thought of the Atacama. Its potential rewards were irrelevant in view of the unlikelihood of anyone being able to settle a land that must once have seemed as daunting as Antarctica. Even as late as 1854, the pioneering Atacama explorer Rodulfo Philippi (a native of the Copiapó region, like nearly all these explorers) could confidently assert that 'this desert lacks all the resources to make it habitable and to allow it to become a major means of commerce and communication.'

Philippi had misjudged his fellow beings; nor had he quite foreseen the world demand for the Atacama's most cruelly ironic commodity – natural fertilizers. The lack of rainfall in this driest of all deserts meant that the earth could maintain great crusted layers of nitrates, which are soluble and unstable compounds that can hugely enrich the soil of places where it does rain. Nitrates had been mined since the sixteenth century, but it was not until the mid-1850s, when a Chilean, Pedro Gamboni, developed a more economic means of exploiting them, that they promised to become an important source of wealth. All that stopped the 'nitrate boom' from taking off was the existence of a rival fertilizer, *guano*, or dried bird shit, which was to be found along the Atacama's coast. The search for guano deposits (*guaneras*) had begun in the 1830s and was responsible for bringing to the Antofagasta area one of its first and most intrepid prospectors, Juan López.

López was looking for anything that would make money, and he was prepared to suffer the greatest hardships in doing so. He had no illusions about the obstacles and dangers facing him in the Atacama; and in later life even claimed that an awareness of these merely strengthened his resolve to pursue his quest for 'guano, nitrate, borax and other substances'. Beginning his explorations in 1845, at the age of twenty, he explored the whole length of the coastline, and was rewarded in 1862 with the discovery of major *guaneras* at Mejillones. But a subsequent dispute with his then French employers soured his triumph. Four years later he moved forty kilometres down the coast to become the first and only citizen of the as yet unnamed Antofagasta, where he lived in a tent made from sewn-together sacks.

López would not be Antofagasta's only citizen for long. Later that year he was joined by José Santos Ossa, a more respectable-looking character who almost immediately uncovered nitrate under a large salt flat twenty-nine kilometres west of the future town. It was the perfect time to have done so: the main *guaneras* were nearing exhaustion, and the demand for fertilizers was continuing to grow. Santos Ossa, as perspicacious a businessman as he was a prospector, succeeded in 1868 in obtaining a government decree granting the newly formed Society for the Exploration of the Atacama Desert the right 'freely to exploit, process and export nitrate' for the next fifteen years. 'Jorge' Hicks, as he was now called, became an associate of the company, the English links of which would be extended in 1869 after its amalgamation with the English-run, Valparaíso-founded, Casa Gibbs to form Melbourne Clark and Co. Under this new amalgamation the first steps were made to create a permanent settlement in Antofagasta. In the early 1870s, workers' houses were built, together with a harbour, a plant for purifying sea water, and the first tiny stretch of what would become the Antofagasta-Bolivia Railway.

But, despite attempts to improve communications inland, Antofagasta remained at first almost entirely reliant on whatever could be transported by boat, including even the drinking water used to supplement that of the plant. The nascent town's fortunes were further hindered by natural catastrophes (such as a devastating earthquake and tidal wave in 1877), and by the worsening political situation.

Ninety-one per cent of the population was Chilean, but the whole of what is now the Second Region then belonged to Bolivia. Regular changes of Bolivian government resulted in regularly changing attitudes towards the Chilean and British mining owners. Economic crisis in Bolivia brought about the reneging of the 1868 agreement with Santos Ossa, and the imposition of a large tax on the export of nitrate. Jorge Hicks, who confessed now to having an 'almost fanatical hatred of the Bolivians', declared them to be the enemies of his company, was promptly thrown in prison, and became a Chilean national hero. The Chileans, gloating over the possibility of annexing to their country the mineral-rich Great North, took heed of Hicks's promptings to declare war on Bolivia. They were cunning enough to do so right in the middle of the carnival season, when they knew that the carnival-obsessed Bolivians would be otherwise distracted. On 14 February 1879, a Chilean fleet landed at Antofagasta without meeting the slightest resistance. Shots were fired and a few people killed when the Chilean troops moved on to Calama; but essentially the Bolivian Atacama fell without a struggle. Thus heartened, the Chileans set their sights on Peru, thereby protracting for three more years what is politely known as the War of the Pacific. Others prefer to think of it as the 'Bird Shit War', though the 'Nitrate War' would be a more accurate description.

The successful outcome of the war for Chile was wholly advantageous to the nitrate boom, and gave a massive boost to the Great North's population, which, from being only 2,000 in 1875, would grow to 234,000 by 1907. A pro-European, free-market policy on the part of the Chilean government meant also that the British became

Bethel Jacobs, *c.*1910

Sophie Solomons and her painter sister Estella, *c.*1907 (Sophie is on the left)

My grandfather's captions are in quotation marks

'Neptune's revels on board the *Oronsa*'

'The *Minas Gerais* in Río Harbour, 19/1/11'

'Soldiers parading before the Intendencia at Valparaíso during the funeral ceremonies of the late President Montt'

'The Palm Valley, Salto, nr Valparaíso. Dr Sturdy of RMS *Oronsa* in foreground'

'Calle Prat. The principal street in Antofagasta'

'The Avenida Ferrocarril, Antofagasta, 8/4/11'

'Dr Williams in front of doctor's bungalow, Mejillones'

Left: 'Chilean mule driver in a nitrate *oficina*'

Below: 'Madame Grillo and her daughter Paulina. Oficina Araucana, June/12'

Above: View of the River Loa, with the Loa bridge in the background

Right: Bethel relaxing by the River Loa

Below: 'The new bridge at Calama. The bridge is in its permanent position and bolted down on its bed plates'

The sail-driven carriage used on the stretch of line between Calama and the Conchi viaduct

'Conchi viaduct'

the main owners of the nitrate mines, the certificates for which had sunk dramatically in price when the war had been in progress.

The main beneficiary of all this was the man whose very name had destined him to make his fortune in the area, the Yorkshire-born John Frederick North. This man who, against all advice, had lasted out the war in the then Peruvian town of Tarapacá, was on hand to profit as much as he could from the arrival of the Chileans. A man who loved in later years to exaggerate the humbleness of his origins, North had begun his career in South America as a railway adviser at Caldera and elsewhere, and went on to become a ruthless entrepreneur and Chile's undisputed nitrate king. From the money he made out of the Tarapacá mines, he was able to spend most of the 1880s back in England, building a showy country house, hosting notoriously lavish parties, and acquiring for himself a title. But with the election of José Manuel Balmaceda as president in 1886, North's empire would be threatened. A politician perceived by British businessmen in Chile to be as damaging to their interests as Salvador Allende would be in the 1970s, Balmaceda was keen to nationalize the mines and destroy the British monopoly in northern Chile. His defeat following the civil war of 1891 was hailed by all foreign investors in the country; but North, soon to die of a heart attack, would never fully recover either his fame or his prodigious wealth.

Antofagasta, meanwhile, continued to expand and to prosper. A brief description of the place in 1889 was given by the then well-known and elderly *Times* correspondent W. R. Russell, whom North had persuaded that year to accompany him on a much publicized return visit to northern Chile. Though Russell thought that 'to the eye there is but little to commend Antofagasta', he nonetheless acknowledged the place's considerable importance, and the fact that it already had 'a church, a hospital, a public slaughterhouse, a band of music, a philharmonic society, a club, hotels, restaurants'. At the time of his visit a huge foundry was being built to process silver that would eventually be transported from Bolivia by railway. The year before, the railway company founded in 1873 by Melbourne Clark & Co. had reorganized itself as the Antofagasta (Chili) and Bolivia Railway Company which, as the largest and most powerful firm in Antofagasta, would be the main factor behind the town's rapid growth. The trains now supplied the town with most of its fresh water which, by 1912, would arrive through pipes laid out by the company next to the track.

The Antofagasta which a rather appalled Bethel was beginning to get to know had already outstripped Iquique to become the seventh-largest town in Chile. Though the streets were unpaved (and would remain so until 1915), a dreary neo-Gothic cathedral was going up alongside the Grand Hotel, a tramway was running, electricity had just been installed, and a much-needed sewage system had finally been completed. As with Valparaíso, it had all the facilities of a modern city, together with such other, less desirable features as exceptionally high levels of crime and disease, and gathering workers' unrest. But what must have particularly struck Bethel was how this once almost exclusively Chilean town in the middle of nowhere had developed a truly cosmopolitan character, at least in terms of its number of foreign communities. There were sizeable populations of Greeks, Chinese, Croatians, Germans, Italians, Spaniards, and even Arabs and North Africans, among whom was a relative of the celebrated Berber leader Abd el Krim. And then, of course, there were the British. These were the dominant foreign element in Antofagasta, and they were mainly employees of the railway company.

Had Bethel studied carefully the *Mercurio de Antofagasta* for 11 February, he would have gained a revealing insight into the character and social make-up of the town. Among the news items that day were reports of both a railway strike and a strike of the 'water-sellers'. The rest of the paper was taken up to a great extent by news and gossip from Britain (a report about George V being accused of bigamy; a tale about an Oldham industrialist's wife who was elected mayoress), and numerous British-produced advertisements, including those for the Pacific Steam Navigation Company, 'W. G. Paton's English Bookshop and Printers', 'Spanish Classes for English Gentlemen Given by Ana Sandford', the '*Colegio Ingles para Señoritas*', and 'House of Lords Scotch Whisky' ('Never let Whisky Get the Better of You, Always Get the Best of Whisky').

Bethel, a keen sportsman with an as yet extremely limited grasp of Spanish, would have probably paid special attention to the columns in English about local football and cricket matches. Before continuing on his way to the offices of the Antofagasta (Chili) and Bolivia

Railway Company, he might well have raised an eyebrow on reading that 'The second cricket match between the "Old Antofagastians" and F.C.A.B. "Newcomers" took place on Sunday last, and resulted in a very interesting game.'

The complex of long wooden buildings comprising the company's offices and the former main railway station seemed, from the regional museum's windows, to take up an astonishingly large area of central Antofagasta. In my imagination it was beginning to dominate the town like the Alhambra does in Granada. I was longing to get inside, Miguel Sepúlveda permitting.

It was now well past ten, and I left the museum to make another attempt to phone him. But again I got the same voice telling me to try again, this time in half an hour. I walked back to the Plaza Colón and then into the pedestrian Calle Prat, where I passed the Union club, founded in 1906, and still with its wooden balcony above a large sign for Coca-Cola. The club's members used regularly to challenge the Antofagastians at football, according to a jovial man sweeping the floor inside, who also told me that the rival Antofagasta Club, which my grandfather would join, was no longer the original institution, and that I would be better off visiting the 'English Club'. This was a five minutes' walk away, though almost certainly closed at this time of day, and in any case not particularly old, or indeed English, but it was a place where I might I find the odd person of English descent, such as its secretary 'Jorge Lyons'.

I tried again calling 'Don Miguel', and was answered now by his personal secretary, a certain Carmen Bailey, who asked me for the phone number of my hotel so that I could be contacted 'when or if' her increasingly mythical-seeming boss appeared. I returned to my wanderings, hunted down the English Club to make sure it was closed (it was), looked around a bookshop to see if there was anything on Antofagasta's history (there was not), and, as the heat became worse, went back to my hotel to be told that someone had phoned, but had not left a message.

Yenko, I now remembered, had suggested meeting up at eleven, but I had not been in a fit state to make any definite arrangement, and had assumed that my morning would be entirely taken up by the F.C.A.B. It was only later, after he had left, that it occurred to me that he might not have said 'eleven' at all, but had merely meant getting together for the Chilean institution of '*onces*', which can literally be translated as 'elevenses'. This has nothing to do with the mid-morning break of tea and biscuits that my nanny Woodsie used to prepare for me, but consists of something between an English high tea and a Spanish supper. My mind, all over the place since leaving the museum, settled for a moment on the word '*onces*', which was surely an example of the English of my grandfather's generation influencing Chilean Spanish, and could not be derived, as Chileans now claimed, from a monk's euphemism for 'alcoholic break', the eleven being a reference to the eleven letters in '*aguardiente*'.

Pulling myself together, I called Carmen Bailey. No, she said, no one from the office had tried phoning me. Don Miguel had still not arrived, though if I wanted I could come and wait for him in the building.

A modern sculpture of a locomotive made from bits of old track and discarded train parts heralded my long postponed arrival at the headquarters of F.C.A.B. Entering the complex was like finding myself in a self-contained territory, protected by formidable railings and armed guards demanding identification. Don Miguel was not in the office at present, I was informed yet again, and Carmen Bailey, the only person who could testify to my being a *bona fide* visitor, had slipped out on an errand. I said I had come all the way from London, mentioning the name of the company's London director. They asked to take a photocopy of my passport, and then at last I was able to proceed into what must have been the ticket hall of the old station.

The station, dating from the 1880s, with a second floor added when the railway line had been extended into Bolivia, was now clearly the showpiece of the whole complex and the seat of power. A woman sitting behind a desk dwarfed by the vestibule told me to take my place on a row of chairs where three cowed and silent men in suits were already seated, obviously overwhelmed by the environment. Carmen Bailey would be back shortly, I was told, and she would tell me what news if any there was of Don Miguel.

My grandfather, finally at his destination, but kept waiting like those three men to find out what the management had in store for him, must have felt all of a sudden incredibly small. He was from one of Hull's leading families; his grandfather had received a patent from Queen Victoria; he had gained invaluable experience working with an uncle who was one of Britain's most successful engineers; he had at last been offered a job, and had travelled to the other side of the world to this God-forsaken hole only to find that he had no significance at all, that he was one of hundreds of engineers the company barely knew what to do with.

I kept still on my seat for about ten minutes, unable to elicit anything but monosyllabic utterances from the three men next to me. I was dying to say something about my grandfather having worked for the F.C.A.B. nearly 100 years ago, but these people did not seem to be the most welcoming recipients of such information. Instead I got up to examine an old map of the railway line, and a couple of framed articles about an aspect of the railway's history that my grandfather would refrain from mentioning to Sophie, for fear of worrying her. In the years before the First World War, the trains across the Atacama were subject to regular hold-ups, often resulting in the shooting of passengers. Antofagasta and its surroundings had been even more of a refuge for desperadoes than I had imagined; and I should have guessed earlier that Butch Cassidy and the Sundance Kid, whom I knew had ended up killed in a shoot-out in Bolivia in 1908, had probably set off on their final journey on the Antofagasta train.

After half an hour more of waiting, I asked if I could go outside onto the old platform and take some photographs. Once again I was made to hand over my passport, after which the woman made a call to see if there was somebody to accompany me. A slightly agitated man came downstairs to lead me to the platform, apologizing all the while that he could not stay with me for more than a few minutes. I enjoyed in the little time permitted the station's green-painted exterior, with its Birmingham-made clock, exquisite wrought-iron benches, and pedimented wooden doors and windows. On a small section of track next to the platform was a beautifully restored old dining car where, my guide told me, the late Pope had been entertained on his visit to Chile in 1987. Privet hedges, flowers, and a neatly mown lawn where the sidings had once stood, gave an English flavour to the whole, enhanced by the presence of a red telephone box. I was walking over to have a closer look at this, and to admire the long wooden balcony of an adjacent block of late nineteenth-century office buildings, when my guide insisted that he had to get back to work. Before he left me back in the vestibule I mentioned my interest in continuing on to Calama on a freight train. He suggested I should have a word about this with Don Miguel, but doubted whether it would be possible.

Carmen Bailey had now returned to her office, and I was allowed to walk on my own up the grand staircase to go and see her. It was after 12.30, and I had resigned myself to not meeting Don Miguel. Carmen proved to be a kindly woman of American rather than British ancestry, and offered me coffee in an old porcelain cup, in a room with a cabinet clock, a tooled leather-covered desk, and other objects of undoubtedly English origin.

'Don Miguel,' she patiently explained, 'is busier now than ever. At the end of last year we took over again the running of Antofagasta's water supply, just like we used to do in the past. Don Miguel now spends his time rushing between this building and the offices of the Water Board. He is hardly still for a moment.'

In the case of his being unable to see me (and, this being holiday time, she did not know when he would next be back in Antofagasta), she told me she would make sure I was attended by the man in charge of cultural activities, Don Victor Maldonado. She also wondered, with a genuine tone of concern in her voice, if there was any way in which she could be of assistance herself.

She introduced me to a burly figure named Pedro, who looked after the passenger train from Calama. Pedro made another photocopy of my passport, faxed it to Calama, and said with a grim expression that a place was reserved for me on the next train from there to Bolivia, which was next Wednesday night, 'unless the Bolivians create any problems at the border, which they did last week.' Then he calmly explained why it would be 'absolutely impossible' for me to travel on one of their freight trains out of Antofagasta.

'Chilean legislation forbids passengers to travel on any train that is not specially equipped for them. Should anything happen to you between here and Calama, and it's a very long and tough journey by train, the legal and insurance problems would be tremendous. Not even Don Miguel would be prepared to take the risk.'

Seeing the disappointed look on my face, Pedro offered as a consolation a visit to the company's private museum, which he said was not normally open to the public. It was looked after by one of their employees, 'a man of English descent called Jorge Lyons, who has done a lot of research on Antofagasta's past'. Ringing the receptionist to put Jorge on the line, he relayed to me what this man had told him, holding his hand over the mouthpiece. 'A visit to the museum is completely out of the question this afternoon. But what about next Thursday?'

I pointed out that he had just reserved for me a ticket leaving from Calama the night before.

'Then you'd better speak to him yourself,' he said, handing me over the phone.

I began by telling Jorge that I had heard all about him, about his position in the English Club, and about his invaluable work on the history of Antofagasta's British community, of which my grandfather, whose life I was researching, had been a part. He replied politely that he would be very happy to meet me one day, but that he was exceptionally busy over the next week. I relayed to him my travel plans, and brought up the possibility of my presenting to the museum copies of my grandfather's letters, which gave a vivid portrait of Antofagastan life at the beginning of the last century. He said he looked forward to seeing me when I was next in town.

I was walking away from Pedro's office, weighed down with frustration, loneliness, and thoughts about my depressing hotel, when a messenger came into the office to announce that Don Miguel was on his way. Upgraded to a comfortable leather sofa in the upstairs vestibule, I awaited almost disbelievingly for his arrival.

It was no cantankerous, impatient old tyrant whom I now saw rushing up the stairs, a great wad of papers under his arm, but a youthful-looking, slightly flushed man in his forties, bespectacled, with a shock of black hair and a preoccupied but by no means unapproachable look. The warmth with which he greeted me reinforced this favourable impression, as did his encouragingly book-lined, old-fashioned office. He said he had tried getting here as fast as he could, and blamed the delay on the onerous new duties that the recent expansion of the company had entailed. 'We're as big now,' he smiled, 'as we were in your grandfather's day.'

Instantly likeable, open in his manner, full of energy and enthusiasm, and radiating cosmopolitanism and intelligence, he was exactly the sort of person my grandfather had dreamt of meeting in Antofagasta but had never found. Learning that I lived much of the year in Andalucía, he talked about his love for Spain, and for Granada in particular, and for the poetry of García Lorca. He had a large family, he added, and a busy job, but he devoted all the spare time that he could to reading. He had a passion for literature, and was keen to get to know me better. On my return to Antofagasta he would like to bring me together with a fellow writer, Hernán Rivera, whose novels were all about 'the world your grandfather lived in'. We would have lunch, supper, go to his house, and have a proper talk the next time, he insisted, looking at his watch and realizing that he had to be in the airport in half an hour, but trying all the same to appear relaxed, and to convey the greatest reluctance in having to curtail this all too hurried but civilized exchange.

'What I can do for you?' he asked, reclining his chair slightly back so as to temper the businesslike directness of the remark. I began modestly by mentioning the company's museum.

'That's no problem,' he replied with complete assurance. 'What about this afternoon?'

I said that would suit me perfectly, but that the man in charge was otherwise occupied.

'There'll be no problem,' he smiled, pushing a button on his interchange and then telling Carmen to get hold of Victor Maldonado.

Emboldened, I spoke about my desire to get to Calama by train, in order of course to achieve a greater understanding of my grandfather's state of mind. He immediately grasped that I was the sort of writer who thrived on direct experience, but expressed slight concern that I might find the journey very long and uncomfortable. I said I was a hardy person who could put up with everything.

'Then there'll be no problem at all. When would you like to go? Tomorrow?'

I felt almost guilty at leaving his town so quickly, so I told him that I wanted to get to Bolivia as soon as possible, just in case there was another crisis like the one that had toppled Goni last year.

'I think that's a wise course of action,' said Miguel, swivelling around his chair as a tall, mustachioed man like some Spanish golden age *caballero* entered the room.

'Victor, I would like to introduce you to Don Michael Jacobs.'

Victor nodded his head as Miguel informed him of Don Michael's requests, and then sorted everything out with two brief calls on his mobile phone.

'There's a train leaving tomorrow at midday,' he said, 'I'll give you all the details if you come back to the office at three o'clock. A man called Jorge Lyons will be waiting then to take you to the museum.'

'Have you anywhere to stay in Calama?' inquired Miguel, who had picked up all his papers and was about to run off finally to the airport. 'There's always our guest bungalow at the station,' he went on as we walked out of the office, 'if you don't mind the noise of trains.'

Goodbyes were said, and I was left alone once again with Carmen, who wrote down a list of names and phone numbers I might find useful in Calama and Bolivia. 'If there's anything else you need,' she emphasized, staring directly at me with an almost motherly concern for my well-being, 'absolutely anything, don't hesitate to contact me.'

Don Michael walked dazed down the stairs, wondering if his grandfather had felt similarly light-headed on emerging from his own meeting with the management. Don Bethel, perhaps pessimistically expecting the worst, had been given the best possible news. He was to leave for Bolivia the next day and help supervise the construction of the branch line from Oruro to Cochabamba. It was a job of considerable responsibility, well-paid, and with plenty of opportunity for him to develop his main professional interest – the designing of bridges and tunnels. More enticing still, for someone immediately convinced that Antofagasta was a miserable place 'where nature does not inspire', he would be based in remote camps in what he heard was a beautiful Andean valley with areas of seductive greenness. This was the first opportunity that had ever been offered to him to fulfil his longing for a quiet and simple life in pleasing, natural surroundings.

I was feeling almost cocky as I confidently strode downstairs past the secretary, in whose manner I now fancifully noted a look of greater respect, as I did in the eyes of the three patiently seated men, waiting philosophically to be told to come back after lunch, and who had now been joined by a fourth man, much younger than the others, dressed in T-shirt and black nylon shorts, and calling my name. I woke up from my daydream to shake hands with Yenko.

'I've brought you some articles about Antofagasta's history,' he murumured, taking out a file from a bag, and opening it at a photo of the Grand Hotel 'at about the time your grandfather stayed there'. Everyone in the lobby was throwing us bemused glances, so I suggested we went outside to have a look at the material in a more congenial place. He said I could keep it.

The once highly suspicious guards could not have been friendlier as they wrote down the time of our departure, and saw us through the gate. I was not quite sure what they made of my young, casually dressed companion; but then I was not quite sure what to make of him myself.

'You couldn't imagine the problems I had getting past them,' he nervously uttered in a slightly louder voice than before. 'I was only allowed through once I had mentioned your name. I was pretty sure you'd be there, as you weren't in the hotel.'

I was puzzled by why he had gone to such efforts to track me down, but was sure he did not want anything from me other than perhaps company. He seemed to be a helpful man who loved Antofagasta and was keen that its few tourists should like it as much as he did. But I had detected in our short conversation the night before a more than polite interest in my grandfather's story. As an introverted and seemingly lonely engineering student, who had already begun searching for a job, he might have identified with Bethel as a fellow spirit. I did not give too much thought to the matter, happy simply to be accompanied by someone with an insider's knowledge of Antofagasta, and a love of its history. With two hours to spare before returning to the F.C.A.B., I asked him if he knew of a good restaurant.

Yenko took me to what he called a 'mid-price' restaurant, which had a white curtained screen dividing the modest bar from a grander dining room with neo-baroque plaster moulding and a head waiter who, in his younger days, might even have worked in a high-price restaurant.

'Antofagasta is the most expensive town in Chile,' Yenko told me after we had sat down to order fish prepared '*à la meunière*'. He talked about the elevated prices resulting from heavy dependency on the import of produce, and from the influx of Chileans from the south in search of work. He himself was from Calama, and had come here with a sister to live in one of the basic, tin-roofed houses in the upper reaches of the town. For a couple of years he had saved money by studying in Bolivia, which he described with an adjective I had heard no other Chilean use in relation to that country – 'lovely'.

'But tell me more about your grandfather,' he asked after timidly accepting the waiter's offer of another glass of wine.

I told him that Bethel's first stay in Antofagasta had lasted, as mine would, little more than a day and a half. On the morning of 12 February, Bethel had taken the 8.30 train to Calama where, after a night at the station, he had continued into Bolivia, arriving at Oruro at 7.30 on the morning of the 14th. Though Oruro had struck him as being as bleak and sordid as Antofagasta, he had stopped off there only for the time it took to receive instructions from the regional boss, a 'Mr Gibson'. Once he had got to the camp on the projected Cochabamba line, he was blissfully happy, especially as he found himself working alongside two Irishmen who, like Burke on the HRS *Oronsa*, knew all about Sophie's rugger-playing, gynaecologist brother Bethel Solomons. He was also in time for the carnival season. He wrote three long letters to Sophie telling her all this and about Antofagasta; but the rainy season that year was worse than ever, making communications with the outside world particularly difficult, and forcing Bethel to entrust the letters to someone whom he later realized had never bothered to post them.

The next time Sophie would hear from Bethel was in a letter begun in Oruro on 21 March. It related bad news. Mr Gibson, after instructing Bethel to report to him at Oruro and then keeping him waiting around unnecessarily for a day and a half, had finally told him that there was no complaint whatsoever against him, either personally or on account of the small amount of work he had had the opportunity of doing so far, which in fact was quite satisfactory. He exonerated him entirely of all blame in the unfortunate state of affairs that, for reasons entirely beyond Mr Gibson's control, obliged B. L. Jacobs, as they now knew him so as to distinguish him from another Jacobs working in Bolivia, herewith to terminate his work on the Cochabamba line, at least for the time being, and report back to head office in Antofagasta where, Mr Gibson was quite convinced, better and more interesting work, more suited to his satisfactory capabilities, would be found for him.

For Bethel all this was 'very trying to bear philosophically', especially as he thought the reasons for his transference to be 'iniquitous'. What had happened was that other engineers on the line, more experienced than himself in this type of work but younger and in his view vastly inferior in terms of their general and technical knowledge of engineering, had discovered that the salary the company was contractually obliged to pay Bethel, was higher than theirs. Their response to this was apparently to threaten to resign wholesale if Bethel was kept on.

Underlying all this were the generally petty frictions between British and American engineers which filled much of the correspondence I had ploughed through at the Antofagasta archives in London. 'Mr Mollet', Bethel's boss in Antofagasta, was English and had been keen to replace the almost exclusively American staff in Bolivia with Englishmen. Gibson, 'a citizen of the USA', had been connected with the railway far longer than Mollet, whom he resented for being officially his superior and for interfering in his business by sending on to him the likes of Bethel.

'Gibson,' wrote Bethel, 'wants his own countrymen in wherever he can get them.' What Bethel did not know was that complaints against Mollet were already being sent from head office in Antofagasta to the London director of the company, A. L. Bolden. Though this would not have been of much consolation to Bethel at the time, his treatment by Mollett was one of the factors that would contribute to the latter's dismissal from the company barely a year later. Bolden, while acknowledging Mollet's 'technical knowledge and engineering capabilities', would be obliged to write that 'he has shown a marked want in administrative ability, and considerable and constant trouble has been caused on that account – friction with his chief and other departments through lack of information and instructions not being carried out, and a constant bickering and backbiting amongst the Americans employed under his orders (this latter I believe proverbial and the one drawback to the employment of American engineers).'

In coping with this new and deeply unfair situation, Bethel's love for Sophie would prove far more effective than any of the philosophical attitudes he would try to adopt, with increasing lack of success. He was feeling profoundly sorry for himself, and believed he had been up against bad luck so many times that he no longer had the strength to go on kicking. Antofagasta, a thirty-eight-hour journey away by train, seemed an almost unbearable prospect after his brief taster of life in the Bolivian countryside.

'Having seen and worked in that fine country in the interior of Bolivia,' he wrote, 'where living costs very little, it is rather rough to have to return to the boiling hot desert where everything is very expensive.'

It would take him, he later confessed, a long time 'to get reconciled to the barrenness of Antofagasta'.

'When he got back to Antofagasta,' I told Yenko, 'he worked at first in the designing office. I think he got a lot of sympathy from everyone. He was given a good room in the company's guest quarters, and was recommended for membership of the Antofagasta Club, where he played a lot of tennis and billiards. He began to like the town a little bit more, but then, after a while he was hardly ever there, being out most of the time doing routine maintenance duties on the track. He wasn't very pleased with this, but the company kept him happy by promising work on the construction of a planned new line from Mejillones. That was a favourite place of his. He used to go there whenever he wanted to relax.'

Of all the places featured in my grandmother's tales of Bethel's time in South America, Mejillones had registered with me mainly for having a comic-sounding name meaning 'mussels'. But mentioning this town now to Yenko had made me remember a curious comment of Sophie's about the place. 'Your grandfather was always so happy in Mejillones,' she had said once with a great sigh of pleasure, convincing me that 'Mussels' was some hedonist's haven.

'I love Mejillones too,' piped up Yenko, breaking into my thoughts and simultaneously reading them. 'I usually go there every weekend. If you want to we could visit the place later this afternoon, when you've finished with your appointments. The local bus there only takes about an hour.'

I arranged to meet up with him later, then walked back to the F.C.A.B., hoping that no unforeseen problem had occurred since the disappearance to Santiago of the miracle-working Don Miguel. But a smiling Victor Maldonado instantly put an end to my worries by handing me a sheet of paper with the number of the train I was to take the next morning, and the name of the man who would make sure I got onto it, Don Rolando Henriquez.

'The train leaves at 12.30,' he told me, 'but I advise you meet up with Don Rolando no later that 12.00.'

I asked what time I would be getting in to Calama.

'Well, the train, as you know, takes slightly longer than the bus,' answered Victor with ironic understatement. The bus, I knew, took just over three hours. 'If you're lucky you might reach Calama by two in the morning.'

Now that Victor had given me my briefing, I imagined that he was going to take me straight to Jorge Lyons. But he appeared in no hurry to do so. 'I'm a passionate traveller,' he volunteered, settling down to what promised to be the 'civilized', leisurely 'yarn' my grandfather had so often hankered after. He admitted to have been to England several times, drawn there by 'a love for your pop music', and had even been lucky enough to have attended a concert given by a group whose name I had not heard mentioned since the 1970s, 'Herman's Hermits'.

'On my last visit to England I had to make a special pilgrimage to the Cavern Club in Liverpool. And do you know what touched me most?' I could not guess. 'Seeing the name of a group called 'Atacama' scrawled on the walls. I thought I would never get sentimental about my distant homeland.'

'We're so far from everything here,' he wistfully reflected.

By 'everything' he meant above all Europe, which for him was the centre of world culture, just as it had been for my grandfather. But it was Italy rather than France that captured the civilized essence of Europe for Victor Maldonado. He and his family were flying off the next day on a tour of his favourite Italian haunts; and as he outlined their itinerary to me, interrupting this occasionally to enthuse over certain artists such as Raphael, Michelangelo and Bernini, I realized that the world he was talking about belonged almost to a past life of mine, as distant from my present existence as the Atacama had seemed from the Cavern Club. I had been born in Italy; I had done a Ph.D. in Italian art; but Spain had made me turn my back on the icons of my youth and led me in middle age to an obscure olive-growing Andalucían village where the Italian names that Victor was now lovingly enunciating meant absolutely nothing. At this particular moment the only name immediately evocative of happiness for me was Mejillones.

'I can see you're anxious now to get on to the museum,' noted Victor, after terminating his Italian speech with an encomium to the frescoes of Piero della Francesca. But we stayed on talking for a good half hour before leaving the civilized calm of Victor's restfully painted office to enter a long white room divided up by low partition walls. Behind these were secretaries, clerks, engineers – people doing what my grandfather had done, sitting behind desks making calculations and diagrams.

'Don Jorge Lyons' stood out by the Englishness of his appearance. He was not English-looking in the sense that my host at Catapilco had been, tall and aristocratic, but rather he was someone whom E. M. Forster might have considered a product of encroaching suburbia: pale, slight, with grey cotton trousers, a sober tie over a white, short-sleeved shirt, and blond hair combed into a quiff – a man in his fifties who could have been mistaken for some faceless civil servant of my grandfather's generation.

But when he talked, Jorge Lyons' diffident smile took on a hint of mischievousness, and he became more expansive than I had expected, revealing perhaps some Latin admixture in his English blood. Now that I had been given the seal of approval from head office, he acted as if he had nothing else to do that afternoon except attend to me, answer my questions, and display with a lack of scholarly reserve the fruits of his thousands of hours studying Antofagasta's history.

'My grandfather came over to work in Chile as a mining consultant,' he said in response to my questions about his family background. 'But he was based in Valparaíso, where I was brought up,' he added, as we left the building to get into his car and drive a short distance along what Bethel had known as the Avenida del Ferrocarril.

Photographed by my grandfather as a wide and empty track bordered by bushes, flowerbeds and a solitary Oregon pine, this was now a busy road parallel to the railway line, passing next to sidings, warehouses, low ramshackle houses, and two incongruously tall apartment blocks. Behind the fencing that marked the company's enclosure was a solitary, peeling white wooden building encircled on both floors with galleries. It would have made the perfect setting for a Chekhov play.

'We're here,' said Mr Lyons, instructing one of the guards to open the door and let us in to an interior smelling of must and floor polish. 'This was built as guest quarters for the company's bachelors.'

Bethel, back again 'amidst the flies and dust', as he described his return to Antofagasta, had been given a room here. Apparently this was a privileged place to be; and he owed it to the briefly guilt-stricken Mollet, now trying to make up for the Bolivia fiasco.

'The bachelors were a notoriously noisy lot,' noted Mr Lyons, 'and got frequent complaints for their drunken piano playing on Sunday mornings.'

It was as difficult to picture the abstemious Bethel joining in on such occasions as it was to imagine the building, in its present mortuary-like state, as having once been the scene of spontaneous joy. Crammed and sombre, it was a museum whose tone was set by the predominance of furnishings in dark, funereal mahogany (tables, bookcases, the ubiquitous clocks, a massive cabinet containing a complex water-filtering system), and the presiding presence of a large plaque, also in wood, with the spot-lit gold letters 'IN MEMORIAM' heading a list of all those colleagues of Bethel who would die fighting for Britain in the Great War.

I scanned the list in search of anyone I might recognize, then went back to reading the names of now probably defunct British manufacturers that were inscribed on every mechanical object, from ticket punches to fire hydrants. Upstairs, I scoured the old photos for Bethel's features, but soon lost myself amidst the miscellany of everyday items which had been salvaged from abandoned British houses and then haphazardly thrown together, like shards and flintheads from prehistoric sites. I assimilated bakelite phones, tin kettles, wirelesses, a Southampton football strip, popular novels of which my grandfather would certainly have disapproved, and a collection of Winchester rifles taken from the bandits who regularly attacked the trains as late as 1918.

'The first patients from the company's hospital were in fact victims of a bandit attack,' Mr Lyons explained before moving on to the subject of the F.C.A.B. as a self-enclosed world with not only its own hospital, dating from 1907, but also an English School, which was founded in 1912 by the woman, who, on leaving the HRS *Oronsa* a few months earlier, had seemed fated to walk out immediately into oblivion – the 'uninteresting' Miss Oldham.

An hour later I would be hurrying past the school on a rickety old bus, with just enough time to note that the building was another Chekhovian apparition, and functioning today as a private college. I had taken my leave of Mr Lyons and was back again with Yenko, heading towards Mejillones. The bus kept close to the railway line as the last of Antofagasta's houses petered out into the desert, and we drove into a loneliness whose only notable landmark was a blue-painted monolith marking the tropic of Capricorn. We rattled our way across the imaginary line, and entered the tropics.

Yenko tried holding my attention with another story involving trains, madness and the desert – a tale of an Atacama stationmaster who was found dead after claiming to be receiving messages from extra-terrestials – while my gaze remained stuck to the window, absorbed by a landscape that I was beginning to find compellingly beautiful. The bleached colours of midday were already being tinged by faint purples, oranges and reds which would gradually crescendo into one of those pyrotechnical outbursts that tend to win over even the most desert-weary traveller to the Atacama. My grandfather, for instance.

Only two weeks after being sent back to Antofagasta, Bethel had travelled for the first time to Mejillones. Colleagues of his had spoken of the town as a place of pleasant relaxation; and I could hear Mollett telling him that a visit there would do him a world of good. But Bethel could not have had his hopes raised too highly as he embarked on another endless-seeming journey across a wasteland hillier than before, but a wasteland all the same, monotonously unwelcoming.

'As far as the eye can see,' he started writing to Sophie near the outset of a journey seven times longer by train than it is by today's bus, 'the country is absolutely bare and barren. Not one single leaf of natural vegetation, not a single product of any description, neither useful mineral or even nitrate is to be obtained from this dreary desert . . . It is just the bed of the Pacific that some great seismic upheaval lifted bodily up when the world was young and giddy. But I don't think it could have been the beautiful Pacific that rolled over this part of the globe then. I think it must have been the River Styx.'

Bethel's black mood, the foretaste of far worse to come, mellowed somewhat as the late afternoon colours began effecting their dependable daily transformation of the desert, shortly before his arrival at the town that would become like an oasis for him. Yenko and I got there at about the same time of day, with only an hour and a half or so of daylight in which to look around the place. Yenko thought that was quite sufficient to see Mejillones's main attractions before sitting down to enjoy one of his favourite seaside bars.

A 'mega-port', planned as the biggest in South America, was said currently to be under construction. But there was no sign of this from the tiny office where the bus left us, nor was it was possible to envisage the present Mejillones becoming a thriving metropolis any time soon. We did not seem to be in a town a all, but rather in a sprawling village of compact weather-worn little houses stranded above rubble. Yenko proposed going straightaway to the former railway building works or Maestranza, which he claimed had also been the largest in South America, and indeed the second-largest in the whole of the Pacific. He pointed vaguely towards a faraway headland, where all I could make out was a cluster of trees, as indeterminate as a mirage, sheltering behind the town's narrow, stony beach.

Mejillones's whole history seemed to be one of spectacular reversals of fortune. With a long, protected bay which made the place a natural port, it should have grown into the great town that Antofagasta had never deserved to become. And there was a moment in its past when it almost did. In 1871, the then president of Bolivia, Mariano Melgarejo, decided that Mejillones, with a population only recently risen from the original thirteen, would become the major port of the area in the place of Cobija, which had been devastated by yellow fever and a major earthquake. A Chilean engineer was commissioned to design a town of 640 blocks. But then Melgarejo fell from power, and the War of the Pacific began. The project was abandoned, and so, virtually, was the town, which suffered the further humiliation of having its Chilean-built mining office of 1866 dismantled and reconstructed in Antofagasta as the future Museum of Regional History.

In 1904 the town was offered another reprieve. The Antofagasta (Chili) and Bolivia Railway sought permission to construct a branch line leading to Mejillones, and to build a harbour, administrative buildings and a Maestranza there. Two years later a plan for a town of 139 blocks was drawn up. Seventy-four years later the Maestranza was closed down, and its large community of workers almost entirely dispersed. In terms of importance Mejillones was almost back to where it had started, to where it was now, but without the projected megaport to create yet more illusions.

As Yenko and I walked closer towards the Maestranza, a handful of imposing half-timbered buildings, utterly different from their humble, bedraggled neighbours, loomed in the distance like remnants of an interrupted dream. A miniature avenue adorned with untended flower beds and an old locomotive, acted as the frontier to the town that had grown up after 1906. We could have followed the avenue down to Mejillones's coastal promenade, but we went in the opposite direction, towards the desert. No more recent attempts at prettification could be observed as we neared a railway station which I was sure had lain derelict for years.

The unexpected sounds of music proved me wrong. Yenko, unsure exactly how to get into the Maestranza, went inside to ask. I followed him through a door marked 'Radio Mejillones', and surprised a DJ with a black T-shirt reading 'FUCK ME!'.

At an appropriate break in the recording, he came outside with us to indicate on the horizon what appeared like the observation post of a concentration camp. We headed off there, along a track which skirted a broken fence with corrugated iron patching up the rotten wooden slats. The observation post lay behind an open gate. At close quarters it looked decidedly less formidable, just a pile of old timber that a carpenter had hurriedly nailed together, adding a megaphone on top as an afterthought. There was also a crudely hand-painted sign featuring a ferocious dog, but I did not have much time to study this before an all too real Alsatian lunged towards me, succeeding in shaking the building to which it was fortunately chained.

The guard emerged from his late siesta. He shook his head. This was private property of the F.C.A.B., this was not a tourist attraction. I uttered the magical name of Don Miguel Sepúlveda, and he weakened slightly in his resolve. Yenko, all too ready to give up, stood amazed as I suggested that the guard call Carmen Bailey in Antofagasta to answer for me. Instead the man insisted I speak on the phone to the general manager in Mejillones who, after listening unconvinced to my story, said she herself would call the head office. The Alsatian fell asleep in the time it took for the answer to come through. The guard then took down my passport details, and waved us on into the vast enclosure.

A light wind was blowing wisps of dust across an expanse of grey sand crossed by telegraph poles, and sections of half-buried track on which were permanently stationed the remains of train engines, freight cars and carriages. Far in the background, mauve clouds, flecked with red and dark orange, were gathering over a coastal range now a russet gold. Closing off the inner sanctuary that comprised the Maestranza itself was another fence whose massive ironwork frame seemed to compete in size with the mountains beyond. We aimed towards a gap in this fence, but before we got there, an old man came rushing up to us on a bicycle. He said everyone knew him as the 'guardia Sánchez', and that he had been sent to take care of us.

The F.C.A.B., as I was fast learning, was a company that inspired great loyalty. Sánchez told us that he had been with for them for thirty-eight years. He had started as a cleaner before becoming one of the several hundred employees who worked on the building of the trains.

'It was tragic when they shut all this down in 1980,' he mused, as we stood within the shell of one of the Maestranza's three giant naves, surrounded by rubble, scraps of metal, and the smashed timbers of upturned wooden carriages. 'It was our whole world. The company provided everything. We had our own church, our theatre, our football club. And then we had nothing. All my friends left. Only a few of us stayed on, as guards. That's all we could do. This is where we wanted to be.'

He took us to every corner of the Maestranza's interior, relating in vivid, precise detail what the place had been like when in running order, what he had done himself, and what parts of the building he had been assigned to. And then he pointed to a modern cabin attached to an upper girder and reached by a metal ladder.

'That's where I now spend my nights,' he said, 'making sure no one gets in here and makes off with all the bits of metal and wood. You wouldn't believe how much all this is worth.' Yenko whistled when he told him, but I was more interested to know how he could stay the night all on his own in this eeriest of empty places, and with all its ghosts and memories.

'You get used it,' he laughed. 'I like my own company, and I like the dark. And I don't believe in ghosts.'

Sánchez was also liking having company. And though he had been instructed to show us only the actual Maestranza, he allowed us to step into a couple of the carriages in the outer enclosure, two of which dated back to the 1920s or earlier. The rust and broken windows should have alerted us to what we would find inside – leather seats with their stuffing hanging out, floors that creaked and broke when you stepped on them, pieces of fallen wood forming jagged obstacles along the corridor, an accumulation of a good twenty years of dust. 'The toilet I'm afraid is out of order,' he joked, opening a door that immediately fell off its hinges.

Afterwards he offered to take us to what survived of 'the English colony' as he called it – bungalows built by the company for the British community and their guests. There was no one of British ancestry left today, but he had worked with many in his time, and some had been neighbours of his in a row of interconnected one-storeyed workers' dwellings at the very end of the town.

'I still live here now,' he said, after we had paused for a moment next to a line of identical olive green painted houses sharing a communal wooden porch facing the sea. 'The fancier people lived over there,' he continued, indicating with his hand the cluster of trees that I had seen from afar without fully believing I had seen correctly. We went closer to investigate.

Under monkey-puzzle trees, Mediterranean pines and Oregon firs was a group of unmistakably English-looking gabled bungalows, with red-tiled roofs and cottage-style front gardens. Only one was inhabited, the largest of them all, and it was a pure slice of Essex suburbia, with perfectly maintained flower beds and the neatest of mown lawns.

'That's our general manager's house.' whispered Sánchez, restraining me from taking a photo on the grounds that her permission would be needed beforehand. He telephoned her, and smiled afterwards with relief. 'She said that's okay.'

The other bungalows were in a terrible state, their gardens overgrown, their once-painted wooden walls left to blister and flake, and the tiles of their roofs replaced by sheets of corrugated iron. We stopped in front of one that I instantly recognized. My grandfather had taken a close-up of the façade, with a tall, mustachioed man in suit and tie posing against the raised porch. In another shot he had photographed the same lanky individual standing in the front garden, his back both to the sea and to a wooden fence identical to the one there now. I showed these two snaps to Sánchez, and he shook his head in disbelief.

'The man in the photos was the colony's doctor, Dr Williams,' I told him. 'My grandfather became a good friend of his. He ended up always staying in this house whenever he came to Mejillones.'

'The engineers,' Bethel had enthused to Sophie soon after glimpsing Mejillones for the first time, 'have very jolly quarters and little gardens attached to the bungalows.'

Not since visiting the Sutherlands at Valparaíso had my grandfather seen anywhere so enticing to live. Here was a place that had much of the charm of England but with perpetual sunshine and an exotic coastal setting which seemed less intimidating and more picturesque when viewed from behind an English garden fence. Tempted by all this to return at last to the healthy outdoor life he had enjoyed so much in Bolivia, he went rowing and bathing in the bay, took up horse-riding again, and made full use of the colony's excellent tennis courts – a facility still lacking in Antofagasta. Moreover, here he was able to relish 'comfortable quarters, excellent grub', and – most important of all in his current frame of mind – company that was 'agreeable and stimulating'.

Dr Williams had yet to take up residence at the time of my grandfather's first visit to Mejillones; but Bethel was wonderfully looked after instead by the colony's chief engineer Tommy Gloag, 'a Scotsman possessed of a grand fund of humour of a very quaint and dry sort'. On this same memorable visit Bethel also had the pleasure of encountering somebody with whom he could talk at length about

'Hull and Hull people'. This unnamed individual, 'a very decent man' according to Bethel, seems to have been one of those expatriates escaping from some scandal or impossible personal situation in his home country; but Bethel, indulging for the moment in life's superficial pleasures, was not in the mood to probe too deeply beneath this man's 'jovial' exterior.

'He must enjoy life on this coast,' he merely speculated, 'for he has been here over two years on a visit; he doesn't do any work, only plays tennis, rides and rows. He is an Oxford man, too; I think he is rather a mystery. Yet he is a jovial sort and, for his age, which will be about fifty, tremendously strong and active.'

Bethel's first stay in Mejillones lasted only three days; but it was long enough for him to feel the place to be 'partial compensation' for his having been forced to leave Bolivia. Circumstances unfortunately would prevent him from going back there until February 1912, exactly a year after his arrival in Chile. The intervening months, spent mainly in the Atacama interior, made him long for Mejillones almost as much as he longed for Sophie. Writing to her in the middle of January to inform her of his imminent return to the town, he said how glad he would be 'to see the sea again', and how 'refreshing' it would be 'after this dreary and stony desert' which, for greater poetic effect, he called also *cet âpre pays surchauffé*, 'this bitter, overheated land.' (French was clearly the language of preference whenever Bethel was overcome with yearning, sexual or otherwise.)

But more than just the sea, it was the company of people like Gloag that Bethel missed. His stay in Mejillones in February, so eagerly anticipated and yet so short, would not disappoint. 'These four days,' he wrote afterwards, 'have been the most enjoyable I have spent since I arrived in the country.' Once again he was the guest of Gloag, but he was actually put up by the newly arrived Dr Williams in the bungalow I was now sentimentally contemplating, 'a delightful place with a gorgeous garden right in front of the beach.'

Dr Williams himself, 'the very best of tonics', was exactly the sort of person needed to raise Bethel's spirits. A bachelor in his late thirties, six foot five inches tall, and a keen athlete, 'he is simply bubbling over with good spirits and fun all the time and has such a keen sense of humour.'

He and Bethel, with their common experiences of living in Paris and New York, became instant friends, and started doing everything together, including taking part in such sporting activities as a tennis tournament against General Management in which Williams gave clear proof of having once been a championship player. Bethel even accompanied the doctor on his medical rounds, including rowing out with him to the ships in the harbour, being rewarded in one French ship by 'a lunch that in this country was something to be spoken of with bated breath', and acting both as his interpreter and, on one occasion, his surgical assistant. I still remember my grandmother telling me Bethel story's of going with Williams to see a badly injured boy, and then finding himself 'helping to administer the anaesthetic, threading surgical needles and interpreting all the time'.

Perhaps more than anything Bethel appreciated how Williams made him laugh. Spontaneous wisecracks may not have been my grandfather's own strong point (I think of him, like my father, as more of a teller of well-rehearsed stories), but he loved them in Williams, particularly when the latter was in the company of the similarly witty Gloag ('the two of them burble nonsense at each other from morning till night'). At the end of his second stay at Mejillones, Bethel confessed to 'have laughed more in these four days than I have so far done in a whole year, laughed until I cried almost, which is very good for the soul.' And the soul was now very much on his mind. Praying more than ever that the long promised offer of work at Mejillones would finally materialize, he told Sophie that the town was 'the one place on the line where I feel (for want of a better expression) "soul space".'

'Soul space' . . . it seemed such a modern Californian phrase, so uncharacteristic of Bethel. The thought of it brought me back to the present with a jolt. Instead of the sounds of riotous laughter from behind the walls of Dr Williams's bungalow, I could hear Sánchez saying goodbye to Yenko. The sun had almost set, and Sánchez had to go home to prepare himself for the night shift.

'We've got just over an hour before our last bus back to Antofagasta,' Yenko reminded me, prompting me to drag myself away from the bungalows and down the darkening coastal past towards the old customs house, seeming curiously luminous under the sun's last rays, with half timbering, a mansard roof, and a resemblance to some grand villa on the Brittany coast. Street lights, scanty and ineffective, were switched on as we walked on this hushed Friday night towards a cabin-like bar with a handful of tables outside, a scattering of couples, and a matronly owner with the dyed black hair and bright red lipstick of the stereotypical French madame. Her seafood *empanadas* were reputedly the best in Mejillones. I clicked my beer glass against Yenko's, and tucked into an abalone-filled pie with a voracious appetite I had not had for days.

'I came away feeling an altogether different person,' I said to myself, quoting a line from my grandfather as I sat in a dark bus under a desert sky brilliant with stars. Bethel's return visit to Mejillones, he revealed to Sophie, had made him better prepared to face the nervous crises that had begun affecting him while stuck in those parts of the desert to which I would be travelling the next day by freight train.

Yenko, sitting next to me, was envious of my journey. Freed by the beer and the darkness, he had lost earlier inhibitions, and was talking non-stop about places on the way to Calama where my grandfather had worked, but which I probably would not notice because it would be night-time, or because these former nitrate settlements were now so ruined as to be indistinguishable from the surrounding rocks and stones. The only ghost town of any size alongside the railway line was Chacabuco, which had been revived by Pinochet in the 1970s as a concentration camp.

'My father,' mumbled Yenko, suddenly hesitant again, 'was a guard in the camp.' Perhaps he was hoping that the night would absolve his family of past sins. 'But he never wanted to be one, he was just a police-man doing his duty, he had no other choice, he did not realize properly what was going on, and when he did realize, it was too late to do any-thing, he had the choice of shooting someone, or being shot himself.'

We were back in Antofagasta shortly before midnight. The sensible thing would have been to go back to my hotel for a well-deserved and much-needed sleep: my train journey the next day across the Atacama promised to be a test of physical and mental endurance. But the indefatigable Sophie had taught me that being sensible was a much overrated virtue; and, in any case, thoughts about tomorrow's journey had made me too tense with excitement to feel tired. I accepted unhesitatingly Yenko's offer of taking me on a tour of Antofagasta by night.

I could not really see my companion as an enthusiastic participant in the town's nocturnal scene, but it turned out that clubbing and drinking were not quite what he had in mind. What he wanted, I realized after another arduous half-hour on foot, without a bar, without a pause, was to go on walking, to walk south of the city centre, and along a gently rising street without pedestrians to a point where a panorama opened up of the southern half of Antofagasta. Here you could see the University of the Atacama, the hospital, the marina, the soaring Holiday Inn, the better-off residential suburbs ('where people like Miguel Sepúlveda live') – and the 'archaeological site'. That was the real reason why Yenko had brought me all the way up here – an 'archaeological site unlike any you will have seen before'.

The ruins of Huanchaca disappeared into the moonlit void directly below us. Their giant blocks of masonry, seen in this mysterious light, could have been those of a forgotten Inca city viewed through the distorted imagination of a romantic artist. Yenko was vague about their history. They were the ruins of a foundry where silver from Bolivia had been processed, that was all that he could tell me. Had I not known otherwise I might have believed them to be a relic of some grand colonial scheme from the years when Potosí was at its height, and not the foundry that had been conceived at the same time as the Antofagasta (Chili) and Bolivia Railway Company, whose trains had been used for the transporting of the silver. Harder still to take in, given its Piranesi-like scale, was that it had functioned for only thirteen years.

Yenko, as an engineer, was more informative about how the foundry had worked, though much of his detailed technical explanation passed over me, concentrating as I was at the time on not losing my footing as we ignored the warning notices and slowly descended towards the bottom of the site. We were between rows of massive piers, walking in the gap down which the silver had rapidly flowed, gravity being somehow essential to the whole processing business. The slope, in other words, was nearly vertical. The surface was rubble, and it was so dark you could hardly see your feet. The notions of caution and foolhardiness were ones that seemed to erode in you the more you entered the spirit of South America.

Safely out of danger, and out the other end into a marina still pulsing with life at 1.30 a.m., with people sitting around on concrete benches, swimming in the floodlit artificial bay, drinking at tempting-looking designer bars echoing with vibrant music and the chat of the young and beautiful, I hoped perhaps we might stop for a moment to reward ourselves, have a *pisco* sour or two before calling it a night. But Yenko appeared to have the foibles of someone of the age I was supposed to be, and did not want to go into too crowded or too noisy places, or where we might be shown up by anyone too glamorous or fashionable. So we walked for another quarter of an hour until we reached a sufficiently gloomy pizza bar, where we ordered two bottles of orange Fanta. And then exhaustion finally hit me. Yenko was again in full flow, murmuring, 'Chacabuco,' and 'Pinochet,' and 'duty,' as I looked at my watch and realized that it was now 2.04 a.m., and that if I had been here exactly twenty-four hours before, the ground would have shaken, and I would have been left in the darkness, listening to the screams of those whose company we had rejected, thinking that the whole world was coming to an end.

'Earthquakes are not the major worry here,' remarked Yenko on the way back to my hotel. I said I could get there on my own, but he replied that he would not be happy until he had left me right outside its door, for Antofagasta, he now admitted, was not the 'safe' place he had claimed it to be, at least not after twelve o'clock at night, when a gringo on his own was like a moving dollar sign. 'The real worry is when it rains,' he said emphatically, ignoring the leers of a couple of leather-skirted peroxide blondes whose large feet indicated that they were men. 'Every time there's been a major loss of life in Antofagasta, it's been after a torrential rainfall, when the ground just slips away, and buildings fall on top of each other, and are swept into the sea.' These rainfalls of course were so rare that Yenko could recite by heart the years when they had happened. 'The most recent one was 1996, when seventy people were killed. 1965 was a rainy year, and so were 1958 and 1947 . . .'

I stopped him before he got to 1911, one of the rainiest years in the Atacama's recorded history. On 15 and 16 February, violent floods caused great destruction in the towns of the province of Tarapacá; and later that year my grandfather would witness scenes of rain and snow unheard of in the desert. Had he been a superstitious man, and not a man of reason and science, he might have thought of these as omens of a worse catastrophe to come, or else as further tests he would have to endure before love could redeem the world and make it green again and peaceful and radiant with life.

4

The Saddest Desert

———◦∞◦———

THE SUN HAD barely risen over the mountains when I was out again on the streets of Antofagasta, happy to have left the hotel, my body alert with adrenalin, feeling as an astronaut must when on the point of being launched into space. I filled up with provisions from a futuristic hypermarket, and went off to look for a novel by the locally much-revered Hernán Rivera, with whom I had been promised a meeting on my eventual return to the town – if I ever returned. I found all his books in a tacky arcade which sold nothing but pirate editions of the latest books, films and music. I chose a novel entitled *The Trains are Headed for Limbo*.

In the hour before my departure to Calama, I sat down on a bench with the book on my lap and my eyes turned towards the Pacific. The sea, my grandfather had written from Mejillones, had always reminded him of Sophie; and I could never work out whether he was just being poetic, or whether he was thinking of a childhood stay with Sophie in her parents' summer home on the coast outside Dublin.

The sea reminded me of family holidays in the Mediterranean. The water on this quiet Saturday morning was so calm and translucent that tiny orange fish could be seen sparkling between the golden rocks below. I thought of summers in Greece, Croatia and the south of Italy; and for some reason I pictured Cesarina, a young Calabrian waitress I had known years ago, telling me with a smile that she would give me a fig in return for a kiss (a Lawrentian moment unappreciated by the then ten-year-old grandson of the 'Innocent from Ireland'). I stayed staring at the sea, assimilating its refreshing tranquility like a mystic drawing sustenance. Then I opened the book.

'The locomotive,' it began, 'advances smokily, solidly, sombrely through the saddest desert in the world.' I did not get much further. The adrenalin was back again and propelling me to my feet.

I reported early to the F.C.A.B. to find a guard waiting to drive me the short distance to the Estación Norte, a station within sight of the former guest quarters where my grandfather had stayed. A call was made to the 'operations manager' Don Rolando Hernández, who came down immediately from the control tower. He was a short, podgy man with a large face and narrow but kindly eyes, and his manner seemed relaxed, leisurely, and full of old-fashioned courtesy.

'You've got plenty of time,' he said, calming me down, and intimating that he had all the time in the world to talk to me and put my mind at rest. Don Rolando had the aura of a happy family man, and indeed it turned out that he had two families – his own and the F.C.A.B. He had been with the latter even longer than had the guardia Sánchez. 'I've been working for the company for forty-four years,' he said, 'I started off when I was fifteen as an errand boy.'

He invited me up to the tower to give me a better idea of what his current prestigious job entailed. Inside were two men methodically writing down on a time graph the whereabouts of each train, at the same time speaking over the radio to the drivers. From a table scattered with papers, Don Rolando picked out at random one of the fully completed graphs.

'You can see from this,' he explained, 'that yesterday's midday train left exactly on time, but didn't get in to Calama until four in the morning.'

The noise of a shunting train brought us to the window, through which we watched the movements of an engine whose blue, yellow and red colouring was faintly visible under an ochre coating of dust.

'That's your train,' he confirmed, 'Train No. 205. With any luck it should be in Calama not much after midnight.'

I picked up my rucksack to go downstairs. 'There's no hurry,' he added, 'it won't leave without you.'

I was not entirely sure what part of the train I was going to be put in, but in the absence of a special inspection car, such as those in which my grandfather often travelled, I assumed I would be in the cab with the driver and his assistant.

'The three of you might find that a bit cramped,' politely commented Rolando. 'You'll be much more comfortable having an engine car all to yourself.' My profound ignorance of freight trains was exposed, for I had no idea that they usually had two or sometimes even three engine cars. I would be travelling in the second one.

Rolando introduced me to the two drivers, the senior of whom was named Samuel. A slight, bespectacled figure, he looked more like a gentle New York Jewish intellectual than the boorish hulk I might have expected to man a train across this toughest of deserts. Horacio, his young co-driver, could have stood in as Samuel's research assistant in a university department. He was the one who was asked to show me to my place. I tried as nimbly as I could to follow him up some iron rungs and into a grimy metal compartment as spacious as a chicken coop. On either side of the central control panel was a round folding seat facing a narrow, dirt-stained strip of glass. Two small side windows, protected by sliding metal shutters so stiff they could barely open, provided the only other main source of natural light, while a tiny ledge with a hand-rail theoretically connected my car to the one in front.

On being told that we would not be leaving quite yet, I left my luggage inside, and negotiated the rungs face forwards. Horacio, having observed my dangerous, clumsy manoeuvre, diplomatically pointed to a sign with a thick red cross over a man doing exactly what I had done. He also hinted that it might not be such a good idea to use the ledge when the train was in motion.

I stood outside chatting with him and Samuel until I noticed that it was already past one o'clock. Samuel explained that there was a slight problem with the main engine, but that this would be sorted out shortly. We then went back to our separate cars. After a while the man in charge of repairs burst into the car where I was sitting, and caught me with a notebook in my hand. By the expression on his face he must have thought I was a stowaway train spotter. I told him what I was doing and he smiled. The train would be leaving any moment, he assured me.

The whole car rattled and we were off, at less than walking pace. A few minutes later we came to a halt. Horacio shimmied along the ledge to switch on a radio monitor above my head, so that I would 'know what was going on'. Then Rolando came running up to my window to recommend that I keep the shutters closed until we had left Antofagasta. 'There are always children throwing stones,' he warned.

And then we were moving again, heading at an increasing speed towards the coastal range, passing my grandfather's quarters, and climbing in a great loop through the upper town, past houses like those of a shanty settlement, through patches of wasteland where children jeered and took aim with slings. And then the sea disappeared, and we slid into a gap between the rocky mountains into a land without even a cactus.

For half an hour the train rested under a road bridge, for no apparent reason other than to muster its strength before heading off into the nitrate pampa, a landscape utterly featureless for miles, just a grey, flat plateau looking like ash, through which we were eventually moving, slowly enough to study the miscellaneous scraps of tin and iron by the track, the mysterious holes in a discarded jerrycan, the lettering on pieces of paper and cardboard blowing in the wind. Slowly the train veered away from the main road with its funerary memorials and almost non-existent traffic, until I felt truly on my own, like a patient having a body scan, sealed within a capsule, sliding along rollers into nothingness.

Pablo Neruda, who went everywhere, once came near Antofagasta, and wrote a poem with that title in which he talks about stopping all alone in the middle of nothingness, in a desert where the air is vertical, where there are no animals (not even flies), where there is only the earth, an earth without paths, like the moon. I carried the poem with me in an anthology of his, just as I carried the novel by Hernán Rivera, and numerous other books which ridiculously weighed down my rucksack and which I should never have taken. I always travel with books as a safeguard against moments such as these, which seem to demand something to break the monotony, to transport me to a more amenable world, to fix my mind on to something else, or to offer the consolation of someone thinking the same thoughts as myself. But, in the end it is usually only the guidebooks I dip into while on a journey; and now I had not the slightest urge to turn even to those. I was finding limbo too exciting.

Distorted, crackling voices bursting occasionally over the radio reminded me that I was not entirely alone; but the codes they were using and the poor quality of the sound deprived the voices of any usefulness in relaying information, and merely reinforced the sensation of being on another planet. I stopped paying them any attention, and listened instead to the music playing inside my head to the rhythm of the train's movements. It was the same snatch of melody, endlessly repeating itself, but with slight variations in tone and intensity, rising in volume and then diminishing, gradually transfixing me with its repetitiveness, like some piece of film music played at first on the piano, switching to the orchestra, and building up to the moment when the hundred-voice choir is ready to appear.

I was crossing the saddest desert in the world, and I was feeling neither sadness nor fear but a mounting elation. This was not an emotion that any of the early accounts I had read of the nitrate pampa had prepared me for. Despite the beauty of the sunsets, and the sometimes sublime desolation, most travellers would once have described the place, in the words of the politician and historian Vicuna Mackenna in 1875, as 'the silent land of death where . . . there is always the same, eternal, unchanging, horrible panorama.' Until very late in the twentieth century this was a landscape that was generally thought best avoided if at all possible, and preferably only to be talked about in the manner claimed by the distinguished British archaeologist Glyn Daniel in 1960: 'looking out through the windows of my College rooms at the temperate grassland and forest of the Backs, a glass of Chilean wine in my hand'.

Conceivably my grandfather, with his positivist philosophy and faith in the modern world, might initially have regarded the Atacama as a place where the unique barrenness needed to be played down in the interests of stressing its positive potential for mankind. But if he did have such an attitude, which the author of a much-praised new study of the Atacama's changing image over history has proposed as typical of his generation, then he soon lost it. The Atacama wore him down physically and mentally, and would assume the role that deserts proverbially do – as a place whose emptiness encourages introspection, and forced you to look into yourself, to question received values, and to face uncomfortable truths. The contemporary Chilean author Ariel Dorfman confessed that it was for that reason that he had spent most of his life avoiding the whole of the Great North, as if it were a part of the psyche he preferred to keep hidden. However, when he finally went there, it was as a mature man, mentally better prepared for the truths the desert might reveal, in a state of humility and ready for catharsis.

And catharsis was perhaps a factor contributing to my elation, as if in undertaking this train journey I was relieving myself of an inter-generational build-up of tensions and anticipations, experiencing the salutary release of all the doubts, unspoken fears, insecurities, disappointments that the desert was nourishing in my grandfather, pushing him to the point of breakdown.

Over two hours had passed, and the landscape was exactly the same – the same infinite aridity, the same distant mountains no less distant than before. Then I focused on a tiny and remote patch of light, which, as we laboriously crept nearer, became identifiable as the tin roof of an apparently uninhabited shack. Three emaciated dogs ran barking from it down to the train, proving that not all life had departed from this enigmatically isolated habitation. The shack, I realized a few moments afterwards, represented both the outskirts and the sole remaining dwelling of a settlement called Portezuelo. The train's whistle sounded as we entered a broken-down station, little bigger than the hut we had just passed. We shunted into a siding where two men were working. We had come to our first stop.

Samuel got out of the cab, and waved to me to do the same. I climbed down the rungs the correct way, and saw my bare arms becoming goose-pimpled in the wind.

'There's always a wind blowing in the pampa,' he told me. Clanking noises were heard from behind, and a good twenty freight cars were added to our already enormously long train which, since leaving Antofagasta, seemed somehow to have become longer still, as if trying to extend itself to the horizon. Another train, of similar extent, was approaching in the opposition direction, carrying, I was told, copper concentrate from the opencast mine at Chuquicamata, from which our now empty cars would also be loading for the return journey. The train jolted past us, allowing just enough time for the driver to raise a hand to Samuel from behind his window. Soon it had turned into a vanishing thread, bringing to an end what must count in the desert as a moment of maximum excitement.

Samuel pointed out to me a British-built tank of *c.*1906, which carried sulphuric acid, and stood on its spindly legs like a Salvador Dalí elephant. Looking at his watch he told me it was nearly four o'clock and we had so far covered only twenty-nine kilometres.

'That's not such bad progress,' he said, remaining standing in exactly the same spot for a few more minutes. Then he put to me a question no train driver had ever asked me before. 'Do you think we should get going?'

I meekly answered okay, and climbed back into my metal hole. We were off again, heading towards mountains which seemed at long last to be getting closer, and to look increasingly like giant drifts of rubble. At five o'clock we neared a fair-sized station with corrugated-iron walls painted a brown so dull as to be almost grey. The grand main door had two of its panels missing, all the windows were smashed, and the only remaining part of the sign contained just the letters 'PRAT'.

We stopped a good half a kilometre further along from the station, which was the only building in sight. Samuel did not get down this time, but Horacio walked along the ledge to tell me that we had reached 'Arturo Prat', one of many places in Chile honouring this great hero and martyr of the War of the Pacific. I knew that several of my grandfather's letters from the pampa had been sent from a nitrate camp of that name, and I thought this must surely be it. Horacio said we were going to have a stop of at least fifty minutes here, which would give me plenty of time to 'investigate'. I thanked him, got down, and started heading back towards the station.

When I had passed the last of the freight cars, and was within a hundred yards or so of the station, I heard the engine starting up. The train began to move. I started panicking. I tried running to catch up with it. The sound of the engine ceased. I laughed off my fear. I had been misled by another of its strange manoeuvres, or even by a practical joke, perpetrated admittedly by a most unlikely pair of pranksters. I resumed my walk towards the station, but when I finally reached it the train set off again, faster than before, and no longer stopping. As it trailed out of sight, a chilling conviction took hold of me. I had misunderstood Horacio. Neither he nor Samuel had any idea that I was still not on board. Nor would there be any way of their finding out for hours, possibly not until Calama. By which time I would have gone mad or died from exposure.

I had read extensively about solitary deaths on the pampa. Julio Requelme, the bank clerk who had stepped off the train at a place probably similar to where I was now, was just another extreme and especially mysterious example of someone who had been *empampado*, become part of the landscape. There were various stories of people whose cars had broken down or who had got lost or had been surprised by the night, with its freezing temperatures. In most of these cases no one had done the sensible thing, and stayed by their cars, or by the railway track. Thirst, cold, panic and insanity had made them walk off into the pampa, wander in circles, and frequently disappear without a trace, or else turn up years later as mummified corpses, perfectly preserved because of the dryness of the atmosphere, and untouched by insects or animals simply because there were no insects or animals to touch them. A soldier from the War of the Pacific was found over 100 years later still in his battle uniform, together with a notebook in which he had jotted down impressions from the campaign. Riquelme was wearing his suit for the christening, and was holding his hat between his legs so it would not blow away.

Trying as hard as I could to think straight, I walked to the back of the station in the hope of finding workers, as there had been in Portezuelo. The sight of a parked tractor raised my spirits, but I could see nobody. I shouted, but there was no response. The station seemed clearly disused, but you never knew in this part of the world: dogs might suddenly appear, or a DJ. There was a single door that had not been boarded up, and so I went inside, and only then remembered the terrible tale of 'El Mariconazo', another of the Atacama's mad, solitary stationmasters, this one a serial killer of the 1920s who preyed on single men seeking refuge or company in the station, and ending up '*empampados*', buried under the rubble, adding to the statistics of the disappeared. I shouted again, and was answered only by the hackneyed sounds from a horror film – the creak of a hinge, the flap of a broken window in the wind. The thick, undisturbed dust on the floorboards was the final proof: no one could recently have entered the building other than in the form of a ghost.

I went back outside, and still there was no one. I looked in all directions, and caught sight of a small white enclosure far away, in the middle of which there appeared to be something I did not really want to see at this present moment of time – an upright tombstone that could have been from an English parish cemetery. However, curiosity drew me towards it. I had nothing else to do; I needed something to keep my mind occupied while waiting in the diminishing expectation of the man in the tractor to return, or even my train.

I got closer. It was indeed a tombstone. There was an English name on it; and as I read it I began to think my mind had gone, or that perhaps I was already dead, wandering among the spirits. The name on the tombstone was that of Harold Blakemore – somebody I knew, not in person, but through his reputation and books. Blakemore was Britain's leading historian of Chile, author, among other works, of the official and, needless to say, only history of the Antofagasta (Chili) and Bolivia Railway, who, I noticed, had paid for the slab. He had only been sixty-one at the time of his death in 1991, just ten years older than I was now. His demise, I was relieved to discover, had taken place not in Arturo Prat, but rather in the more homely setting of the London borough of Barnet, described here quaintly as 'near London', as indeed it had been when my grandparents bought there their house at 30 Meadway.

Why had Blakemore asked to have his ashes scattered here, of all places, in the desolate heart of the Atacama, not even near a main road, in a spot likely to be visited only by the drivers of freight trains? Even Barnet, where I had been brought up, and where my father had died on a grey wet day, in a home for Alzheimer's patients, seemed alluring in comparison. The more I thought about it, the more I indulged in a fantasy about some sinister conspiracy whereby the F.C.A.B. made sure that any British author who wrote about them would finish up, dead or alive, at Arturo Prat. Before I could work out the finer details of this theory, however, I saw a man with a yellow construction helmet walking onto the platform.

I almost ran to embrace this person, but fortunately contained myself. Had I done so I would have felt even more of a fool when he responded to my story with the matter-of-fact statement that the train would be back at any moment. I asked him if there were any remains left of the nitrate camp where my grandfather had worked.

'The *Oficina* Arturo Prat wasn't here,' he replied, 'it was further along the line, just after Chacabuco. But I don't think you'll find much there.'

I sat on the platform, next to the sign whose remaining letters seemed right now the best way of describing how I felt. The back carriages of my train were shunting towards me and came to a halt just outside the station. Too embarrassed to say anything to Samuel and Horacio about the turmoil I had just been through, I returned to my engine car, which was becoming ever more welcoming as the day progressed. Dingy, uncomfortable, and probably soon to be freezing, it was nonetheless my refuge from the desert, and I was almost wishing by now that we would never arrive at Calama, and that I could just go on sitting here for days, with my bottle of water by my side, my rucksack with its unread books under the seat, and my provisions, as yet barely touched, hanging in a supermarket bag on the hook behind me.

I peered out of the window for a last sighting of poor Blakemore, and then, as the train pulled away, sat down to await the revival of the melody inside my head, soon surely to attain its climactic chords now that the drama of daylight's last hours was about to commence.

Little more than two kilometres out of Arturo Prat, we stopped again.

There was no station, no shack, no siding, no passing place for any other train, absolutely nothing. Samuel and Horacio said nothing either. Getting down from their car, they walked past me and headed towards the end of the train. I stayed this time happily in my seat. For the first fifteen minutes. I put my head through the window, but saw no sign of them. I climbed down, checking first to see if they had not slipped back past me. Then I set off in the same direction as they had taken. Twenty carriages further down, and still no sighting of the pair, visions of *empampados* were back again to haunt me. I found the two men hidden under the penultimate carriage, with Horacio about to hit a wheel with a huge spanner.

Samuel distractedly got up, and, without saying a word to me, scoured the ground near the track. Among the rusting debris was a piece of wire, which he picked up and then attached to the wheel. 'A faulty wheel,' he explained at last, breaking the silence. 'But I think that'll do the trick.'

I talked to Samuel as the three of us returned to the front of the train. It was already 6.30 p.m., and he doubted if we would get to Calama before 2.00 a.m. at the earliest. If we were going to be very late he would call for replacement drivers, and he and Horacio would continue to Calama by car. I could go with them if I wished. I said I would stick it out to the end. 'The night shift,' he said, to encourage me in my resolution, 'that's the worst part of this job. That's when you really begin to feel lonely.' 'And cold,' butted in Horacio, 'No matter what warm clothes you put on, the cold of the desert just gets to your bones. Perhaps it's psychological.'

The train persevered in fits and starts through a landscape that was rapidly changing as the night approached. The darkening folds in the hills created sensual forms, like entwined bodies, and the grey of the rubble became streaked with luminous, metallic yellow. The wind was rising, and every so often miniature whirlwinds ran meanderingly across the foreground like spirits in search of a home.

At 7.30 we were back for a moment in the land of the living. Baquedano, the only surviving settlement between Antofagasta and Calama, was a metropolis with a population of at least 500 inhabitants spread out on either side of the main road to which we had briefly returned. We crawled across the historic intersection of the F.C.A.B. and the now defunct Northern Longitudinal line, and continued without stopping, past the station that was now a railway museum, and then past a group of decrepit old steam trains terminally parked inside ironwork sheds.

Further along the line some irregularly spaced orange letters announced that we were passing alongside the 'Nitrate Museum', a comically lopsided structure in plasterboard and the ubiquitous cor-rugated iron, adorned with an ox skull and a row of dusty green bottles. Graffiti-like writing was daubed over an open door, insist-ing that the place was 'Open'; but the train resisted this tempting invitation and relentlessly pursued its slow advance towards Calama. Baquedano came to an end a few yards further on, beyond a sorry stall selling bedraggled cacti, from which protruded a sign in English enigmatically inscribed 'Positive Energy'. We were not even a third of the way to Calama; and an even greater emptiness lay ahead of us.

Imperceptibly we were climbing, and had passed the 1,000-metre mark just as the orange purple light of sunset was spreading across a broadening expanse of stones, deserted mines, and strange rock formations resembling piled-up sandbags. We had reached what my map called 'the Pampa of the Dead Indian', and I thought I could see far, far in front of us the dark pink cone of a snow-capped volcano. Then the sun disappeared, and the train stopped.

I sat in near-total darkness, staring through my side window at the black profile of a hill crowned by a tall chimney.

'Chacabuco,' said Horacio, entering my carriage, and showing me where the light switch was. Outlined against the remaining dark red glow of the penumbral sky, the former nitrate *oficina* and concentration camp could not have appeared more dramatic, or more sinister. Horacio went off with a lantern to 'inspect the back of the train', and Samuel came in to confirm that there would be a change of drivers in about 'two hours time'. He asked me again if I was sure I wanted to stay on the train; and again I said yes. I pulled up the zip of my pullover, and prepared myself for a long night.

The train moved on, and the temperature descended further. An hour before, I had been warm enough in a light summer shirt; and now I was on the point of donning a polar fleece on top of the zipped-up pullover, so as to snuggle up as warmly as I could inside my sparse mobile home. We were rumbling through a landscape where all that was faintly visible were the ghostly silhouettes of ruined walls – a long succession of nitrate *oficinas* from which all life had departed decades ago. I could not decide which of these was Arturo Prat, or which ones were Anibal Pinto, Pampa Unión and Araucania – all places where my grandfather had worked, and which had registered in me as a child as symbols of endurance.

When all was black outside, and nothing of the landscape could be seen, I pictured Bethel late at night at one of these *oficinas*, alone in his hut, and with a pen poised in his hand. This was his preferred time for writing to Sophie; no one would disturb him at this hour. The workers had gone drunk to bed, and the silence of the pampa, so oppressive 'it could almost be felt', ensured that all he could hear were the sound of his breath and the ticking of his watch.

My grandfather had dreaded coming here. Weeks before, in October

1911, he had voiced to Sophie his fears about having to stay in places that would be entirely staffed by 'natives (Chilians)', or in the case of Araucania, Italians. His loneliness, he had envisaged, would be absolute. But as it turned out, life in the *oficinas* was not quite as bad as he had thought. There was no one whom he could talk to about Hull or Sophie's brother, or French philosophy, but he was able to practise his Spanish among hospitable people who enjoyed the occasional game of billiards. Life was also relatively inexpensive. Food and drink were free, and the well-equipped stores sold goods such as bath towels and underclothes that were of better quality and far cheaper than in Antofagasta. He also welcomed the availability of 'some grand Munich beer' which, he guilty admitted, he found very welcome after trudging around for hours in the scorching sun. 'I am afraid,' he confessed, 'I am sufficiently "animal" to appreciate such things under the circumstances.'

What wore him down, and contributed more than anything to his growing depression and nervousness, was having to work in an environment where everything seemed to conspire against him. The glare and refraction, particularly over the snow-white salt flats, made 'accurate instrument work' an impossibility for most of the day, as did the wind, which started early in the morning, and built up to hurricane force by mid-afternoon. To avoid both these hazards, he had to do most of his work between the hours of 5.30 and 9.30 a.m., thereby fully experiencing the most extreme climactic fluctuations in the world: the temperature, below freezing at 5.30, had already risen to 100°F four hours later. 'It is not much fun working on the pampa,' he concluded with English understatement.

I saw him putting down his pen and raising his head to the window. The world outside, which was gradually defeating him, making him, by his own reckoning, a tetchier, emptier and more 'animal' person, seemed almost benign and inspirational by night. The hideous *oficinas*, where life had been reduced to its ugliest basics, had acquired in the darkness a poetic aspect, and, with their electric lamps, now dotted the landscape like 'so many little clusters of stars'.

From the windows of my car the only lights to be seen were those of the train and the stars in the sky. I had stayed resolutely in the darkness, half-hypnotized by the insistent, stroboscopic effect of the engine's lights shining on the tracks. The train's constant stopping and starting had achieved a rhythm of its own, echoed by the control box above me, which flashed and made siren-like noises every time we got going again, announcing to the orchestra inside me the change of pace, the acceleration that preceded another opening of the window, in turn a signal for the choir to start up, to compete against the sudden blast of bitter air, and to welcome a night sky that forced me almost to applaud the brightness of the stars and the crescent moon.

At around 11.00 p.m. the train shunted backwards and forwards, then came to an abrupt halt. The engine suddenly went quiet; and the silence that followed was like the aftermath of a shock. Then a scene from a *film noir* began to take place outside. A Land Rover had caught up with us, and two men were getting out. Samuel and Horacio went down to join them, and advanced in their direction as if going to a shoot-out from which they would not return.

The train had now been taken over by Aldo and José. The pensive expressions of the New York intellectual and his assistant were replaced by the warm, open looks of two men of obviously indigenous blood. Each came in turn to shake my hand, introducing themselves not just as Aldo and José, but with their full complement of names, and treating me with the hushed respect of people who had been entrusted with smuggling out of the country some ageing revolutionary.

The engine started up again, and soon I was rubbing my eyes to try and prevent them from closing. The adrenalin that had kept my senses all day in a state of high alert was slowly losing its force. At around 1.00 a.m. I fell finally asleep, to be woken up two hours later by the cold. The lights of Calama were shining in the distance. I gathered up my belongings and prepared myself for what had promised in Antofagasta to be like a scene from a tale by Borges: a meeting at the dead of night between the solitary passenger of a freight train and a stationmaster mysteriously named Fuad Yacsic, a man of 'Croatian Arab descent'. He would definitely be there to meet me, Don Rolando had confirmed at midday, no matter what time I arrived. It was his 'duty' as stationmaster to be there.

Don Fuad Yacsic was neither on the platform, nor inside the station. I was met instead by the more prosaic-sounding Freddy.

'Don Fuad went to bed hours ago,' I was told by this friendly, smiling guard who went on to identify himself as a Mapuche from southern Chile. 'And you?' he asked, becoming visibly excited when I said where I was from and what I was doing.

'I've never met a writer before,' he exclaimed, pleased also to have found someone who appeared delighted at the prospect of a thorough tour of Calama's old-fashioned station at well after 3.00 a.m.

'As someone who likes history, you're going to love this,' he said, pointing out to me the date, name and royal patent on an English clock, and then taking me into another room to show me a old framed photo of a group of engineers and railway workers lined up in front of a steam train. Among the tiny, grainy figures in the background I spotted a familiar mustachioed man, slightly taller than the others, and with a slight, distracted smile. Sleepiness was almost certainly leading me to delusions. I told Freddy in my excitement that I had recognized my grandfather.

The station's guest house, at the end of the platform, was like another vision. When Freddy unlocked the door to this modest wooden bungalow, I found myself in an English holiday home in the Lake District. There were the comfortable floral-patterned sofa and matching armchairs, the electric plastic kettle, the blue and white teaset in 'Cambridge' porcelain, the glass-fronted wall cupboard with an array of hanging mugs, and a bowl filled with sachets of Nescafé and bags of Tetley tea.

The illusion stayed with me until after the sun had risen. A couple of trains had shunted loudly past during the night; but they might have been vestigial memories of the day before. They had not disturbed the sensation, often experienced on waking up after a first night in a rented house in the English countryside, that you have misjudged the number of blankets necessary to keep warm, and are consequently freezing. Your nostrils are assailed by the dank stale smells of a place only fitfully occupied. You long for what my grandfather so often longed for during his years in South America – marmalade on thick, buttered slices of toast.

The reality on opening the door was not nearly as harsh as I had expected. The sun was already blinding at 9.00 a.m., and the station sign on the other side of the track denoted an altitude of 2,100 metres. But the view of the large railway enclosure embraced trees, hedges, patches of green, and some distant tennis courts, from which I thought

I heard the sounds of an early Sunday morning game. Calama was an oasis watered by the River Loa; and the land belonging to the F.C.A.B. was like a private garden at its centre. The station was locked, and so I walked across to the frontier post protecting this land from the world outside. The hostile guard on duty had no idea where Freddy was, and considered Sunday morning an inappropriate time to bother Don Fuad. I left a message to say I would be back in Calama early on the Wednesday morning, to have a full day in the town before taking the night train to Bolivia.

I passed the intervening time pleasantly at the nearby oasis village of San Pedro de Atacama, an age-old travellers' rest which lay below a range of volcanoes crowned by the perfect cone of Licancapur. The sight of these mountains at sunset had always moved my grandfather as he wandered alone around the outskirts of Calama.

'The long range of snow-clad mountains,' he wrote, 'all lie to the east, and as in these latitudes the sun sets very quickly and behind some relatively low hills, one can watch these mountains change colour in the space of a little more than half an hour from gold to glowing orange, then crimson, and finally to violet, before they are lost and disappear imperceptibly in the darkness.'

This was a spectacle I observed for the first time in less solitary and dignified circumstances as I scampered behind a guide clad in a Spiderman outfit, together with hundreds of other people who had signed up for the converging evening excursions offered by San Pedro's multitude of travel agencies. At this pretty village of adobe houses I had suddenly hit the well-trodden backpacker's route from Peru to Patagonia, and had been brought back with a jolt to a world where travel as exhilarating uncertainty had declined into one of travel as prosaic dependability.

Over a candle-lit dinner just before returning to Calama I found myself discussing the behaviour patterns of today's gap year students and backpacking young professionals with a locally resident young anthropologist and his inevitably beautiful, blonde and French wife (an apparent *sine qua non* of the Chilean intellectual). Somehow the conversation naturally turned to the subject of Balzac, for whom the Frenchwoman had a passion she had hitherto been unable to share in the Atacama. I told her what a shame it was that she had not met my grandfather who, in one of his bleaker letters from Calama, revealing more sensitivity than ever to the fundamental tragedy and absurdity of the human condition, had regretted to Sophie that there was no one around with whom he could discuss Balzac's *Comédie humaine*.

I went off cheerfully to bed, and rose the next morning full of optimism about the next stage of my journey. But almost immediately something happened to tarnish my mood a little – a minor incident, but one which touched on my Westerner's guilt at the way South America's indigenous population had been brutalized by the conquistadors, marginalized by my grandfather's generation, and patronized by so many of today's backpackers, for whom this continent was merely a giant adventure playground.

This guilt had started to surface as I prepared to go deeper into the Andean world, and that was perhaps why I reacted so strongly to the behaviour of the young German couple who had rushed onto the Calama bus at the very last moment. Finding an elderly indigenous woman occupying one of their reserved seats, they had ordered her, though she was blind and could barely walk, to go to the back of the now moving bus without even a thank you or a smile.

'I suffer from car sickness, I need to be in the front,' one of them curtly explained to me after I had got up to surrender my own seat to the blind, limping woman.

Irritation was perhaps still affecting my judgment when we reached the Calama approach road, which had lost its tranquil pleasantness of before, and now seemed just a busy dusty thoroughfare. On arriving at the town I went straight to the station of the F.C.A.B., where my good spirits momentarily returned after at last meeting the charming and gentle Don Fuad Yacsic.

Don Fuad had Syrian blood on his father's side, but his mother was Croatian 'like so many of the Europeans who came to Calama', he told me as walked to the tennis courts at the other end of the railway enclosure. Beneath a clump of trees facing the courts was a long and attractive wooden bungalow with disproportionately large bay windows.

'I think this is where your grandfather must have lived,' he said, taking out a key to let us inside.

The place had obviously not been lived in for years, but deterioration had affected mainly the back of the house, where there was a rotting terrace and a wildly overgrown garden. The interior, though overwhelmingly musty, and stripped of all furnishings, seemed structurally unchanged since the beginning of the twentieth century; and there was even a room that must have been the one my grandfather had described as having 'three doors, a white painted ceiling, and a fireplace about ten times too big for it, a perfect architectural aberration'.

This fireplace, a sturdy, unornamented concrete block now painted a dark maroon, was mentioned several times by my grandfather, who had stayed in Calama in the middle of an especially harsh winter. It was early in June 1911, and his period in the drawing office at Antofagasta had just come to an end. He anticipated spending only a week or so in Calama, for him 'a miserable town' redeemed only by 'a few traces of natural vegetation'. But he was impressed by the size of the bungalow that had been put at his disposal.

'Here I am,' he wrote to Sophie on arrival, 'sitting alone in a room which might almost belong to an English country house, instead of that of the Sectional Engineer, and which I have all to myself for the present.'

The walls were decorated with hunting prints and cartoons from *Vanity Fair*, 'a big red-shaded hanging lamp' was casting 'a cheerful glow', and 'a bright wood fire' was burning. He had just finished a 'solitary dinner' prepared and served by a 'rather stupid but willing boy' who 'turned out to be quite a dab hand at cooking'.

The meal had been an unusual experience. 'Dining alone in this big, comfortably furnished room, with its huge fireplace, the well-appointed table service and this boy to wait, gives one a particular feeling of solitariness.'

Afterwards, however, when the boy had gone, and he was sitting in an armchair before the fire, Bethel began to feel more comfortable and in the mood for thinking. And he had not been entirely alone. A black kitten was lying beside him on a rose-coloured cushion, while at his feet was a sleeping mastiff identical, from his description, to the one currently at my own feet, keeping me company as I sit late at night writing these lines, all alone in my Andalucían house, during a winter also unusually severe, with icicles hanging from the roof, a foot of snow on the ground, and a wood fire blazing.

'It is a young dog,' he wrote, 'but already big enough to put its paws on my shoulders; in fact it has grown very fast for its years and doesn't seem to be aware of the fact, for its behaviour is most undignified, more like that of a small puppy.'

Fuad asked me what work my grandfather had done in Calama, and I told him once we were back in the station, and sitting down comfortably in his station office. The task for which Bethel had come here, I said, had been a curious one. There was an old bridge across the River Loa that was clearly not strong enough for the ever-increasing railway traffic. A new bridge had been built alongside it, and was waiting for the old one to be removed so that it could occupy its position and be bolted down. So as not to cause too much delay to the traffic, Bethel had been given precisely fourteen hours to carry out the switching of the bridges.

Everything had to be meticulously prepared beforehand; but right from the beginning Bethel knew he was going to have problems. The 'old johnny of a foreman' assigned to help him was an 'awfully garrulous old bird' who headed 'the most awful crew of beachcombers I ever struck'. The beachcombers, like most of their kind, were 'mainly deserters from ships and forever grumbling and dissatisfied', not to mention 'drunk on every possible opportunity'. The only cause for optimism was that they were not going to be paid until three weeks' time, for if they received money any earlier they would 'all be hopelessly drunk, and I have very strong suspicions that the foreman will be as bad as any of them.' Drunk or not, they proved largely useless; and their incompetence, combined with a long spell of freak bad weather, endlessly delayed the moment when the actual operation could begin.

Bethel's estimated week in Calama had already been extended to four weeks by the time the beachcombers were finally all sacked and replaced with a crew of 'Bolivian Indians'. The change was welcomed at first by Bethel, but not for long. He went on to develop attitudes towards his Bolivian workers that underlined, as I sat talking to Fuad in his office, all that had troubled me about the incident on the Calama bus.

My grandfather had been a kindly man; but he had the prejudices of his generation, together with an inability to comprehend those with a different background to his. The European beachcombers had been difficult enough for him to handle; but at least he had had a glimmer of understanding about what went on in the minds, knowing, for instance, that the offer of increased pay would have been an incentive for them to work harder and for longer hours. However, he was incapable of motivating the Bolivians in this way, and thus believed them to be unintelligent rather than the products of a world where money did not have the same meaning, where life was lived at a different pace, and where the immediate comforts of sleeping and drinking were sometimes more attractive.

Bethel, prompted by the work ethic embedded in his genes, unfavourably compared the Bolivians to Americans he had known in New York, who had been prepared to slave away day and night in the interests of completing a job. And even the 'incurably lazy' French workmen were preferable in his view, for 'though they cannot do anything without a cigarette in their mouth and are forever going on strike and have eternal grievances, they are at least extremely intelligent.' The 'Bolivian Indians', in contrast, were 'the crudest kind of unskilled labour', and totally unsuited for the job of changing the bridges, which required 'a very good class of man'.

Another month passed before a date was finally set for the lowering into their foundation plates of two '60 ton spans about 15 ft. long', a delicate operation with a margin of error of only one-eighth of an inch. For the whole week beforehand Bethel was forced to work like a 'galley slave', and not just as an engineer, but also as foreman and jack of all trades.

'Besides all the careful measurements and setting out and instrument work, I have done the work of carpenters, mechanics, stonemasons, and indeed every kind of work. I have hauled on ropes and lugged bars and beams about myself to try and get things going.' In an attempt to persuade people to work into the night he brought in 'a huge five thousand candle power acetylene flare light', which only he knew how to operate.

But all was to no avail. Only six people chose to work overtime, and the others responded instead to their 'natural laziness', displaying in so doing an intelligence half the size of 'the veriest farm labourer at home'. Bethel's 'nightmare of a week reached its high watermark of rottenness' early on the morning of 20 August, when the new bridge was due to be put in its place. Orders had been given for the workers to be ready to start work at exactly 5.00 a.m., after the night train had passed. But when Bethel arrived at 4.30, not a soul had turned up. 'I routed out the foreman and went to the men's tents with him, but they only replied with grunts and curses.' It took another two and half hours for them to be in a fit state to do anything, by which time Bethel had telegraphed Antofagasta to postpone the operation until the following Sunday. 'Next week,' Bethel had warned, 'I shall take my revolver with me and threaten to shoot the beggars.'

Fortunately there would be no need for this. Miraculously, when the time came, everything would be realized with 'a success that far exceeded my most sanguine anticipations'. After the last train had gone by, at 5.45 a.m., the girders had been jacked along the greased rails laid down for them 'as easily as shelling peas', and had then been effortlessly lowered and bolted to the ground. Bethel managed to have the track relaid and ready for traffic six and a half hours ahead of time, and was even able to go back afterwards to Calama, have a change of clothes, wash, and then go and play two sets of tennis.

'I came in for such a lot of kudos and congratulations that I am ordering a size larger in hats,' he excitedly told Sophie in a letter detailing every tiny aspect of the operation, his greatest achievement so far in South America, his only real achievement.

I showed Fuad my grandfather's pictures of the new bridge, and he looked blankly at them. It no longer existed, he said, the railway track had been rerouted and did not have to cross the river until much further up. I brought out a photo of the nearby late nineteenth-century Conchi viaduct, which my grandfather had been asked to inspect at the same time. In the photo a chugging steam train, as diminutive in its context as the one in Turner's *Rain, Speed and Steam*, was pictured right in the middle of what had been the world's highest railway viaduct.

'It's ages since a train has crossed that bridge,' smiled Fuad, 'but the pipeline is still in use. We can take you there if you're interested.'

Freddy, my friend from before, was not around, so the task of driving me to the viaduct was entrusted to a stocky, middle-aged guard called Oswaldo. He did not seem particularly pleased by the prospect, and was as silently grumpy on the way to the car as one of my grandfather's beachcombers. Attempts to engage him in conversation by asking questions were repeatedly met by the phrase '*Correcto, correcto,*' though in a moment of rare expansiveness he revealed how much he missed the greenness of southern Chile, where he was from. But there was no point in regretting, he said. Calama was where his roots were now, where his children had been born, where the money was.

Beyond the grid of streets between the railway station and a landscaped main square, Calama came to seem progressively larger than I had first thought, and progressively uglier and less innocuous. The dust blown up by the wind had blanched all the colours, and we were rushing under a white sky through an endless hazy sprawl of hypermarkets, industrial estates, and concrete residences. Then we accelerated over desert.

The road ran in a completely straight line between the new railway track and the pathetic, polluted trickle of the Loa, along whose banks was a sudden eruption of dusty green as we bypassed the tiny village of Chiu-Chiu.

'Do you want to see the village?' Oswaldo asked before suddenly swerving round when I said yes. Driving speedily down a track where the name 'Lord Cochrane' was scrawled in red on a corrugated-iron door, we pulled up violently next to a solitary reminder of the days when this ramshackle, decayed little community had been a major stopping place between Potosí and the coast. It was a seventeenth-century parish church, said to be one of the most attractive in Chile. Oswaldo waited by the car as I went inside to view the simple interior, with its white adobe walls, and doors and ceiling made from the now protected bark of cacti. I stood motionlessly for a few moments. It had been some time since I had taken in a work of man-made beauty.

We seemed to speed up as we shot out of Chiu-Chiu and into a landscape pockmarked with copper mines. The asphalt ended, but we barely slowed down, and continued in a cloud of dust as the unpaved road came right up against the old railway track, on which I pictured my grandfather literally sailing from Calama to Conchi and back on the small sail-borne car used by engineers only on this particular stretch of the line. And then, all of a sudden, the once insignificant Loa dramatically split the landscape in two, creating a deep, wide chasm. A modern branch of the railway veered well away from this, while the old track headed sharply towards it before being cut off by a barrier marked 'Danger, Keep Out, Private Property'.

Getting out of the car we climbed over the barrier, and walked over the viaduct that for my grandfather had been one of the great marvels of modern engineering. The engineer had been French, and a model of his creation had been placed almost immediately in the Musée des Arts et Métiers in Paris. For Bethel this was the sort of engineering achievement that justified his faith in the modern world, his faith in his profession. And it was a privilege to be associated with it, if only through investigating how well it was bearing up to the greatly increased railway traffic and to the terrible stresses caused by constant winds.

Only a light wind was blowing as I trod fearfully across it with Oswaldo. This was enough to heighten my sense of exposure and vulnerability as I neared the middle of the eight-feet-wide structure, and took a look down to the water 320 feet below. The steel girders appeared as insubstantial as stilts, and I felt that the slightest sudden increase in the wind would be sufficient to blow either me or the viaduct over. I hardly dared imagine the structure buffeted by the gale force winds my grandfather had known. Passenger trains had been prevented from crossing, and Bethel, standing where I was now, had been forced to hang onto the guard rail for all he was worth.

Back safely in the car we drove for a while along the canyon of the Loa to the point where the river had been dammed and became a large modern reservoir. Oswaldo, more taciturn than ever, was able to volunteer the information that water levels were exceptionally low this year, before he fell back into silence. As we returned towards Calama, a wild man of Biblical appearance emerged from out of the empty desert, and started hysterically waving his hands at us. We pulled up besides him. He had thick matted hair and a white-streaked beard so long that it trembled in the wind, rather as artists had imagined that of Moses. He asked if we were going to Calama, then jumped into the car, and placed on the seat next to him the large wooden box he had been carrying on his shoulders.

The desert was a place of strange beings and strange ways of making a living. The wild man apparently survived from catching trout in the reservoir. He had not seen a soul in three days, he said, and had almost died from the cold at night. He had never known such a bad year for trout, and had had to wait around until his provisions had been completely exhausted to catch the thirty he now had in his box. After we left him on the outskirts of Calama, Oswaldo reckoned that the man would get a good price for the fish. His near fatal hardships had probably been worth it.

I asked Oswaldo to leave me at the entrance to Calama's cemetery. It was not even one o'clock, and I had nine more hours to kill in this town that was beginning inexplicably to fill me with foreboding and trepidation as I waited to go into Bolivia. The haziness was worse, barely a trace of blue was left in the drained sky, and the warm midday wind was grating on the nerves. In the cemetery, I found the tomb of a contemporary of my grandfather who had stayed on at Calama and died here in 1944. Its anachronistic inscription seemed to be admonishing me in my over-heated state.

'Along the cool sequestered vale of life,' it read, 'he kept the even tenor of his ways.'

I took a taxi to the town square, and in a now desperate ploy to pass the time, hunted down the surviving pale-blue house of Bolivia's sole hero of the War of the Pacific, Eduardo Avaroa, a former mayor who died on 23 March 1879 while organizing Calama's brave but futile resistance against the advancing Chilean troops. His words of defiance against the Chilean general, unsurprisingly not recorded on the house, are today enshrined in Bolivia's history:

'Surrender? Me? Let his grandmother surrender, damn it!'

It seemed to me a telling example of history's underlying complexities that one of this man's descendants should be Luksic Avaroa, the celebrated Chilean magnate of part-Croatian origin, and the current owner of the F.C.A.B.

More out of curiosity than hunger, and still with eight further hours to spend in Calama, I went to have lunch in the Croatian Club. Under the ornamental friezes of the white plastered walls were posters dating back to the days of communist Yugoslavia, with photos of the original bridge at Mostar and of a smilingly innocent Dubrovnik. I ordered the very un-Croatian set menu and asked if I could speak to someone who could tell me something about the club's history. The manager came over to sit next to me for a few minutes. He was another Chilean from the south. There were no more first-generation Croatians left in Calama, he said, and virtually no one who could speak the language. If I wanted to find out more about the club's history, he continued, I should have a word with its president, Don Fuad Yacsic. Politely concluding our meeting with the words '*Con permiso*', he went back to sit with his friends.

In that moment the sense of unease that had been with me for much of the day took a sudden turn for the worse. As I alternated my glance between the dog-eared posters and the unsmiling people around me, a chill spread out from the pit of my stomach, my forehead felt clammy, and I thought I was finally succumbing to one of those phobic crises that deserts are said sometimes to bring on. The sensation was momentary but strong enough to bring up afterwards a memory of Sophie gently chiding me for being too sensitive and morbid, telling me that life had these moments when there seemed no way out of the greyness, but these times always passed, and you had always to be brave and determined, for life was so full of beauty and excitement, so full of things worth living for. And I wondered now if these consoling platitudes would have had any effect on Bethel as he sat alone in his cold Calama bungalow, restlessly dividing his attention between the fireplace and the empty chairs around him, his heart 'too full of unutterable things to write any more'.

If places can eat into your soul, then this is the effect that Calama and the nitrate *oficinas* would have on Bethel, condemned for nearly one and a half years to go backwards and forwards between them, moving slowly towards despair. The gods had been against him from the start.

Within a week of his first moving to Calama the sky had turned an apocalyptic black before releasing a deluge which had continued for days without easing, devastating a town wholly unaccustomed to rainfall. There was not a single house in Calama that did not 'leak like a sieve', or whose inhabitants did not spend their time pushing their beds away from places where water was dripping. Any potential cosiness that Bethel's own house might have had was now becoming ever more difficult to imagine. Revealingly focusing his concerns not on his bed but on a cottage grand piano, he moved this from one spot to the other before eventually drilling a hole in the ceiling to release the accumulated water and prevent the whole bungalow from collapsing on top of him. By then water was oozing up under the floorboards, and running in steady streams down the wallpaper. His supply of wood and coal had run out and the house was 'as horribly cold and dank as any charnel house'. He also had no bread; every oven in the town had been flooded.

In the earliest of Bethel's impressions of this part of Chile to have reached Sophie, he had jokingly remarked, 'This must have been the site of the cities of Sodom and Gomorrah, and the ancient curse of the God of Genesis still rests heavily on this parched and arid land.' The advent of the rains made this seem not such a joke at all.

'It appears now,' Bethel wrote to Sophie, 'that as the wicked (including me) continue to flourish, as is their wont, like a green bay tree, a second Deluge is being sent to wipe us off utterly from the face of the earth.'

'The climate has gone cranky altogether,' he was writing at the end of July, by which time the rains had stopped, the dust had returned, earth tremors had become more recurrent than ever, and a bitterly cold spell had set in, climaxing in snowfalls that had given Calama 'the very curious appearance resulting from snow lying on thick dust'.

Up in the mountains, the situation was even worse. For weeks snows had blocked the railway, causing huge financial losses for the F.C.A.B. (which Bethel said was entirely their fault, as they had not invested in a snowplough), and nearly leading to loss of life after an assistant sectional engineer and his crew had been trapped up there trying to clear the former branch line to Collahausi. Bethel himself went later to investigate, and took a photo that brings to mind the Victorian painter Landseer's great canvas of an Arctic disaster, *Man Proposes, God Disposes*. Instead of a wrecked ship jutting among icebergs, there is a tilted steam engine, with its coal wagon spilling its contents on the snow – a no less effective image of the helplessness of modern man in the face of sublime nature.

Yet Bethel's battle with the elements was at least something he could share with everybody else, and, as with the problems and challenges associated with the Loa bridge and Conchi viaduct, prevented his mind from dwelling too much on morbid issues. The real test for Bethel came with the return to dusty normality at the end of his first August in Calama.

My grandfather had realized quite soon into his stay in Chile that he was not going to acquire either great fame or great fortune there; but he had not anticipated, after his triumphant switching of bridges on the Loa, being relegated afterwards to routine maintenance and inspection work. Tired of being endlessly fobbed off with the promise of a job at Mejillones, for a while he contemplated leaving the F.C.A.B. An Italian millionaire proposed putting him in charge of a nitrate *oficina*. More tempting still was the offer of a job in southern Chile that would have meant working for better pay on interesting commissions in a pleasant green environment.

However, Bethel had a strong belief in loyalty, and told Sophie that it would not be 'quite right' for him to forsake the employers to whom in principle he was committed. The F.C.A.B. did not reward him for this loyalty. Though Mollet, the manager in Antofagasta, appeared appreciative of Bethel's qualities, the 'G.M.' in Calama certainly did not. This nameless individual, reported to be 'the worst bully and most hated man in this part of the country', was held in similar contempt by Bethel, who thought of him as a 'miserable "glorified ticket puncher"' with a shocking ignorance of science.

Bethel feigned not to mind the G.M.'s 'apparent view that engineers are on an inferior social plane to others in the railway'; but what he could not forgive was the man's organizational incompetence, and the resultant lack among his staff of any '*esprit de corps*' – a quality which had a vital importance for Bethel's public-spirited family. A low point in his relations with the man was reached when the latter accused him of incompetence, a charge from which Bethel would be entirely exonerated by Mollet. The G.M., unforgiving of this slight, was to make doubly sure that Bethel's career in Calama would never advance.

One of the features that had most troubled me on reading Bethel's letters from Calama was the way they reminded me of my father – another model and loyal employee whose integrity had been held against him, and who would be constantly passed over for promotion in favour of less experienced and often less competent colleagues. Particularly frightening was to discover how many of Bethel's words to describe his frustrations would later be inherited by my father to describe his own, above all the words 'cope' and 'iniquitous', which, as my father's vocabulary was gradually pared down by disease, became ultimately the only words that were left to him. An iniquitous state of non-coping was also reflected in the Calama letters, not so much in their hints of a mind being worn down, but also in my father's annotations on the envelopes, which touched me deeply with their list of places in Spain I happened to be visiting while he was editing the envelopes' contents.

'We don't mind what you do in life, Michael, as long as you're happy,' my father would often tell me, which was not really true at all, for I think my parents would have minded greatly had I become, say, a toilet attendant or a drug dealer. But what interested me now was that the sentiment was exactly that of my grandfather, who, in a letter to Sophie written during the middle of his Calama period, when his career was looking bleaker than ever, had stated that the only failure in life was the failure to be happy.

And happiness for Bethel was entirely contingent on his being reunited with Sophie, a prospect that was beginning to seem as vague and impossibly distant as that of paradise. In the meantime he was not happy at all. He could have put up (I almost wrote 'coped') with the unwelcoming environment and the disappointments of the job; but what he could not bear was the lack both of 'congenial souls' and of what he defined as culture and civilization. The social and intellectual snobbery I had once found so unacceptable in the letters had begun to seem more comprehensible in the light of Bethel's genes and his daunting background. Now I was almost coming round to pity him for being such a snob, for I had begun seeing this as the main factor militating against his immediate happiness.

In his attempts to define to Sophie the malaise that was affecting him, Bethel repeatedly lamented being in a 'semi-civilization', in a land where there was little understanding of culture.

'I have been feeling very restless lately,' he wrote to her in October 1911. 'There is so much I miss in this country. You can imagine after living in New York and Paris what it means to be landed in a place where there are no concerts or art exhibitions, where good books are scarce and people who appreciate these things even scarcer.'

He would have certainly been less lonely had he accepted people more on their own terms rather than his, had he indeed made a greater attempt to socialize with those whom he considered his social and intellectual inferiors. He made not a single friend among the Chileans. The 'natives', as he called them, were culturally the lowest of the low; and, when he once had the rare treat of witnessing at Antofagasta 'a fine German opera company', he concluded that these German musicians were 'really far too good for the place, at least as far as the natives are concerned (it is a question of casting pearls to the swine).' On another occasion, observing how the native staff in the nitrate *oficinas*, 'never seem to read', he went on to express his belief that 'they live the most stupid inane lives imaginable, vegetating I call it.'

Yet the British in whose company he was thrown proved mainly to be no better. The staff at Calama, from the G.M. downwards, were a particularly depressing crowd, with the exception of the head of the railway works, who reminded Bethel of a 'character out of a Kipling novel'. This man, despite his 'awful accent', 'little education', and having 'evidently risen from the lower ranks', was redeemed by being 'a thoroughly decent sort' endowed both with a 'keen sense of humour' and a 'natural keen intelligence'; he also had the advantage of coming from Hull. For the most part, however, Bethel found himself surrounded at Calama by 'hopeless mediocrity and indeed vulgarity'.

Underlying such dismissiveness was a fearful and growing realization of what could happen in a barbaric environment even to the 'best' and most 'interesting' British people. Soon after his frustrating return from Bolivia in March 1911, he had been saddened but unsurprised to hear what had occurred in grim Talcahuano to his Hull friend Tom Somerscales: the man had suffered such a bad nervous breakdown that the doctor had forbidden visits from anyone, even his wife.

Bethel was able to witness for himself the pernicious effect of South America on a number of people of whom he was very fond, for instance the two Dubliners whom he had got to know on his first foray into Bolivia, 'Samuels of Trinity', and 'Murphy'. Both these men turned up several months later in Calama, and Bethel was shocked by the change in their appearance and behaviour. 'Poor old Sammy', now missing a few front teeth, was looking and acting less like the intellectual he had once been and more like 'a prize fighter'.

Murphy too had 'absolutely deteriorated through mixing with the Yankee crowd in Bolivia, a tough lot'.

But the most tragic case Bethel knew was his friend from Mejillones, Tommy Gloag, now rapidly turning into a character from a novel not by Kipling but by Graham Greene. Little more than two months after Bethel's delightful and exuberant four days in Mejillones in the February of 1912, Gloag came to stay in Calama. He was hoping to continue on to Bolivia, but the state of his health would prevent him from travelling any further or higher. Tommy Gloag was in an advanced stage of consumption, and kept alive only by his 'natural vitality and good spirits'. Bethel lamented both his physical decline and the way the man had wasted his life and talents. 'Had he been a man in good health, and had he not sought forgetfulness in drink, he would have been in a very high position today in all probability.'

Sophie, whose last news of Tommy had been of him engaging in non-stop comic banter with Dr Williams, must have been surprised now to read Bethel's comment that 'he is one of the saddest lives I have ever known,' and that 'he seems in a way to be such a lonely person.' Perhaps she might have started worrying about what was happening to Bethel himself.

For Bethel was indeed changing. Lack of mental stimulus, combined with deepening experience of life in the raw, and growing bitterness about being in South America at all (for which he now entirely blamed his uncle Charles) were dulling his mind and allowing cynicism to taint his ideals. In his earlier letters to Sophie he had enjoyed philosophizing at length, as he did, for instance, in relation to Tom Somerscales's illness, which inspired a pompous yet lucidly argued meditation on pain and sorrow. The rather less cerebral Sophie was clearly impressed by such discourses, and responded by quoting from books that she admired but which Bethel, more often than not, was able brilliantly to demolish for their woolly thinking. However, the huge gaps in time between the writing of a letter and the receiving of a reply (one of Sophie's letters took a record eleven weeks and five days to arrive) limited the amount of intellectual satisfaction to be derived from such exchanges.

What Bethel needed was someone nearer at hand with whom he could have such discussions; but, even had he encountered such a person, he was finding that life in the desert was gradually making him more apathetic, and less inclined to argue. 'Too much calculations of whys and wherefores doesn't lead one anywhere,' was a statement typical of his new way of thinking. At the same time he was having to question his previously held belief in the supremacy of reason over intuition, and reluctantly to conclude, for instance, that the French philosopher Henri Bergson 'is right after all, and that pure intelligence is really unable to give a satisfactory explanation of the world.'

The only important subject on which his views remained completely unbending was that of love and marriage. Trapped in his literal and spiritual desert, he could not entertain even the remotest possibility that union with someone he loved might not necessarily rid him of his new-found pessimism, and turn him into a 'better person' than the mentally stagnating character he thought he was becoming. And so he vehemently rejected Robert Louis Stevenson's opinion that 'in marriage a man becomes slack and selfish and undergoes a fatty degeneration of his moral being.' Such an outlook on life, for Bethel, was 'pessimistic enough to have been written by Schopenhauer, and worthy of La Rochefoucauld for cynicism.' For good measure he added that 'as a generalization it is also a glaring inaccuracy,' a comment lacking the scientific authority he might once have demanded.

The inflexibility of his thoughts on love and marriage was perhaps the predictable consequence of a view of Sophie which remained firmly fixed in the past. Rather than thinking too much about what was happening to her in her present life, he preferred, like a spurned lover, to dwell obsessively on their past moments of happiness together. He had even brought with him to South America everything she had ever written to him, right back to the time of their momentous first meeting at Baker Street.

'I was looking through your letters the other night and rereading them. I have them all, from the very first notes you wrote me when I came over to London the first time from Paris, a year ago last March. I suppose at that time you would have been rather surprised to learn how religiously I treasured them. For you see, chérie, I knew from the first moment I met you on that occasion (it was outside Baker Street station, and we afterwards went to the little tea shop opposite the Blenheim, and stayed disgracefully long), that I was most desperately in love with you. Yes, every little detail of that visit stands out amazingly clear in my memory.'

As did those few special times in their courtship when he had gone back with her to 9 Aldridge Road Villas: 'Do you remember the famous occasion when we returned there one night (after a glorious day) and found everybody had returned to roost, and you hunted up supper down below? I don't believe we had much appetite for supper, we had too many things to say to each other, or to think and leave unsaid.'

There was perhaps a side to Bethel that wanted Sophie to stay unchanged from the young woman featured in the photos I have of her in her early twenties – timid and inward-looking in comparison to her rebellious sister Estella. He hated the prospect of her eventually having to leave Aldridge Road Villas, and the protective care of those 'dear old souls' the Isaacson sisters, who had recently started advising her in such womanly tasks as knitting a green tie for him. But, whether he liked it or not, Sophie and the circumstances of her life were changing as much as he was.

The 'Innocent from Ireland' was becoming less innocent in matters of the world, and turning into an independent woman with strong views of her own. Though Bethel had always supported Sophie in her career, and repeatedly claimed that her happiness was everything to him, he appeared put out when she ignored the wishes of her parents and became a chorus girl in the 'Covent Garden Company'. He had not heard of the organization before; and had to take her word for it that it was 'a company of repute'. But what really upset him was that this was a touring company on the point of going to his beloved Paris, a place to which he had so wished to take Sophie himself. And this somehow added to his other and greater fear that she was gradually slipping away from him into a world of glitter, ambition and superficial celebrity. Such were his worries now about Sophie that he started warning her of the dangers of too much ambition, and even attempted to persuade her that she had achieved something far better than fame – 'the art of making everybody love you'.

These were kind and truthful words, but they may not have gone down so well with an increasingly emancipated young woman trying to establish a life of her own. Furthermore, Estella and Louise were encouraging in her a developing interest in the suffragette movement, much to the concern of a Bethel still shocked by the news that she was keen to go up in an aeroplane ('On no account should you let your curiosity persuade you to do that!').

He now implored her never again to send him any more copies of the *Free-woman*. Though he said he believed in women's right to vote, he found it difficult to accept that some of the *Free-woman*'s more fanatical contributors 'could ever have been on speaking terms with that little Mr Cupid'. Nor could he reconcile the 'mistrust and antagonism' between the sexes evident in this journal and the memories he had of the two people he loved most in the world, Sophie and Louise. If only the eighteenth-century cult of the salon were reintroduced, he said, then there would be no more need of suffragettes.

At heart he was jealous, and not without reason. A letter from his mother describing a chance meeting with Sophie in London commented on how radiant and confident she had looked; and this was also an impression he was gaining from Sophie's own letters. She seemed to be putting into practice a philosophy of life summarized by a line she had once quoted to him, and he had duly torn apart: 'True life is to be alive in every fibre.' Her time, as he had feared, soon became taken up by glamorous social and cultural events, tours round Europe with her opera company, visits to such favourite old haunts of his as 'Le Petit Riche' in Paris, and meetings with interesting new people, such as 'Mr Campbell', a friend of Louise mentioned so many times by Sophie that Bethel's curiosity in the man, as indeed in all those 'other interesting people you have met, and other cousins who have the inestimable privilege and good fortune to be able to take you out to concerts and dinners', was reaching an unbearable pitch. Sophie was well on the way to becoming the future muse to artists and writers; and Bethel had to confess to 'feeling horribly envious'.

The waiter from the Croatian Club brought my bill as I remained distractedly at my table, steeling myself for the moment when I would have to get up and go out into Calama's hot and sleeping midafternoon streets. The last clients had just left, and I had become conscious of the loud ticking of an old clock similar perhaps to the one that had grated on my grandfather's nerves as he had sat in his Calama bungalow, tormenting himself with thoughts of Mr Campbell, incapable of writing another line to Sophie, and trying ineffectually to block his ears to those 'deep chimes and steady monotonous ticking that seem mockingly to proclaim the thousands of hours that must elapse before I see you again.' I thought about him for a few moments longer, waiting for him to move on to his 'lonely bed in this lonely house, in a lonely spot, in a world that is lonely because you are not here.' Then I paid the bill, rose sharply to my feet and walked out of the door.

I was feeling shaky, insecure and vulnerable, an easy prey to the gypsy woman who blocked my path. She had long flowing hair and a colourful dress, and looked young and sprightly from a distance. From nearby she became the wrinkled old hag from a horror film, with evil smiling eyes which froze you to the spot. Unthinkingly I handed her a small note; and in a flash she had leant forward to pluck out one of my hairs. She said I was on the point of embarking on a long and dangerous journey, and that I needed some protection. Because I had been so kind to her, she continued, she was going to be generous and give me an amulet that would save my life. But first I would have to give her more money.

I refused. She held up the lock of my hair, and said she had me now in her power. Stupidly I gave in, but the new and larger note I handed over was apparently not large enough. She demanded more money, I started walking away. She asked me if I had heard of the gypsy curse. 'It would be a shame,' she said, staring angrily, 'to put the curse on someone as young as you.'

Contrary to my grandfather's spirit, and contrary to all that had been instilled in me as a child, there was an irrational side to me which believed in curses, just as there was one that believed in amulets and in the saintly faith healer who looks after my Andalucían village of Frailes, the Santo Custodio. I slipped her another note, at which she sneered more than before. I began to hurry away from her, and she started shouting and cursing, and pointing a finger at me accusingly. Several other gypsies appeared from out of the shadows, and converged towards me in the empty street. I prayed to the Santo Custodio, and a police car arrived.

The police asked for the papers of the gypsy woman, as well as those of two young men who had caught up with her. I hurried away down a side street and on to the town's main pedestrian street, now thankfully filling up again with people. I walked as fast as I could to the railway station, and was pale and sweaty and feeling slightly ridiculous as I sat down again in Fuad's office. He laughed when I told him what had happened, and immediately changed the subject.

'Here's your ticket for tonight's train,' he said, presenting me with a faded piece of coloured matt paper which could have dated from my grandfather's day. This was appropriate to a passenger train service that, from what the guidebooks said, had been reduced over the years to the basic minimum, with nothing being done to improve comforts, and no more than essential repairs being carried out. The service made a loss for the F.C.A.B., but they were committed to keep it running by the same nineteenth-century treaty that had allowed them to extend their operations into Bolivia.

'We're not that hard on our passengers,' Fuad laughed again after I had shown him a guidebook complaining that all the windows were broken, thus making the freezing temperatures more unbearable still as you climbed up one of the world's highest railway passes. 'But there's no heating, that's true.'

The train would be leaving at the scheduled time of 9.30, and no problems were expected on the Bolivian side, where we would be arriving at around seven in the morning. 'There won't be a spare seat tonight,' he warned, 'this is the time of year when all the Bolivians here start going home for the carnival. You'll be in for quite a spectacle, it'll be pure folklore.'

I had had enough of Calama, and longed for the spectacle to begin; but I still had five more hours of waiting in a town that was coming to seem ever more threatening. Fuad suggested that Oswaldo should drive me to nearby Chuquicamata, the site of the world's largest opencast copper mine. I was in the mood for anything that would keep me off Calama's streets, and this mine was a place I had been hoping at some stage to see.

So once again I set off with the sombre Oswaldo through Calama's desiccated suburbs, passing this time through a new outlying district where Chuquicamata's 3,000 miners and their families were gradually being rehoused. Chuquicamata itself, a further twenty minutes' drive from there, was already halfway to becoming a ghost town, and dark grey residential blocks, a cinema, and two large restaurants stood in grim abandon on rubble slopes.

At the centre was the mountain sacred to the Chuco Indians, now a giant open wound aggravated by daily doses of dynamite. The copper deposits had been known in pre-Columbian times, and I had seen in Santiago's natural history museum the mummified corpse of a fallen miner known as 'the Copper Man'. But, once again, it was left to a foreign power, the North Americans, fully to exploit and desecrate the place that had been regarded for centuries as the 'Magic Mountain'. The year of my grandfather's arrival in Chile was also the year that the Guggenheim Foundation of New York was given the rights to mine Chuquicamata. The place would remain a 'Yankee state' until nationalized under Allende.

Che Guevara and his motorcycle companion Alberto Granado, whom I had last recalled smuggling themselves onto a boat at Valparaíso and heading towards Antofagasta, had visited Chuquicamata at the height of the Yankee dominion. It was an experience which contributed more than anything else to turning Che towards revolutionary politics. They had spent the night before sleeping by the roadside at Calama, next to an impoverished couple whose communist sympathies had prevented them from finding work.

The cold had been so intense that Alberto had suggested to Che that they should give up one of their blankets to the couple, who had no covering whatsoever. 'It was one of the coldest times in my life,' wrote Che, 'but also one which made me feel a little more brotherly towards this strange species that constitutes for me mankind.'

The couple had gone off the next day to some sulphur mines to the north ('where the climate is so bad and living conditions so hard that you don't need a work permit and nobody asks what your politics are'), while Che and Alberto, overcome with a sense of injustice, reported to the manager's office at Chuquicamata.

The American bosses had been 'blonde, efficient and arrogant', and spoke in 'primitive Spanish'. They had told Che and his friend that Chuquicamata wasn't a tourist town, but they would provide them with a guide to give them a half-hour tour if 'you then do us a favour and leave us alone, we have a lot of work to do'. A strike was imminent, and closure meant the loss for the company of 1,000,000 dollars a day – a figure whose obscenity was underlined for Che and Alberto by the fact that the workers were striking for an increase to their salaries sufficient just for the men to subsist. The guide who was showing them round had thought that the workers' demands were excessive. Che and Alberto would have liked to have thrown him into one of the acid vats, but instead they had asked him about work-related accidents.

'Many people like you,' he replied, 'ask me technical questions but it is rare they ask how many lives it has cost. I can't answer you.'

Oswaldo parked the car next to a large sign promoting daily tours of the Chuquicamata mine. There were only two tours a day, and the last one had left some time before. The woman who sold the tickets said that in any case the numbers on each tour were quite limited, and that at the height of the tourist season it was advisable to start queuing early in the morning to make sure you got in.

We drove away from Chuquicamata after an aimless wander by car to see the last of the inhabited prefabricated houses ('of course the Yankees and their lackeys,' Alberto Granado had written, 'have a special school for their children, as well as golf courses, and their houses aren't prefabricated.') There was nothing I could do now except return to Calama and hope that my sanity and wallet would survive intact until the night.

Alone back in the town, after Oswaldo had dropped me off, I checked the streets for signs of the gypsy woman and her accomplices. There were a few errands I wanted to accomplish before enclosing myself in the railway station, the only place in town I felt safe. I needed to change some money, buy some provisions, purchase a woolly hat for the journey. But every step I took in the town centre seemed laden with danger. I was becoming more paranoid than ever, more absolutely convinced that there was something evil about Calama, and that this something had to do with greed, and the cycle of corruption, oppression, resentments, quashed hopes and desperation that this had set in motion in a part of the world largely unfit for human habitation.

I was holding a large wad of dollars in my hand and was about to exchange these for some Chilean and Bolivian money when there was a tap on my shoulder. I shuddered, and then gave in to an almost exaggerated sense of relief when I discovered who was behind me. In the midst of all my thoughts about evil, I could not have hoped to have found a better counterbalance than this young French couple, Mathieu and Axelle, whom I had met in San Pedro. They had recently married and exuded happiness and well-being. They asked me now if I wanted to join them for a drink.

The difficulty was finding a place to have one. Mathieu and Axelle's knowledge of Calama was even worse than mine, and they were only here to catch a plane early the next morning. We walked the whole length of the town's main streets, and all the many bars and cafés we passed had insalubrious exteriors, sounds of drunken voices from within, and signs outside displaying an uplifted leg in a cancan position. We found out what this sign meant when, tired of walking, we decided to enter the next place we came to, no matter what its appearance. The leg turned out to be a reference to the Chilean slang for woman, *pierna*; and we were in what is known in Chile as a '*bar con pierna*'. A group of women dressed in nothing but white T-shirts stood smiling at the counter, while some gambling men looked up from their table and whistled at Axelle. A waiter kindly approached us to suggest that we might be better off elsewhere.

And so we returned to our traipsing, in a darkening atmosphere where shoppers and returning office workers were fast becoming outnumbered by inebriated men and *piernas* of the night. I would not have been surprised if I had known then what I would learn from a Chilean friend several weeks later: Calama had more prostitutes per capita than any other town in Chile, and perhaps in South America; and it was also the murder capital of the country. 'Did you know,' my friend said, 'that on the week you were there two people were knifed to death simply for not handing over their money?'

As I continued roaming the streets with Axelle and Mathieu, I was already beginning to think that my grandfather had not been so flippant in comparing Calama with Sodom and Gomorrah, and that the town had always been a notorious centre of vice. It was here that, disturbed and sexually frustrated but faithful to the last to his vision of reason, civilization and pure monogamous love, he had begun seeing human nature for what it was, violent and base, and controlled by the animal instincts against which he was struggling like a priest who holds up his cross to the Devil.

We ended up in an Italian restaurant near the station. Instead of just having a drink, we had supper of partially reheated ravioli with pungent sawdust as parmesan cheese. Even my cheery dining companions, with their love-tinted view of the world, had to confess to be not entirely taken with Calama. I told them that my grandfather had almost gone mad here. When the Mejillones job had finally fallen through, in the August of 1912, he had had another of his crises of depression, which had made him question the wisdom of coming to South America in the first place. But then his luck changed. He was sent back to Bolivia.

It seemed as if the folkloric spectacle evoked by Fuad was already underway when I got to the station. The small ticket hall was completely obstructed with passengers, of whom only half a dozen were backpackers, sticking closely together on the floor like a strange, threatened species. Almost everybody else was Bolivian, mainly women with colourful alpaca waistcoats, several layers of pleated skirts, huge wickerwork baskets, and of course the famous Andean bowler hats that had always struck me as such a bizarre legacy of the British presence in South America.

'To go from Chile to Bolivia is almost like switching planets,' wrote the British journalist Alistair Horne in 1972; and the same appeared as true now as it had been in my grandfather's time. The scenes in the ticket hall reminded me of those at Spanish border towns during Franco's rule: scenes that came as a sudden shock but mentally prepared you for a country whose rural areas had largely escaped Americanization, and where you were brought back instantly to the era of Laurie Lee and García Lorca and all those other nineteenth- and early twentieth-century writers who propagated the romantic image of Spain on which I had been raised.

But Freddy the guard, to my embarrassment, was now shouting out my name across the crowded hall, and telling the crowd to move aside so that the venerable English writer, as yet unrecognized in his country, could make his way to the platform. As invisibly as I could, I followed Freddy to the guest house where I had left my luggage.

'I've reserved the best seat for you,' he winked, as I went into the bathroom to put on some long johns and a thermal vest. I emerged still feeling rather naked and poorly equipped in comparison with the travellers in the hall, with their blankets, sleeping bags and multitude of pullovers, jackets and skirts, and was led on to the as yet empty train.

I could not see much difference between my hard seat and any of the others on the train, but it was by a window, and I was able to lay claim to it before the invasion that followed. Within half an hour, there was not even space in the passageway that was not occupied by baggage and passengers. A family of six was crowded around me, with a young man and his fiancée pressing against my side, and his parents and young brother pushing my knees towards my chin. They were going to the border town of Ollagüe, where the fiancée had never been before. She was worried about what life was going to be like in a tiny village nearly 4,000 metres high. 'Very cold,' smiled the husband-to-be.

The lights went out soon after the train had left the station, an hour late. The darkness was so intense that only the sounds of snoring alerted me to the presence of people of indeterminate sex sleeping head to toe in the passageway. I was sitting up as rigidly as if in a state of rigor mortis, my immobile legs stiff from cramp, and my extremities numb with the sharpening cold.

The train started climbing in fits and starts, like an old man pausing repeatedly for breath. It was well past midnight before my head slumped forward in sleep, only to be jerked back almost immediately as I woke to the sight of the old gypsy woman smiling at me from outside the window. Surely I was entering the mountainous realm where the Devil ruled. I began panicking blindly until I pictured my grandfather reprimanding me for giving in to what Goya had called 'the sleep of reason'. My eyes closed again, and then half-opened for a few moments at around three in the morning, conscious this time of my legs being wrapped mysteriously in a blanket, which I then realized must have been placed by the young woman by my side, who was straightening out its folds and adjusting it to fit more comfortably around my body, just as my mother had done when I was child and had fallen asleep in the back of the car.

5

The Good Angel of the Altiplano

THE FIRST GLIMMER of light came just after six in the morning. I was fully awake, and aware of the cone of a volcano taking gradual shape in the darkness. The Devil had disappeared back into the crater, banished by the beginnings of a 'beautifully pure' dawn, such as the ones my grandfather had known at nearby Ascotán, the highest point on the main line from Antofagasta.

'I have had some ups and downs in life,' Bethel had joked to Sophie, 'for I have worked over 100 feet below the sea as well as 13,000 feet above its level.' Four months before his transfer to Bolivia in August 1912, he had been sent for a few days to Ascotán, where he had had his first experience of working at high altitudes. The 'intensely rarified air' had taken his breath away at the slightest exertion, and made him always wake up with 'a dry and parched throat'. It also had the effect of 'diminishing the sense of distance', which explained why the volcano forming in front of my eyes was becoming so luminously clear that I felt as if I could reach out and stroke its snowy crest, then warm my hands in the wisp of smoke floating at its summit.

I was not exactly sure where I was, nor whether I was still alive. The state of calm I was experiencing was so profound as to be suspicious, while the clarity of the developing light and colours was so vivid as to be preternatural. The train appeared to be neither climbing nor descending, so that I could not tell whether we had reached or were about to reach the pass of Ascotán. We were moving in a slow, hushed fashion, without a halt or jarring movement, through a bare, broadening landscape in which other volcanoes were coming into view. We could have been in a realm beyond the clouds.

Mutterings from the some of the passengers about nearing Ollagüe finally brought me back to the real world. We must have passed

Ascotán when I had been fast asleep. We had now descended about 500 metres and were approaching the Bolivian frontier. The rest of the carriage was waking up, and a man had begun treading over bags and bodies to distribute coffee from a giant tin kettle. A few of the women were bizarrely re-distributing the contents of their overflowing wicker baskets, and a good twenty bottles of wine ended up under my seat. I cheerfully agreed to this, though not to the offer of a black leather jacket from a man who had been wearing seven of them and was going round the carriage persuading people to 'borrow a jacket' until we were across the border. I had been slow to grasp that I was in a train filled with smugglers.

At Ollagüe the train was entered by the Chilean border police, who strolled down our carriage with apparent lack of concern about everything, even the bottles whose presence behind my legs had begun to worry me. We then all had to get off the train to have our passports stamped, a process that took little more than ten minutes. A Bolivian in the queue told me not to bother about getting back on board for the time being. 'We'll be here for a good two more hours,' he said.

The family who had been with me on the train waved goodbye as they headed off with their caravan of luggage into the distance. I wondered what the young woman was thinking of as she took her first steps through her future home village – a place consisting of a dozen or so widely scattered prefabricated buildings, including a white church. While a young Australian backpacker stood next to me enthusing over the beauty of the surrounding ring of volcanoes, I remembered what a Bolivian villager had said once to a leading British geologist engaged in field work:

'You people,' he had said, 'you only come to stare, then you go away again. We have to carry on living here.'

I started talking to the rest of the backpackers, who formed a fairly representative group of types and nationalities: an extrovert Israeli woman with her soulful, guitar-playing Argentinian boyfriend; two very young and down-at-heel Frenchmen whose coffee I had had to pay for on the train (they thought it was free); and an intensely serious German couple of my age who clearly considered themselves 'real travellers' and had hated San Pedro de Atacama for being too touristy. The already burning sun gave me the excuse to move away to the small amount of shade provided by the overhang of a corrugated-iron roof.

There were two others from the train who had taken refuge in the same spot – a decidedly Bolivian-looking woman, possibly in her early thirties, and a slightly younger man, large, stocky, with a sharply trimmed black beard, khaki-coloured combat trousers, a padded waistcoat and a baseball cap. The couple had already attracted my attention on the train because they were so different from everybody else. They were not backpackers, nor did they seem like Chile's downtrodden Bolivian workers returning to be with their families during the carnival break. They appeared instead to be the sort of intellectual revolutionaries whom Che Guevara might have recruited. I was curious to find out more about them.

This curiosity would have significant consequences. Within a few moments we would be talking together as if we had known each other all our lives. In fact they instantly reminded me of my two closest Italian friends, whom I had first met in similar chance circumstances, during a particularly unstable period in Italy's political history. They had drawn me into a world where naively anarchist ideals and precarious finances had gone hand in hand with an ability to derive intense enjoyment from the simplest pleasures.

My new companions were called Jorge and Marbel, and they lived in the Bolivian town of Sucre, the country's official capital. From the doom-laden conversations I had recently been having about Bolivia, such as my exchange in London with the ex-president's niece, Susana Sánchez de Lozada, it had seemed that anyone with Chilean blood was likely to be strung up at the moment of crossing the frontier. So it was a relief to find myself on the point of entering Bolivia with a couple whom I soon discovered to be Chilean-Bolivian.

Jorge, a trainee doctor with an endearing straightforwardness bordering on innocence, was from Antofagasta, where he and his Bolivian wife had just spent a short holiday. He was one of many Chileans who had gone to study in Bolivia because the universities there were as good if not better than those in Chile, and much cheaper. He said he was now much happier in his adopted country than in his native one, where life had become too Americanized and too stressful. I asked him if as a Chilean he felt he now belonged to a beleaguered minority, and he said not at all. He had been living now for five years in Bolivia, and had never been the victim of any hostility.

The sense of reassurance that Jorge projected was more than matched by Marbel, the more talkative and sophisticated of the two. With her calm, mask-like face, thick jet-black hair, and large eyes underlined with black eyeshadow, she had the look of a benign witch. She spoke approvingly about her country, but commented on the corruption of its politicians, which in her opinion was as true, sadly, of the indigenous opposition as it was of the governing elite. She was coming to the end of a five-year law degree, and had had contact with many of Bolivia's major public figures, including the trade unionist and indigenous leader Evo Morales, a man of humble background and lifestyle whom I had thought of as a true people's hero.

'The heroes of our country,' she said, 'are its drivers. They're the ones who keep this country going. The apalling roads they have to face daily, and the vehicles they have to maintain. Every time I go on a bus I'm amazed by their skills. They have to be the best drivers in the world.'

Through Marbel I began to glimpse a Bolivia which existed independently of the turbulent world of its politics. I had always thought of the country essentially as a tragic place (the 'most tragic' in South America, according to Alastair Horne), whose mainly indigenous population was torn between a seething hatred of the West, and a sullen indifference and resignation that, for some of the more fanciful commentators, was a legacy of the Incas. Rarely before had I heard someone defining Bolivia as a place with some of the proverbial characteristics of my beloved Andalucía (easygoing, welcoming, and pleasure-loving), or claiming that its so-called backwardness was made up for by qualities lacking in countries that more obviously lived up to Western notions of progress.

'We are meant to be one of the poorest countries in the world,' said Marbel, 'but you can get a meal here for virtually nothing; and everybody tries to help out those who are worse off than they are. I'd far rather be poor here than in somewhere like Chile, where if you don't have money you're much more likely to be on your own and treated as a failure.'

Even the way Marbel talked was almost as revealing as what she was saying. Bolivian Spanish seemed so much purer than Chilean Spanish, less contaminated by Americanisms, more formal, closer to the Spanish of Cervantes, and with charmingly archaic usages such as that of the adjective '*amoroso*' which, together with '*tranquilo*', was a word Marbel was constantly using to describe people. I had concluded at first that the Bolivians must be a race of sensualists and Casanovas until I realized that '*amoroso*' (whose every syllable was slowly and softly drawn out by her) was used here to mean 'lovely.' The Bolivians, in her view, were 'lovely' and 'tranquil'.

The train's whistle blew, and all the passengers slowly got back on board, only to get off again a couple of kilometres further down the line, when we reached the Bolivian frontier village named after the great hero of the War of the Pacific, Avaroa. I had a battered old passport that was shortly to expire, and guidebooks had warned me that unscrupulous Bolivian border guards were prone to demand that passports should have at least a year left before expiry date: if you failed to offer a bribe, you might be refused entry into the country; and if you did offer one, you might find yourself in trouble for trying to corrupt officials. I mentioned this to Marbel, but she just laughed. And she was right. The smiling Bolivian guards were 'lovely' and 'tranquil', and barely looked at the documents.

There was another hour of waiting while a few Bolivian carriages were added to the train. I managed to find a seat next to Jorge and Marbel when we finally moved off into the Bolivian Altiplano, the high plateau that averages an altitude of 4,000 metres and covers an area larger than the whole of Britain. The mountains and volcanoes slid back to the horizon, and the foreground became a flat sandy emptiness whose only vegetation was the low, scrubby plants known locally as *tholla*, which Marbel told me had resinous branches that made excellent firewood. There are Bolivians, she added, who believe that the Altiplano was once entirely covered in trees; but that these had all been cut down by the Spaniards to use for burning in the mines.

I had lost all sense of time and season. At the border, watches had been put back an hour, and we had gone from summer to winter, or rather the 'Bolivian winter', which is the name given to the summer's rainy season, when the daylight temperatures can be lower than in the real winter because the sky is often covered by thick clouds coming from Bolivia's tropical forests. So far it had rained little this year, and the sky remained clear up to the far horizon, where black clouds blew over a mountain range far away but visible in such intricate detail as to seem painted by a miniaturist.

Marbel asked if I would be going to Sucre, and I said yes, but I didn't know when. I was in a country of imponderables. Unreliable and irregular transport, appalling roads that were often impassable, and the constant possibility of strikes and other protests (not to mention an all-out revolution) were said to be endemic to Bolivia, and to make nonsense of the most carefully worked-out plans. And my intention of travelling as much as I could along the tracks laid out by the F.C.A.B. would only be adding to my potential difficulties. I knew now that there was a passenger train as far as Oruro, and that from there to La Paz there was just a road running roughly parallel to the old line. But big question marks hung over the branch lines to Cochabamba and to Potosí: the first appeared currently unusable, and the second was served only by freight traffic, though none of the information I had received so far about these lines had been consistent. It seemed that my best bet now was to go as soon as I could to La Paz, and then try and sort things out with the head office of Bolivian Railways.

Before doing anything, however, I needed a good night's sleep, and I hoped to get one at the next official stop on the Ollagüe line, Uyuni, where we would be arriving at a still undisclosed time.

'We should be getting there quite early,' said Marbel, 'possibly by six o'clock this evening. Certainly by midnight. What about having some lunch?'

We went to eat in a dining car that had been attached at the border. It was the sort of dining car I remembered from train journeys of the past, with proper tables and chairs, and a waiter in a white jacket. However, it was probably just a shadow of the 'salon-restaurant' that had existed in my grandfather's time, when the train had been dubbed 'the Good Angel of the Altiplano.'

In 1912, an employee of the French ministry of commerce, Paul Walle, gave a description of the 'more than adequate facilities' of the express train that left Antofagasta twice weekly at six o'clock on Wednesday and Saturday evenings, and arrived at La Paz only forty-eight hours later. He was impressed by the sleeping cars, whose two- and four-berth cabins had comfortable couchettes that could be turned by day into seats, and by the 'extremely well-equipped restaurant', which had electricity, and 'highly effective' heating and air-conditioning. Even the food, he thought, was 'relatively satisfying given the high altitude'.

The purpose of Walle's mission to Bolivia was to research his 500-page *La Bolivie et ses mines* (1912), a book that my grandfather would surely have got hold of, for it was the most exhaustive study on the country yet to have appeared. The idea behind this project, backed by the French government, was to stimulate foreign investment in Bolivia at a time when its financial fortunes seemed finally poised to take a dramatic turn for the better.

Up to 1900 the vast and still only partially exploited mineral wealth of Bolivia was widely recognized, if only for the lingering fame of legendary Potosí. But the country itself, unlike Chile, did not inspire confidence. It was the epitome of the unstable South American republic, with an average change of presidency every six months, and a reputation for crackpot leaders such as the notorious General Melgarejo.

This man, whose rise to power had coincided with the birth of Antofagasta, was a person of mythical cruelty and madness whose humiliation and expulsion of the British consul in La Paz had reputedly led the irate Queen Victoria to strike Bolivia off the map, saying that from now on the country no longer existed. Whatever the truth of this, there would be no British consular representation in Bolivia until 1900, by which time attempts to redeem the country's international image, and to bring the place more firmly into the modern world, had been initiated under the presidency of Aniceto Arce.

Arce recognized that one of the major factors preventing his country from capitalizing on its resources was the lack of good roads and the absence of any railway system. As one of his country's biggest silver-mine owners, it was of course as much in his own interests as in those of his country that he set about radically improving Bolivia's transport network. In addition to a massive road-construction programme, he encouraged the activities of the newly founded Antofagasta (Chili) and

Bolivia Railway Company, and thus made possible Bolivia's first rail link to the sea. By 1889 the line from Antofagasta had already reached Ollagüe, and three years later would be extended to Oruro, with a branch from Uyuni to the major silver mines at Huanchaca.

The Bolivians, still humiliated and enraged by the loss of their coastal territory to Chile during the War of the Pacific, were widely critical of Arce's collaboration with their oppressors, and thought of the projected railway between Antofagasta and La Paz in terms of an extension of Chilean dominion into the heart of their homeland. Arce tried defending himself in the speech he gave to mark the opening of the line to Oruro in the May of 1892:

'I have struggled,' he declared, 'not only with nature, who has fought hard against my project, but also with you, who believe that I have been serving purely the interests of our former enemies, the Chileans. Well let me tell you now that my efforts have been carried out solely in the name of progress, so that our Fatherland should be set on the path of eternal greatness. If I have done well, I have merely done so out of a sense of duty; if I have done badly, then I stand here accountable before you. Kill me.'

If Arce managed with this speech to win over some of his Bolivian detractors, he still had a long way to go before convincing the Americans and Europeans that his country was on the way to becoming a stable modern nation. It was not until after the bloody Federal Revolution of 1899, which brought to power Bolivia's first Liberal President José Pando, that the country showed signs of settling down to a period of relative stability, untroubled by political coups. Remarkably this would last right until 1920.

Foreign investors, swayed by this promising new development, as well as by the signing of a peace treaty with Chile in 1904 by Pando's successor Ismael Montes, naturally turned a blind eye to the corruption that kept the country tightly under the control of a political system known as '*la Rosca*' or 'the Screw'. But the era of liberalism that Pando's presidency seemed to herald was nominal and short-lived. Pando, despite being helped to power through collaboration with the indigenous leader Pablo Zárate Willka, immediately repudiated his indigenous allies, and carried on little differently from the conservatives. His policies, like those of his successors, were effectively dictated by the wishes of the home-grown tin-mining elite, which came to ascendancy with the collapse in the price of silver at the end of the nineteenth century.

'A country in itself has nothing,' wrote the twice-elected Montes, whose second term of office began shortly after my grandfather's arrival in Bolivia in 1912. 'Its wealth is nothing more than the sum of private wealth. Therefore it is scientifically necessary to stimulate the growth of the latter so that it will contribute to the greatest effectiveness to the national prosperity.'

The extent to which national prosperity grew under Montes is doubtful; but individual fortunes certainly benefited, as did the foreign companies which controlled Bolivia's nascent railway empire. In 1906 an American consortium drew up a scheme for a proposed railway network that would have covered most of Bolivia. The perennially perspicacious F.C.A.B., worried about competition, forged an alliance with this consortium, and, during the years of my grandfather's stay in South America, would take direct control of three of the more important of the new routes. While the largely British-owned Peruvian Railways created a link between Lake Titicaca and La Paz, the F.C.A.B. persevered with the line between Oruro and Cochabamba, extended the Antofagasta line all the way to La Paz, and constructed a branch line to Potosí. With the opening of the latter in May 1912, the government official in charge of the ceremony referred to railways as the 'valve of progress', and predicted the imminent day when a prosperous Bolivia would be the envy of South America.

Only one remaining obstacle seemed now in the way of Bolivia's prosperity: the apparent unwillingness of the indigenous population to share the white man's vision of their country's future. The potential enormity of this problem was due to this population being by far the most dominant element in Bolivia's make-up. There were the 'peaceful' Quechuas, whose language was inherited from the Incas, and who were settled mainly in the inter-Andean valleys; and there were the 'violent' Aymaras, who ruled the Altiplano, and whose strength and resilience were reflected in their having one of the few Andean languages to have survived both Inca and Spanish rule. A third category was the mixed race 'cholos'. Despite having Spanish blood, these were generally subject to the same white prejudices and discrimination, were not allowed to vote, had their properties ruthlessly appropriated, and were often mistaken for 'Indians' by people such as my grandfather.

Small groups of South America's white intellectuals, mainly in Peru, had begun by this stage to champion indigenous causes, and to take an interest in their culture and history, the past splendours of which were brought to light by Hiram Bingham's discovery in 1911 of the Inca citadel of Machu Picchu. However, this liberal concern was as yet barely transmitted to the white population at large, and particularly not in Bolivia where, as the Spanish traveller Ciro Bayo commented in 1912, 'nothing has been done to alleviate the lot of the poor Indians, who continue to live under the same conditions of misery and servility as they did in the time of the conquest.'

The feelings expressed by my grandfather towards the 'Bolivian Indians' of Calama were typical of almost all white professionals who had to employ an indigenous work force.

'The Bolivian Indian of the Altiplano,' wrote Bethel's contemporary A. V. Guise, a British mining engineer who lived in the Bolivian Altiplano for much of the second decade of the twentieth century, 'is not a prepossessing specimen of humanity.' As with all early writers on Bolivia, Guise could not refrain from commenting on the 'dirtiness' of these people, and was amused by the idea that the women never washed or changed their skirts, but simply accumulated more of the latter in tandem with their growing social status. He initially hired as a housemaid 'an Indian girl who, in personal appearance, worthily upheld the Indian standard of dirtiness'; but he succeeded neither in improving her standards of hygiene, nor in preventing her from getting frequently drunk, nor in instructing her in 'the mysteries of European cooking'.

Guise had little more luck with the miners under his care. As Bethel had found, and as the horse-riding Tschiffely would later discover, the men were prone to sulking, superstition and drunkenness; and were more likely to respond to the offer of coca leaves (the chewing of which was integral to their culture) than to money. For Ciro Bayo, the great tragedy of Bolivia's indigenous peoples was that, despite the awfulness of their lives, they 'did nothing to further the progress of the nation'. In fact they often did the very opposite. According to

Bayo the completion of the railway between Antofagasta and Oruro had been constantly delayed due to Aymara attacks and willful destruction of the line.

Bolivia's 'Indian problem' was one that appeared to have little solution, except to Paul Walle, whose job of course was to portray the country in a wholly positive way. He could not help displaying some of the characteristic white man's contempt for the 'Indian' (for instance, the women's skirts had for him a 'very disagreeable smell of ammonia'), and took it for granted that 'the Inca empire was a civilization inferior to European civilization.' Nonetheless, he believed that many of the faults commonly attributed to the Indians, such as laziness and drunkenness, could equally be found among the whites, and that it needed only a proper education and the withholding of alcohol to correct these failings. Already he had heard encouraging stories from mine and factory workers about Indians who had become hard-working and conscientious citizens under their care; and the Bolivian government's recent institution of military service seemed to be producing comparable results.

Another cause of optimism for Walle was the indigenous population's high rate of infant mortality. With any luck, a continuing decline of this population, combined with a growing influx of whites and mestizos, would end up producing a 'unified race just like there is in Chile'. But whatever happened, Walle had not the slightest doubt that Bolivia was on the verge of a breakthrough. In the course of his long train journey across the Altiplano he had had plenty of opportunity to reflect on how the sad, barren and monotonous landscape might give the passing traveller a completely wrong idea of Bolivia's future. The outer appearance of the country, he emphasized, was deceptive, for the Altiplano alone was a 'table of gold standing on columns of silver', and waiting properly to be discovered.

My grandfather, returning excitedly to Bolivia in the summer of 1912, had had similar thoughts. On the train journey back to Oruro he had entertained himself by weighing up the pros and cons of this country. Among the drawbacks were the 'rotten climate', 'mostly impossible natives', and 'almost non-existent game' ('this latter objection may not be very serious but it is undoubtedly a disadvantage; it makes it much less attractive to foreigners working in the country and it is a decided inconvenience having to rely so much on tinned food taken with one.')

But there were also good reasons to feel positive. The very fact of his being on a train, and on the point of using the newly opened lines to La Paz and Potosí, meant that the hitherto 'wholly inadequate transport facilities' were being 'improved to a considerable extent'. The discovery of oil was another great new asset, and would reduce the reliance here on coal, which was prohibitively expensive. Then there was the almost certain return to office of Montes, 'a fairly enlightened man' from whom 'a good deal for the benefit of the country is expected'. Above all, however, there was the knowledge that the 'greater part of Bolivia's incredible mineral wealth' had not been touched as yet, and that there were 'still fortunes to be made in rubber and coffee from the Yungas'. 'One thing is absolutely certain,' he predicted to Sophie with the same conviction that Walle had shown, 'and that is that there is going to be a tremendous mining and industrial boom in Bolivia over the next two years.'

The waiter in the dining car had just brought us a pot of hot water and some sachets of instant coffee when the train violently jolted to a halt, spilling some of the water over the table and onto my knees. We remained talking as before, and continued doing so for a further twenty minutes or so, while quietly finishing our drinks. The ticket collector told us that there had been a problem with one of the freight cars, and that we would probably be stuck here 'for some time'. Eventually we got up from our seats and followed the example of nearly everybody else in the train: opening one of the outer doors we went outside to stretch our legs by the tracks.

The Israeli backpacker had chummed up with the Australian and was doing ambitious stretching exercises between applications of sun cream. Her boyfriend played his guitar badly while a couple of nearby Bolivian women hitched up their skirts and let out abundant streams of urine. The others from the train stood around talking and thinking, indifferent apparently to the burning high-altitude sunshine, which came and went in ever briefer intervals as large clouds moved rapidly across the sky. Dogs appeared out of nowhere to sniff quietly around our feet, followed soon by their owners, who advanced unhurriedly towards us across the desolate flat plateau. They were carrying pastries and bread, and glasses of a pale yellow liquid. No one paid them much attention; nor did they make any determined attempt to sell their wares, not even to the foreigners. They just waited there silently, the expression of one of them turning into a faint smile when my eyes fleetingly caught his.

I could not work out why this whole scene before me, so superficially bleak and pathetic, seemed so reassuringly familiar. I might have been here in some past life, or I might simply have been reminded in a curious way of early travels in Italy and Spain, or even of my current existence in a modest village, which had made me question material and professional ambitions. I could not really explain why I was already feeling so at home in this country whose history had taken such a different course from the one my grandfather and his generation had foreseen.

The ticket collector came out to warn us that the train was about to leave. A few more women squatted to do their ablutions. A man purchased a pastry. Then slowly everyone returned to their seats and the vendors disappeared. The whistle sounded, and we were off again, heading in the late afternoon towards a distant thunderstorm.

The sky went black, the rain poured down, and a rainbow as perfect as any I had ever seen formed an arch across the track. The sun had reappeared low on the horizon, pushing through the darkening clouds to streak with light a distant, watery white band like the shores of a vast ocean.

'The famous salt flat of Uyuni,' murmured Marbel, waking up from the drowsiness into which we all had fallen. 'We'll soon be at the station.'

The sun stayed for a brief period, long enough to cast an eerie light over the skeleton of a llama before the rain returned and night fell. I thought I saw the profiles of some old steam trains as we struggled towards the apparently ever-receding lights of a town.

At Uyuni there were scenes of confusion as passengers overladen with luggage tried to get out of the train, and a large group of backpackers heading towards Oruro fought their way on. Jorge and Marbel remained characteristically calm as the three of us manoeuvred our way down to the platform. They only had five minutes in which to catch the night bus to Potosí and Sucre, so we had to curtail our fare-wells. But they made me promise I would go and see them.

I caught a taxi to the hotel used by the F.C.A.B., but I need not have bothered. Uyuni was hardly a town at all but a barely lit grid of unpaved streets lined with humble tin-roofed dwellings. The Andean Jewel Hotel was little more than a few minutes' walk from the station, but the taxi driver made sure I got my money's worth by making a huge detour through outskirts largely indistinguishable from the centre.

For a good quarter of an hour I sheltered under the hotel's narrow porch, waiting in the rain for someone to open the door. The friendly young woman who eventually did so turned out to be the owner. When she saw my name on the passport form, she asked me if I was any relation to 'Jacobs the engineer'. I stood there, puzzled and excited, until I realized that the man she was talking about had died just a few years ago, 'when he was still quite young'. He had been a good friend of her grandfather, and had been responsible for planting Uyuni's first and only trees, along the promenade leading up to the railway station. Together with a Protestant missionary called Willy Hill, Jacobs had been the last of the town's British residents. He had worked on the railway, just as the young woman's grandfather had done.

Everyone in Uyuni seemed to have elderly relatives whose lives had been spent with the railway. Indeed, the railway was originally the only reason for the town's existence. Like La Calera in Chile, it had been conceived as a major junction, serving not only the lines to Antofagasta, Huanchacha and La Paz, but also the one to southern Bolivia and Argentina, along which Butch Cassidy and the Sundance Kid had presumably set off on the last stage of their journey to their deaths. Uyuni had been Bolivia's main gateway to the outside world, and when its foundations had been laid in 1889, its planners had envis-aged a thriving cosmopolitan centre symbolizing progress, modernity, and the country's hopes for a prosperous, industrial future.

When the rain stopped, I walked out into Uyuni's streets, whose very width, so disproportionate to the buildings they supported, said much about the town's former ambitions. The streets were sinisterly quiet, and the few voices I heard at first came from distant, conspirato-rial groups who wove their way in and out of the shadows. These con-verged onto a central axis that had obviously been planned as a grand

promenade leading out from the station, and which had now disintegrated into a long market where vendors sat contemplatively behind
tiny stalls selling biros, tinned foods, Korean-made bags, crude Andean
flutes, and a large selection of floppy canvas hats to protect tourists
from sunstroke. Only as the station loomed into view could some ves-
tiges at last be found of Uyuni's brutally truncated heyday – a classical
fountain, a bandstand, a handful of eclectic plasterwork buildings and,
as in Antofagasta, a squat and swollen 'reproduction of London's Big
Ben', resembling the original merely in its chimes, and whose purpose
today seemed largely to mock the urban pretensions of yesteryear.

None of the hopes for Uyuni had been justified. Before even the
town could properly be built it had begun to decline, neglected by a
country continually weakened after 1920 by economic recession, a
disastrous war with Paraguay, and a resumption of interminable coups,
uprisings and violent strikes. The radical cutting back in the 1990s of
Bolivia's by now nationalized railways might well have turned Uyuni
into yet another ghost town had it not been for the concurrent arrival
on the scene of the most unlikely of saviours: the backpacker. The
town became the base for progressively less hardy generations of backpackers wishing to cross the outlying salt flat – something I wanted to
do myself, but not until I was on my way back to Chile.

I wondered where the foreigners had all gone until I stepped into
one of the several internet cafés in the vicinity of the station. Here I
was able to secure the last available seat, but was too distracted by the
loud conversations going on around me to send any message.

'When do you think we'll hit Rio?' an American asked his girlfriend.

'There was this place in Mexico where they served scrambled eggs
with onion!' exclaimed a disgusted English teenager, chatting up the
Italian woman next to him.

'Let's hitch up in San Pedro next week,' proposed an Australian man
slapping the hand of another. But what finally made me want to leave
was a German losing his temper with the café's quiet and reasonable
owner.

'You fucking charge me all that money for a computer that doesn't
work properly and I'll call the fucking police,' he shouted before eventually storming out without paying anything. I discreetly asked the
owner how much the man had owed, and paid the tiny sum myself,

for I which I was promptly reprimanded by a Frenchwoman sitting near the till. 'If it wasn't for us,' she said, 'these people wouldn't exist.'

The next morning, when I walked towards the railway station, I found the backpackers around the bandstand, sitting at its base, lying on the ground, making jokes, and waiting for the four-wheel drives to take them to the salt flat and away from the town they had saved. I entered the station to keep an appointment with the melancholy stationmaster.

This man took me across the track to see the former Maestranza, where most of Bolivia's trains had once been made and repaired. The place was not nearly as big as that of Mejillones, but its sidings contained a larger group of seriously decayed engines and carriages than any I had seen over the past weeks. They were lined head to toe, side to side like corpses after a massacre.

'This is not to be confused with the railway cemetery,' said the stationmaster, referring to a famous Uyuni attraction that lay a good half-hour's walk away. 'These trains are still salvageable. We could make an excellent museum of all this.'

I nodded in agreement, while casting a pitying glance over what was difficult to perceive as little more than a scrapheap of wood and iron.

I started walking towards the railway cemetery, trying to imagine how there could possibly be trains in a worse condition than those in the Maestranza. On my way past the last of Uyuni's half-built dwellings, I heard the sounds of soldiers parading behind their barracks walls. 'THE FATHERLAND HAS TO LIVE, AND SO WE HAVE TO DIE' was the cheery slogan attached to the building. Stray dogs and children accompanied me outside the town and into a flat rubble landscape strewn with the tattered remnants of black rubbish sacks. The intense blue sky was rapidly marbled by clouds as I lost sight of the path and aimed as straight as I could towards an outcrop of rusting metal forms. Even the dogs stopped following me.

The railway cemetery occupied an immense area of ground which in turn was made insignificant by the endlessness of the plateau, with its outer ring of diminutive mountains dusted with snow. The rust had eaten so deep into the metal that the trains were pockmarked with large holes, out of one of which appeared the heads of two smiling children who asked me to take their photo. Their giggles broke the silence, which soon was further disturbed by the noise of an ancient four-wheel drive from which emerged a group of excited back-packers, who ran towards the trains, got out their digital cameras, and set in motion a couple of wheels still attached to their axles. 'This place is really neat.' I heard one of them shouting as they ran back to the car.

Left again on my own, I approached one of the more battered of the steam engines to look more closely at the graffiti daubed over it by some itinerant philosopher.

'SUCH IS LIFE,' it read, 'AN EXPERIENCED ENGINEER IS URGENTLY WANTED.'

I spent the rest of the day waiting to leave Uyuni. I would have loved to have moved on earlier, and seen by daylight the huge Lake Poopó, which a deluded American researcher has located as the site of the lost Atlantis. But the only public transport out of Uyuni went by night: and, as the next train was not due until the end of the week, I felt reluctantly obliged to go by bus and to leave this stretch of railway line for my journey back from Oruro. I occupied my time having a long lunch with an Argentinian teacher who was also waiting till night, to return to his home country. He had recently come from Chile, which had disappointed him by being so much more materi-alistic and less politicized than the country he had remembered from ten years earlier. And he did not feel strong enough for Bolivia. 'The food always makes you ill, you've got to keep a constant watch on your belongings, and the buses are atrocious.'

It was dark and pouring with rain when I picked up my luggage from the Andean Jewel Hotel and ran towards the office of the bus company I had chosen. The bus had yet to arrive, and the wooden benches and concrete floor within the office's sombre interior were as crowded with people, bags and baskets as the ticket hall at Calama had been. The scene was like that of a colourful market place on the move, except that everyone was quiet, patient and stoical, and completely unconcerned by the bus's eventual appearance two hours later.

I contorted my body to fit the hard, broken seat, and shook hands with the old man next to me, who was only travelling as far as the next village. His son and daughter-in-law sat down in the passageway, once the last of the vendors had moved off with their unsold pastries and drinks. The bus left, and the rain increased to such an extent that drops of water began falling on my immobilized knees. Beyond Uyuni the surface of the road became so bad that you felt as if you were inside a pneumatic drill. Objects began falling from the luggage racks.

More than three-quarters of Bolivia's roadways are still without asphalt, and are often blocked, during the rainy season, by floods, landslides and deep mud. The old man by my side said that he had been waiting for two days to get back home. If the rain kept up, he thought it likely that the road would once again become impassable. But the rain eased, and the bus stayed moving until nearly one in the morning, when we reached the man's village. Those who had not pissed on the floor of the bus went to do so outside. I asked one of the villagers if there was a toilet, and he pointed to a space in between two squatting women. It was too dark to find a more isolated spot.

There were no more stops until Oruro. We got there four hours later; but the driver did not open the doors until 6.30, to allow the passengers to continue sleeping.

'It's also safer this way,' he explained. 'There are bad people who hang around the station at night. They come from Peru every carnival season.'

Oruro's carnival celebrations, the most famous in South America after those in Rio, were not due to begin until two weeks' time, and I had already reserved for that date one of the town's few remaining hotel rooms. I was now just passing through on my way to La Paz; but I needed to pay the deposit on the hotel in advance, and used this as an excuse for a preliminary look around what had been my grandfather's first base in Bolivia.

Bethel had known Oruro during its days of greatest prosperity. The silver deposits in the surrounding mountains had been second only to those of Potosí; but it was the beginning of the world demand for tin, which fortuitously coincided with the coming of the railway to Oruro, that enabled A. V. Guise to call the place 'Bolivia's most important town'. Few observers of the time could think of much else to say about it. For the normally over-enthusiastic Paul Walle it was a town 'with a totally mediocre apprearance', while for Guise it was 'an unattractive place where one lives in an atmosphere of sand and street dust raised by the miniature sandstorms which continuously sweep in from the plain.'

Bethel, though taking numerous photos of llamas and picturesquely attired natives in the market place, was similarly negative. The town was for him another example of 'semi-civilization', made still worse by the awfulness of the ramshackle warren of a building where he was put up from the August of 1912 onwards.

'The new house for staff quarters and offices,' he wrote 'is the most amazing architectural abortion I have ever seen. It seems to be built mostly of old scraps of packing cases, it is all windows and doors, and it is fatal to try and walk upstairs quickly, for the stairs are so badly proportioned and the treads overlap the risers by about three inches.' He rapidly came to the conclusion that 'the less I am at headquarters at Oruro the better pleased I am.'

Under the beautifully clear dawn that awaited me, Oruro did not seem the cold, grim and melancholy place I had been led to expect. What it did seem like was a town whose development had been abruptly curtailed in the mid-twentieth century. There was something about the place that reminded me of a small Eastern European town of the communist period, a likeness I began to feel on leaving the concrete station and seeing in front of me an incongruously big high-rise hotel. Later the similarity was reinforced by the clash between the town's predominant functional architecture and the decayed neo-baroque buildings in the centre, such as a theatre, a Grand Hotel with gilded furnishings, and the former ostentatious palaces of the tin-mining elite.

The main streets of Oruro sloped upwards towards the town's spiritual focus, the Sanctuary of the Socavón or 'mineshaft', which stood outlined against gaunt slopes of ochre-coloured mountains. On my way up I paused to glance at the main symbol of the town's former prosperity, the blue-painted palace of Bolivia's 'king of tin', Simón Patiño. Coming from a poor Cochabamba background, Patiño rose to become the fifth-richest man in the world during my grandfather's time, as well as, later, a person of reputed Nazi sympathies who was said to have financed Franco's victory in Spain's civil war. The way the local miners were treated both by him and others of his kind would later make Oruro one of the main centres of the 1952 revolution, leading to such reforms as the nationalization of his mines, and the granting at last to Bolivia's indigenous population of the right to vote.

The miners had not been able to enjoy their victory for long. Economic crisis, and the consequent compromising of ideals through the need to turn to North America for aid, was followed by dissent among the unionists, a military takeover, and a collapse in the price of tin that, after 1985, made Oruro the economically depressed town it was now. The houses along the street I was climbing became progressively humbler and more scattered as I moved away from the tightly packed centre and neared the sanctuary containing the image of the Virgin sacred to the miners.

A festive atmosphere was building up on this Saturday morning; and a carnival band was rehearsing on a square where an elderly Aymara woman in a bowler hat appeared to be exorcising, with the use of a cigar and an amulet, an old man sitting in a wheelchair. A gilded bronze tableau of miners emerging triumphant from a shaft preceded the recently rebuilt sanctuary, a rambling structure in grey stone and white plaster as seemingly haphazard in its construction as my grandfather's quarters at Oruro.

I went inside to pay my respects to the Virgin, and to descend into a former mine, now a museum displaying halfway down its shaft a realistic statue of the dying Chiru-Chiru, the bandit hero who had bled to death here after a shoot-out with the police. At the bottom, I had my first brush with El Tío, the horned underworld spirit whom the indigenous miners had come to think of as the ruler of the kingdom which the Catholic church had identified as hell. The stubs of several cigars dangled from his grinning masked face, while at his feet were some of the other offerings that miners still give to El Tío in return for his protection – coca leaves, bottles of alcohol, packets of cigarettes. Simon Patiño had also been a believer in El Tío, which made sense given that he was rumoured to have sold his soul to the Devil.

The Devil and the Virgin were the two protagonists of Oruro's carnival, the vitality of which was becoming easy to imagine as I headed back towards the bus station, through a centre ever more animated by the sounds of fast multiplying bands. I returned by way of the steep residential area where I had booked my hotel for the carnival; but my path was blocked by soldiers demanding my passport. More soldiers stood guarding the newly opened hotel, an endearingly kitsch pseudo-colonial construction with a staircase emulating the mineshaft of the

Virgin of the Socavón. The charming receptionist was cheerful and talkative before suddenly lowering his voice at the emergence from the lift of a tall bearded man resembling one of El Greco's mournful and elongated noblemen. 'Carlos Mesa,' he whispered, 'our country's president.'

The pace of my stay in Bolivia already seemed to be speeding up. I had seen the president, and now I was travelling from a carnival-rehearsing Oruro to the notoriously volatile La Paz. Oruro's bus station, unrecognizable in the early afternoon as the quiet place where I had arrived at dawn, helped to prepare me mentally for any revolution into which I might soon be dragged. The whole of the country appeared to be on the move, orchestrated by the shouts of rival vendors trying to drum up customers for the many imminent departures to the two main destinations served by Oruro. 'Cocha-bam-baaa! Cocha-bam-baaa! Cocha-bam-baaa!', a name I had so rarely heard since my grandmother had articulated it, but given now a musical, drawn-out lilt, competed with the more strident and urgent 'La Paz! La Paz! La Paz!' which echoed around the crowded concrete halls and corridors like a round of machine-gun fire.

The bus I chose did not leave for La Paz until every seat had been taken, and then set out on a well-surfaced modern road. We ascended almost imperceptibly towards Bolivia's unofficial capital, and as we did so the mountains bordering the Altiplano drew more closely towards us before retreating again to the distant horizons. The monotonous scenery resumed, and all that was left to distract me visually was the odd glimpse of adobe hamlets, and of the now defunct track that had been extended all the way to La Paz only a couple of months before my grandfather had used it, in the autumn of 1912.

Bethel, as excited to be approaching La Paz as I was now, had travelled there in the company of his new boss in Bolivia, H. S. Brown. It was Brown's appointment as the F.C.A.B.'s chief engineer in Bolivia, replacing the biased and disgraced Gibson, that had facilitated Bethel's return to the country. Brown had for my grandfather all the qualities that his predecessor had lacked. He was courteous, diplomatic, temperate and fair, and had soon begun reversing the F.C.A.B.'s policy of sending all its unwanted riff-raff from Antofagasta to some remote Bolivian camp in the hope that they would be 'out of sight and out of mind'.

However, Brown's 'extreme reserve', though helping him to keep his cool in a crisis, made him also seem distant and difficult to get to know. On the journey to La Paz, Bethel had managed to break through this at last and get him to talk a bit more about matters other than 'shop'. The tales he extracted from him put engineering on the same heroic, adventurous level that he must have imagined as a child while listening to stories about his Aunt Henrietta's itinerant husband Elim d'Avigdor (the Wanderer), who had built the main railway line across Transylvania. Brown, a youthful forty-year-old with the appearance of a 'naval officer in mufti' (an impression confirmed by 'his way of speaking like a man used to command'), turned out to be 'an explorer of note', who had carried out major reconnaissance surveys in Central Africa, had crossed most of the African continent on foot, and was currently studying the possibilities of getting a railway from La Paz to some Amazonian port.

'One is not likely to do that sort of thing without having many exciting and unpleasant adventures,' observed Bethel, for whom the calm, silent, and authoritative Brown was like the hero of one of the romantic novels of the immensely popular but now forgotten Edwardian novelist Seton Merriman.

This man of almost mythical stature for Bethel was perhaps the perfect person for him to be with when catching a first sight of La Paz – an experience that for many has seemed like a sudden confrontation with the world of make-believe. 'It was as though the brown and arid plain we were crossing had cracked,' wrote A. V. Guise, 'revealing a fairer – perhaps fairy – land within.'

Whereas Guise eventually settled on *The Arabian Nights* to describe the 'atmosphere of the spectacle', Bethel invoked instead the works of the Anglo-Irish fantasist and friend of Sophie's family, Lord Dunsany. He thought that Dunsany 'might well have got his inspiration here for some of his descriptions in *Beyond the Fields We Know*', a reference to a collection of tales set in 'Elfland'.

Today's glimpse of Elfland comes preceded by a taste of shocking reality: you have to cross El Alto. My eyes, glued to the window throughout the scenically ever less interesting drive from Oruro, now started taking in the urban equivalent of the flat, featureless and unending plateau. A chaotic expanse of tin-roofed adobe and red brick dwellings stretched right into the distance, interrupted only by some disproportionately high church steeples of Bavarian baroque appearance. None of this had existed in my grandfather's day. El Alto had begun life a few decades ago as a shanty development that had grown up around the airport of La Paz. Successive new waves of Aymara migrants had now created a township with an independent status, an estimated population of over half a million, and fame as a centre of indigenous opposition to government rule.

The traffic became intense, as did the crowds of pedestrians, and within half an hour an hour the bus was trapped within a maze of lorries, other buses, taxis, people, and battered cars. Everyone was trying to go in different directions, undirected by any policemen. The driver managed to escape into the unplanned confusion of dusty side streets, where there were houses and shops which appeared on close inspection to have been built from any materials and architectural elements that happened to be to hand. We got stuck again before finally extricating ourselves an hour later, reaching a main road that dropped vertiginously down to La Paz from a height of over 4,000 metres.

The slum dwellings that for Bethel had already begun to spoil the view of Elfland from above had now spread almost all the way up to the top of this steepest of valleys, and thick clusters of modern high-rise buildings covered most of the lower slopes, shielding what little remained of the colonial city. But what was so remarkable about the panorama was how utterly unimportant the human contribution still seemed in comparison to the terrifying grandeur of the setting. I found myself thinking not of fairy tales but of sublime canvases of the romantic period, and in particular of the works of the visionary Englishman John 'Mad' Martin, whose *Sardak in Search of the Waters of Oblivion*, with its tiny figure struggling up a crevice, is one of the most memorable nineteenth-century images of human futility and insignificance.

I was fortunately lucky with the weather. My grandfather, also travelling in the rainy season, had been enveloped on his return from La Paz in a 'Scottish mist' so thick that 'nothing could be seen except an occasional Indian, who, standing on some little summit, would loom up out of the fog like some spectral wraith'. But now, on this late Saturday afternoon, the light was penetratingly, blindingly clear. Though the uninterruptedly blue sky I had enjoyed earlier at Oruro had become streaked with fast-moving storm clouds, not a detail of the fantastically cragged and fissured landscape was hidden, from the snow-capped, 7,000-metre-high Illimani down to a faraway outcrop of menacing, eroded peaks which looked, in my grandfather's description, like 'colossal fingers'.

The bus, as if to make up for lost time at El Alto, negotiated the hairpin bends with stomach-churning speed. The near perpendicular descent from the plateau into La Paz had held comparable thrills for my grandfather and his generation. Those coming by train from Oruro had once been forced to undertake this last stage of the journey on an electric cogwheel railway built in 1905 by the Peruvian Railway Company. According to A. V. Guise, travellers had been kept entertained by tales of the occasions when the train had 'jumped the rails and continued its journey by a short cut down the almost vertical sides of the valley, which diversions had invariably brought most unpleasant consequences to the passengers.' One of the worst of these 'mishaps' had unfortunately occurred when President Montes had been on board. The coupling between the second and third carriages had broken, and though Montes's coach had been brought automatically to a halt by the air brakes, the English manager in charge of the railway company had been arrested and charged with complicity in an assassination plot. He had eventually been released only on payment of a very large fine.

But the rapid descent into La Paz made me think not so much about the possibility of accidents as about the city's extreme vulnerability to sieges. This helter-skelter of a road was the sole important route into the city, and could easily be blocked off at El Alto, which is indeed exactly what the rebel Aymara leader Tupac Katari had done during his violent uprising against the Spaniards in 1780–1. The first siege he had laid against La Paz had endured for 109 days, and all the people of the city would have starved to death had it not been for the arrival of a relief army from Sucre. For the second siege he had had the brilliant idea of damming the river that passes through El Alto and creating a massive build-up of water with the intention of releasing a flood of Biblical proportions on La Paz. Unfortunately for him the dyke had burst before a sufficient amount of water had accumulated, causing only a relatively moderate loss of life and property.

Tupac Katari ended up gruesomely executed by being torn apart by horses; but his example has been an inspiration to subsequent rebels. In the course of the recent events which had led to the flight to Miami of ex-president 'Goni', many citizens of La Paz must have convinced themselves that Katari was about to exert his posthumous revenge. For weeks beforehand, Aymara peasants had been setting up camp in the surrounding countryside, and by October 2003 the city was isolated from El Alto and its airport. Goni went in with his troops to rescue a group of trapped tourists; several Aymaras were killed in the process; the country was paralyzed by a general strike; walls of sandbags went up around the presidential palace; and a bloodbath might have ensued had not Goni taken the sensible course of action and resigned.

Newspaper accounts of those troubled weeks were still fresh in my mind as the bus entered a grand ironwork bus station, and an atmosphere of mounting anarchy. La Paz hit me like a shot of pure alcohol. No sooner was I out of the station than my body already appeared under the control of some superior force which compelled me to avoid the line of taxis and hail down instead one of the thousands of worn, Japanese-built mini-buses or *micros* which seemingly account for most of the city's traffic. The *micros*' fixed routes were shouted out at great speed by boys leaning out of the front windows, or clinging on even more perilously to the open sliding doors. Squeezing my body and rucksack into an interior filled with probably twice the amount of people and luggage ever intended for it, I secured a few inches of spare seat by the window, but soon forgot the extreme physical discomfort as I surrendered my senses to the human spectacle around me.

La Paz, as the guidebooks had said, was truly a giant market place, an extraordinary blending of the urban and the rural, of the European and the traditional Aymara. And I felt instantly at home here, perhaps because of years of subjecting my senses to the compelling energy and mayhem of Spanish festivals such as the pilgrimage to the Virgin of El Rocío, whose mix of chaos, colour and kitsch was coming back to me now in sudden flashes of recognition. If I had paused to think, I might have contemplated the possibility of what would happen to all this diffuse energy if it were suddenly focused on a particular target; but this was not the time to think or to pause, just to watch and to feel, and to do what so many of the citizens of this city reputedly did: put all my faith in the protective powers of the inexplicable and the supernatural.

The flow of *micros* and people was slowing down to the speed of molten lava as we continued descending, past the higgledy-piggledy concrete and red brick constructions of the poorer upper part of the city, and into a centre where American-style office blocks were randomly thrown together with examples of 1950s functionalism, sombre art deco, grey nineteenth-century domestic architecture, granite neo-baroque, and genuinely baroque colonial ecclesiastic such as the massive dark-brown convent church of San Francisco. Here we came to a complete halt, impeded by what appeared to be a major demonstration of placard-waving Aymaras, but which, I was assured by my relaxed and friendly co-passengers, was merely a typical Saturday afternoon activity.

I got out and walked past a row of twenty hooded shoeshine boys, looking like joke terrorists, past several men with mobile phones attached by chains to their wrists (the phones were rented out by the minute), and then into a more sedate, more consistently old grid of streets. Here multi-skirted women squatted on the pavement at every corner, with whatever goods they had to sell on the ground in front of them – a dozen tomatoes, folding umbrellas, batteries, husks of corn, a radio, packets of tissues, biscuits. The Plaza de Murillo, core of this city of more than 1,000,000 inhabitants, symbolic heart of Bolivia, was like a square taken from a nineteenth-century novel of Spanish provincial life. A dully neo-classical cathedral, a presidential palace as unimposing as an old-fashioned gentleman's club, and some balconied stone buildings in a Parisian style, enclosed a square that appeared to have chosen on this weekend afternoon to distance itself from all the nearby confusion and take a well-deserved siesta.

I went straight to the corner of the square, where I had been told I would find the Grand Hotel Paris, which my grandfather had called 'the only hotel in La Paz worth staying in, or, as I should say, fit to stay in'. It had been opened the year before Bethel's visit to the city, and was generally known by the name of its French proprietor, Monsieur Guibert who, according to my grandfather, 'had enough capital to kill any opposition hotel that might want to start', and for that reason took little care in looking after the place. Despite its credentials, and its position on 'a rather decent Plaza where an excellent military band plays on Sunday nights', the hotel was actually 'pretty rotten'. The guidebook I had with me spoke about it as a luxury establishment in a 'delightful *belle époque* style'. I thought I would treat myself to a night or two there.

I quickly spotted the building my grandfather had photographed; but there was no hotel sign.

'The hotel is temporarily closed,' explained the waiter of an adjoining café. 'Perhaps permanently closed. There is a management dispute.'

I went off to look for another, more down-market place to stay, and climbed up one of the 'frightfully steep streets' that had put Bethel 'badly out of puff'. He had been hoping to encounter a wealth of picturesquely cobbled colonial streets adorned by seventeenth- and eighteenth-century palaces. But all that he had come across was the solitary Calle Jaén, a street whose palaces have all been turned today into museums, including one dedicated to the polemical subject of Bolivia's coastline. I spent an exhausting half-hour carting my luggage around the vicinity in search of an available hotel room, but then gave up on this quiet, dark area. I jumped into another *micro*.

I was back on the city's animated main thoroughfare, but further down, where it turns into what my grandfather called the 'rather fine wide avenue known as the Prado', with its verdant central reservation still in existence, and with occasional buildings of early twentieth-century pomposity squatting among the soaring glass, and monotonous concrete and stone casing. My grandfather, so thrilled by Elfland from afar ('I don't suppose any other city in the world possesses a more amazing natural site and scenic surroundings'), was disappointed by the place's lack of 'attractive or interesting buildings'. But he could not help commenting on the examples of architectural extravagance and pretentiousness to be found 'on either side of the long road of suburban villas' in which the Prado had ended.

'I think these villas,' he wrote, 'must have been built for the most part with a view to counteracting the depressing influence that having to traverse such forbidding-looking country in order to get away from the town may have on its inhabitants. The average French suburban villa is a fearsome sight but quiet and inconspicuous compared with some I have seen in La Paz.'

One of these villas must surely have been the present Hotel España. The suburban road of Bethel's time was now a noisy prolongation of the Prado, from which the hotel stood slightly set back and on top of a tall flight of steps flanked by stone cherubs, rather incongruous in the context of the street's tall modern office blocks, but in keeping with many of the older residences in the middle-class district of Sopocachi extending behind. The hotel was a rambling hotchpotch of styles, but so much past its prime that the door of my room, over-looking a large garden at the back, half collapsed when one of the staff opened it for me.

Barely had I settled in than I did what my grandfather always seemed to do immediately on arriving at a new place: I got in a touch with a member of the city's British community. This person's phone number had been given to me by a friend of his in London; and it seemed to me, briefly adopting my grandfather's way of thinking, that it would be pleasant in this strange country to exchange views about the place with someone of a similar cultural background. The friendly, open-sounding young Englishman who answered the phone told me I had arrived in La Paz just in time. In time to avoid the revolution? No, he laughed, in time for tonight's Burns Night party.

Wasn't Burns Night in January? Yes, he admitted, but Bolivia was always slightly behind the rest of the world; and, in any case this was the first Saturday in several weeks when all his British friends in La Paz could get together. He said he would come and pick me up at my hotel at 8.30. I would have no difficulty in recognizing him, he added. He would be wearing a kilt.

A Burns Night party in La Paz with a group of British people seemed as absurdly decadent a prospect as the toga party to which I had once been invited at the American embassy in communist Leningrad. But after so much time on my own, I quite looked forward to experiencing the sort of activity I imagined my grandfather had got up to in Mejillones with Dr Williams and Tommy Gloag. However, within twenty minutes the Englishman rang me back at the hotel, his tone as awkward as Mr Gibson's probably had been when sending my grandfather back to Antofagasta. He said he had just spoken to his wife, who had reminded him that numbers at the Burns Night party were strictly limited. He and his wife would love to meet me on some other occasion, perhaps for a coffee or a pre-supper drink, but not at this particular event, where the presence of a single additional person might throw the organizers into a complete tizzy.

I had the phone numbers of other people in La Paz, but I was not sure if contact with any of these would result in the sort of relaxed, informal meeting that I was now more in need of than ever. Most of the phone numbers had been given to me in London by Susana Sánchez de Lozada, and were of members of her politically disgraced family. I feared that I was of neither the right age nor generation to do as the renowned travel writer Patrick Leigh Fermor might have done during his youth, and in my dishevelled condition pay a social call on the country's élite. But I was keen to get to know someone in this city, and thought it in my own interests to inform myself a bit more about Bolivian politics. So I gave a ring to Macri Bastos, a woman whom I had been told knew everyone, and who appeared to be a mentor to Susana and her circle. The warmth of her welcome over the phone helped boost spirits deflated by the recent de-invitation, and I arranged to meet her late the following day. She told me she lived in the Zona Sur (southern zone), near the 'Valley of the Moon'.

La Paz, despite its compelling strangeness, proved to be a city much easier to get a superficial feel for than Santiago de Chile. Unlike any city I had ever known, the poor lived in the top of the city and the rich at the bottom, a reversal of the normal hierarchical order that allowed the former the satisfaction of knowing that all their effluence and rubbish would finish up polluting the territory of the latter. As you descended by *micro* from one end of La Paz to the other, the city became ever more prosperous and North American in appearance, so that by the time you reached the Zona Sur you were in a place indistinguishable from a well-to-do North American suburb, complete with shopping mall, designer boutiques, pizza parlours, strolling groups of smart young people, and complete absence of street vendors. Its blandness was redeemed only by the backcloth of eroded peaks – Bethel's 'colossal fingers' – which seemed to be indicating the spiritual wasteland to which all this capitalism was leading.

Macri was a psychiatrist, a charming person whose artistic modern villa included the statutory live-in Aymara maid. My grandfather would have been completely at home, especially as the conversation turned almost immediately to Hampstead Garden Suburb, where Macri's best friends in England happened to live – in a house near my grandparents' former home at 30 Meadway. We continued talking in a Mexican restaurant patronized by wealthy American students who had come to Bolivia to learn Spanish. I learnt nothing about Bolivian politics, but I did gather an interesting piece of information about an art historian cousin of Susana Sánchez de Lozada with whom I had already been in touch by email: this woman was none other than the daughter of the late General Barrientos, the Bolivian president responsible for the killing of Che Guevara in 1967.

Guevara, who had enthusiastically defined La Paz as 'the Shanghai of the Americas', came here for the first time in the winter of 1953, a year after returning from his trip with Alberto Granado, and a year after the Movimiento Revolucionario Nacionalista had seized power in Bolivia. The place had seemed to him a 'polychromatic and mestizo city' where 'a rich gamut of adventurers of all nationalities flourish and vegetate.' Though putting up at a dingy hotel in the same area that I had myself originally looked for a place to stay, he was to spend a schizophrenic month in La Paz divided equally between the city's 'low life' and 'high life'. He was interested in getting to know the Bolivian revolution better; but his new and well-connected travelling companion was forever bringing him into contact with members of the country's racist white elite, to whom the revolution was anathema.

'The so-called *good* people, the cultured people,' he noted, 'are astonished at the events taking place and curse the importance given to the Indian and the *cholo*.' A counter-revolutionary uprising was rumoured to be in the offing, and Che was keen to be around in La Paz to witness it.

I did not have Che's desire to see history in the making; but my earlier fears about being caught up in a violent social upheaval in Bolivia had given way to a masochistic fascination about the possibility of this happening. This possibility, which had seemed so remote when viewed from the placid normality of the Zona Sur, began to appear much more likely after I had talked to Denise Arnold, a friend of the anthropologist I had met in San Pedro de Atacama. Denise, an Englishwoman my grandfather and his contemporaries would have considered as having 'gone native', had married an Aymara, and together they had founded in one of La Paz's poorer areas an institute devoted to defending Aymara rights and propagating Aymara culture.

'You've arrived at La Paz at a key time,' Denise told me when I called her on the phone. Her tone of voice did not seem to be that of an enthusiast of Burns Night parties. 'Things are quite calm at the moment. But I'm sure the storm is about to happen.'

She said it would be better if we met up in the centre of La Paz, as the institute was difficult to find. I waited for her outside the place she had proposed as a convenient rendezvous, although she clearly disapproved of it: one of a new chain of American-style cafés that were springing up in all the city's better locations. She was immediately recognizable from a distance, even in a crowded street. Blond and contemplative, she stood out as a middle-aged, middle-class English academic who had just emerged distractedly from a library or seminar.

Shortly after we had sat down in a quiet upstairs room to sip our double cappuccinos, she talked to me about her experiences during the recent uprising that had ousted Sánchez de Lozada. She and her husband had been at a conference in Germany at the time, and had had to fly into La Paz on a military plane on the last stage of their return home. Spotted as a white woman on her way back to her house, she had had stones thrown at her, a cruelly ironic occurrence given her marriage to a widely respected Aymara, and her almost life-long dedication to indigenous causes.

I suggested that for the moment at least Goni's successor Carlos Mesa appeared to be doing a good job of holding the country together. According to newspapers I had read in Spain at the time of last year's crisis, this former television journalist was an approachable and enormously popular man who enjoyed the support of a large section of Bolivia's indigenous population.

'You have to remember,' said Denise, 'that he comes from a family that owns half of Bolivia's media.' As she launched into a speech about

Mesa and his family, she said with a faint smile that she always referred to him as 'Charles Table', a literal English translation of his name that allowed her to talk more openly in public about a man whose tentacles seemed to be everywhere.

Even after just a few days in Bolivia, I had become aware of his family's dominance in this country. The main books on Bolivia's art and architecture were written by Table's art historian parents, and published by the family printing press, which also brought out the one widely available book on Bolivia's history, written by Table himself. A daughter of Table was responsible for the largest painting in Bolivia's National Museum of Art, while another daughter was a model regularly featured in television programmes, gossip columns, and fashion magazines. Table's mother – a woman with questionable theories about mestizo influences – had arranged the current layout of the Museum of Ethnography and Folklore, a large part of which was taken up by a dreary and incongruous numismatic display publicizing the Banco Central de Bolivia, in which the family was also closely involved.

'Have you read Table's History of Bolivia?' Denise asked. 'It gives an extraordinarily partial picture of the country's history. It's a history written entirely from the point of view of the European settlers.'

Despite the 1952 revolution, Bolivia was still a country with a strong apartheid mentality, where discrimination against its indigenous peoples extended throughout the whole education system. Denise told me about an art student she knew who had been accused of 'deviousness' for wanting to take a course on 'Andean art'.

The prejudices and limitations of Bolivia's teaching institutions offered an explanation of the paucity of potential candidates for the role of Bolivia's first indigenous president. Evo Morales, the most touted candidate, had a limited grasp of complex political ideology, and was widely thought to have 'sold out to the government'. The only other much-publicized indigenous leader was Felipe Quispe, a citizen of El Alto who claimed descent from a general in Tupac Katari's army, and had written a book urging the rekindling of Katari's revolution. But Quispe, apart from being thought of as a lunatic fanatic, was another compromised individual, and was rumoured to be in cahoots with the CIA.

The mention of Quispe gave me the opportunity to bring the conversation around to the 'Inca cycles of revenge' which had been sporadically on my mind since Susana had told me about them in London. Was this, I asked, a typical obsession of Bolivia's paranoid white elite? Denise, revealing now her academic manner at its most measured and clear-headed, used the wonderful term '*pachamamismo*' (derived from the ancient Andean word for 'earth mother') to describe a cultural phenomenon prevalent today among a huge spectrum of woolly thinkers from New Age travellers to indigenous radicals of the Quispe variety, from fanciful travel writers to the knee-jerk politically correct. It included romantically inclined Western intellectuals such as the popularizing Chilean anthropologist Malu Serra, whose books Susana had urged me to read. For Denise, this was a phenomenon that greatly detracted from the serious and dignified consideration of Andean culture.

My first meeting with Denise extended well into the evening and led to my taking up her suggestion to see a film she rightly suspected of *pachamamismo*. She had no idea of how good or bad the film was going to be – the important thing was that it was the only film being shown in La Paz by a Bolivian director, Jorge Santesteban. I had never been to a Bolivian film before, nor had I read a Bolivian novel, nor, until the last days, had I seen any works of art by modern Bolivian artists. Bolivia was possibly the South American country whose contemporary culture was least known abroad.

On the basis of Jorge Santesteban's *Children of the Last Garden*, I could see why. The film, shown in a huge and almost entirely empty old cinema like the Odeons of my youth, had a grainy, crackly quality reminiscent of radical Cuban films of the 1960s to which I had once been addicted. The film quality matched the sophistication of the plot, which concerned a group of young Aymaras from the La Paz slums who decide to steal from a stereotypically unpleasant wealthy bourgeois family. They do not want the money for themselves but intend instead to give it to the villagers of an isolated and desperately poor Aymara community, which can only be reached on foot.

For days they traipse through beautiful Andean countryside until they finally reach the village, whose inhabitants remain understandably unimpressed by the argument that the money is rightfully theirs, a small token of what the whites have been robbing from them over the centuries. The politically motivated thieves return to La Paz and are arrested. The film ends with a group of their friends having a celebration in the ancient, pre-Inca site of Tiwanaku, a temple to devotees of *pachamamismo*. The Aymara words '*MARKASAM CHAMAPA*' (power to the people) cover the screen, a sentiment dutifully applauded by the solitary intellectual couple sitting twelve rows behind me.

Outside in the foyer, the dozen or so takers for the next showing were standing in front of a television screen, watching an address to the nation given by Charles Table. I stopped for a few minutes to listen, concerned that a dramatic new development in Bolivia's history was taking place. But the gist of his speech was to persuade all Bolivians to accept a five percent drop in their salaries – a measure that Denise would doubtless have viewed as bringing Table one step closer to his surely imminent demise.

I would see Denise again two days later, when she kindly set up a meeting for me with an eccentric employee of the institute who came from a Scottish engineering family. The idea was that I would rendez-vous with this man, Ian Mare, near his home in the centre of La Paz, and then go with him up to the institute. Ideally I would have liked to have done this in the morning but, as Ian explained to me on the phone, his sleeping patterns of late were 'completely up the spout'. He never managed to get to sleep until about five in the morning, and only woke at around midday. We agreed to meet up at two o'clock in the afternoon at La Paz's main post office; but he told me not to worry if he was 'an hour or two' late.

I decided to bide my time with a visit to the Club de La Paz, a grand, forbidding, vaguely art deco structure on the other side of the Prado from the dreary 1960s post office building. The club seemed to have a touch of Nazi Germany about it, though this was an impression quite likely to have been influenced by my knowledge of the place's reputation. This was where Klaus Barbie and fellow Nazi émigrés had brushed shoulders with Bolivia's no less numerous Jewish refugees, who likewise were welcomed in Bolivia when no other country would accept them. Numerous coups had reputedly been hatched at the club, and Klaus Barbie's former bodyguard was still said to be one of the more regular clients. I would have contented myself with a glimpse of the latter; but my way up the club's grand staircase was blocked by two stocky guards straight from a gangster film. They told me there was a public café at the side of the building.

The Café Club de La Paz more than satisfied my desire to see something of the European La Paz of yesteryear. As I sat having lunch in my fleece and jeans, I felt not only remarkably scruffy but also extremely young. The smoky, mirrored room was entirely occupied by elderly men in grey suits which could well have been those they had packed in their luggage on fleeing central Europe. One mustachioed gentleman had a monocle and shaved head just like a Hergé caricature of a Ruritanian army officer. But the sight that truly chilled me was of a man resembling my childhood Jewish dentist, Dr Rosenkratz, a Boris Karloff lookalike who had regularly featured in my early nightmares. As I glanced a second time at this reincarnation of my childhood ogre, the man horrified me further by rising up from the table and starting to shuffle towards me. When he stopped directly in front of me and began to open his mouth, I waited in dread for that terrifying Rosencrantz phrase, 'Michael, open viiide!' But instead he proffered an apology. 'I'm sorry,' he said in heavily accented Spanish, 'I mistook you for my son.'

I was so absorbed by the café's atmosphere that I arrived a quarter of an hour late for my appointment with Ian Mare; but I need not have worried. He was not there; nor was he there by four o'clock, by which time I had made a thorough survey of the users of Bolivia's postal service. I had no idea what Ian looked like, so I was forced to sidle up to anyone who seemed as if he might have British blood. Mare finally turned up two and a quarter hours late, just as I was on the point of leaving before someone denounced me for suspicious behaviour.

Ian Mare was as instantly recognizable as Denise had been, as British in appearance as the habitués of the Café Club de La Paz were Central European. But whereas the latter seemed to have found a comfortable niche in Bolivia, the comparably elderly Ian had the look of someone who had been sent to the other side of the world and then forgotten; he could have been a gentleman tramp. Over a frayed grey sweatshirt covered in stains he sported a black herringbone jacket which must have been a prized item of clothing when first purchased, about forty years earlier. He had thick yellow-white hair and was holding one of the black rubbish sacks used by many Bolivians to carry their belongings.

'I just can't get my sleeping patterns right,' he said chirpily, in a voice of indeterminate British origin.

I kept up with him with difficulty as he darted across the Prado and hailed a characteristically jam-packed *micro*, into which he manoeuvred himself with the agility of a lifelong practitioner of the art. Untying the knot in his sack, he rummaged through its contents in search of some old photos he wanted to show me, 'pictures of trains, engineers, that sort of thing'. He finally realized he had left them at home, but managed to extricate instead a small notebook in which he had written down every detail of his family's history. He barely needed to refer to this. He had an extraordinary ability of recall, as well as unstoppable verbal energy.

The journey uphill by *micro* was sufficiently slow to allow a full exposition of his ancestral background. The Scottish link was more tenuous than I had thought. His mother was from Newcastle, while his father, though coming from a long line of horse and cattle dealers from Inverewe, had been born in London's East Ham.

Soon after the end of the First World War, Ian's father had set off to Antofagasta, sailing on the HRS *Orcona*, a sister ship to HRS *Oronsa*. Like my grandfather, he had worked as a railway engineer, first in Chile and then in Bolivia, where he had been stationed for a while in Potosí. Many years later, during a prolonged return visit to Britain, he had fallen in love with the woman who would become his wife, and had done what my grandfather had often thought to do with Sophie: he had brought her back with him to South America. Ian was born on the sea crossing, two years before his father's premature death in 1938. His mother had stayed on in Bolivia but, fearing a Japanese invasion of the country during the Second World War, had sold off the family home there for a pittance, thus condemning herself and her children to a precarious existence. Ian had survived intermittently as an interpreter and tour guide, and now was retained almost on a charitable basis by the Aymara Institute. On arriving at the institute and finally alighting from the *micro*, I asked Ian if he had ever gone to Britain. 'No,' he said, 'and I don't imagine I ever shall.'

We were now in a rundown area that apparently was completely un-policed late at night. On the outside the Aymara Institute, which was also Denise's home, proved to be a shabby red-brick building little more prepossessing than its neighbours. Inside, however, it had a cosily English look, with folkloric artefacts tastefully arranged on the walls, and a well-groomed Siamese cat stretched out on a sofa draped with an ethnic rug.

Denise brought in some tea and digestive biscuits, which Ian wolfed down during short pauses in his continuing monologue. Occasionally I lost track of what he was saying, distracted as I was by the view from the panoramic window in front of us.

'This is something that the rich people in the Zona Sur don't have,' commented Denise, as I enjoyed a bird's-eye view of crepuscular La Paz. Her Aymara husband, a solidly impressive figure, came into the room to shake my hand, but left again at the very moment when the sacred Illimani, a peak considered impregnable during my grand-father's day, briefly emerged from hiding to stand like a giant white phantom over a city now sparkling with lights.

Ian now ceased to talk about his curious family background, turning instead to recent Bolivian history, on which he displayed a wonderfully vivid and gossipy knowledge. After telling a scandalous story about how Goni's wife had touched up colonial canvases prior to getting them illegally out of the country, he then proceeded to give me the low-down on the sex life of General René Barrientos, a former president about whom I was beginning to show a particular interest now that I knew I was going to meet his daughter. He told me about Barrientos's notorious womanizing, and about the man's fatal love of helicopters which had led to him to be known as 'Renécóptero'. I became especially excited on hearing that that his famous crash had taken place between Oruro and Cochabamba, directly above a stretch of railway line laid out by my grandfather.

'Tell Michael about the time you had tea with Che Guevara,' inter-rupted Denise, just as I was thinking about the curious way that these diverse themes which had been recently on my mind had converged. Ian, delighted to launch into another long story, began by saying that his tea with Che had taken place in November 1966, a week or so after the now celebrated revolutionary had flown in from Cuba in disguise.

'He had shaved his head, was wearing glasses, and pretending to be a Uruguayan economist called Ramón Benítez,' continued Ian. 'Though he was officially staying in a suite at the Hotel Copacabana, he seemed to be spending much of his time in a flat just above where my mother and I were living. We decided one day to invite him in for tea.'

There seemed to be one major flaw in this story. If even some of Che's closest comrades had not recognized the disguised revolutionary, how come Ian and his mother had done so? Ian gave a convincing explanation. 'Of course,' he said, 'we had no idea who he was at the time. It was only a few weeks later, when the story came out that he was in the Bolivian jungle, and photos appeared in the papers of the disguise he had used in La Paz and of the car he had hired, that we realized who our neighbour had been. My mother had had her suspicions about him all along, and had had the foresight to write down his car's licence plate. It was the same licence plate as the one in all the newspapers.'

Mulling over Ian's strange life, and over the possibility that it could have been mine had Sophie come to live with Bethel in Bolivia, I left the institute, walked quickly through the darkness to the nearest main street, caught the first passing *micro*, and started thinking of the strangeness of La Paz itself. What a shame it was that the French poet and founder of surrealism André Breton, who had called Prague the 'most surrealist city in the world', had not come here instead, to this place which truly seemed to exist 'beyond the fields we know', in a magical dimension that my rational grandfather could perceive only as indigenous superstition, but which perhaps offered an explanation for the bizarre new directions in which the search for his spirit seemed to be taking me.

Before going back to my bed in the Hotel España, it had become my habit to have what the Spaniards call a 'penultimate' drink in the bar located a few yards from the hotel's steps. Dark, modern, and poky, and with the grim dirges of Leonard Cohen playing constantly in the background, this establishment had little to recommend it except for its owners, a Chilean-Bolivian family in whom I had become increasingly interested, and who would soon greatly further my thoughts about the esoteric.

The most normal member of this family was young Alejandro, a welcoming figure who generally served the drinks. On my first night in the city, he had introduced me to *shufflay*, a drink as popular in Bolivia as *pisco* sour was in a Chile, and which consisted of a cocktail of Seven-Up and the Bolivian brandy called *singani*. This was a drink originally invented by British mining engineers, Alejandro had told me before expressing a random thought that attracted my curiosity even more:'My mother was engaged to a British engineer.'

He mused over this for a moment, then joined me for a second glass of this deceptively strong cocktail. 'He was more of a railway than a mining engineer, but I always find my mother's stories about him confusing.'

The mother had then fallen in love with Alejandro's father, a Chilean intellectual who had somehow drifted into La Paz and had got a job at the university.

'You'd get on well with my dad, I'm sure,' said Alejandro, 'he's a philosopher, a poet, an illustrator, a bit of everything.'

I met this Renaissance man the following night, and he immediately instructed his son to put a whole bottle of *singani* on our table, together with a litre of Seven-Up and an ice bucket. He was about my age, with thick, curly black hair and an intensely serious expression tempered by the occasional ironic smile. Telling me no more about himself than that he gave classes in both industrial design and English literature, he took out a sheet of paper on which he wrote down a list of his intellectual and literary idols, beginning conventionally enough with Chaucer, Newton and Jonathan Swift, but going on to such recherché figures as George Ripley ('the nineteenth-century American Transcendentalist') and Thomas Vaughan, a seventeenth-century Welsh alchemist, poet, cabbalist, Rosicrucian philosopher, and brother of the better-known poet, Henry Vaughan.

Before I could question him properly about this choice of names, other oddballs had begun gravitating to the table, including a young Argentinian who said how much he too admired Vaughan, but had recently veered away from 'purely alchemical and mystical works' and was reading only travel writers such as 'the Tibetan explorer Ferdinand Ossendowsky'. This Argentinian, Alejandro's father told me when the man had wandered back to the bar, was making a name for himself for his solo mountain climbs and his solitary, reckless wanderings on foot across such inhospitable parts of the continent as the Salar de Uyuni.

'He's a hero of mine,' Alejandro's father said. 'Even when he's in Buenos Aires he never stays in his parents' comfortable apartment. He prefers to lay down his sleeping bag on the pavement.'

On subsequent night visits to the bar, I also got to know Alejandro's wife and brothers, and a range of adventurers whom the young Che Guevara might have engaged in conversation. But it was only on the night of my meeting with Ian Mare that I finally became acquainted with Alejandro's mother and her mysterious past. This was not the day she normally worked in the bar, she said to me right from the beginning. But she had heard a lot about me from her husband and son, and so she was curious to know what the fuss was all about. She was a bubbly short woman with close-cropped blonde hair and huge eyes that were alternately flirtatious and mad.

She brought out a bottle of the 'family wine', which had the German name Weissbrun printed on it. The Weissbruns, her father's family, were Germans who had settled early last century in the Bolivian wine-growing area of Tarica. They still had large vineyards in the region, but the copper mines they had once owned had been confiscated by the government.

'My father,' she continued, 'was always a very proud German. He went off to fight for Hitler in the Second World War.' She poured me out another glass of wine, stared straight into my eyes, and said something that no one had ever told me before. 'I think Hitler was a very great man, a much maligned man.' She took a closer look at my face. 'But I've always liked Jews.'

I said that I was glad of that because the person she was talking to, though strictly speaking a Roman Catholic, was called Jacobs. He huge eyes opened even wider. 'You're not,' she asked disbelievingly, 'from the same family as Jacobs the engineer?'

'If you mean the Jacobs who died recently and worked in Uyuni, then I'm not.' I said.

'Is he dead?' she enquired anxiously.

'That's what they told me in Uyuni.'

'But he cannot have worked in Uyuni in over twenty-five years! The last I heard of him was that he was in Venezuela.'

'You must be thinking of another Jacobs,' I ventured. 'It's not exactly an uncommon Jewish name. It's like Pérez in Spain, or Jones in Wales.'

'There's only one Jacobs family in Bolivia,' she said quite adamantly.

'But how can that possibly be?' I retorted. 'There were thousands of Jews who came to Bolivia at the time of the Second World War.'

'The Jacobs family I know, the only Jacobs family in this country, came over to Bolivia long before that. The father of my friend was from somewhere in the north of England. He was also an engineer, and worked on the railway between Oruro and Cochabamba. He married a Cochabamba woman when he was very old, and there are still descendants of his there. If you go to Cochabamba I can put you in touch with a great-niece of his called Jenny Jacobs. She's a lovely woman, she's a good friend of mine.'

There had been times during my researches when it had crossed my mind that my grandfather might have gone astray in South America, and had a secret affair just like his uncle in New York. Cochabamba, moreover, would have been the most likely place for him to have done this. He loved the town, and the gaps in his correspondence with Sophie during the times he was working near there are unusually long. I had actually amused myself with fantasies of encountering in Bolivia the illegitimate progeny of the illustrious Jacobs seed. But, of course, even if my worthy, morally upright and Sophie-besotted grandfather had had such children, the idea of their having inherited the name of Jacobs totally defied plausibility.

'But I know of at least one other Jacobs family in Bolivia,' I said, persisting in trying to disprove Alejandro's mother.

'Who?' she questioned almost aggressively.

I was in fact thinking of a Jacobs family whom Susana Sánchez de Lozada had told me about as soon as she had heard I was researching family history. These Jacobses ran a beauty salon in La Paz that Susana frequented whenever she was in the city.

'Oh you mean the two sisters Carmen and Adela Jacobs? The ones who run the beauty salon round the corner? They're cousins of Jenny.'

I gave up arguing. I thought it best simply to listen to what else Alejandro's mother might have to say about a family who appeared to have been the descendants of the namesake my grandfather had mentioned during his first brief period of working on the Cochabamba line.

She opened another bottle of Weissbrun Riesling. I noticed that behind her lively smile tears were forming.

'Jacobs the engineer, my friend,' she continued, 'was the great love of my youth. We were very close, I would have loved to have married him, but it would never have worked out. He lived on another planet, he always had these mad schemes and ideas. I trusted him. He had special powers, he had a gift for divining water. He was obsessed by alchemy. The first time I met him he turned up at my father's house carrying a large wooden box. My father was too ill to attend him, so it was left to me to ask him what he wanted. He said that he had heard about the family copper mines, and that he had a scheme that would make my family greatly increase its fortunes. I asked him what he had in his box, but he wouldn't say at first −'

Her train of thought was suddenly interrupted, and she turned around to shout at her son. 'Oh, Alejandro, could you take that dismal music off, and put something livelier on!'

'I'm sorry,' she said, resuming her story, as the soft deep voice of Leonard Cohen gave way to the Ride of the Valkyries played at top volume. 'Well, I wanted to find out more about this man, so I invited him in for lunch. He told me he had trained as a civil engineer, and that he worked between Oruro, Cochabamba, Uyuni and Potosí, undertaking repair work on the lines his grandfather had helped to build. But he said he also had a degree in chemistry, and was very interested in alchemy. In fact the main reason he had come to Tarica was that he had heard about a seventeenth-century treatise on alchemy that had been written by a local priest and was kept in the library there. It was a very rare document, and the only other known copy in the world was kept in the secret archive of the Vatican.'

At this point of her narrative I paused briefly to wonder what my grandfather would have made of me continuing to engage in conversation a self-confessed lover of Hitler with a clear susceptibility to esoteric nonsense comparable to *pachamamismo*. But I found her curiously likeable and believable, and I was beginning to think that Borges must have been a great realist as I listened to this tale of a Jacobs whose life had run parallel to mine, and whose name, I now heard, was Miguel, the Spanish equivalent of Michael.

'Well, Miguel, or Miguelito, as I began calling him when we became intimate, went to the library at Tapica and asked if he could see this treatise. But the librarian said that he needed special permission from the bishop, and that the bishop would be unlikely to give this unless he had dispensation from the papacy. But it so happened that I was very friendly with the librarian, and that I was sure he would let me photocopy the book on the premises. Miguel said he would do anything for me if I could manage that. I said that all I wanted in return was to have a look inside his box.'

It was now after 3.00 a.m., and Alejandro was anxious to close the bar, so his mother was forced to distil her tale to its essential remaining elements. She had succeeded in photocopying the treatise, she said, and Miguel had opened the box to reveal the tools of his alchemical trade. A couple of weeks later, after they had started 'going out together', she had gone with him down into her family's copper mines. Miguel had explained to her there that the treatise confirmed what his own scientific investigations had led him to conclude: that there was a way of turning copper into silver and into gold.

'He went back to his work on the railways, and I went to stay with him several times in Oruro and Cochabamba. Then he disappeared, and no one in his family could tell me where he had gone. Five years ago he wrote to me from Venezuela to say he had found paradise. I can't believe he's dead, he's just probably got into one of his usual scrapes, and has had to change his identity.'

Alejandro succeeded at last in getting his mother out onto the street, but she had still not finished, and was now telling me that Miguel had been a Mason, and that I should visit the Masonic Lodge in Potosí, a place with which so many engineers of British descent had been associated. A taxi stopped beside us, and her son was almost pulling her into it, giving her only the briefest opportunity to display another side to her nature: her claim to be a psychic.

'I can see through people; and I can see their future. And I can see that you're on the verge of great success. You're a man much loved by everyone; and you love people. But there have been negative and evil forces working against you, as there were against your father and your grandfather. You're going to have to fight hard to overcome these. I see difficult times ahead and dangerous situations; but it's in your destiny and in your genes to win out in the end . . .'

Even as she was closing the taxi door she managed to keep talking. 'No one really knows you, nor do you know yourself. You seem so open, yet you're hermetic; there's a void in your life that needs filling . . .'

Her last words, spoken through the open window of the departing taxi, were largely drowned by the screech of a passing ambulance. I thought she said something about a woman who was now waiting for me 'at the end of the world', and that this woman had a 'glass eye'. But by now I was sure that drink and an over-susceptible imagination were influencing me. The only woman I had ever known with a glass eye was my grandmother.

My alarm clock went off four hours later. Wine, *shufflay*, lack of sleep, and high altitude were not a good mix; but I felt unaccountably sprightly, as if I had sold my soul to the Devil in return for the secret of a permanent sense of well-being. The sun was shining over the hotel's garden, and I was full of optimism as I got ready for the meeting I had finally succeeded in arranging with the head of Bolivia's railways, Eduardo MacLean.

I needed to see him before I could leave La Paz; and much as I was enjoying the city, I needed to leave the place soon. There were still three more weeks to go before the carnival season was over, but already there were signs that the country was heading again towards paralysis: a general transport strike had been called for the following week, and the president's deadline to sort out Bolivia's problems was appearing ever more unrealistic. If matters were going to reach a crisis, I wanted at least to complete the next major phase of the journey, and follow my grandfather as he worked on the one stretch of the railway line he had helped lay out himself, between Oruro and Cochabamba. But I still had no idea how I was going to do this.

The Bolivian railway network, which had been completely nationalized by the mid-1960s (when the F.C.A.B. finally relinquished direct control over the Bolivian side of its operations), had been drastically reduced over the past two decades, so that the only public services still running by the beginning of 2003 were between Ollagüe and Uyuni, and between Oruro and the Argentinian border town of Tupiza. A few days before my departure to South America, a friend who had written the *Rough Guide to Bolivia* had rang me up excitedly to say that the line between Oruro and Cochabamba had recently been reopened. However, this proved to be a red herring: the line had indeed been reopened in October 2003, only to be closed down six weeks later because of the rainy season. I now looked to Eduardo MacLean for a solution to my travel plans.

The Ferrocarriles Bolivianos occupied an attractive early twentieth-century villa just five minutes' walk from my hotel. As with the head-quarters of the F.C.A.B. at Antofagasta, the building was covered with old British clocks and other items of furniture dating from the days when the main railways in the country were British-run. Don MacLean was waiting for me in an office that could have been mistaken for an Edwardian lounge.

His appearance did not correspond to his British surname, and was more that of the swarthy, heavily mustachioed generals who feature on old South American postage stamps. I asked him about his ancestry, and he said that on his father's side he was descended from British shippers who had worked in Peru. In his manner he was as charming and open as Antofagasta's Miguel Sepúlveda had been; and he displayed a similar interest in history and in what I was doing. When he finally came round to asking what he could do to help me, I had every faith that he would prove another miracle-maker.

My first request was to be allowed to travel by freight train on the branch line to Potosí, which goes over the highest railway pass in the world. Sadly, he said, that would not be possible, as regulations about carrying passengers were extremely strict, and I would be an insurance hazard. Then I asked him about travelling along the line between Oruro and Cochabamba, and whether it would be possible to do so on one of the inspection cabs used by maintenance engineers.

'That would be totally out of the question,' he replied, 'for the simple reason that much of the line has been removed until the rainy season is over.'

'But, let me think about this a bit more,' he added, furrowing his brow. He took up the phone, dialled, and left a message for someone to call him back. 'There's this man who owes me a favour,' he told me. 'His company does all the maintenance work for us. You might be able to borrow one of their jeeps. Do you drive?' I said I did not. 'Well, that might be a bit of a problem then,' he mumbled, getting up to take an album of photos from his bookshelf. He tantalized me by showing pictures of all the places on the line where my grandfather had worked. The photos showed a green and wildly beautiful mountain valley.

The phone rang. Don MacLean nodded as the man on the other end was speaking, and then gave me a thumbs up sign.

'Well, that's all arranged then,' he said after putting down the phone. 'You'll be travelling all the way to Cochabamba in a jeep, accompanied by an engineer. It'll mean going in and out of the valley, and losing sight of the line for long stretches, unless of course you're prepared to walk in parts.' I said I was. 'There might be some hairy moments negotiating those areas where the mountain side has fallen into the river. But I'm sure you'll manage.' I laughed off any potential dangers. 'And I hope you're not in any great hurry,' he added, showing me to the door. 'The bus from Oruro to Cochabamba takes about four hours. You'll be taking about four days.'

I had to report early the following Monday to the railway station at Oruro, which gave me plenty of time to make two essential purchases in preparation for next week's trip. First of all, I wanted a good map of Bolivia, which was not as simple a request as one might imagine. After visiting all the best bookshops in La Paz, only to be shown the most schematic maps of the country, my one remaining option was to go to Bolivia's Military Geographical Institute, which was situated in the middle of a large army barracks inconveniently far from the centre.

Once I had left my passport at the entrance, had been subjected to a full body search, and had convinced the guards of my *bona fide* status as a map lover, I was all but frogmarched past parading soldiers to a building in the middle of the complex. There, a further half-hour was spent being introduced to officers of the institute in ascending order of status until finally the director himself, in full army uniform, walked down the stairs, shook my hand, talked to me pleasantly about literature, and then asked for my email address.

'Our detailed map of the country,' he explained, 'is currently out of print, but we'll be happy to notify you of its reissue, which might even be as soon as the end of this year.'

In the meantime, all that he could offer was a black and white photocopy of the military survey of the area I was visiting. This took another half-hour to produce, and was so blurred, dirty and illegible that its only use was as a nostalgic reminder of the first map of Spain I had ever bought. It was also remarkably expensive, but, as the man in accounts who took the money from me said, 'you're paying for military expertise.'

My second purchase proved infinitely easier, and was probably going to be of greater use. The little time I had spent in Bolivia had already convinced me that the best protection you could acquire in this country was a supernatural one. I had in my wallet an image of the Santo Custodio, guardian of my Andalucían village; but though it had served me once in good stead in a car accident in Scotland, I was not sure of its efficacy on the other side of the Atlantic. I needed something more specifically Andean, and so stopped off on my way back from the barracks at the Feria de Alasitas (literally the 'Fair of the Little Wings'), a giant market held once a year where hundreds of covered stalls sold statuettes of and miniature offerings to the smiling, mustachioed Ekéko, said by some to be the modern manifestation of an ancient Aymara deity.

I bought a rosy-cheeked figure with green trousers, a brown jacket and a yellow woolly hat. Though he was already overloaded with bags of food and wads of miniature dollars, the man who sold him to me said I needed to keep him happy with regular supplies of cigarettes and alcohol, give him a name, and provide him with miniatures of anything I particularly desired myself. I baptized him Custodio, and bought him a pan of paella and a pair of climbing boots. Then I asked another of the vendors if he thought that Custodio would look after me when travelling. The man, after pondering for a moment, said that an Ekéko was essentially a god of abundance whose sphere of influence generally did not extend much beyond the household. He reckoned that for safe measure I should also get an amulet.

Accordingly, I went to the centre of La Paz to visit the city's famous Witch's Market. A young, squatting mother, breast-feeding her baby under a poncho, carefully explained to me the particular function of each of the many types of amulet she sold. After much consideration I decided I needed two. One was an all-purpose *pachamama* that would ensure me good luck, wisdom, many children, and a happy love life. The other was of more immediate relevance: it was a tiny vial in whose clear liquid floated some coloured grains, and miniatures of a train and a bus. 'That's specifically for travellers,' the woman said.

Three days later, on the eve of setting off to my appointment at Oruro, I would already have cause to feel grateful for having this vial in my pocket. I had spent the weekend at Lake Titicaca, where my grandfather had also gone, carrying with him the spare part for one of the three British-built ferries used for transporting passengers and goods from Peru into Bolivia. An English friend had invited me to stay on one of these boats, the *Yavari*, which she had salvaged from the scrapyard and was currently bringing back to full working order. Whether or not this had been the same boat Bethel had helped repair, it was a wonderful late nineteenth-century vessel, captained by a quiet, handsome and mysterious man whom I saw as a reincarnation of my grandfather's boss in Bolivia, H. S. Brown, the man he had likened to a hero out of a Seton Merriman romance. This man was another loner who had also trekked right across Africa, in his case alone and on foot.

On my last night on board, after I had managed with the aid of a few drinks to get this person to say something about his remarkable African journey, I talked about Tschiffely's solitary ride across South America, and about how he had regularly had to fight off people trying to take away his money, his horses and even his life.

'Michael,' the captain responded, 'there are two main things that travelling teaches you. The first is that you can always tell someone's personality from his eyes, which allows you to spot any potential danger immediately. The second is that you have to be disposed to trust everyone, and to accept that every person, whatever his race or creed, is fundamentally the same, and governed by the same set of emotions. If you accept all that you begin to lose all sense of fear.'

Reflecting on this on my way back to La Paz, my thoughts were brusquely interrupted just as I was entering El Alto. The *micro* on which I was travelling was halted by police near the scene of an accident which must have resulted in several fatalities. A bus had careered off the road and was lying mangled and upside-down at the bottom of a twenty-foot drop. The old Aymara who was pressed up next to me began to speak.

'In Aymara we have an expression that probably every language has, because the truisms and clichés of the world cannot change so greatly from one place to the next. But I doubt if there are many countries other than Bolivia where you so constantly find yourself in situations that remind you of this expression.'

He told me what it was before I had time to look into his eyes and tell if he was wise or mad.

'Live each day,' he said, 'as if it were your last.'

6

As if it Were Your Last

———————

I CHECKED MY watch as I strode into Oruro's railway station. It was 8.58 a.m., and I was already twenty-eight minutes late for the start of a week whose exact timings and activities had been set down in a two-page document awaiting me on my return to the hotel in La Paz late the night before. I had been told to report to 'Engineer' Ricardo Rosales.

'You're nice and early,' smiled Ricardo after a station guard had walked me down the platform to an office marked 'SOCAIRE', the name of the company responsible for the upkeep of Bolivia's railway tracks. 'I didn't think you'd get here until at least midday.'

Ricardo held my hand firmly with fingers that were soft and clammy. He was a tall, olive-skinned man with a belly heavy with sensuality and a love of the good life. Nor did his thick glasses modify this impression with any look of scholarly seriousness, for, despite his thinning black hair, his face was that of a playful, misbehaving child.

Addressing me as 'Mister Meechell', he clasped his hands together excitedly, and said how much he was looking forward to the next few days, and how pleased he was to be able to assist in a project 'of such enormous sentimental importance'. Quickly going over the itinerary, he explained that he thought it best to take it 'relatively easy' today, and to come back to spend the first night at Oruro. I was worried that the transport strike which had been called for the next day might prevent our leaving. The newspapers had warned of blockades, and pickets being set up around every major town. Ricardo dismissed all this with another of his broad smiles.

'I only believe a strike is going to take place when it actually happens,' he said, 'and if it does happen I know all the escape routes.'

I could already see that Ricardo was one of life's optimists. I could not have predicted how vital his irrepressible optimism would prove to be.

A jeep was waiting for us outside the station, together with a quiet young Aymaran called Jesús, a trainee mechanic who worked as SOCAIRE's general dogsbody. Though looking little more than sixteen years old, Jesús had an efficient, conscientious manner that inspired confidence. This was more than could be said for the jeep, which spluttered to a halt almost immediately after the engine was turned on. Ricardo opened the bonnet, rearranged some wires, and successfully restarted the vehicle. 'There's nothing to worry about,' he smiled, 'just a minor problem with the electrics. Fortunately all of us in Bolivia who know how to drive a car know also how to repair one.'

We drove into the centre of Oruro to buy some 'emergency provisions' and to go to the bank. I got ready to cash most of my remaining traveller's cheques to pay for the expedition. 'You'll hardly need any money at all,' Ricardo told me. 'SOCAIRE will take care of the main expenses. We just want you to be happy and find what you are looking for.'

I learnt a bit more about my guide as our morning of preparations at Oruro proceeded at a comfortable pace. His home, he said, was in Cochabamba, where his wife and three grown-up children lived; but his job obliged him to be based mainly in Oruro. Did he mind being away for so long from his family? 'In life,' he replied, 'you have to accept what comes your way, otherwise you'll never be satisfied.' In fact, he seemed rather pleased with his current professional and domestic situation. 'It's very boring being always in the same place,' he insisted, before saying how he hated being stuck in an office, and how he loved the freedom his job allowed him. The freedom, I wanted almost to add, of being able to devote nearly a whole week to doing nothing else ostensibly but look after me.

Ricardo's exuberant enthusiasm became more exuberant still when directed towards his three apparent favourite topics of conversation – women, the Oruro carnival, and food. I was glad to be able to talk about something other than politics; but I was surprised to hear somebody rave about food in a part of the world where the gastronomy was usually mentioned only in terms of the filthiness of its preparation, the poverty of the soil, the shortage of crops, and so on.

Delaying slightly our afternoon trip, we went off to lunch at one of Oruro's best restaurants, where a dish of roast lamb was accompanied by a staple of Bolivian diet that had driven my grandfather and his European contemporaries almost to despair. Known as *chuño*, this was potato traditionally prepared by being frozen overnight in a field, and then stamped upon repeatedly when thawed so that every drop of water was gradually squeezed out. This 'horrible article of diet' was viewed by A. V. Guise as a 'dark, shrivelled-up object' looking like 'old cork', having 'about the same flavour', and, 'as with the bagpipes', impossible to like unless you happened to be 'native-born'.

'What do you think?' asked Ricardo, watching me like an amiable dog waiting to be patted.

'Delicious,' I said.

Eating with Ricardo reminded me of meals with one of my Spanish friends: his enjoyment was so contagious that it made you appreciate food that in other circumstances might seem unremarkable or even awful. The enthusiasm of my own response had in turn the effect of making Ricardo fantasize about all the wonderful dishes that we would be enjoying over the coming days, especially in the province of Cochabamba, 'the gastronomic capital of Bolivia'. He shook his head when I described how my grandfather had resigned himself on the Cochabamba line to a near-continual diet of 'Indian corn and tinned beans and large quantities of mustard pickle'.

'Poor man,' he sighed. 'In the few days that are given to us in this life, we must try and enjoy everything, even the simplest things. If we complain or are miserable, we achieve nothing except waste time.'

Ricardo's exposition of his philosophy of life was soon peppered with sexual allusions that had the hitherto silent and serious Jesús smiling occasionally, and even giving the odd chuckle.

'Meechell,' said Ricardo (the 'Mister' had been dropped soon after we had entered the restaurant, and was used only for introducing me to others), 'a plate of food is like a woman. Some plates appeal more than others, but all can give pleasure in the right circumstances.'

My grandfather's problem, in Ricardo's view, was that he had focused all the love he had inside him on one person. 'He had as it were put his eggs into the one basket,' he added, making a pun on the

Spanish slang for testicles that made Jesús turn his head away in a gesture of suppressed laughter.

'If you're ready,' he said, 'we should get going.'

I downed the last drop of 'our excellent Oruro beer', and walked outside into an afternoon that had become as cloudless as Ricardo's outlook on the world. 'Every morning when I wake up,' beamed Ricardo, 'I say a prayer to San Ricardo, and he always grants me what I want.'

With Ricardo at the wheel we started on our afternoon outing to a place called Banderani, which was as far as the railway had reached at the time of my grandfather's truncated first visit to Bolivia in the February of 1911. Our first stop came shortly after we had turned off the modern Cochabamba road and reached a large and pathetically solitary white sign welcoming the traveller to the 'ORURO GOLF CLUB'. 'Another legacy of your grandfather's people,' commented Ricardo as I studied the sign, which featured a coat of arms formed from a pair of golf clubs, and a foundation date of 1902. The golf course beyond was the sparsest I had ever seen, and wholly at odds with the newly repainted, English-looking clubhouse. A light covering of weeds and grass pushed through the stony ground like the stubble on an unshaved face. 'Outside the rainy season,' said Ricardo, 'there is no green at all.'

The narrow dirt track hugged the unused railway line closely as we continued into a landscape of barren mountains and gorges thinly carpeted with pale, threadbare vegetation. The jeep's battery, shaken by the ever-rougher surface, detached itself completely at the small village of Paria, a place known for its orphanage, its celebration of the Devil at carnival time, and its onions. While Jesús undertook an emergency repair, Ricardo strolled with me along the railway line, pointing out some fields where onions were being harvested.

'This was a line different from the others you've seen in Chile and Bolivia,' he said. 'It was built to transport the country's agricultural produce and not its minerals. It was built to feed the miners and the engineers.'

The jeep was already repaired when we returned from our walk. We drove off again, at first away from the line, past the spa hamlet of Obrantes (where 'men from Oruro come to spend the weekend with their mistresses'), up to view-points of crumpled panoramas so immense as to appear infinite. Then we came back into the valley through which the railway had run, framed now by mountains whose smoothly undulating ridges were indented with rows of upright boulders, making them appear like the crawling bodies of dragons.

At Banderani the road ended. A few inhabited adobe dwellings, cube-shaped and almost windowless, like the elements of an austere abstract composition, stood in the distance, behind the ruins of stone buildings more obviously contemporary with the railway. Ricardo and I got out again to walk, leaving Jesús this time with the task of turning the car round in preparation for our eventual return that evening to Oruro.

The former station, daubed in Aymara graffiti, cast a long shadow in the sharp late afternoon sunlight. We paused at the point where the platform must have stood, staring at the line as it disappeared between the dragon-shaped mountains. Around the corner, Ricardo informed me, the valley broadened out to begin its dramatic descent towards the green paradise in which Cochabamba lay. We walked just a few yards further on to look at a small garden entirely enclosed by fencing made from the railway line's rusting sleepers. These metal sleepers, Ricardo said, had all been made in Europe, but had been progressively replaced in recent years by the more flexible wooden ones. He took a chalky stone to rub against some embossed lettering, so that I could read the words more clearly. The letters on the sleeper spelt the name of Krupps, the German steel and arms manufacturer. Thus I learnt something new about this company: while producing arms that would soon be turned against Britain in the First World War, it had been helping Britain with her railway empire. The date was 1911.

My grandfather had first come to Banderani shortly before this shipment of sleepers had arrived there. His state of mind had very probably been similar to mine at this moment – buoyant, fresh, and open to new adventures. After his bleak and disappointing first impressions of Antofagasta and Oruro, he was now at last in an environment which satisfied his sense of beauty, and would have been in the mood to get started as soon as possible on the job he was sure would bring him professional satisfaction, independence from his unreliable Uncle Charles, and the financial security to be able to marry Sophie.

Bethel's three weeks in Bolivia before being ignominiously sent back to Chile in March 1911 were clearly unforgettable. Alone in his house in Calama several months later, sure now that his letters describing those critical weeks had never been posted, he distracted himself from his solitude by again writing up every detail of his first Bolivian trip, beginning with the memorable train journey from Oruro to Banderani.

'If I remember rightly,' he wrote, 'it took about 7 hours to do this journey of 73km (45 miles) by train.'

Bethel was travelling, as I was, in the height of the rainy season through a landscape that, as I was soon to find out, was of extraordinary instability. Recent flooding had 'undermined the line, and you could hear the water squeezing out underneath the sleepers.' The exceptional heaviness of the locomotives on this stretch of the line (130 tons when loaded) did not help matters, nor did the fact that great rock falls were a regular hazard. Three times the train had to be stopped so as to remove these rocks; and during one of the delays, lasting more than two hours, it even had to be backed for safety round a turn in the line so that large quantities of dynamite could be used.

'You see,' Bethel wryly noted to Sophie, 'travelling in these countries is not quite the simple affair that it is at home, even on the Dublin, Wicklow and Wexford line.' But the compensations were the scenery, which, 'as the train wound its way across the Bolivian Andes', gradually became wilder and more rugged. With the decreasing altitude, 'vegetation, chiefly represented by alfalfa and various forms of cacti, began to appear.' Bethel anticipated the day when the completed Oruro to Cochabamba line would 'form one of the most wildly picturesque railway journeys in the world.'

The train, on reaching Banderani, was met by three members of the railway company who had ridden up there from the construction team's base camp at Cona-Cona, ten miles further on. By an oversight typical of Bethel's whole time in South America, his own presence on the train had not been announced; but happily a spare horse was available, and so, after a meal 'which would hardly have appealed to a Brillat-Savarin', he was able to ride off with the party from Banderani to Cona-Cona. His real Bolivian adventures were about to begin.

★

As they would for me after Banderani. But before continuing on my journey towards Cochabamba, I had a night in Oruro ahead of me, and, if Ricardo was to be believed, the prospect of wonderful food, plentiful drinking, and scores of beautiful women. In my current, slightly dazed state, I could have believed almost anything. As we drove back to Oruro under the setting sun, I confessed to Ricardo that I still could not get over the fact that, thanks to him and SOCAIRE, I was about to realize a stage of my journey I had almost come to think of as impossible.

'Meechell,' he said, 'nothing in this life is impossible. Things are only impossible if you believe they are going to be so. For instance, how many times have you seen an absolutely gorgeous woman and thought with a sigh that she's well out of your class, and that you'll never be able to have her. Well, if you think like that, then you never will. But if you can convince yourself that you have as much to offer her as any Sean Connery, then you can be guaranteed that she'll fall for you, absolutely guaranteed.'

'But what,' I pointlessly protested, 'if she's happily married, totally besotted with somebody else, or else physically repelled by you?'

'Meechell,' he replied, 'there are no obstacles in life other than purely imaginary ones. You must always remember that.'

We returned to the less controversial subject of food and drink, and to the specific culinary and alcoholic specialities he wanted me to try, such as guinea pig ('a magnificent dish'), viper ('surprisingly tasty') and an alcohol of fermented corn (*chicha*) which my grandfather refused to touch once he knew how it was made.

'In the meantime,' he said, as we approached Oruro at dusk, 'it's high time to introduce you to a *Charqekanería*. There's an excellent one on the outskirts of the town.' A *Charquekanería*, I gathered, was a popular eatery specializing only in one dish – dried reheated llama.

Ricardo had identified me not only as a fellow lover of food (or, as they say in Bolivia, a *buen diente*, or 'good tooth'), but as someone generally happier to eat in popular than in more sophisticated establishments. This particular one was probably as popular as they get. Dark, with long benches, a dirty, slithery floor, and with urinals barely hidden from the dining area, it had an all-pervading smell of urine. We queued as in a soup kitchen to collect a plate on which a layer of *chuño* formed a bed on which were heaped the sorry, stringy remains of the llama. I looked in vain for some cutlery, but discovered you ate this with your hands.

I soon took to the experience, aided undoubtedly by the company, and by several shared litre bottles of beer which, Ricardo told me, was often mixed in Bolivia with Coca-Cola to form an *encholada* ('excellent for hangovers'). By eleven o'clock that night, after more than seventeen hours on the move, and with an early start lined up for the next day, common sense and a pleasant state of exhaustion should have dictated my going straight back to the room reserved for me in Oruro's Grand Hotel. But unfortunately I too had now been converted into a fanatical proponent of *Carpe Diem*. While Jesús went off to bed, I was persuaded without difficulty to explore 'Oruro's exciting pre-carnival night life'.

When, at seven the following morning, the still perky Ricardo turned up as agreed in the lobby of my hotel, I could only admire both his punctuality and his stamina. I was still at the stage of regretting having had only a few hours to sleep off the effects of a whole bottle of *singani,* drunk in what Ricardo had enigmatically described beforehand as 'a bar with company'. Confused recollections were now swimming in my head of a garishly pink interior occupied mainly by bored miniskirted young women on whom there would have been little need to try out Ricardo's theory of seduction.

'What you really need now,' said my guide as he took me off to have breakfast with Jesús in Oruro's market, 'is a *'caldo de caldán.'*

Sadly, this broth made from ox penis ('a well-known pick-me-up') was unavailable, and I had to make do with a more usual Bolivian breakfast of cheese fritters accompanied by a hot maize-based drink of porridge-like consistency. As we were tucking in to this, an old man came up to Ricardo to warmly shake his hands.

'A former colleague of mine,' Ricardo smiled, introducing me to him. 'Mr Ernesto was an engineer on the Cochabamba line for more than fifty years.'

Mr Ernesto, finding out where I was from, said he had once worked with an engineer of British parentage. 'He was called Jacobs. A lovely man, very quiet, very down-to-earth. He retired years ago to La Paz.'

'Shall we go now, Meechell?' interrupted Ricardo, wisely prevent-ing me from getting carried away on yet another wild-goose chase. We had no more time for distractions.

The sky was still clear, and there were no signs of a transport strike. 'I have already said my prayers to San Ricardo,' my cheery guide reminded me as we drove quickly and unimpeded by traffic along the modern and asphalted Cochabamba road. We went over a pass that was nearly 4,500 metres high before turning onto a track that Ricardo reck-oned would get us back to the railway line at a point near Cona-Cona.

Clouds now began gathering at an alarming pace, and the sky had turned a uniform grey as we looked down into the valley we were heading for. The sharpness of the light was nonetheless as great as ever, and the magnitude of the panorama even greater, so that I found myself revising my previous day's notions of infinity. If there were any man-made dwellings within this landscape, they were so microscopic as to be invisible within the millions of miniature terraced plots of land laid out, it seemed, by some super-race long since vanished from the earth.

We began our hairpin, hair-raising descent. Ricardo had never driven this particular route before, but he remained characteristically unworried as he continued down a track barely wider than our vehicle, heavily worn away in parts, and with little more than a centi-metre or two to spare in which to turn a corner. 'We'll continue on foot from here,' he said, once we had thankfully reached the bottom and the jeep was half-stuck on a stony bank projecting into the fast-flowing river.

Poor, long-suffering Jesús was given the task of driving back the way we had come and meeting us ten hours later at the village of Talcapayo, where we would be staying the night. Ricardo was not entirely sure if Jesús would make it. 'You never know about the state of the roads in the rainy season. Some villages can be cut off for weeks by flooding or landslides.' As a contingency plan, we would meet up with Jesús at Arque the following night. 'And failing that,' he laughed, 'we'll hope-fully find the jeep waiting for us this weekend in Cochabamba.'

That Ricardo and I would reach our destinations without any problems was of course never doubted, at least not by Ricardo. I tried not to think about flooding or landslides, but, as I looked at the dark-

ening sky, I could not refrain from saying something about the possibility of torrential rain. I was duly admonished.

'Remember, Meechell, what I told you about San Ricardo. He's
been good to us already. If the weather had continued as it was early
this morning, we would have been worn out within a few miles. The
clouds have been sent to stop us from having sunstroke. And they
aren't rain clouds, San Ricardo has seen to that.'

I took out from the jeep a small backpack, and put in it a medical
kit, a thermal vest, a plastic cape, and a litre of water. Ricardo looked
at me appalled.

'Why on earth are you taking all that?' he asked.

As a concession, he allowed me to bring the water and to exchange
my city shoes for some sturdy walking boots. He himself intended to
keep on his trainers and carry nothing. I wondered about the provisions we had bought. 'We'll eat those now,' he said, opening a tin of
Mongolian ox tongue. 'It's always better to travel as light as possible.'

Ricardo quickly finished his snack and stared for a few moments at
the landscape in front of us to work out the best approach to Cona-
Cona. I produced my photocopied military map to try and help him,
but he discarded this with a single glance, telling me to leave it behind.
The two of us walked to the river's edge, where I turned round to
wave a sad goodbye to Jesús. I was not entirely confident that I would
ever see him again.

My grandfather too must have wondered what he had let himself in
for as he journeyed from Banderani to Cona-Cona. The supposed
road was little more than a 'rough trail' that often disappeared altogether owing to rock falls and the swollen river. Progress would have
been almost been impossibly difficult had it not been for the
Argentinian mountain horses that he and the other riders were using.
These 'wonderful creatures' almost never lost their footing, even while
descending slopes so steep 'that one had to stand in one's stirrups to
prevent describing a graceful parabola over one's horse's head.' An
English horse under these conditions, commented Bethel, would have
given up after five yards.

The regular river crossings were Bethel's greatest worry. 'The man
with the largest horse was sent across first, and if he reached the other

side without getting too wet the rest followed.' Even with the water 'swirling up over the stirrups', the horses negotiated the rocky river bed with their usual sure-footedness. However, on one occasion, one of them put its foot into a deep hole, ejecting the rider into the gushing brick-coloured water. The person might well have drowned had not his progress downstream been hindered by a large rock. He luckily escaped with just a few cuts and bruises.

'We're going to have to try and cross the river here,' announced Ricardo, after we had skirted the banks for twenty minutes in search of an obvious crossing place. 'I'll show you how.'

He took a running leap and landed on a slippery-looking rock from which he hopped kangaroo-like on to a central island.

'The secret,' he calmly announced, 'is never to hesitate for a second. And of course to think of San Ricardo.'

With my heart in my mouth I followed his example, and succeeded. We were now surrounded on both sides by rushing water, and with no other option but to do the same thing again across a wider branch of the river.

'I can see you're getting the hang of it,' Ricardo beamed, once I had made it all the way across, and had paused to wipe my brow and calm my beating heart.

Then, without waiting for me fully to recover, he started to scramble up a dauntingly steep slope of loose earth and stones. He had an agility remarkable for his girth, and left me panting a long way behind, struggling, as my grandfather had often done, with the rarefied air.

I was relieved to reach the railway track, after a sheer climb of a good 400 metres. I was convinced that the greatest physical hardships of the trip were now over. All I had to do was to walk along a railway line that had been in use only three months earlier. I knew that large sections of the track had been taken up for the rainy season; but, as it had rained this year much less than normal, the damage done to the ground could surely not have been that great.

I maintained this illusion for the first hour of the walk. The sun peered periodically through the clouds to illumine a valley that was becoming noticeably greener as the track leisurely descended. Ricardo all the while kept me diverted and informed with his huge fund of botanical knowledge, much of which had an inevitably strong culinary and sexual element to it. I soon learnt what to do should I ever have a crisis of impotence in the Andes: if an infusion of *alfalfa* grass failed, I only needed add to this brew a teaspoonful of powder made from a type of potato grown at over 4,200 metres.

'We call this the Andean Viagra,' said Ricardo, showing me a small box of the stuff which he carried with him.

After less than twenty minutes of walking along the track we came to Cona-Cona, which now consisted of little more than a roofless station and some similarly ruinous brick buildings that my grandfather had described as 'grandly situated on one side of a deep ravine'. He fortunately had to stay there for only one night, for the place was almost entirely taken over by 'Yankees of a very undesirable class'. His opinion of the type of American employed on the Cochabamba line was corroborated by A. V. Guise, who spoke of the Yankee workmen here as 'people of dubious past' who were frequently still active as criminals. All of them, according to Guise, carried guns.

'An Indian boy' had guided my grandfather the next day down to the 'location camp', which was right on the river, just before the then hamlet of Aguas Calientes. This ride had been even more difficult than that of the day before, and there were patches so precipitous that Bethel had felt safer dismounting and leading the horse by hand. The dangers he had experienced during this stage of the journey seemed pleasantly distant to me as I leisurely ambled with Ricardo down the well-graded track. But then we reached the first of the landslides.

A huge segment of land, which Ricardo calculated as being twenty metres deep, had fallen into the river below, leaving a long stretch of the track hanging in the air like one of the narrow and perilous swing bridges you see in adventure films. Ricardo took a photograph of this, and noted down the location, so that his boss could prepare a report assessing the damage this year to the line. But he remained as insouciant as always.

'Meechell,' he said, 'this is nothing. There are always landslides such as these, however little it might rain during this period.'

I asked him how long it would take to repair the damage.

'Not so long, four or five days perhaps. But to be honest, Meechell, I don't think it's worth doing any more repairs. This whole line to Cochabamba is no longer commercially viable, especially now that there's a good modern road. It was reopened for a couple of weeks or so in the autumn partly as a publicity exercise, and partly because our president at the time, Goni, is the owner of some nearby mines. But to keep such a railway going you need a huge maintenance staff, which today there simply isn't the money for. When railways were Bolivia's most important means of transport, a line such as this would have had a team of at least eight maintenance workers for every fifteen kilometres of track. But that would be impossible now. Meechell, it's sad to admit this, but I don't see this line ever being used again.'

He led the way nimbly down the hole left by the landslide and then up the other side. I focused my gaze on his shoes rather than on the sharp 300-metre drop to the river below. 'Don't worry, Meechell, when we get to Aguas Calientes, the track is almost at the same height as the river.' Once again I was lulled into a sense of what would prove to be false security.

As we approached Aguas Calientes, there were fields of maize, a scarecrow made from a real dead bird, and a couple of fenced gardens of the kind we had seen in Banderani. My grandfather had given a detailed description of the 'location camp'; and from this I had optimistically anticipated immediately recognizing the site.

'But Meechell, you've already seen how much this landscapes changes from year to year. If your grandfather said that the camp was on the only strip of land exactly level with the river for miles around, you can be sure it's gone by now. The river's level is getting higher all the time what with all the accumulated stones and rubble from the mountains.'

A few hundred metres further on, at the point where a tributary stream formed a small waterfall as it neared the opposite bank, Ricardo paused once more.

'Your grandfather did mention camping opposite a waterfall, didn't he?'

I nodded.

'Well, let's say, Meechell, that this was the spot right below us. I want you to be happy.'

All the railway staff had been out at work at the time of Bethel's arrival at the location camp, which consisted of a group of tents pitched unwisely close to the water. The only people around were the camp boys and chef ('all Bolivian Indians'); and he had to wait almost until sunset before finding out who his colleagues would be for what he still envisaged as the next three years.

After the Yankees of the night before, the staff at the location camp turned out to be 'a generally agreeable lot'. The man in charge, the only American, was 'a big, slow-speaking, raw-boned Kentuckian who spoke seldom and then in the softest of Southern drawls.' He had started his career as a cowpuncher and had then slowly worked his way up the old Bolivian Railway Company. Though 'a queer retiring character', and 'terribly deficient in technical knowledge of any kind', he was 'not a bad sort all round'.

There were just four others, two of whom, a 'levelman' and a 'chainman', were 'mere boys' in comparison to Bethel. Together with a much older 'rodsman' ('a most blatant Cockney from the lowest walks of life, and altogether unspeakable'), these 'boys' were adventurers who had 'drifted into this country to pick up any rough job that fell their way, from brakesman on a freight train to mere labouring work, and were, of course, 'more or less uneducated and illiterate'. Bethel's favourite of the three was the 'picturesque-looking' Australian chainman, a 'good natured and good tempered' youth, who, though leading 'a wild and dissipated life' (when the opportunity offered) was the 'least obtrusively vulgar'.

The final person in the team, the 'ridiculously underpaid instrument man', more than made up for the limitations Bethel perceived in the others. This person was the Dublin-educated Samuels, who was not only acquainted with Sophie's brother, but also belonged to that relatively elite clan comprising Ireland's Jews. Bethel was totally astonished and elated by the encounter; and though he would later meet up in this area with another 'Trinity man' ('an Irishman with the not uncommon name of Murphy'), the empathy he felt for Samuels was altogether stronger.

What cemented Bethel's liking for the man was their shared passion for music, which, as the rainy season got worse and camp life became harder, would lead to moments of bathos and absurdity.

'It seemed,' wrote Bethel, 'a trifle incongruous to be discussing, say, modern French composers with a man squatting on a rock in the heart of the Bolivian Andes, whilst endeavouring to get some nourishment out of the horrible meals that the Indian boys brought out to us during that time when the floods had reduced our camp almost to a state of siege, and provisions rapidly failing us.'

The stretch of river in front of the camp 'tumbled in a seething brown cataract over huge boulders' that were carefully studied each day to see how much the water had risen. But, despite this precaution, Bethel woke up one morning to find, as he had feared, the river on the point of sweeping away the tents, which had to be taken down in a matter of minutes and moved to higher ground. With the continuing rain high in the mountains, and the accompanying ceaseless volleys of small stones being swept downstream, the mule pack trains that brought provisions from Cona-Cona were unable to reach the camp, which was soon without bread, butter, sugar or meat.

The surveying work went on regardless, and had a banality that contrasted with the dramatic conditions in which it was undertaken.

'The work,' Bethel admitted, 'presented no features of particular interest; it was just the usual (American) procedure for locating a line, setting out curves and calculating earthworks.' All that was novel for Bethel was 'setting up one's instrument on most uncomfortably steep slopes which were apt to collapse and slide from under one's feet. And if you slipped or fell whilst scrambling through the undergrowth the chances were ten to one that it would be a cactus you clutched hold of to save yourself.'

By far the most notable event of my grandfather's weeks at the camp was the expedition to a carnival at Talcapayo, the village where Ricardo and I were now heading. Their journey there and back, along a riverside path largely hidden under earth, water and rocks, was an integral part of the experience, and had climaxed on their return with a thunderstorm from which they had been unable to shelter through fear of not reaching the camp by nightfall. 'To make the last and worst crossing of the river in the dark would have been simply suicidal, especially as half an hour's rain sometimes makes a considerable difference in its volume.'

Smugly I walked with Ricardo towards the railway bridge that now made it unnecessary to endure the hazards suffered by my grandfather and his party. The structure had a reassuringly sturdy metal frame; but once I was on the bridge I was disconcerted by the lack of a metal gangway, and by having to tread instead on the wooden sleepers, the gaps between which seemed greater than they had been on land. The sensation was like walking on a horizontally placed ladder, through the rungs of which you looked down to a terrifyingly fast and sinisterly coloured river three metres below. At first I followed Ricardo's example and strode confidently along the middle; but halfway across, and with the noise of the water disturbingly loud, I had a sudden feeling of insecurity, and kept closer to the side of the bridge, where I consoled myself with the thought of grasping hold of the metal frame in case I fainted or one of the sleepers broke. I did not like the idea of placing the full weight of my body on a potentially rotten piece of wood attached to the underside of the track merely by a couple of pins.

'Are you okay?' asked Ricardo, as he sat waiting for me on the other side of the river, at the entrance to Aguas Calientes. I said I was fine. I was pleased to be on land again, and was enjoying the sight of the grove of Chilean pines and eucalyptus trees that announced our arrival at this hamlet of ten or twelve houses.

'The trees were planted by your grandfather's people,' said Ricardo, who also drew my attention to the brick 'water breakers' that had been constructed a year or so after the abandoning of the location camp and the conversion of Aguas Calientes into an 'important' station on the Cochabamba line.

Ricardo lifted up some vegetation near where he was sitting to reveal an old 'water extractor' dated 1913, and marked 'G. & J. Weir Ltd., Cathcart, Glasgow'. Rust had unfortunately eaten away the serial number which, according to an inscription, had to be quoted 'when ordering spare parts'. We continued on to the shaded station, in front of which, directly on the track, were some playing children, a sleeping dog and a squatting woman. A man with an ox-drawn cart advanced slowly along the railway line towards us. He greeted Ricardo and, after yoking his animal to a tree, sat down next to us on the station bench, as if expecting a train. After remaining silent for a few minutes, he asked Ricardo when the railway would be functioning again.

The squatting woman, overhearing him, said that she wanted to know as well, and that their community could not exist much longer without the railway. As buses did not come to Aguas Calientes, nor to most of the other places on the line, the railway was their only link with the outside world. They needed it for their hospital visits. They needed it every time they wanted to go into a town and sell their goods.

All eyes were on Ricardo, waiting for him to give an answer. He looked unduly hesitant and ruffled. 'Soon,' he eventually said, 'when God wills.'

I wanted to talk more with him about the future of places such as Aguas Calientes once we had resumed our walk; but he seemed keen to avoid the subject, and was soon telling me instead about 'a sure-fire way' of calculating the width of a man's penis by the size of the nail of his forefinger. Within half an hour we had lapsed into silence, and were anxiously counting the kilometre posts so as to work how much more we had left of what had turned into a route march.

After a while I became almost blasé about the numerous incidences of landslides and subsidence that had left long stretches of the track dangling in space. None of the resulting large cavities in the ground were too difficult to negotiate; and the only remaining physical challenge of the day came almost within sight of Talcapayo, just at the point when I thought that the day's quota of dangers was at an end. Flooding had swept away a good 500 metres of the line, creating a bare, steep slope of rubble falling straight down to the river. A path of sorts had been made by the villagers, but this was just a four-inch wide indentation cut into a slope where there was not even a single cactus to break one's fall into the water. 'Remember,' said Ricardo, 'whatever you do, don't stop to think too hard. Just keep on going.'

Walking along this path was how I envisaged balancing on a trapeze; but for the last metres I gained heart by the welcome sight in the distance of Jesús standing next to the jeep and waving. Talcapayo was on the other side of the river, separated by one of the railway bridges I would increasingly come to dread. The car could not get any nearer the village, so we took out what we needed and walked across a bridge rather worse for wear than the one at Aguas Calientes, and with at least one sleeper missing. The knowledge of having to cross the same bridge again the next morning was not a particularly pleasant prospect; but Ricardo humoured me by saying I would feel an entirely different person after a good night's sleep, a 'guinea pig or two' inside my stomach, and several litres of *chicha*.

My grandfather, after his arduous ride from the location camp, had been greeted at the end of his journey to Talcapayo by the raucous sights and sounds of his first South American carnival. Murphy, who was based at a camp near Bethel's, had already reached the village in the company of a large German colleague, and the two men, dressed up in 'false noses, pigtails and weird attire', were contributing to the overall hilarity by 'sprinkling the crowd with flour and distributing largesse in the form of very small copper coins'.

The throwing of flour, water, coloured streamers, and even eggs, had continued all day, accompanied by the 'clamour' of an 'Indian band' playing repeatedly the same two tunes on a vigorously beaten big drum and 'a sort of reed mouth organ'. What had interested Bethel most was an elaborate ceremony involving the hurling of peaches and potatoes by 'two Indians in masks and a gorgeous costume', which he believed was 'an imitation or survival of an old Inca costume'. But the anthropological curiosity this had aroused had been offset by the bathetic spectacle of the two men, gravely kneeling 'with all the seriousness of abject superstition' to receive the blessing of a village priest ('a most repulsive-looking old ruffian, as I am afraid they all are in these Bolivian villages') as absurdly 'bespattered' as most of his parishioners.

The growing drunkenness of the revellers, combined with worsening weather, had led Bethel and his party to set off back to their camp by the late afternoon. I arrived with Ricardo and Jesús in the early evening. The clouds had gone, as had most evidence of human activity, and all signs whatsoever that Bolivia was already into its carnival season. The village itself, largish in comparison with places we had seen earlier, had the makings of one of those European showpiece communities mainly taken over by weekend and holiday homes. The stone and adobe brick houses were filthy and graffiti-covered, with thatched roofs falling into disrepair; but the two main streets, with their beautiful stone paving and central stone gutters, had something about them of the traditional rural architecture of central and northern Spain.

One of the streets formed a long, level row of buildings which included a small school and a town hall distinguished by a projecting wooden window and a main door with a proper stone lintel. The other street climbed uphill before trailing off in front of a shaded area embracing the outlying parish church. Jesús had gone ahead earlier in the day to book three beds for us in a government-restored hostel at the convergence of the streets, above the riverside 'village green' where the villagers had gathered on the day my grandfather had visited Talcapayo. The hostel was clean and pleasant, and with an enchanting garden filled with flowers and hummingbirds. To Ricardo's regret, however, Jesús had failed to persuade the owner to prepare guinea pig for our supper. Chicken was on the menu instead.

While this was being cooked we went off to search for *chicha*, which my grandfather too had first encountered at Talcapayo (he would thereafter stick to whisky). We walked towards a house whose red flag outside indicated that *chicha* was available. On the way we stopped to sit down on a stone step to talk to the young village schoolmaster, whom Ricardo had not seen in some while. The teacher asked me what the scenery was like in Britain, and whether there were volcanoes and an Altiplano as in Bolivia. I replied that Britain's scenery was rather different from Bolivia's, but that I knew few villages in my country as beautiful as his.

'This is a beautiful village,' he agreed, 'but we have our problems.'

The village was not just suffering from terrible isolation and the gradual departure of its young. It also had an infestation of Chagas beetles. 'The Chagas beetle,' elaborated the teacher, just in case I needed being reminded of its fatal effects, 'is a flying beetle that swoops down from the rafters of a house to bite you at night. The bite is extraordinarily painful; but what is worse is that the disease to which it leads gradually destroys your immune system, and swells your heart, leading to certain death many years later.' Ricardo butted in to say that a government 'anti-parasitical programme' had fortunately now made this a 'negligible problem'; but the teacher was keen to have the last word.

'This village,' he insisted almost as a matter of local pride, 'is famous for having an adult population over forty that is almost entirely effected by Chagas disease.'

'Mister Meechell is now greatly in need of some *chicha*,' said Ricardo rising from the step, and bidding the teacher goodbye before he could alarm me further. We went into the house with the red flag, and sat down in its courtyard on a bench made from Krupps sleepers. A young girl with mud-coated arms rushed off to get some *chicha*, whose alcoholic effects, Ricardo had enthused, were instantaneous. In case of losing control, I took the precaution beforehand of studying the tiny section of overhanging roof above us. I was looking out for unusual insects.

The *chicha* arrived in a jerrycan and was poured into a coconut bowl to be shared between Ricardo, Jesús and myself. The girl had offered us glasses, but these were spurned by Ricardo who, giving me a wink, had explained to her that 'Mister Meechell is a real man'. The deceptively mild-seeming drink, which was still fermenting, reminded me of some millet beer that I had drunk from a communal gourd in an African hut. My grandfather had told Sophie that *chicha* was a 'native beverage to be religiously avoided if one's mind is ever likely to enquire into or dwell on the methods of its manufacture.' The details that he delicately spared her would later be outlined in print by Tschiffely, who wrote that those making the drink would chew the corn into a paste which was spat out into a wooden bowl. The saliva with which the masticated corn became impregnated contained an enzyme, diastase, which, when 'added to a mass of hot boiled corn . . . acts upon the starch of the corn, converting it into malt sugar.'

Was all this true, I asked Ricardo? Yes it was, he admitted, 'but it's better just to drink it, and not think too much about how it's made.' With every mouthful he took, he said the Aymaran word for 'Cheers!' – '*Choncaricuna*!' – which he made me repeat every time I too had a drink.

After ordering a second jerrycan of *chicha* , he taught me the only other Aymaran phrase I would learn in Bolivia, '*Ñoca ancha munaquqi*.' He wrote this down in my notebook before telling me what it meant. 'Hopefully,' he said, 'you might find someone on whom to practise this expression before the trip is over. It means "I love you very much."'

'How are you feeling?' he enquired the next morning, when I had woken up after a good nine hours of deep, uninterrupted sleep. The *chicha*, which contained only 'healthy human spittle' and no chemical additives, was said by Ricardo to leave no trace of a hangover. And he was right.

'It'll be a relatively short day,' announced Ricardo, before confessing that we might run into a few problems near Changolla, about two hours downstream. That he himself was aware of potential difficulties on today's walk should have put me on my guard. But the optimism and good cheer induced by my night at Talcapayo had, as Ricardo predicted, made me almost ashamed of my earlier worries; and I was even able to cross the railway bridge this time with a confidence that matched the early morning sunshine.

Once again we said our farewells to Jesús, who was told to make doubly sure that we would have 'something decent' to eat on arriving at Arque. Ricardo estimated that we would get there as early as lunch time; and the spanking pace at which we set off promised that this would be the case. By 9.30, just as the heat was rising, the clouds returned to keep us cool and help us maintain our speed. My faith in San Ricardo was now almost limitless.

Our last glimpse of Talcapayo came just before we followed a bend in the valley where dynamite had blasted a great segment out of the cliff face so as to allow trains to pass. I recognized this distinctively shaped opening from one of my grandfather's photos; and Ricardo confirmed that it had been made 'around 1912'. We had now moved on from the scene of my grandfather's first stay in Bolivia, and were walking along a stretch of the railway which had been completed just before his return to the country more than one and a half years later.

Progress on the Cochabamba line had been slower than my grandfather might have expected. He found the track completed only as far as Changolla, where he set up camp from the late autumn of 1912 onwards. Samuels was the only remaining member of the original location camp; and he now had with him a twenty-three-year-old assistant from the north of England who 'has not an H in his composition, and talks without a break until you want to gag him.'

Working in this new camp helped Bethel lose many of his earlier misgivings about the 'Bolivian Indians', whom he now described as 'a very harmless and cowed lot; their worst feature is their ugliness.' His earlier prejudices were now transferred to the British working classes, whom he increasingly perceived at Changolla as lazy, interested only in money, and lacking any 'sense of personal responsibility'. He focused these unattractive criticisms on one man in particular, a 'Cockney' train driver who was 'a liar by nature' and had 'an accent you could cut with a knife'. Bethel went on, in a statement likely even to have shocked Sophie, to confess to being 'an adherent to the cause of woman's suffrage if only for the thought that men such as these have the vote'.

Bethel, with his concern for the truth and the scientifically verifiable, found especially distasteful the way everyone in the camp spent their evenings telling the 'most frightfully far-fetched yarns'. One of the worst offenders in this respect was the 'cockney', who exchanged tales about his experiences in India and South America with an 'extremely morose and worried-looking Australian' whom Bethel nonetheless really did admire and find interesting. This man, despite a tendency to exaggerate, had tales that Bethel found genuinely believable ('and which were corroborated by others') about his experiences when building railways in India, mining in remote parts of Mexico, Ecuador and Peru, and fighting as a soldier in the Boer War.

But the only person in the camp with whom Bethel could enjoy any form of deeper friendship remained as before Samuels. Though the man's many months in the Bolivian outback had coarsened him, he was still someone who could share Bethel's sensitivity to landscape and the higher pleasures of life. It was with Samuels that Bethel went on a memorable expedition on horseback into the steep mountains directly behind Changolla. After climbing up through a landscape coloured with brilliant green splashes of cultivation, and fields of flowering cactus and acacia, they were able from the top to observe the valley though which the future railway would run, snaking its way towards the distant snow-capped ranges behind Cochabamba.

'A year's location work,' noted Bethel, 'looks as though it might be done in a few weeks.'

As we approached the great loop of the valley in which Changolla was situated, Ricardo's normally untroubled brow seemed to furrow slightly.

'There's absolutely nothing to worry about,' he quickly reassured me, 'it's just that we've reached a point in the river where's it's joined by several tributaries. This is usually where we get the worst flooding along the line.' I already knew this from what my grandfather had written, and from photos that he had taken starkly captioned 'Flooding at Changolla'.

'The water does not seem particularly high today,' continued Ricardo, as the valley broadened into a massive bed of stones streaked with rivulets of widely varying width. What I could not see were any signs of a railway track. 'That's because a stretch of track extending several kilometres was dismantled here at the start of the rainy season.' And what about Changolla itself? 'There's not a single stone left standing. After rebuilding the station and surrounding buildings every year for about fifty years, the railway authorities finally saw sense, and gave up completely.'

From the pensive expression on Ricardo's face, and the way he was pausing periodically to gather his bearings, it became obvious that we would be unable to stick to the river bank as it curved in a near circle around the valley. We were going to have to cut a large corner and walk directly across the loop.

'Are you ready for some more jumping?' Ricardo asked. I looked at the rows of murky torrents ahead of us, and reluctantly said yes.

A series of increasingly risky long jumps managed to get us three-quarters of the way across. Then we came to a branch of the river at least twenty feet wide, and so loud, dark and fast-flowing as to be as fearful as the Styx. Short of singing 'Hey, nonny no, nonny no!' there seemed little now that we could do other than to return by the precarious way we had come. But Ricardo, unwilling to be defeated, took a huge stone and threw it as far as he could into the water.

'I was just testing the depth,' he explained, before sitting down on a rock and removing his shoes and trousers. 'We're going to have to wade across.'

An individual on his own, he confessed, might experience some difficulty struggling against the rush of the water. But if we were to stand side by side and lock arms we would create a barrier strong enough to resist the pressure. I was sufficiently convinced by this theory to follow him into the river; but as soon as I had done this my doubts were instantaneous.

My frozen naked feet, in pain from the stones underneath, and struck by rushing pebbles, were barely able to keep their balance in only a few inches of water. But Ricardo was pulling me further into the river until the water was well above our waists. His strength was phenomenal, whereas mine was slowly ebbing.

'Don't turn against the current!' I thought I could hear him saying, as if from a great distance, for by now the water had loosened one of my feet from its place in the river's bed; and it was only Ricardo who was keeping me from being dragged away. I managed after a struggle to straighten my errant foot; but panic had now set in, and I turned round to face the full force of the river, which resulted in the two of us being soaked all over and making a mad, disorderly scramble to reach the other bank.

'That was a fundamental error you committed,' gently chided Ricardo, whose face had registered a brief moment of terror before our safe arrival at the river's bank. 'But fortunately San Ricardo is still looking kindly upon us.'

I was more inclined instead to thank my grandfather as I sat, still a little shocked, putting on my socks and boots and picturing him smiling at me from his deathbed. Perhaps something of his spirit had attached itself to this land and was taking care of his foolish grandson. Then I thought again and concluded that the only spirit I was likely to encounter here was a vengeful one filled with hatred towards the Western intruder.

I became more thoughtful still as we got up to continue our walk towards Arque, which was still at least four hours away. Ricardo claimed that there were no more hazards facing us; but his words hardly registered with me, for I was back again in the past, thinking about how my grandfather had changed since his first visit to Bolivia. He had become more realistic in his expectations, more hardened by life, less fuelled by hopes and high ideals.

A symptom of this was that he was now writing to Sophie far less often than before. From penning almost daily missives on the boat journey out to South America, at Changolla he had been reduced to one letter every five or six weeks. Usually he made the excuse that he had been exceptionally busy; but on one occasion, attempting to write to Sophie at 5.30 a.m., with 'two very tough nuts' snoring away on the floor of his tent, and then waking up to talk, he had also to confess that 'there is something about living in a camp that is not conducive to letter-writing.' The unreliability of the postal service in Bolivia must have been another disincentive; and Bethel clearly became fed up with sending long letters when only two out of three could be expected to arrive. As for Sophie's replies and occasional gifts (a silk scarf, a photo of herself as a chorus girl, a woollen tie she had knitted), these were either lost in the post or kept in storage at Antofagasta. He would have to wait more than half a year before seeing the promised tie.

'Don't misinterpret my silence,' Bethel once urged Sophie, who must indeed have worried occasionally that his love for her, perhaps like hers for him, was wavering. The letters she did receive did not have quite the same intensity of yearning as before, either for her or for 'civilization'. After having been prey in Calama to the most disturbing extremes of passion and self-pity, Bethel had now adjusted himself to a life of boy-scout adventures, campfire bonhomie, minor frustrations, and longings for the 'most trivial things – show windows, afternoon tea in the shop, and going about in a taxi'. Perhaps he had come now even to regret his earlier outpourings of despair, for he wrote to Sophie on 18 November 1912 to 'repudiate' any worries she might have on his behalf.

'So far,' he insisted, 'I have not been at all lonely, and I don't think I am likely to be.'

With his mental equilibrium apparently restored, and his planned return to England and to Sophie rapidly approaching, Bethel should have been the happiest of men. Yet his mood seems to have been an ambivalent one: the Bolivian environment might have appealed to him far more than that of Chile; but his work here was even less fulfilling than it had been in the Atacama, and there was no longer the prospect of his being offered something better. In his next letter to Sophie, written just before the close of 1912, he admitted that his one real professional challenge to date had been the bridge on the River Loa. As for his present job, he sighed, he was 'beginning to detest this, as one often has to work so much, and there is so little to show for one's work, which in itself is deadly uninteresting.'

Unaided at first by any of the assistants he had been promised, Bethel was engaged in surveying the land between Changolla and Cochabamba, and working out the right of way. If he had been allowed to confine his attention 'purely to the surveying and engineering end of the question', he would not have minded this so much. But he had also been put in charge of purchasing – at prices as favourable as possible to the railway company of course – those parcels of land that were going to hinder the train's path. He had entered morally dubious territory, for this was a time when President Montes was forcibly making many of Bolivia's indigenous landowners sell off their property for ridiculously small amounts of money.

Throughout 1912 and 1913 articles regularly appeared in the Cochabamba press urging the speedy completion of the railway line from Oruro, which was described as the 'great hope of the town', and a project whose endless protraction had been the source of 'much tension and anxiety'. The local newspaper *El Comercio* saw the railway as a vital means of fostering 'industry, commerce, art and science' in the area, and implied that those who tried to impede its progress by refusing to let the railway company appropriate their land were putting their own selfish concerns before the national good.

Though Bethel would have agreed with the tone of these articles, the actual task of trying to make patriots out of the 'small owners' was one so mindlessly boring and mentally exhausting as to drive from his mind any higher thoughts and moral concerns he might have had.

'There is no job on the line,' he wrote, 'that involves more petty little worries than mine. I have to carry in my head a mental picture of everyone's little mud hut and cabbage patch over 70 miles of line, listen to a thousand absurd little claims and complaints, scarcely any of them justified, and with all the discomfort of continual travelling about in the middle of the rainy season.'

Added to all this was the irritation caused by the constantly changing and delayed decisions of the railway company, and the consequent impatience of the small owners to be paid immediately. The one aspect of the job that might have appealed to someone such as myself or Ricardo was sadly regarded by Bethel as 'another of its objectionable features'. This was 'being always asked by someone or other to have drinks or invited to one of their wretched native meals at ungodly hours, where one has to burn one's mouth with red peppers and swallow horrible home-made wine.'

Bethel, as he himself confided to Sophie, did not really mind what sums of money the company had to pay up; but his sense both of company loyalty, and of what he considered 'fair play', made him hate the idea of his employers being swindled, and particularly through emotional blackmail on the part of the 'natives'.

'These natives, our own rascally lawyer included, make my blood boil. They come weeping and wailing and saying that by cutting down a narrow strip of their crops we are taking the bread from their mouths. As a matter of fact, it scarcely makes any difference to them; many of them have pots of money and never spend a penny, living like pigs.'

The 'rascally lawyer' was a widely respected Cochabamba man called Jorge Galindo; and Bethel's feelings towards him would change entirely after he had got to know him better. The man understandably irritated him at first with his habit of suddenly cancelling appointments, or turning up for them as much as six days late. He also greatly offended Bethel on another occasion by failing to arrive on time at a dinner to which he and the sub-prefect of Arque had been invited at Changolla camp. The two Bolivians had decided to stop off beforehand at 'some filthy little *chola's* hovel', where they had got half-drunk on *chicha*. However, by the August of 1913 Bethel would end up liking Galindo 'very much'. Theirs was a friendship that would be cemented in the course of many arduous trips together, of the kind I was currently experiencing.

Knowing that Ricardo was also from Cochabamba, I asked him if the name Galindo meant anything.

'Of course,' he replied. 'The Galindos are Cochabamba's most famous family. My wife Susi, who's a teacher, could put you in touch with one of them who made the mistake of marrying into the family of our last president. They have a daughter who is often in London.'

'Susana Sánchez de Lozada?' I asked.

'Yes, that's her,' he said, sounding not in the slightest bit surprised that I already knew the woman. 'An aunt of Susana's, also a Galindo, married General Barrientos, who, as I think you know, was killed at Arque in a helicopter crash.'

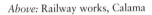

Above: Railway works, Calama

Right: 'Myself and new engine', Calama

Below: 'Mr Gibbes and Mrs Pearson, Calama. May/12'

Above: 'On the way to the accident. In foreground the inspection car in which I have travelled many weary hours'

Left: Clearing the line of snow, north of Calama

Below: Derailed engine in snow, north of Calama

Right and below left: 'Oruro Market'

Above right: An Indian band in Oruro

Right: 'Street scene, Oruro. Balcony of railway offices'

Left: Bethel surveying on the Cochabamba–Oruro line

Below: 'Changola Camp, Bolivia. Kilometre 110, Cochabamba–Oruro line'

Above left: Bethel sitting in his tent at Changolla

Above right: '"Me" in Sammy's camp'

Right and below right: 'Wash out on line near Changolla'

The mule-drawn carriage used by Bethel while staying at Orcoma camp

La Paz

Street scene, Potosí, with Mint on right

Main square, Potosí, with Cerro Rico in background

View of the Cerro Rico, Potosí, with the church of San Benito ('the parish of the Indians') in the foreground

The Pass of El Condor, highest point on the Río Mulatto–Potosí line, and highest railway pass in the world

I was still trying to assimilate these coincidences when we turned a corner and saw in the far distance a bridge spanning a tributary of the main river. The railway track, which had been slowly ascending ever since we had rejoined it after Changolla, was now a good twenty metres above the river, and continuing to climb as it veered towards the bridge. The carefree mood with which I had begun the day had already been dented, and, as the bridge got nearer, I had a sudden feeling of imminent danger. When we were finally there, I noticed that the first two sleepers were missing, and that at least three others were half-hanging off, suspended above the void.

'Are you up to this?' asked Ricardo, attempting his most un-convincing smile so far. I did not appear to have much of an option, so I nodded.

'Just try and do what I do,' he advised, as he jumped over the gap at the beginning of the bridge, where the drop was fortunately not as high as it became a couple of metres further on. But then, instead of walking right down the centre of the sleepers as he had boldly done at Aguas Calientes, he stepped instead on their projecting edges. These were about two feet wide and separated from the bridge's outer metal frame by four feet of space.

I could not decide whether Ricardo's chosen tactic of crossing the bridge this way had been determined out of sheer bravado or for some genuine technical reason connected either with the state of the wood or the laws of physics. But like a soldier following his leader unquestioningly into battle, I did the same as he did, and managed to get a third of the way across before beginning to hesitate. I had heard of mountain climbers who, halfway up a cliff, are too frightened to continue either going up or coming down. I felt I was nearing that same situation.

'Don't look down, whatever you do,' shouted Ricardo, rather too late, for I had already peered down to the cataracts thirty metres below and had completely lost my nerve.

'Just look straight ahead and go quickly,' instructed my leader, as I forced myself to place my foot on the next sleeper, which promptly wobbled, giving me such a shock that I did exactly as I was told, and started rushing forward careless of the consequences, jumping over the broken sleepers, and landing so hard on one that I thought I heard the wood creak, knocking one of the rusting pins into the chasm, badly stubbing a toe, but never looking down again, never stopping, never thinking, only accelerating, until finally, shocked and clammy, I set my feet down again on solid earth, grateful for having survived, worried about what was coming next.

There were still fifteen more kilometres to go before reaching Arque; and I was unconvinced by Ricardo's promise that we had crossed the first and last of the high bridges. The only reassuring development of the morning was coming across the first human beings we had met on the line since Aguas Calientes, beginning with an old man who, it seemed, made his living by stealing pieces of metal from the track. Ricardo, losing his temper for the first time, borrowed my camera to take a photo of the man doing this. He threatened to expose him to the authorities.

The old man returned to his illicit work soon after we had moved on, by which time we had been distracted by the appearance of two young men who gave us encouraging news. They had walked all the way from Arque that morning, and had not encountered any problems. One of them was collecting rare flowers which he hoped to sell. The other had come along simply to keep his friend company and to play tunes for him on a reed pipe, of which he gave us a demonstration.

'Until recently,' Ricardo told me afterwards, 'everyone in the Andes used to have some musical instrument that they played whenever they went on a journey. Nowadays they nearly all have Walkmans.'

When we were just five kilometres from Arque, I began unwisely to relax. Ricardo was singing the songs I was likely to hear in the Oruro carnival, and the sun was making ever longer reappearances, creating patches of bright emerald in the rocky valley. Dreamily, unconcernedly, I watched the valley's sides draw gradually together and become higher and steeper, until a deep gorge had formed before our eyes.

I was thinking more of the gorge's sublime, Turneresque beauty than of any practical difficulties it might present until I looked more closely at the river. Greatly swollen from all the tributaries and waterfalls that had cascaded into it, this rushed madly ahead, covering all traces of a bed or a track as it squeezed past the sheer slopes of rock and rubble at the promontory marking the gorge's neck. There seemed not the slightest possibility of continuing further.

'But how did the two young men make it? And what on earth where they thinking of when they said that we would have no difficulties?' I asked Ricardo, dismayed by the idea of having now to turn back after all that we had been through.

'Firstly, Meechell,' he answered, 'didn't your grandfather himself say that half an hour makes a huge difference in this part of the world? It might not be raining down here, but there might be big storms higher up in the mountains that are helping to swell the river.' He paused to study more carefully the view in front of us.

'Secondly, you must have noticed by now how everyone in this country always tells you precisely what you want to hear. Thirdly, the two men did exactly what we're going to do.' There was no point in asking Ricardo what this was, for I had already observed him surveying the bare slope that rose at an angle of about seventy-five degrees from the water.

'We're going to have to be careful, Meechell, but there's really very little to worry about.'

Without this time making even a token enquiry about my feelings on the matter, he found a foothold in the rock that enabled him to start climbing. Grabbing onto a shrub above, he pulled himself up on a narrow ledge, from where he continued his ascent by similar methods until he reached a bare expanse of rubble twenty metres above the water. There he waited for me to follow.

I had never done any rock-climbing before; but the childhood friend who had once tried to persuade me how easy it was had been killed doing so in the Andes. I hoisted myself onto the first ledge without too much difficulty, and then onto the one above; but, as I clung to a shrub higher up, this loosened all of a sudden, causing me to transfer my hand speedily to a tiny crack. Ricardo was shouting instructions about how I should proceed from this point; but I preferred to trust my own instincts, as I pulled myself slowly but surely towards him. The sheer physical exertion needed to do this took my mind briefly off the dangers, the greatness of which became obvious once I had reached Ricardo, and looked down to the river, and to the similarly steep descent that we would have to make before rejoining the railway track.

While stopping to regain my breath and composure, I was surprised to see three boys scurrying up towards us in a matter of minutes, smiling and saying hello, and then effortlessly heading on down in the direction we ourselves would soon be going. At least, I thought, my grandfather had got one thing right about the 'Indians'. The 'Indian boys' were truly as 'surefooted as cats or goats', worthy of being entrusted with 'the carrying of the delicate and costly theodolites and levels when running surveys on these precipitous and treacherous hill-sides.' Without their assistance, he observed, 'we would soon have had to shut up shop for want of instruments.'

Seeing how easily the boys had descended to the river on the other side of the promontory was comforting in the sense that it demon-strated that what we were about to do was humanly possible; but I was unconvinced when Ricardo told me that going down would be 'infi-nitely easier' than coming up. Twenty steep metres of loose soft earth led to a ten-metre-high cliff, below which were boulders that were being violently attacked by the water. Ricardo, as goat-like as the boys, reached the cliff in no time, and turned round to beam me a smile and make the thumbs up sign. The secret, he had told me, was always to stay confidently upright, and never to waver.

Within a few seconds I had slipped, fallen on to my backside, and was hurtling towards the cliff and what seemed a certain and ignomin-ious death. Ricardo reacted quickly, and rushed towards the point where I was falling. But in the meantime I had grasped a shrub which, though not strong enough to hold my weight, slowed me down before my feet finally came to a rest on a small, rocky overhang. Blood was seeping through my trousers, and my hands were lacerated by thorns; but I would have been happy to stay where I was indefinitely. I was still ten metres above the cliff, and it needed much persuasion on Ricardo's part to make me continue to where he was standing.

The cliff was where the real difficulties began. Even Ricardo looked slightly worried as he went first to find the 'easiest way down'. I checked my trouser pockets to see if my amulets were still there, and opened my wallet to look at the photos I kept of my dog, my partner, and the Santo Custodio. I wondered if I would find any dogs in the other world.

'Are you ready, Meechell?' screamed Ricardo, his voice barely audible above the torrent.

He was trying to tell me where I should next place my feet and hands; but the phrases 'To your left!', 'To your right!', soon became indistinguishable. I was fine for the first three metres, but then I was unable to find a hole to place my left foot. Simultaneously my right foot lost its grip, leaving me for what was probably the longest minute of my life hanging on to a ledge just with my hands.

In retrospect I would come to view the whole morning in terms of famous cinematic moments of suspense. From having started off as Jon Voight up to his neck in water in *Deliverance*, I had gone on to become Robert Donat making his perilous crossing of the Forth bridge in *The Thirty-Nine Steps*. And now I was Cary Grant stuck on Mount Rushmore in *North by Northwest*. Of course, no such thoughts came to me at the time. In fact, as I hung desperately to the ledge, I had no thoughts at all, just a momentary desire to plunge directly into the water and bring all my fears to a sudden end. This was probably the closest I had ever been to death; and there was nothing remotely glamorous about the experience.

I started to behave more rationally, found a foothold, and climbed down to the bottom of the cliff without further difficulties. We were sprayed with water as we negotiated the boulders along the river's edge, but were soon beyond the promontory, and walking along a section of exposed river bed towards the next surviving stretch of railway track. Once we were through the gorge, I speculated about the probability of death or serious injury had one of us truly fallen.

'Meechell,' said Ricardo, 'if you stop and think of all the terrible things that can happen to you in life then you'll never do anything.'

This was probably the soundest advice he ever gave me.

Arque was now visible in front of us, preceded by an isolated crane that turned out to be inscribed 'Beyer Peacock & Co., Ltd., Manchester, 1913'. We had survived another stage of the journey, and were back firmly on my grandfather's trail. This village, though only of 1,000 inhabitants, was the first of the reasonable-sized communities between Oruro and Cochabamba; and the coming of the railway here had been eagerly anticipated. To the frustration of my grandfather and others, however, the construction of the last stretch of the line here, as well as the fate of the whole line from Arque onwards, was delayed for several months in 1913 as a result both of bureaucratic hurdles and the inability of the railway authorities to make up their minds.

'I am, Micawber like, waiting for something to turn up,' wrote an exasperated Bethel on 16 April. 'For some reason, which I cannot understand, the powers-that-be continue to maintain an impenetrable silence with regard to the work ahead on this Cochabamba line. Already it is five days past the date when it was decreed that some 12 miles of line should be located, staked out and all ready for the contractor to begin work on, and as yet it has not been decided which side of the river the line is to go.'

So that he could go straight ahead with the necessary purchases once a decision had been made, Bethel took a chance and made a survey of the Arque side of the river. Fortunately, by the end of the month, when word from the authorities finally came through, his instinct proved to have been right.

The line was built at the lower, riverside end of this steeply sloping village, on a now wildly overgrown strip of land along which Ricardo and I, exhausted but victorious after our adventures, prepared to make what deserved to be a triumphant entry into Arque. A couple of grunting pigs ran out to greet us, but no one else. The railway track, half buried in the earth, and largely covered by grass and wild flowers, ran past a terrace of attached houses resting on the mossy ruins of the station platform. A tasselled red flag, blowing in the wind like an oriental kite, was hanging above one of the doors. It gave us hope.

Before we got there, a young man who had been asleep under a tree suddenly rose to his feet on hearing our voices. It was Jesús. He had arrived only a couple of hours before, but had had the time to make our culinary requirements widely known in the village. Three roast guinea pigs, he announced with a broad smile, were waiting for us in the bar off the main square. Ricardo congratulated him for this, but said that he and I were first of all desperate for some *chicha*.

We reached the house with the red flag, the owner of which, a retired school teacher called Walter, had known Ricardo for years. Recently widowed, Walter was now looked after by a sister-in-law who brought us *chicha* and a coconut shell to drink it out of. We rested for twenty minutes on a stone step which, as Ricardo admiringly pointed out, had been made from a fragment of an ornamented lintel dating from Arque's boom years, 'after the arrival of the railway'.

Walter was prepared to sell it; and while he and Ricardo negotiated a price, I gulped down the *chicha* contentedly, and looked down across the platform in the direction we had come from.

The mountains of the gorge, projecting upwards against the clear blue sky like the fantastically narrow peaks in a Japanese print, were elements of an idyll in which even the rustic neglect of the foreground played a part. Only the open sewer was to be regretted; but a half litre of *chicha* helped play down the prominence of this pungent visual obstacle.

'If only you had known this place when the English were still here!' lamented the woman serving us. 'There was no open sewer then. The station was surrounded by beautifully looked-after gardens with flower beds and trees that were pruned. The English would not have allowed pigs to wander all over the place.'

I was puzzled by her suggestion of a recent English occupation.

'I mean, when Mr Williams was still around,' she explained.

Ricardo further clarified this by saying that Mr Williams was a district engineer who had worked in the Cochabamba and Oruro districts right up into the 1970s.

'He had a motor car and everything,' the woman added. 'When he was around, things seemed to work in this village. There weren't the problems with the trains we later had.' She appeared distracted for a moment. 'Poor man. He would only have been in his early seventies if he had been still alive.'

When I asked what had happened to him, she talked about the landslide. 'It occurred just outside the village, on the way towards Orcoma. He was caught right in the middle of it and dragged into the river. The railway's team of fourteen maintenance staff died as well.'

I said that a similar catastrophe had taken place when my grandfather was working at Arque, and three or four people had been drowned. Her response to this was as matter of fact as my grandfather's description of the incident to Sophie. 'That's not so many people,' she commented.

'The guinea pigs will be getting overcooked,' interjected a now impatient Ricardo, rising up from the step, and rubbing his belly. 'We'll be back for the step after lunch.'

We walked up a cobbled street overhung with trees in blossom. Arque was as old-fashioned in appearance as Talcapayo, but more enticing still with its well-preserved streets in rough-hewn stone ambling off from a lush central green. This seemed at the time like a paradise, or at the very least like a strong candidate for inclusion in *The Most Beautiful Villages of Bolivia* , should ever a publisher bring out such an unlikely-sounding coffee table book.

The hostel at the corner of the green where Jesús had left the car and luggage had a certain resemblance to rural French hotels of my grandfather's time, down to the one solitary bathroom to be shared by the many, in this case a party of fifty trainee schoolteachers. Some of these were finishing their lunch in the unadorned bar, where we found the owner much concerned about the state of the guinea pigs, which had charred rather badly on the outside. It was already past three o'clock. I tucked in with a hearty appetite to a creature I had previously known only as a much-loved family pet. Burnt or not, it was like a flavourless, bony chicken with a repellently fatty texture. Only hunger, a lot of accompanying beer, and Ricardo's enthusiasm, made it in any way enjoyable for me.

After finishing lunch, we returned as planned to the house with the *chicha*, this time bringing a pickaxe with us. Ricardo started hacking away at the step even before Walter, the owner, had emerged to greet us at the door. When the stone was finally removed, Jesús dragged it back in the direction of our hostel. Ricardo and I stayed on to take up an offer of what I had been told would be an 'excellent digestive'. Walter showed me a tin marked 'Drinkable Alcohol, 98° proof'.

In the absence of the outside step, we went to drink this in a stark sitting room, painted pink and pale blue. The only decoration was an old photograph of a man whose bronze bust dominated the village green – General Barrientos. The photo was a commemorative one, with the dates 1919-1960 preceding the quote, 'I prefer sacrificing my life to seeing my people suffer.'

'He was a magnificent person,' said Walter of this Bolivian president who had extinguished the last embers of the worker's revolution of 1952, and had instituted what would turn into eighteen years of military rule in Bolivia.

'He was a strong man, unlike Paz Estenssoro,' Walter continued, alluding to the workers' leader who, on being elected to a third term of office as Bolivian president in 1964, had chosen Barrientos as his vice-president, and was then promptly deposed by him. 'Without Barrientos we might have ended up as a communist state.'

On coming to power, Walter explained, Barrientos had turned immediately against the left while also cleverly maintaining the support of the peasant federations. 'Thanks to the loyalty of these federations, Che Guevara's attempt to launch a continent-wide guerrilla war in our country was suppressed without gaining a single peasant's support.'

I took another sip of the supposedly drinkable paint stripper and, prompted by Ricardo, turned the conversation round to Barrientos's death at Arque, to which Walter had apparently been a witness.

'Yes,' he said, 'I was there on the day he died, I even saw his dead body. He had come for an official reception, and was going on afterwards to Talcapayo. If he had taken your grandfather's railway and not gone up in a helicopter, he'd probably still be alive today.'

Walter recognized that his hero had many enemies, and that his views about the suffering of his people did not appear to apply either to his own wife or to the many husbands whose wives had gone off with him. But he challenged the idea that the general was assassinated.

'That's total nonsense,' he said, 'I was standing right outside this house when the accident happened, and I saw everything. The helicopter took off okay, but then hit a telegraph wire and collapsed into the river. It was as simple as that.'

I would hear an entirely different version of the story at the end of this long day. Ricardo had taken Jesús and myself to have *chicha* and supper prepared by one of the woman friends whom I suspected he had in every village. This woman, María, was a large person with a sharp wit and healthy cynicism, quite capable of putting into his place the flirtatious Ricardo, who claimed to have been engaged to her once. Unmarried, and clearly wary of men, María lived with her mother above a curious cross between a bakery, an ill-equipped grocery store, and a bar with a single, rickety wooden table. The filth and darkness of this place were off-putting at first, as was the knowledge that some more guinea pigs had been cooked for us. However, none of this really mattered after everyone had started chattering away amidst general exclamations of '*Choncaricuna!*'

María's mother was the one who remembered Barrientos's death. What she recalled above all were two men in black suits and white shirts whom she had assumed were bodyguards. She had seen them in the crowd welcoming the general as he stood in the village green; and then had noticed how they had mysteriously disappeared after the helicopter had fallen.

'I heard a shot,' she said, 'I definitely did, and then I saw the helicopter plunge straight onto the railway line. It didn't fall into the river, as some people later said, for otherwise it wouldn't have burst into flames. I'll never forget the sight of the general's burnt leg as they took out the body.'

I could not decide whether to believe her or Walter, or simply to take both versions as examples of the unreliability of memory, or the impossibility of recreating even the recent past. Later during my stay in Bolivia I would mention my visit to Arque to the late general's daughter, Rosemarie, who had been a small girl when her father had died, and could not shed any new light on the matter. But she did tell me about a related experience she had undergone while travelling on the railway my grandfather had helped to build. She had been on her way to Cochabamba when a landslide blocked the track, and everyone was told that the train would be unable to move until the morning. When she heard that they were just outside Arque, she was overcome by 'a strange, ghostly feeling'. Some mysterious genetic force had led her to spend the night where her father's spirit roamed, just as it had led me to her, Rosemarie Barrientos, the granddaughter (as I would discover) of Jorge Galindo, my grandfather's future friend.

I woke up to another brilliant cloudless morning, free of all worries about what this new day would have in store. Before doing anything else I knew at least that we were going to have breakfast with María, who had a wood-fired oven and made 'the best bread and pies in the province'.

She was in an excited state when we arrived. The bus from Cochabamba, which had been prevented from reaching the village for much of the rainy season, had arrived during the night and was on the point of setting off back. She was finishing preparing a consignment of sixty pies to be sold in Cochabamba's market. Her livelihood largely depended on sales such as this. She gave us some pies to try, while her mother prepared some herb tea made from coca leaves. Ricardo sprinkled some 'Andean Viagra' into my tea so that I would be 'fully alert'.

'But what are we going to do today?' I anxiously asked, tasting a liquid that now had a granular texture and an unpleasant potato flavour to it.

'We'll be driving slowly to Cochabamba,' Ricardo answered, 'unless, of course, you want to walk.'

He was fully prepared to walk to Orcoma, the next stop on the line, he said, but Santo Ricardo had warned him of heavy rains, and in any case the track immediately ahead of us was especially problematical. 'Remember, Meechell, what that woman yesterday said about Mr Williams.' He did not need to argue his point any further.

When I said goodbye to the kindly María, I expressed the genuine hope that I would come back to Arque one day, and see her again.

'You will never be returning to Arque,' she insisted, shaking her head and turning to Ricardo. 'I'll never see Mister Meechell again, I'm sure of it. This is the last time I'll see him.'

The road out of Arque left from the top of the village and climbed through steep cultivation up to a high pass, before descending towards a tributary of the main river. A modern suspension bridge could be seen at the bottom of this small valley, but once we were alongside the water, I realized that the road turned away before reaching it, and that the bridge was just an isolated shell.

'They've been wanting to finish that bridge for years, and I don't know what the problem is,' observed Ricardo as the road ahead of us appeared, cut off by cataracts. 'The bridge will make such a difference to the village.'

We got out of the jeep to look at the cataracts that blocked our path. Jesús had had no difficulty in crossing them yesterday; but the water level had obviously risen considerably since then, and, despite the cloudless sky, was continuing to do so almost as we looked at it.

'We're going to have to be quick,' announced Ricardo, 'in ten minutes this is going to be impassable.'

He backed the car one hundred metres down the road, and then pressed his foot down on the accelerator. We rushed at full speed towards the cataracts. Water sprayed the windscreen and rose above the wheels as Ricardo made some manic movements that at one stage tilted the vehicle at an angle of about forty-five degrees. For a few moments we seemed stuck, with two of the wheels madly rotating without engaging; but after some painful scraping noises Ricardo righted the car and drove us onto dry land.

'That was close,' he admitted, once we were steeply climbing again up the other side of the valley. The Cochabamba bus could be seen descending towards the cataracts. 'It's going to get there too late,' Ricardo predicted, 'It'll never make it.' I spared a thought for María and her lovingly prepared pies that would now be going to waste.

As we ascended in a long series of hairpin bends up to the main Oruro-Cochabamba road, the panorama before us was the one my grandfather must have seen with Samuels after their climb from Changolla camp. But reaching the modern asphalt road, after what had seemed like an incursion into a lost world, somehow made the sublime views more pedestrian. We were driving through more familiar-looking territory, with lorries, cars and petrol stations; and soon we were making a well-graded descent into the fertile hills and plains of Bolivia's market garden.

Thirty kilometres from Cochabamba, and with black clouds beginning to obscure the distant snow-streaked mountains behind the town, we left the main road a final time to return to the valley of the railway. This had become gentle, lush, and almost tropical in its climate, with large, rambling villages, densely cultivated fields, and extensive orchards covered in apple and peach trees. Images of bosky retreats from Bourbon Spain were suggested by the name of Buen Retiro, a village once renowned for its important railway-building yard of 1913, now looking like a neglected pleasure pavilion in the middle of a shaded green.

'Meechell,' said Ricardo, 'we need an injection of life.' So we went off to have lunch at a favourite restaurant of his where I was promised a tapioca soup as tasty as any 'woman from Santa Cruz' ('the women from Santa Cruz, Meechell, are the most beautiful in Bolivia').

The restaurant's owner said that the riverside road to Orcoma was passable despite some recent landslides.

'We'll give it a go,' declared Ricardo, more optimistic than ever after a delicious cider-fuelled lunch in a patio embellished with palms and exotic flowers. We finally got moving at around three in the afternoon, and headed again in the Arque direction, following the river as it became hemmed in once more by steep mountains. The sky ahead was turning a terrifying nocturnal black.

'We should get there just in time,' said Ricardo, keener now almost than I was to make a long and difficult detour to the place where my grandfather had spent a short, insignificant period between September and October 1913.

Orcoma, a hamlet only thirteen kilometres downstream from Arque, had been the site of Bethel's new location camp after Changolla was abandoned. I knew only two things about his stay there. First, he was finally joined by his long-promised assistant, who proved to be 'scatty', morbidly touchy, and incapable of 'turning out a neat plan for toffee'. Second, he forsook his 'long and weary trips' by horse in favour of going about in a 'light two-seated buckboard driven by a pair of mules'.

My grandfather was immensely pleased with this 'much more comfortable form of transport', and had enjoyed his frequent drives along a road that was now beginning to be a challenge for us. A few heavy drops of rain had hit the windscreen just after we had reached a point where a recent landslide forced Ricardo to drive along rubble at a sharply raking angle to the river. The sky over the mountains in front of us was not improving, but the drops of rain eventually petered out as, inevitably, did the road.

'It's only about a three kilometres' walk to Orcoma,' said Ricardo, getting out of the jeep, and leaving Jesús to look after it again while he and I went off on our trek. 'We shouldn't be gone for more than an hour.'

Ricardo, a fast walker at the best of times, now set a pace I found difficult to keep up with. Though telling me to pay no heed to the sounds of a distant thunderstorm, he was nonetheless keen to hurry me along a section of railway track spanning a wide tributary river with water gushing just a few inches under the sleepers. To fill those gaps where the sleepers were missing, the inhabitants of the hamlet of Orcoma, now finally within sight, had placed some bundles of twigs tied together with twine.

I had just photographed a beautiful thatched hut, and was about to take a photo of the exquisite wrought-iron columns of Orcoma's tiny railway station, when a flash of lightning was followed almost instantaneously by loud thunder. I suggested to Ricardo that we weather the storm under the station's covered platform; but he firmly rejected this idea.

'We can't afford to do that, Meechell. We've got to get back to the jeep as fast as possible.'

In a torrential downpour, with lightning all around us, we began sprinting back to the car, not even slowing down while crossing the bridge whose sleepers were now slippery and lashed by the water underneath. We ran through deep mud, past two women who were struggling in their many skirts to catch up with their husbands some fifty metres ahead of them, and whom we passed as well. One of the men begged us to wait and give them all a lift, but Ricardo, without stopping, shook his head, and said that our car was too small.

'We can't lose even a minute, Meechell,' he explained to me, as we continued our dash towards the distant Jesús, who appeared to have lost his usual unflappability and was pacing about wildly.

We jumped into the car, and were off in a flash, as if being chased by gangsters firing on all sides. A horrendous rumbling could be heard behind us, and Jesús and I turned our heads round to see what looked like the whole mountain falling into the river, entirely obliterating the patch of land where he had been parked seconds before. The next day, in Cochabamba, I would read a small news item recording the deaths in a landslide of four villagers from Orcoma.

'There are times in life, Meechell, when you have to put your own survival before that of other people. Look what would have happened had we stopped to wait for those villagers. We wouldn't be driving now.'

But how did he know that a landslide was so imminent?

'Working as an engineer in Bolivia, Meechell, gives you an instinct for disasters. And of course I always take heed of the advance warnings from San Ricardo.'

We kept to the river and the railway line once we were past Buen Retiro and back into a green hilly landscape which, in the grey damp aftermath of the storm, seemed almost more Irish than tropical. We were going to Parotani, my grandfather's base from November 1913 onwards, when the 'headquarters construction office' was transferred there from Oruro. It was a period in his life when he began at last to experience the happiness that had so often eluded him in South America.

'I can see why your grandfather liked Parotani so much,' commented Ricardo as we drove through this tranquil village, whose outskirts had several European-style villas 'where rich people from Cochabamba come to stay'. The 'railway compound' was just outside the village and was well-known to Ricardo, who remembered many happy visits here when he was younger, 'when Bolivian railways bothered to maintain the place'. There were, he said, excellent tennis courts, a football field, and comfortable houses surrounded by trees and 'lawns like I imagine you have in England. What a shame it was all left to ruin.'

We parked the jeep as close as it would get to the first of the houses, and walked through a gate into a sodden field where cows were ruminating. 'This is where we played football, Meechell.' Further on, past a train carriage half-buried in mud, and ingeniously recycled as a chicken coop, were two pools with protruding posts that had once supported tennis nets.

'You could swim there now,' said Ricardo, leading me on without pausing to a residential area of bungalows with porches and corrugated-iron cladding. In better days, I imagined, this whole compound must have like one of those North American cabin complexes where I had spent some of the best country holidays of my childhood.

'And these were the quarters reserved for the engineers,' said Ricardo, kicking open the door of one of a group of three particularly spacious buildings.

The interior looked as if someone had deliberately set about smashing it up with a sledgehammer. This was the house where Ricardo often stayed, and he showed me what had been the kitchen, two bedrooms, a large bathroom, and a sitting room with French windows.

'As you can see,' he said, confirming what my grandfather had written, 'these houses were intended not just for bachelors, but for engineers who had families.'

At Parotani, Bethel had had a taste of the pleasures of home-making: he was obliged to buy curtains ('a new experience for me'), and could not hide his delight at being offered 'a ripping armchair' by the company. For the first time since Valparaíso, he had found a place in South America where he could almost see himself living happily as a married man. And it was perhaps because he felt so much at home at Parotani that he was not as upset as he might otherwise have been when he realized he would have to stay on in this continent for six months longer than he had originally intended, 'so as to be able to bring my work to a satisfactory conclusion'.

In addition to his other duties, he had been asked at Parotani to take on those of 'irrigation engineer'. The construction of the railway line here was apparently seriously interfering with a traditional system of irrigation that was 'vital to maintain cultivation during the dry season'.

'Ma chérie,' he anxiously wrote to Sophie on 18 December 1913, 'I came out here full of brave hopes and most optimistic views. It scarcely entered my mind that I should not leave the moment my agreement expired and that nothing would prevent me coming home and carrying you off there and then. Events have proved that there was no particular justification for such hopes and I have now got to look at the practical side of the question very carefully. Sophie, will you wait for me until June or July?'

He urged her to answer him as quickly as possible; and though she obviously wrote back to say yes, his letter must have fermented any doubts she might have had about their relationship. She had been twenty-four when they had become engaged, and she would now be twenty-eight when he returned, if 'circumstances over which I have no control' did not conspire to delay him yet further. Her singing career may not have taken off in the way she had hoped; but she was in the prime of her beauty, gaining ever more distinguished admirers, and maintaining an undiminished faith in the suffragette movement. My grandfather's persistently old-fashioned views on female emancipation, and his recently expressed desire for her 'glorious voice' to be heard just by him and their friends, must have irritated her, and made her wonder how much longer she could remain a virtuous Penelope.

The additional six months in Parotani would have unfortunate consequences for Bethel himself. To try and augment the money he had saved up for his marriage, he unwisely invested it in the nitrate business, which collapsed early in 1914 as a result of the development in Germany of industrial fertilizers. By May of that year he was laid up with a bad dose of malaria, which took several weeks to clear. And when he was finally in a position to book his return passage to Europe, towards the end of June, the world situation was looking more precarious than ever. His last letter from Parotani, indeed his very last letter from South America, was dated 30 June, the day when the habitual reports in the local press about progress on the railway line was superseded by a news item of greater international consequence. Spread in giant letters over the front page of the *El Comercio de Cochabamba* was the announcement that the Archduke Ferdinand had been assassinated at Sarajevo.

Slowly we returned to the early twenty-first century. Past the once 'very pretty little village of Vinto', from where an 'electric tram' had led into Cochabamba, the ever more congested main road shot along a plain dotted with warehouses, small industries, and spreading townships. The lights were shining in a rainy Cochabamba when we left the ever-patient, uncomplaining Jesús to take the night bus to Potosí, where another assignment awaited him.

Ricardo drove me off instead to his suburban home, where he briefly reinvented himself as a responsible family man, surrounded by three delightful attentive children and his quiet, shy schoolteacher wife. We celebrated our still being alive with several jugs of a *singani* cocktails, in the course of which Ricardo again became his familiar immature self, donning a funny wig, and persuading his elder son to put on for my benefit part of the devil's costume worn by dancers at Oruro's carnival.

Nausea and stomach pains coloured my next day's impressions of the town, and made me not fully receptive to the budding carnival spirit due soon to erupt into a nation-wide riot of singing and dancing. The carnival tradition of throwing water-filled balloons at unsuspecting passers-by was one I first discovered on entering what my grandfather had called the 'ripping Plaza'. I remained afterwards, damp and slightly miserable, observing a military ceremony intended to remind the public that not everything to do with the carnival season was fun and games. This was the day when Bolivia had lost its coast to Chile.

★

My momentarily low and sickly mood was at odds with the unusual buoyancy that had come over my grandfather at the time of his first visit to Cochabamba in July 1913. His first impressions were of 'a rather jolly town, and the most attractive I have seen so far in Bolivia'. His good spirits were undoubtedly helped by his always staying at what he considered the country's best hotel, the Hotel Unión, which then stood at the corner of the arcaded nineteenth-century main square. After two and a half years of 'the most terrible deprivations' it was a real treat for him to find an establishment providing 'absolutely top-hole fresh butter, cheese and milk'.

In almost every respect Cochabamba was like civilization as he had once known it, and was in danger of forgetting. He admired the town for following the 'continental custom of having one's drinks at little tables outside the cafés', and he was enthralled by the 'absolutely tip-top military band' that brought 'all of Cochabamba society' out into the main square two nights a week, and had 'the girls putting on their best black lace mantillas'. Furthermore there were electric trams, electric street lights ('a trifle feeble I admit'), and places showing 'the latest Pathé Frères cinematograph films'. 'In fact,' he summed up, 'it is a remarkably developed city when one remembers that every scrap of machinery and material has had to be transported for several days journey on the backs of mules, donkeys and llamas.'

Though he was still dismayed by the general 'want of critical faculties' among the colleagues who came with him to Cochabamba (one of them, at an exhibition of Japanese prints, 'could not even distinguish between a Hokusai and a tea-chest advertisement'), he could always rely on meeting 'interesting people' in the town itself. One of these, the English-born managing director of some nearby tin mines, was 'the most delightful old man I have met in South America'. Known variously as 'old man Read' or 'Don Juan', he was 'a handsome-looking old Johnny' ('and very interesting to talk to') who was married to a Peruvian and had lived out here for over thirty years. He and Bethel soon got into the habit of playing together 'a mild game of what is known as whisky poker before dinner to see who is going to pay for cocktails.'

And then of course there was Jorge Galindo, mention of whose name alone was sufficient for Bethel to get preferential treatment in the Hotel Unión. Seeing the high regard in which the man was held in Cochabamba might perhaps have played a part in Bethel's radical change of opinion about him. From being an unpunctual, unreliable and *chicha*-drinking 'native', Galindo was transformed into 'a most unassuming man who, though an almost confirmed invalid from kidney troubles, is always "merry and bright", always smiling, honest as daylight and a great friend of all the "gringos".' In all Bethel's time in South America, Galindo was the only native-born friend he would make, and among the very few he could trust. 'Although a lawyer and a native, it is generally said of him that he has not an enemy in Cochabamba, and that says a great deal.'

Thanks to Ricardo's wife I had been able to contact Julia Galindo, mother of Susana Sánchez de Lozada. I was invited to have lunch at her apartment, and slowly made my way there, feeling increasingly shaky but unwilling to cancel a meeting likely to throw some light on the distinguished Galindo lineage. Around the corner from the main square I had to make the first of the day's several emergency visits to a toilet. I rushed into the lobby of a cold and unfriendly concrete hotel of the 1980s, picking up a leaflet on my more dignified way out. Unknowingly, I had been throwing up in the modern reincarnation of the Hotel Unión.

The rain did not flatter Cochabamba's dirty and untidy nineteenth-century heart; but I could see it was a lively town, and probably a pleasant and relaxing place to live for those who had money, and could afford the green and exclusive districts immediately beyond the centre. Julia lived just off a broad green avenue that had been the town's out-lying Alameda during my grandfather's time. Her apartment was high up on a smart modern block of flats framed against a backdrop of mountains. A maid answered the door, and showed me through a suite of apparently unlived-in rooms decorated in a neo-rococo style.

Julia, a friendly, motherly old woman who would have been an acceptable presence at tea at 30 Meadway, apologized for the fact that we were going to be eating in the 'breakfast room'. Now that she was a widow, she said, she was very informal in her lifestyle. When I asked for a glass of water she blew a whistle for the maid.

'I'm not very good at family history,' she confessed, 'so I've invited my cousin Augusto along for lunch. He's the family historian.'

I asked her all the same if she knew anything about the lawyer Jorge Galindo. 'Oh, I can tell you about him,' she said with a broad smile, 'He was my father.'

He had died of kidney trouble when she was very young, she told me, after having held for several years, as my grandfather had predicted, the post of governor of Cochabamba province. She took down from the wall an official photo of an aquiline-nosed man proudly wearing a governor's finery. She said that I would find many other photos of him in the 'museum' Augusto had set up in what had been her father's country property.

Augusto, a bespectacled figure with a trimly clipped, military-style moustache, turned up ten minutes later, shortly before the arrival of an old family friend who had been a high court judge at Sucre. The judge, a tall and severe man, talked to me about Bolivia's culture and history in the manner of a formidable professor reluctantly imparting his knowledge to a not particularly bright student. The maid meanwhile served a lunch I did not feel like eating at all.

'A few days of bread and water will do you a world of good,' counselled the judge at a moment when I thought I was about to be sick all over the table and cause irreparable damage to the good relations my grandfather had established with Cochabamba high society. Augusto, who said he had a limited amount of time at his disposal, proposed that the two of us should head off immediately to the 'Galindo Museum'.

We drove beyond the town's outskirts and to an English-style mansion set in a large garden protected by a tall hedge.

'Jorge loved entertaining his friends here,' Augusto told me. 'Perhaps your grandfather was one of them.'

A repulsive, furless hound came up to be stroked as Augusto opened the upper door of a large outhouse. We entered a loft as crammed with diverse objects as my grandparents' attic had been, but with everything methodically arranged in well-ordered table and cabinet displays, neat piles of papers, and walls papered with long rows of photos.

Augusto was immediately able to single out the photos featuring Jorge Galindo, including a picture of him at the opening in 1916 of the Oruro-Cochabamba railway. He then handed me a heavy, vellum-bound volume in which he had penned in an italic hand the names and details of every member of his family. After I had dutifully copied down what he had written about his uncle Jorge, he showed me numerous books, manuscripts and newspaper articles so that I should be left in no doubt about the formidable pedigree of the family I was dealing with.

As with all Bolivia's ruling families who had risen to power in the nineteenth century, the Galindos had made strenuous efforts in the past to establish ancient and aristocratic Spanish roots. One genealogical work I skimmed through insisted that the family were direct descendants of the Goths who had come into Spain after the sixth century AD, and that a later member had been a knight who had fought with El Cid. There was of course not a shred of evidence to support this, and the Galindos were more likely to have been the offspring of Spanish peasants down on their luck. But whatever their Spanish origins, there was no question that they had achieved great honours since settling in the New World. One had been an officer of Bolívar and a hero of the battle of Ayacucho; many had become governors of Sucre and Cochabamba provinces; and several had even been elected vice-presidents and presidents of Bolivia.

What ended up entirely absorbing my attention, however, was a recently published book by General Eduardo Galindo entitled *Chronicles of a Soldier when We Confronted Che*.

'That's a work by my brother,' remarked Augusto. 'Although he's never been properly credited with this, he was the soldier who captured Che. He was the real hero of the day.'

I had never thought of the Bolivian army's easy capture in 1967 of Che's puny guerrilla force as being in the slightest bit heroic, least of all their subsequent summary execution of him. Che's attempt to turn the South American jungle into another Vietnam may have been, as Alistair Horne has written, 'one of the greatest flops of the century'; but the only person out of this whole sorry episode who deserved to be called a hero was surely Che himself.

I have never been politically active in my life, nor have I ever been fired by burning political idealism; and yet there was a time during my teenage years in the 1960s when, almost concurrently with the discovery of my grandfather's letters, I had become obsessed by Che and the Cuban revolution. I filled my bedroom in Hampstead Garden

Suburb with books and posters supplied to me by London's Cuban embassy; I regularly attended the Cuban film festivals at the National Film Theatre; and I won my first and as yet only literary prize with a school essay on 'Post-Revolutionary Cuban Literature'.

Augusto was holding a Rolex watch for me to look at. 'This belonged to one of the soldiers who were killed fighting alongside Che.'

I took it into my hand, and fingered it as respectfully and thoughtfully as if it were a saintly relic. My passionate admiration for Che had survived my disillusion with Cuba, which I had finally visited in the 1990s. And though the watch I was touching was not actually his, and though the fact of its being a Rolex was somehow incongruous in the context of revolutionary socialism, the very touching of it seemed for a short while to bring me closer to his spirit.

I did not want to let go of it; I had begun almost to believe that it would also absolve me of some of my guilt, both as a Westerner in South America and as the grandson of someone complicit in the exploitation of the continent. 'When my brother gave the watch to me,' Augusto now muttered, 'it was covered in blood. I made the great mistake of wiping this all off. I felt better at the time for doing so.'

7

Dancing with Devils

———◇◇◇———

'LEFT LEG FORWARD! Right leg across! And step! Sway to the left! Sway to the right! Right leg forward! Left leg across! And turn!'

A loud, monotonous, hypnotic cacophony of bugles, trumpets, voices and drums was resounding from a pair of speakers, and competing with the muffled instructions issuing from the metallic, pipe-smoking mouth of the devil standing before me. I was in Ricardo's home, taking my first lesson in carnival dancing from Ricardo's elder son Pablo.

I am a terrible dancer; I was genetically disposed to be one. 'I never was a dancing man. You'll have to teach me,' Bethel wrote once to Sophie, who would later try on frequent occasions to persuade me to take up dancing lessons. I foolishly thought this ridiculous, being a serious young man at the time, wary of frivolity, busying myself by going to Bergman films at the Hampstead Everyman, attempting to read the whole of *Don Quixote* in the original, and doing the sort of things I would have been better advised leaving for my middle years, had not my life been strangely lived in reverse, causing me in my late forties to live for five years above a Spanish village disco.

I now love dancing, but I do it in the same way that my father was said to have danced – chaotically, manically, in mad bursts of sudden energy and enthusiasm, uncontrolled by any sense of rhythm or coordination, and with arms, body and legs acting irrespective of the music and of each other.

'You're getting better,' said Pablo kindly, persuading me with these unwise words of encouragement to pursue my dancing beyond the sitting-room floor of Ricardo's Cochabamba home, and on into the streets and discos of a Bolivia infected by a mounting carnival fervour impervious, so it seemed, to the country's growing political instability.

The truce given to President Carlos Mesa by his opponents was coming to an end; road blockades were threatening soon to spread everywhere; and indigenous demands for the nationalization of Bolivia's newly discovered reserves of natural gas had become so intransigent that violence appeared the only solution to the country's problems. Thinking about all this as I thought about my grandfather's final, war-shadowed weeks in South America would lend an occasional grotesque element to the spectacle of carnival. Parading devils would be turned in my imagination into marching soldiers, and pipe-smoking masks into gas masks; and all the dancing would come to seem like the final act of defiance of a world headed towards apocalypse.

My pilgrimage to the places in Bolivia where my grandfather had worked was nearly over. I had library research to do, a carnival appointment to keep at Oruro, and a personal ambition to cross the salt flat of Uyuni. But as far as my grandfather was concerned, the main destination I still had left to visit was Potosí; and to get there from Cochabamba I would have to pass through a town that Bethel might or might not have been to, but which I was desperate to see for myself – Sucre.

'I must see Sucre before I leave,' wrote Bethel early in 1913, and I was sure he would have loved the place as much as I did. In my case the love affair was instantaneous. I treated myself to the half-hour flight from Cochabamba, and was met at the airport by the young couple whom I had got to know on the Calama train, Jorge and Marbel. Their warm, emotional welcome was like that of the town itself, which, white and shining in the morning sun, was waiting for me like a familiar friend in the luscious green bowl of its mountain setting.

It was officially the capital city, yet Sucre had the feel of a quiet and sophisticated university town, barely troubled by industries or glaring modern buildings. As I went with my hosts on a preliminary walk around the centre, I took mental note of the features my grandfather would have liked – the relaxed atmosphere, the European-style cafés, the landscaped central square, the elegant French neoclassicism of its theatres and official buildings, and even the miniature imitation of the Eiffel Tower that stood shaking in the wind in the Parque Bolívar.

But what made Sucre so pleasantly recognizable for me was its pervasive Spanishness. The architects who had worked here after Bolivia's independence from Spain may have tried to impose a French look on their country's new capital, but for all their efforts they had not eroded the impression of being in a small aristocratic Andalucían town such as Carmona. I felt as if I already knew the place intimately, and, what is more, had been there in my teens. When I entered the law faculty of the university, one of the oldest in the Americas, my nostrils were assailed by a smoke-infused, sweetish mustiness that had as strong an effect on me as the *madeleines* had had on Proust. I was back in the austere collegiate world of Salamanca university, taking a language course there at a time when the statue of its former rector Unamuno was still regularly daubed with red to show that his heart still bled for Spain.

Staying with Jorge and Marbel was another nostalgic experience, in this case one that evoked student days of sleeping on other people's floors, using outdoor toilets, and doing things together in large groups. Their cramped and informal quarters, more comfortable for me than any smart hotel, helped make me feel immediately part of an extended family that included Jorge's child-like student sister, Marbel's eight siblings, and two young children who, like all the Bolivian children I had met, were exquisitely mannered.

A key figure in the household was Marbel's younger brother Oswald, a tall young man, whose good looks were as old-fashioned as his clothes. Oswald was like the mischievous hero of an old Spanish film, and had bundles of charm, and an enormously complex love life that he was fortunately able to combine with his work as 'cultural officer' at Sucre's Town Hall. His duties were particularly onerous at carnival time. He had the job of organizing the competitions to choose each year's Carnival Queen and '*Cholita*', the latter competition being among the mestizo people in the surrounding villages.

Oswald thought I might find the *Cholita* competition of 'particular ethnographic interest'. It took place in one of Sucre's old theatres, where I was made to sit alongside a judging panel comprising the town's leading intellectuals, who were immediately recognizable as such by virtue of attributes like neckties and broad-rimmed felt hats. They sat with notebooks in hand as each of the multi-skirted *cholitas* stepped with varying degrees of shyness onto the stage, answered challenging questions from Oswald (e.g. 'What is your favourite food?'), and did a dance involving the waving of a handkerchief.

The judges, identifying me as a fellow ageing intellectual, asked me which of the *cholitas* I personally would choose. I made the great mistake of going for vivacity, intelligence and confidence.

'You've got it all wrong,' I was politely corrected by the author of the leading study to date of Sucre's carnival traditions. 'What we're looking for in a *cholita* is a certain naïve village awkwardness.'

The general agreement of the judges was that I would be better suited to help them elect the Carnival Queen in a few days' time, a more straightforward task. Sadly, I said, I would be elsewhere by then. As a consolation I was able to accompany the potential candidates to one of the several Sucre discos regularly visited by Oswald and his circle.

The dancing in these places was inevitably preceded by karaoke, a craze that has probably lasted longer in Bolivia than in any other country of the world. My singing is on a par with my dancing; but as this night was going to be my last before Potosí I was persuaded with the aid of copious quantities of *singani* to take up the microphone and sing a Beatles song whose lyrics well matched the sentimental mood the town had put me in.

'Yesterday,' warbled my discordant voice, 'all my troubles seemed so far away . . . Yesterday, love was such an easy game to play . . . Oh, I believe in yesterday.'

I did not want to leave Sucre, where I could have seen myself happily living for ever. But my grandfather was waiting for me at daunting Potosí, where I was also being pulled by a morbid curiosity going back to the days when I had learnt my first Spanish phrase, '*Vale un Potosí*,' – 'It's worth a fortune.'

After enjoying the relaxing intimacy of small-town life, I now had to prepare myself for a place I did not think of as a town at all but rather as a cautionary tale about the rise and fall of civilizations. Potosí alone had made Spain rich, and had almost single-handedly financed a golden age as magnificent as any that a nation has ever known; but Potosí, with a history that Bethel had described as 'romantic' but others have generally perceived as terrible, had also done much to foster Spain's still lingering image as a country where greatness had been achieved through acts of immeasurable cruelty.

My grandfather had luckily gone to Potosí for the first time without any preconceptions at all. The place, as he himself confessed to Sophie, was one whose name had conveyed almost nothing to him before he had come to South America. His subsequent shock at discovering, in the middle of nowhere, a town that for a while had been one of the largest in the world, was so great as to inspire not only the longest letter he ever wrote to Sophie but also a passion for history that would be inherited by his descendants. At a time when his job had become more prosaic than ever, Bethel's contact with 'wonderfully interesting, historic and picturesque' Potosí was like a brush with the sublime.

My grandfather had been one of the first to have travelled by train to this once famously remote destination. I was going in a shared taxi along a modern asphalt road that reduced the journey from Sucre to only two hours, and probably managed even more than the branch line had done to make the trip to Potosí seem remarkably unchallenging. The landscape too was much greener than I had imagined, and only disintegrated into bleak expanses of rubble in the very last stages of the gentle climb, when Potosí's legendary Cerro Rico (rich peak) was finally identifiable. Seen from the Sucre road this mountain, which had made Spain's empire, had the disappointing appearance of a giant slag heap.

Like Chuquicamata, the Cerro Rico had been a mountain sacred to the Indians. Its extraordinary mineral wealth had been known to them for centuries, but was kept secret from the Spaniards. Even when the secret was finally out, revealed by an indigenous servant (who in turn had it from another servant who had worked for the Inca ruler Huayna Capac), few Indians would have believed the Spaniards mad enough to establish a township at well over 4,000 metres high, where the nights were freezing even at the height of summer, and where the air was so rarefied that only those born to such an altitude could move energetically around without becoming, in my grandfather's phrase, 'horribly out of puff'.

But this is exactly what the Spaniards did, a year after the indigenous servant's treachery in 1545. Two years later Charles V gave the town at the foot of the Cerro Rico the status of '*Villa Imperial*', and awarded the servant's Spanish master Juan de Villaroel the title of 'Discoverer of the Hill and Founder of the Town'. Mining was carried out at first on the uppermost part of this conical 'hill', where the richest veins were to be found, and where the silver was of such high quality that traditional Andean refining systems featuring primitive 'wind ovens' could be used. However, as the purer silver near the earth's surface began to be exhausted, and demand for silver increased, the Spaniards had to consider new and more sophisticated systems of processing which involved amalgamation with mercury and the use of water-powered 'crushing refineries'.

Until the early 1570s the Indians had had a considerable degree of control over how the silver was produced and marketed; but all this would change with the arrival at Potosí in 1572 of Viceroy Francisco de Toledo. Viceroy Toledo was the man responsible for finally implementing the new techniques of silver production, and the consequent building of twenty-four artificial lakes that were among the marvels of sixteenth-century engineering. He made many other major improvements to Potosí, including the widening of its streets, the founding of a mint, and the creation of a canal spanned by twenty-two bridges. But sadly he will always be popularly remembered not for these enlightened acts but for the establishment of the notorious *mita*, a system of forced labour based on Inca institutions.

As a result of this particular ordinance, 1,600 men could be recruited each year from all over the Andes, and sent to work for a token payment in the Potosí mines. This was part of Toledo's policy of slowly transferring the mountains' inhabitants from hamlets into more governable towns, which ultimately had dire consequences for Andean agriculture. Potosí itself grew almost to the size of London, and its silver production increased fourfold; but the unhealthy climate and dreadful working conditions in the mines caused massive fatalities among an indigenous population divided from the Spaniards by Toledo and housed in a separate part of the town.

This strict racial segregation, in force right up to the revolution of 1952, was unmentioned by my grandfather, whose main references to the local Indians was to their being 'much more interesting than in Oruro, less influenced by the European habits and costumes, and nearly always bare-legged and wearing sandals'. As for their role in

Potosí's history, he thought this barely worth mentioning other than to emphasize that they 'were in a very dangerous majority against the Spaniards', whose achievement here he perceived as another example of the West's heroic endeavours in civilizing an environmentally hostile South America.

He was even optimistic about the future of modern Potosí, an insignificant place in comparison with the seventeenth-century city. Though remaining the largest town in South America right up to the beginning of the nineteenth century, the near exhaustion of the silver seams soon brought about a dramatic decline that was only halted by the boom in tin mining from the 1890s onwards.

When Bethel came here, in continuing pursuit of absentee land-owners from the Cochabamba area, the population was a mere 25,000; but, with the imminent 'handing over of the railway to regular public service', he predicted that 'things will begin to liven up pretty considerably in this old town.' As it was, the Potosí he found was not the sad place living off past glories that one might have envisaged. It was, like Cochabamba, a town with all the necessary modern facilities and comforts, including street lighting 'even in the poorest streets in the purely Indian quarters' ('power is cheap, and so no doubt it is adopted in such quarters in view of keeping down crime'). Much to his delight and amusement, he was also able once again to see 'the very best of Pathé Frères' films', and to do so this time in a church converted into a 'combined roller-skating rink and cinematograph hall'.

By chance I discovered, within half an hour of my arrival from Sucre, just where this cinema had stood. The building was now the headquarters of a local organization called PRAH, an acronym standing for the 'Proyecto de Recuperación de sus Áreas Históricas'. I had set off there immediately after booking into a shabby, unheated hotel with a deceptively magnificent baroque façade. In my hand was a letter of introduction to the organization's director Luis Prados, with whom the Andalucían government was collaborating in the restoration of a town that still contains one of the finest and most extensive complexes of Spanish colonial architecture in the world.

The task of restoration was an urgent one. Following the collapse of the world market in tin in 1985 Potosí had become Bolivia's poorest large city; and this was noticeable even in the five minutes it took me to get to the PRAH from my hotel. After white and shining Sucre, Potosí seemed a town of grubby ochres and maroons, collapsing plasterwork, diseased stone, and sad glazed balconies in rotting painted wood. Even the recently rehabilitated PRAH building, with its incongruous plate glass façade intended to symbolize the town's resurgent spirit, had already a worn and tattered look. The glass main door, cracked in one corner, needed a mighty push before I could get into the building's cold and gloomy lobby.

I had high hopes of Luis Prados, and a mental picture of him as a warm, modest and almost saintly person. A childhood friend of President Carlos Mesa, as well as an architect and restorer of international reputation, he had been offered major jobs in La Paz, and throughout the world, but had turned down all these so that he could devote himself to his beloved Potosí. This was at any rate what I had heard from a mutual friend from Seville, who was working with Prados on an architectural guide also to be financed by the Andalucíans. The finished product was going to have an unrecognizably glamorous cover photo of the PRAH building's façade, together with an English text acknowledging the 'valuable contribution and sacrifice of thousands and thousands of Andean men' in the building of Potosí. 'Today we owe them recognition, sincere respect and a profound commitment to preserve both their memory and their achievements.'

The small, white-haired man in the dark, wide-lapelled overcoat who came up to shake my hands in the waiting-room did not have the appearance of a humble saint. I saw him more as the melancholy dictator of some banana republic. He took a brief glance at the letter I had brought, and instantly offered to help me in any possible way. Such was the apparent extent of his power that I soon was promised the use of a car and driver, 'should you need them', and virtual carte blanche to visit any of Potosí's countless closed churches and palaces.

Over breakfast the next morning at my hotel, after a night so cold that I was shivering even in long johns and a thermal vest, the mild-mannered middle-aged woman who ran the establishment came up to talk to me.

'I hear you went yesterday to see Luis Prados,' she said. Before I could ask her how she had known this she started to criticize him forcefully.

'He acts as if he owns the town, and speaks always about his great love for the place. But I doubt if he even lives here. There are not many people in Potosí who care for him.'

She claimed that his so-called restoration was doing more harm than good ('He pays a pittance to young boys who haven't a clue'), and that the money coming in from Spain was being used in a 'dubious fashion'. She hinted at a web of corruption centred on Spanish business interests.

I tried momentarily to put aside dark thoughts and to become absorbed instead by the undeniable architectural achievements of the Spaniards. To a greater extent even than in Spain itself, the architecture of Potosí was one of violent contrasts, with portals and soaring altar-pieces of breathtakingly intricate elaboration and richness contained within essentially simple structures, some with bare adobe walls and wooden ceilings that looked like the upturned hulls of ships. The famous mint, where my grandfather had been overawed by the thought of the 'small army of Indians' necessary for the transport of 'the huge baulks of timber', was like a secular version of Spain's terrifyingly austere Escorial, and conveyed more than any other building I had ever seen the megalomaniac grandeur of Spain's imperial ambitions.

But the churches of the 'poorer, Indian quarters' were the build-ings that most moved me. Their ornamental and material wealth stood out against the humility of surroundings where I found myself, more often than not, the only white man. Greetings of 'Mister', to which my grandfather and his Anglo-Saxon contemporaries had probably been frequently subjected, alternated more bizarrely with ones of 'Padre' or 'Father'. The former Sucre disco dancer was now being mistaken for a Spanish priest, which led to some unusual situations.

'Father,' asked one man, anxious to benefit from my priestly fund of learning, 'are the Spanish gypsies of Norwegian origin?'

At least three women genuflected in front of me, and one of them touched my black T-shirt in case it might confer on her some of my holiness. Another woman asked me for my blessing, which put me in a particularly difficult position. Unwilling by this stage to be exposed as an impostor, I eventually made the sign of the cross, muttered some words in Latin, and told her to go away in peace. She went off with a beatific smile.

Throughout all this pleasant time of wandering and sightseeing, I paused periodically to cast a respectful glance at the Cerro Rico, which, since my first sighting of it as a grey slag heap shiny with rain, had undergone several spectacular transformations, including into a starkly sombre red pyramid, and into a delicate Fuji-like mountain crowned with snow. Sooner or later I knew I would have to confront the demons who lay inside.

'There are those who, having entered only out of curiosity to see that horrible labyrinth, have come out totally robbed of colour, grinding their teeth and unable to pronounce a word; they have not known even how to ponder it nor make reference to the horrors that are in there.' So wrote a Spanish historian in 1701 of the thousands of 'rat-holes' (my grandfather's phrase) that make up what is now Potosí's principal tourist attraction. All modern guidebooks warn of the dangers of a visit to the Cerro Rico's old mines, where the conditions of working have not changed since the sixteenth century, and where, in the words of the *Rough Guide to Bolivia*, 'safety precautions are largely left to supernatural forces.' The almost gloating descriptions of crawling for hours along muddy passages, avoiding falling rocks and speeding mine trolleys, suffering temperatures ranging from freezing to forty-five degrees centigrade, and breathing in air fetid with dust and poisonous gases, have had of course an effect opposite to the one purportedly intended. To those following the backpacker trail around South America, a visit to Potosí's mines has become an activity comparable to bungee-jumping or hang-gliding.

This last thought alone was enough to make me opt out of going down into one of the sixteenth-century mines. Instead I compromised by taking up Luis Prados's kind offer of a private visit to a modern and easily accessible mine that the PRAH was currently turning into a museum. The director of this, a retired miner, led me down a large and gently sloping shaft, off which there was a group of spacious interconnected chambers where minute particles of silver could still be detected. I was shown the future locations of a conference room and an 'audio-visual centre', told about plans for realistic sound effects and waxwork mock-ups, and left with the revealing news that the Cerro Rico was so criss-crossed with horizontal and vertical shafts that one day the whole mountain would collapse on top of Potosí, destroying all the rehabilitation that the PRAH might by then have succeeded in achieving.

I had no idea whether my grandfather himself had been brave enough to descend into one of the 'rat-holes' he had mentioned; but what I did know was that he had walked to the top of the Cerro Rico. Any unexpressed pangs of conscience he might have felt about the Indian miners would have taken secondary place to the emotion he had experienced near the summit of discovering 'a steel girder bearing the name of the Frodingham Iron and Steel Works'.

'Frodingham,' as he went on to remind Sophie, 'is not 30 miles from Hull and they were the first steel works I ever went over.'

Potosí might have awakened in Bethel an interest in a culture different to any he had known before; but it was also a place, like Cochabamba, full of reminders of those aspects of Europe he loved above all others. Paris in particular was a town he now had frequent opportunity to recall, thanks to the many hours he spent with two of Potosí's most 'interesting' residents, 'Señor Isidoro Aramayo', and 'Don Luis Soux'. The former, a brother of one of Bolivia's leading tin barons, had been a seventy-year-old mining engineer who enchanted Bethel by going around Potosí in a top hat and frock coat, and by having been educated at Paris's École des Mines at a time when this institution was situated in the centre of the Quartier Latin. Bethel could barely contain his excitement at the thought that Aramayo 'must have been almost a contemporary of the students of Mürger's *Scènes de la vie de Bohême* or of De Musset's *Mimi Pinson*.'

With Luis Soux, a Frenchman who had been living in Potosí for over thirty years, Bethel formed an even closer friendship. My grandfather had gone originally to see him about land purchase, but immediately had got talking about other matters. He later described Soux, then in his mid-fifties, as 'the most delightful and unassuming old man to talk to'.

Soux's story was an especially intriguing one. He had originally been persuaded to come to Bolivia after meeting the future Bolivian president Aniceto Arce at the inauguration of the Eiffel Tower in 1881. After saying goodbye at Marseilles to the parents he would never see again, Soux set sail with Arce to work as an engineer in one of the latter's mines. When Arce moved into politics, Soux went his separate way, and soon settled in Potosí to became a mine owner himself. Always abreast of the latest technological developments, it was he who had introduced electricity to Potosí, as well as such other innovations as an English-built 'ropeway' whereby loaded buckets coming down from the mines on the Cerro Rico pulled up the empty ones. By December 1912 he was on the point of installing in his mines some pioneering 'compressed air drills', on which Bethel 'was able to give him some tips'.

By this date Soux was 'turning out more than a quarter of the whole mineral production of Potosí today'. As Bethel rightly reckoned, Soux was already a 'very wealthy man'; and his wealth would become far greater over the next two decades, when he came gradually to acquire the majority of the town's mines. Only towards the very end of his long life did his fortunes begin seriously to dwindle, as a result of his wife putting huge sums of money both into the building of a local hospital and into Bolivia's disastrous war with Paraguay. Soux's children (two of whom married into English engineering families) did not share their father's business acumen; and the family's decline was hastened further when the state confiscated the Soux mines in 1952.

When I asked Luis Prados what he knew about Soux, I discovered, as I had suspected, that the man who had once been one of the most important in Bolivia was now a forgotten figure even in Potosí. But I was told that three of his grandchildren still lived in the area; and I was able to track one of them down to a bar on Potosí's tall and sloping main square.

This grandson's name was Arturo Layton, and the bar, of which he was the owner, was dwarfed within a monumental eighteenth-century church that my grandfather had mentioned as having been transformed into a theatre. The theatre, controversially remodelled by Luis Prados, was still there, and its auditorium now rested on giant columns above a handful of bar tables, where a group of half a dozen tourists listened in respectful silence to an Andean band playing 'El condor pasa'.

Arturo was a stooped chain-smoker whose blue eyes and blonde hair betrayed his northern European ancestry. When I introduced myself to him as the grandson of one of Luis Soux's English friends, his worn, troubled-looking face relaxed into a smile. When the music was over, he sat down with me at one of the tables as if to take up a conversation that had been interrupted more than eighty years before. After an hour of catching up on what had been happening in Potosí over all that time, we were joined by his lively and glamorous wife, whose Italian origins were revealed in the dish of food she asked the waiter to bring us – 'llama *involtini*'. Arturo went out to look for a bottle of the family wine on which their hopes had largely been placed of being able one day to make enough money to return to Europe. We made a toast to the meeting which our ancestors had ordained.

'Friendships that are made in this way,' said the wife, 'are always the most special ones.'

With the car and driver that Luis Prados had promised, I went with Arturo one sunny morning to the Soux country property, the Hacienda de Cayara, which was twenty kilometres further down the mountain from Potosí, and had a 'less demanding climate'. At the entrance to the narrow green valley in which it lay was a huge and abandoned factory, the one ugly note in an otherwise idyllic landscape. I was told that it was a Soviet-built 'tin purification plant'.

'When my grandfather decided in the 1880s to export tin and not silver,' Arturo said, 'everyone thought he was mad. Then the First World War turned tin into the world's most sought-after commodity. The boom managed to last for much of the century. But, like every boom, it suddenly ended.' The factory we had passed had never properly functioned, and would not have the time to do so. 'The world tin crisis of 1985 saw to that.'

The hacienda reclined among willows, cypresses and pines at the end of the valley, in front of rocky cliffs streaked by a distant waterfall. Painted a reddish ochre, it was now occupied by two other grandchildren of Soux, one of whom, Juan Jorge Aitken, had turned part of it into an exclusive country retreat for tourists. Aitken had gone away on a business trip to Cochabamba; but in his stead we were met in its large stone courtyard by another of Arturo's cousins, Edgar Soux.

The two men were utterly unlike in appearance. The smiling, moustachioed Edgar, the older of the two by a good ten years, was a man in his early sixties dressed in a casual country suit and deerstalker hat. He looked like an amiable Inspector Clouseau on an English country-house weekend. 'Welcome to the Hacienda de Cayara,' he said, shaking my hand before proceeding to give me a short account of the place in a low, gentle voice. I had already heard from Arturo that Edgar was a gentleman scholar who devoted his time to writing and studying history.

'This estate,' Edgar continued, 'was the first to be created after Charles V had granted Potosí its royal charter. The family who owned it went off to Spain in 1616 to buy the title of marquis. But the place was in a terrible state when my grandfather bought it in 1898. There was even a sheep in the sitting room.'

We walked into an intimate, crowded interior that seemed tailored to fit both my passion for Spain and my inescapable roots in Hampstead Garden Suburb. Sixteenth-century suits of armour, a Moorish-crafted writing desk, heavy oak chests, stone coats of arms, and other furnishings from Spanish colonial times, happily shared space with the sort of objects that had filled up 30 Meadway – dog-eared Gallimard paperbacks, framed sepia photos, glass cabinets, French-polished mahogany tables , a mah-jong set – I felt as if I had reached a destination I had been heading towards all my life.

While Edgar went off to 'make a pot of tea', Arturo took me outside to walk towards the waterfall.

'One of the reasons why my grandfather bought the property was that it came with the local water rights,' he told me. 'He needed these to build Potosí's first electrical generator.'

The generator, installed within a now decrepit outhouse, was still in good working order, though it only produced electricity now for the Cayara valley and not for Potosí itself. Above it hung a warped portrait canvas that made Luis Soux look like a bearded Spanish hidalgo gone prematurely white.

Back in the hacienda, sipping our cups of tea, Edgar expressed views about history that could have been my grandfather's, and he did so in the unassuming tone that Bethel had characterized as that of Soux. In Edgar's view South America had never been the same great continent ever since the influence of Europe had been succeeded by that of the United States.

'It was our grandfathers and their generation who were responsible for the major technological innovations in this country, and who brought here culture, civilization and hope for the future. Bolivia, alas, is no longer the same place.'

His smile remained a wistful one as he went on to define Europe essentially in terms of France and Britain, 'the two great nations of modern times'. Italy, another country whose culture he loved, had sadly rested too much on its past laurels; and Spain had been in terminal decline since its golden age. 'No,' he repeated, 'there's no question about it. The most important scientists, politicians, artists and writers since the nineteenth century have all been French or English.' He asked me who I thought his greatest heroes were. I could not guess. 'Napoleon,' he said, 'that goes without saying. And Winston Churchill.'

He paused for several moments as if waiting for my reaction to this statement, allowing Arturo to butt in and say that I was anxious now to see the tomb of Luis Soux. Edgar led me outside immediately to a sixteenth-century chapel where, for a few moments, I stood with bowed head before a slab placed directly in front of the high altar. I was doing what Bethel would surely have done himself. The slab's inscription read 'Luis Soux, Sainte Croix de Voluestre, November 5, 1855 – Potosí, October 18, 1939'. He had died only a couple of weeks before his 84th birthday.

Perhaps it was seeing this inscription that spurred me on to pursue what was becoming a developing mania during my last days in Bolivia – to find something here in writing that recorded my grandfather's stay in this country, something that showed he had not passed through here completely unperceived. On our return later that day to Potosí, Arturo became a willing assistant in my quest.

Though there was said to be material in the provincial archives relating to the railway and its staff, we thought it best in the little time we had to concentrate our researches on local institutions with which British engineers were likely to have been associated. Hearing of my grandfather's sporting interests, Arturo telephoned Potosí's English-founded 'Lawn Tennis Club', and then a football club which had originally been called 'Highland Place'; but neither institution, he discovered, maintained records earlier than the 1930s. 'We're bound at least to find something in the Club Internacional,' he assured me, referring to an old gentleman's club that now occupied premises of athenaeum-like grandeur on top of the town's main square.

The overwhelmingly charming president of the club greeted us in the building's library. 'We have annual records going back to 1897, the year of the club's foundation,' he announced, delighted to be of assistance. He then produced the earliest of a large group of cloth-bound volumes containing summaries of debates and discussions, financial accounts, and the names of each year's members. He agreed that my grandfather, as a regular visitor to Potosí from November 1912 right up to June 1914, would almost certainly have taken up temporary membership of the club. I skimmed through the records until I reached October 1912, when the last of the volumes I had been given came to an end. The president went back to the shelves, and returned with dismaying news. 'I'm afraid that the records for the two years you're looking for are missing.'

Sitting afterwards with Arturo having a coffee, I suddenly remembered what the woman from the strange late-night bar in La Paz had told me. As a long shot I asked if there was any point in visiting Potosí's Masonic Lodge. 'I should have thought of that immediately!' said Arturo, 'Almost all the British railway engineers in Bolivia and Chile were Masons.'

Through the intercession of the all-powerful Luis Prados, we managed to arrange a meeting at the Lodge for that evening. The door of the modest-sized old building in which this was housed was opened by the institution's secretary, who took us across a shabby courtyard to a small room decorated with a symbolical canvas featuring the words 'Honour and Prudence'. The secretary reminded me that I was not to take photographs.

'This Lodge,' he said, 'was the first in Bolivia. It was founded in 1913 by engineers who had belonged to the Antofagasta Lodge.'

He showed me a photocopied article from a Masonic magazine in which was described this historic inaugural meeting of 'January 17, 1913', the date of one of my grandfather's letters from Potosí. The surnames of the Lodge's twelve founder members were all listed, together with their countries of origin. There were two Chileans, a Pole, a Frenchman, an Italian, a Dalmatian, three Scots and three Englishmen. One of the Englishmen was called Jacobs.

Reading the rest of the article made me soon realise that the Jacobs referred to was not Bethel Lyon, but rather a person whose first names were David Maurice. High hopes had again been dashed, though in the process a further twist had been given to the ongoing Borgesian mystery connected with Bethel's engineer namesake in Bolivia. Was the latter none other than the Potosí Mason? Was this Mason the father of future Mason 'Miguel Jacobs', better known as 'Jacobs the Engineer'? And was it pure coincidence that David Maurice Jacobs happened to be the full name of my own father?

I had no more time to pursue all this. The main carnival celebrations were due to begin at Oruro in less than thirty-six hours; Rosemarie Barrientos was already waiting for me there; and my newly learnt dance steps were in danger of being forgotten. I purchased a ticket for a bus departing for Oruro at seven in the morning.

Unable to find a taxi I walked in the cold wet dawn all the way down a long steep hill to where the bus was leaving, and was told that it had been cancelled. The replacement was not expected until three in the afternoon, so I went unhappily back up the formidable slope, pausing to regain my breath next to the town's surprisingly grand and well-maintained railway station. Here, oddly enough, my grandfather, also on his way to Oruro, had turned up early one morning to find that the once-weekly train had left long before it was scheduled to do so. 'My feelings on trudging back a mile of steep hill to the hotel can be better imagined than described!'

I returned to the bus stop just before three o'clock, and the bus arrived at five. Stepping aboard, my right foot slipped into a pothole, causing a sudden stab of pain. I could still walk, but once I had got to my seat and had been sitting for half an hour, I was conscious that my foot was rapidly swelling up. The pleasant young Aymaran next to me had begun talking about the Oruro carnival, to which he had been looking forward for months. 'You can't go to Oruro without dancing,' he said, 'Everyone dances at Oruro.'

I mentioned having badly hurt my foot. 'Just soak it in a hot infusion of coca leaves when you get to the hotel, wrap it tightly in a bandage, and you'll be absolutely fine.' I wondered if this man was related to Ricardo.

The pain was soon almost constant and so strong at times that I turned pale and sickly. My travelling companion, noticing this new development, offered further words of wisdom.

'It's quite clear to me now what has happened. You had doubts about dancing at Oruro, and the Virgin of the Socavón, to whom the festival is dedicated, has punished you. But the Virgin is very forgiving. If you pray to her she will come to your aid.'

Arriving that night at Oruro I almost fainted on getting out of the bus, but managed slowly to hobble into a taxi, and from there into the lobby of my booked hotel. I had surely broken some bone in my foot, and was thinking about the irony of having done so in so stupid a fashion after having survived up till then so many dangerous situations. My crippled entry into this smart hotel was certainly not that of a returning hero. A group of elegant people observed me as if I were a beggar upsetting their world.

I hoped that Rosemarie Barrientos was not among them. Before seeing her, I needed to get to my bedroom, freshen up, try the experiment with the coca leaves, and pray for a miracle from the Virgin of the Socavón.

'Are you Michael?' asked a smiling woman as I waited at the reception desk for the bedroom key. She had thick shoulder-length dark hair, and looked much younger than someone in her early forties, as I had calculated General Barrientos's daughter to be. 'I'm Rosemarie.' She seemed warm and easy-going, and showed immediate concern about my injury. 'Don't worry,' she reassured me, 'the restaurant I've booked for supper is just round the corner.'

But before letting me up to my room, she introduced me to the others in the lobby. They were different from her, displaying the pampered, over-manicured look of tetchy South American soap stars. Later that night she would tell me in more detail who some of these people had been. One woman was the sister of Sánchez de Lozada's predecessor as Bolivian president, Horacio Quiroga; another was the anorexic-looking fashion model daughter of current president Carlos Mesa; and a third was the daughter of the most notoriously brutal of Bolivia's military rulers, General Luis García Meza, now serving a prison charge for smuggling drugs. The incestuousness of Bolivia's political elite could not have been better illustrated.

Rosemarie was the only president's daughter to come with me to supper, accompanied by her younger brother, freshly over from his Miami home, and his sensual Hispanic girlfriend. The brother, who had barely lived in Bolivia and spoke imperfect Spanish, was a decent, straightforward young American with ambitions to open a Bolivian fast food joint. Rosemarie, in contrast, displayed what my grandfather would have characterized as a European sophistication, and was probably a more complex personality. But my growing state of physical discomfort prevented any deeper insights, and eventually made all the dinner chat seem as alien as half-heard sounds from a background television set. It was the second time I had eaten in Bolivia with members of the Galindo family; and on both occasions I had been too ill properly to appreciate the conversation. Theirs was a world I was beginning to associate with a sense of unease.

Giddiness overtook me as I stumbled back from the restaurant's toilet, causing shocked looks from a well-dressed couple whose baby was being coddled by a young *cholita* seated at a respectful distance away from them. I managed just about to return to the hotel, where I woke up in a fever at around five in the morning. My whole leg was red and swollen. My chances of seeing anything of the carnival did not seem high. I had abandoned all thoughts of dancing, and saw myself being flown back to England with my leg in plaster. I prayed to the Virgin of the Socavón.

And she came to my help. Three hours later the swelling had gone down, and the pain had all but disappeared. I trod disbelievingly onto the floor, and found I could move without limping. Sun shone into the room, as firecrackers and the distant hum of massing crowds announced that the celebrations had begun. I dressed hurriedly, and wanted almost to skip as I headed off, thankful and elated, towards the festive din. Fighting through the mounting numbers of revellers and tourists, some already drunk by as early as nine in the morning, I found my way to my reserved seat on a tiered row of benches under the principle arcade of the town's main square, where Rosemarie and her friends, distracted for a moment from the gaudy motorcade heralding the first of the day's dozens of musical troupes, stared at me as if I was Lazarus risen from the dead.

★

'Left leg forward! Right leg across! And step! Sway to the left! Sway to the right! Right leg forward! Left leg across! And turn!'

I could almost hear the voice of Ricardo's son Pablo rising above the hypnotically monotonous sounds of brass and percussion, and giving instructions to the infinite-seeming rows of dancers who swayed and twirled, and made occasional kangaroo-like jumps into the air, as they passed through the square in the course of their punishing advance towards the still distant shrine of the miraculous Virgin. Some came as conquered Incas, others as wild tribes from the Amazonian lowlands, or as African slaves brought over to die in the Potosí mines, or even as cruel gringos in the guise of mine owners and capitalists. And thousands came as devils – rulers of the mineral-studded underworld, ever-multiplying enemies of the pathetically outnumbered St Michaels, who madly pirouetted with Lucifer at the head of these diabolical processions.

The women were a cross between cheerleaders and ballet dancers: they had mini-skirts and tutus, and flimsy tops barely appropriate to weather conditions in which bursts of blinding sunshine were eclipsed by sudden spells of chilling gloom. The men, by contrast, had costumes in which they could hardly move, weighing up to fifty kilos, costing sometimes more than several months' salary to hire, shiny, armour-like, futuristically baroque, so cumbersome as to determine the strange, stately steps of the dance that was making me feel restless on my seat within minutes.

'Left leg forward! Right leg across! And step! Sway to the left! Sway to the right! Right leg forward! Left leg across! And turn!'

And as they approached to where I was sitting, the grotesquely masked black slaves could be seen mouthing occasionally the songs whose heartfelt lyrics Pablo had taught me along with the dance steps. And I thought I began catching some of the words of the late 'J'alcha' Flores, the 'Great' Flores, a musician of legendary popularity who was known as the 'Solitary Man', and had sung of his worldwide wanderings in search of the elusive female love he would bring one day to Oruro, to dance before the Virgin of the Socavón, who would rid him of all sorrows (just as she had rid me of all pain).

And the drink flowed, and inhibitions broke down. Bottles of beer and improvised *shufflay* were passed from one mouth to the other, first from friends to friends, and then from strangers to strangers, all of whom started standing on the benches and swaying to the music, waving bottles like batons. Rosemarie's brother, revealing his North American upbringing, became drunk too quickly, and progressed rapidly from lively to surly to pugnaciously macho, finally provoking a fight that only the Virgin's intervention managed abruptly to stop.

Rosemarie herself self-consciously attempted to integrate with the crowd, unlike most of her companions, who continued resolutely to stay on their seats, watching the whole spectacle with serious detachment, and eventually leaving for La Paz before night fell and the mayhem intensified with the long-awaited arrival into the square of the Morenada Central de Oruro, the musical troupe to which the great Flores himself had belonged.

'Coca is not cocaine! Coca is not cocaine!' rang out the voices of the slaves, implicitly criticizing the ever-intervening North Americans whose anti-drug activities had ruined the lives of the coca growers, or *cocanis*, founders of the Morenada Central de Oruro.

'Coca is a sacred leaf,' the voices continued, before switching to the song that Flores had penned in violent response to former president Goni's comment that Bolivia was not a 'viable' country.

'Bolivia is viable,' they screamed, 'my people are not poor or miserable, I do not want robbers or the corrupt in my beautiful land.'

And by now I too was standing on the bench, moving frantically about on the foot I thought I had broken, making friends with my neighbours, sharing their drinks, and joining in the dancing and singing until I had lost all track of time, and Saturday had merged imperceptibly into Sunday, and I was apparently being harangued by a devil who had stopped directly in front of me and was removing his mask. I did not know what he wanted.

'He wants you to put on his mask, it's the greatest of compliments,' one of my new friends explained. 'He thinks you're famous, he thinks you're Sean Connery.'

'Left leg forward! Right leg across! And step! Sway to the left! Sway to the right! Right leg forward! Left leg across! And turn!'

And still the same mesmerising music ceaselessly played, accompanying me even after I had finally left the square to wander with my new companions through slithery streets cloudy from the smoke of stalls selling grilled meats and intestines and the supposedly energy-giving broth made from bull's penis. Then I went to my bed, but only for a few hours, for I was up the next morning for what seemed like a repetition of the previous day's events, but more fervent still, and with an atmosphere tense with anticipation of the climax, due to take place after many more hours of drinking and dancing and listening to music whose beat had now come to seem as vital to my body's existence as that of my heart.

It was near the start of another dawn when everyone who was still awake started slowly to climb towards the sanctuary of the Virgin of the Socavón. At the top of a town now turned into a giant urinal in which drunks were slipping and falling, the countless musical bands of the past two days were gathering with their drums and brass instruments to play all together once the new sun had risen. While waiting for this moment of unimaginable raucousness, I went inside the church to see the Virgin who had saved me.

The scene within was strange and unexpectedly moving. The dancers were shuffling towards the Virgin on their knees. Forming an endless line of souls, they dragged their exhausted legs across the marble floor, the men holding their masks in their hands, the women pathetically out of place in costumes more in keeping with a nightclub than a sanctuary. And, as they filed behind the high altar, and I could glimpse their watery eyes as they looked up at the Virgin, I remembered once more the great J'alcha Flores, who had sung of 'never wanting in this life to cry or to suffer', but who had cried whenever he had sung and who would die as he had always feared, all alone in a sordid flat in La Paz, his body undiscovered for days.

A terrifying commotion outside dragged me away from the Virgin and from thoughts of the 'Solitary Man'. The first of the sun's rays had touched the sanctuary's dome, and the hundreds of assembled musicians had begun playing all at once, discordantly, and with a volume so loud that the walls of Jericho would instantly have collapsed. Firecrackers and rockets were exploding, and a blitz of water-filled balloons drenched the fervent, drunken masses. The Seven Riders of the Apocalypse seemed already to be advancing, in step with the rising dawn.

★

I escaped from Oruro later that day, on a train heading south to Uyuni. The train, destined eventually for the Argentinian border, ran along the one surviving section I had yet to see of the main Antofagasta–La Paz line. It was also Bolivia's last remaining passenger train of any importance. I decided to savour it in a first-class compartment, which I found improbably occupied by a Japanese film crew and the family of an ageing Argentinian hippy with a house in Tiwanaku and a passion for rail travel.

The arrival in the late afternoon at Lake Poopó reduced us all to silence. The lake had expanded with the rains, and a thin layer of water washed against the sleepers of the track. The train appeared to glide miraculously across an apparently boundless mirror that reflected a sky streaked with preternaturally luminous clouds. After all the agitation of the past few days, I was suddenly filled with a profound sense of calm. I wondered if my grandfather had experienced such a feeling as he travelled past this lake for a final time, on his way back to a Europe on the verge of war.

Bethel had left Paratani for good on 10 July 1914. After a few days of errands in La Paz and Oruro he was able at last to take the Antofagasta train, where I could imagine him, his business in Bolivia finally complete, settling down in his seat to enjoy the soothing, sea-like immensity of Lake Poopó . But the tranquillity he might have felt at this stage of his long journey home would only have been transitory. Though he had spent his years in South America desperate to return to England and be reunited with Sophie, he was assailed by sudden doubts and fears now that he had a fixed date for this – the last week of August.

'It seems so futile to write, for I shall be seeing you so soon,' he had announced to Sophie on 30 June in a letter in which he also admitted how especially hard these remaining few weeks of waiting were going to be. He worried about how Sophie would receive him, and how he would find her. Feeling guilty about 'the disgraceful way' he had been 'neglecting' her in recent months, he said he would not be surprised if she were 'coldly distant' towards him. Furthermore, his four years of disappointments, and what he thought of as vegetating, had greatly eroded his self-confidence.

'Sophie, *mon âme*, I am longing for you so, and yet feel so unworthy. You have met so many fine people that I wonder if I shall not appear to you horribly mediocre.'

His fear of feeling out of place in Sophie's increasingly glamorous circles in Europe made more attractive an idea he would once have instantly rejected – the idea of getting her eventually to come back with him to live in Bolivia. He warned that the life they would lead here would be a simple and frugal one, but he reckoned that they could be wonderfully happy 'without the income of a Pierpont Morgan'. Bolivia itself, he had to confess, had so far failed to live up to his expectations of its future, and was in fact in a particularly bad way by June 1914. Crop failure resulting from a recent drought, together with a 'tremendous fall in the price of tin', had brought the country to the verge of bankruptcy. And yet, he added, Bolivia had come to seem a remarkably quiet place in comparison to the rest of the world.

'One might do far worse than elect it as a home,' he insisted. 'The bitter strife and dissension, the clamours of a proletariat that hates its betters, but does not exactly know what it does want, the ineffectual kicks of an aristocracy against what it considers an invasion of its privileges, the hard lot of the middle classes who really have to pay the piper. None of these things have come to disturb the peace very seriously as yet in South America.'

Outside of South America, in contrast, the world was disintegrating in a way that had begun threatening Bethel's projected idyll with Sophie, as well as his hitherto unquestioned faith in the future. The British and French newspapers that had once been his refuge in Chile and Bolivia now made him increasingly depressed. 'Political unrest, labour troubles, suffragettes on the war path, squabbles between Dukes and Ministers, murders galore, unemployment in Canada, general strikes and martial law in S. Africa, famine and earthquakes in Japan, a sorry state of affairs,' was how he had summarized the contents of these papers in February 1914.

By the end of June the world situation had become even worse. 'More Balkan troubles seem to be brewing, if not a more general conflagration. Financial depression, political unrest and scandals, war scares and increased armaments seem to be the order of the day.' He was worried that Sophie was going to think of him as an 'awful old croaker and pessimist'.

I was heading back now towards the Chilean frontier, and would soon have to be thinking about my own return to Europe. But already I was finding it hard to imagine any other existence than that of wandering eternally around Bolivia, a country to which I had become addicted. The carnival season was ending, and chaos was looming, but I no longer had any sense of hurry or of imminent troubles, and was enjoying a serene present coloured by the sight of a slowly disappearing Lake Poopó.

By the time I had alighted at Uyuni, in the middle of the night, I had had a change of travel plans. Instead of going straight from here to Chile across the outlying salt flat I would postpone this journey for a little while to return to Sucre by way of Potosí. I did not mind the extra travelling that this large detour would entail, or the partial retracing of my footsteps. The prospect of staying longer in Bolivia and seeing again my Sucre friends made everything worthwhile; and I still clung to two distant hopes: that I would finally encounter some mention of my grandfather, and that I would find a way of travelling by train along the Potosí branch line. Relieved at having made my decision I went off to the hotel where I had spent my first night in Bolivia – the Hotel Andean Jewel. I felt as if my time in this country was beginning all over again, and that it would never end.

The woman at the hotel who had first told me about 'Jacobs the Engineer' sleepily opened the door. I asked about buses to Potosí and Sucre, and she strongly recommended me to stay put at Uyuni until at least the Wednesday.

'Tomorrow is a public holiday,' she explained. 'I doubt if there'll be any buses running; and if there are, the drivers will be drunk. It's not a safe day to be on the road.' It was the day, she said, when everyone drops in to the houses of friends and family 'to give the blessing'.

Her own household was going to be visited by a group of people whom she referred to as the 'Yankee Boys'. She invited me to hang around her house so I could meet them. It was fate, she thought, that had wanted me to be in Uyuni on this particular day. The Yankee

Boys, she beamed, were a carnival fraternity founded 'many years ago' by the town's American and British engineers.

They turned up at the hotel well after two in the afternoon, their arrival so delayed that doubts had arisen about whether they would be coming at all.

'They'll be coming,' said the grandmother of the household, who had spent the morning ensuring that they would be welcomed with sufficient supplies of food, beer and *singani* cocktails. The news that they were only 100 metres or so down the street, and approaching rapidly, was relayed by a couple of excited children, who rushed into the narrow courtyard where we were all sitting, drinking and getting drunk. Outside bugles had started blaring and drums beating. I took up my place at the gate, poised as instructed to garland each of the Yankee Boys with streamers.

They filed into the courtyard one by one, wearing baseball caps and plastic visors, and shiny tops and trousers in garishly coloured nylon and viscose. Once inside the gate they broke into a trot and then into a dance, round and round the courtyard, their speed now governed not just by the drums and the bugles, but by a giant stringed instrument plucked with devilish gusto. They continued for a long while without stopping, men and women, young and old, all with smiles on their faces and streamers round their necks. Then, one by one, they picked up a drink and went on into the dining room, where I helped out by carrying around big jugs of ice-cold *shufflay*, which quickly disappeared down throats otherwise busily engaged in chattering and laughing.

A glass was tapped, and for a few minutes a serious silence ensued while the head of the household said a few words of welcome, to which this year's new president of the Yankee Boys responded with a speech of thanks. This was followed by a blessing ceremony in which a few drops of *shufflay* were thrown on the floor for the benefit of the *Pachamama*, the earth mother. Then the sounds of enjoyment resumed, and soon I was hearing stories about the Yankee Boys and their ancestors.

They gathered every year from all over Bolivia and the world. They had all been born in Uyuni, many of them being the children, grandchildren or great-grandchildren of foreign engineers who had come to the town during its heyday. Some had gone on to marry foreigners themselves: one told me she had married an American university lecturer and was living in Austin, Texas; another was engaged to an English doctor working in Africa; one couple had brought with them their teenage American daughter who could barely speak Spanish. And then they asked me about myself and what I was doing in Bolivia; and of course I let slip that I too was the grandson of a British engineer, and that his name was Jacobs.

I explained to no avail that my grandfather had nothing to do with 'Jacobs the Engineer', the presumed son of Bethel's American namesake. But drink had made everyone blind to such subtleties; and, in no time at all, word had got out that I was a member of the family of 'Jacobs the Engineer', a Yankee Boy legend.

Many of those present had known him well; others knew him only by reputation. No one had seen him for years, and though generally thought to be dead, he was said by one person to be now living in New York, while another claimed he had moved to London. But the one detail that made any real impact on my by now confused brain was provided by an elderly businessman long resident in Buenos Aires.

'He loved dancing,' the man said, 'but he danced appallingly, just like he claimed his father had done.'

'And just like Che Guevara for that matter,' added the wife of the Texas lecturer at the point when the music had started up again, leading everyone out again into the courtyard, to dance in endless circles into which I too was finally dragged.

'Come with us into the town!' the Yankee Boys implored, persuading me without much difficulty to join their conga formation as it slid through the gate and into Uyuni's grand but dusty streets, now crimson with the setting sun. Without breaking for a moment our snake-like chain, we danced all over the town, around 'Big Ben', and down the station avenue, until we came to a waterless fountain where the men jumped up onto its massive basin, encircling the monument with their hands before engaging in an Apache-like stomp and howling the Yankee Boys' song: 'We are the Yankee Boys! We are the Yankee Boys! We come from far and wide, we've got balls, and we've got pride! We are the Yankee Boys! We are the Yankee Boys!'

I felt the next morning as if I had danced all the way to the bus station. After the interlude at the fountain, the conga chain had reassembled to skip off into an echoing old dance hall where we had danced for most of the night, allowing me just a few hours in my hotel before I had to rush off to catch a bus which, inevitably, would turn up two hours late.

I was half-asleep when the bus eventually took off. Dazed from so much dancing, and remembering all the talk about 'Jacobs the Engineer' as if it had been a dream, I sat bleary-eyed at the window, watching the scenery as we jolted along a narrow dust track up into the bare mountains. The white ocean of the Salar de Uyuni extended in front of a barely perceptible horizon of volcanoes marking the Chilean frontier. The views took my mind briefly away from the groans and screeches of the bus as its wheels hugged the sides of precipices.

After less than an hour on the road the bus spluttered to a halt. The driver got out to inspect the engine, and the passengers followed suit a quarter of an hour later. Water was dripping from the broken car-burettor, which was later refilled with water from a nearby stream. Under the blinding sun all the men present began pushing the vehicle, which started up and even managed ten more kilometres before breaking down again. We found another stream, and this time used empty litre bottles of Sprite and Coca-Cola to supplement the water collected in a couple of jerrycans. We managed to get a further half-hour's journey down the road; and then the bus had another relapse. We would maintain this pace up to Potosí, where we arrived by miracle only ten hours later than we should have done. The bus had several more years of life ahead of it, reckoned the man next to me, who compared the vehicle to an ageing and ailing dancer, determined to keep going until he dropped.

I got to Sucre at the weekend, in time for the last day of the carnival season. My friends had planned an event for this day that they said would make me truly remember Bolivia. We were going into the country in search of 'ambrosia'.

We woke up on Sunday morning rather later than we had intended, and delayed our departure further by looking for a shop that would sell us sugar and a litre of '98° drinkable alcohol' – ingredients that were apparently essential to the experience that was in store for us. By nine o'clock we were outside Sucre's grand and bosky cemetery, waiting for a *micro* to take us towards the village of Yotalla, whose annual saint's day festivities this year coincided with the end of the carnival.

It was a day my mother would have described as making you 'happy to be alive'. The blue of the sharp and cloudless sky brought out all the rich colours of a mountain valley brushed in emerald green by the recent summer rains. We alighted just before the village at a farm whose owner was known to Jorge and Marbel, and was said to have 'reliable cows'. I was still not entirely sure as to what 'ambrosia' consisted of; but I knew we were looking for cows on the point of being milked. Unfortunately we had arrived at this particular farm two hours too late. Told to come back in the evening, we walked on to Yotalla, normally a peaceful village but now receiving the first of the hundreds of festive visitors who would be choking the place by nightfall.

After an early lunch at a makeshift restaurant under the trees, we walked down to the river, where families were swimming, youths were drinking, and lovers lay embraced on shady, grassy patches. Armed with a bottle of *singani*, we hopped across to the other side of the river on stepping stones, and found a quiet place to spend the next two hours toasting our happiness, and taking it in turns to sing.

The sky went black in a matter of minutes. As the first drops of rain began to fall, we darted back across the river, just in time to avoid being trapped. The rain poured down with a cataclysmic vehemence, tearing off festival decorations, flooding streets, swelling the river to an impassable size, even leaving stranded the outside restaurant where we had had our lunch. The village band marched on oblivious, giving encouragement to those determined to enjoy themselves whatever the conditions. There were people, such as us, who tried at first ineffectually to find shelter; but we all soon gave up when the rain showed no sign of stopping. We paraded the streets laughing in our drenched clothes, and went to dry ourselves in a dance hall where pools of water covered the floor.

In the late afternoon, with the rain at last beginning to ease, we left the village on foot to continue our search for the drink of the gods. The *micros* and taxis were all taken, or else trapped, like the buses, in the congestion of traffic trying to enter Yotalla to celebrate the carnival's last moments. We attempted to return to the farm that we had called at before, but realized the road leading to it would be flooded, obliging us to head off onto a much longer road back towards Sucre. We hoped to come across other farms that would serve our purposes.

It took two more hours of walking to find the right cow. Its swollen udder, glimpsed in the dusk just when I was sure our search would have to be abandoned, was a sight as satisfying as that of sunken treasure. The farmer was already advancing towards the creature, pail in hand, when Marbel stopped him, saying that we would like to buy all the milk the cow would be producing that evening. The farmer put down the pail and ordered his wife to bring out some seats, on which we sat while Marbel's brother added sugar and 'drinkable alcohol' to a glass placed directly under the udder. The udder was squeezed, and a steaming, frothy concoction was produced. My friends insisted that I, as 'the guest of honour', should be the first to try this. I put the warm liquid to my lips, closed my eyes, and murmured, 'Pure ambrosia!'

In near total darkness we shared glass after glass of this soothing and reviving brew whose alcoholic content was reputedly strong enough as to kill off any microbes the untreated milk might contain. I was not wholly convinced by this theory, but drank on regardless, enjoying without worrying the intense pleasure of the moment, until I started almost persuading myself that this ambrosia was truly like its ancient namesake, not really a drink at all, but a substance conferring immortality.

The post-carnival dawn brought with it no hangover, nor any immediate sense of impending tragedy, but rather a feeling that I had almost discovered the secret of life in Bolivia, and that this involved doing exactly the opposite of what my grandfather and his ancestors had done, and to live only for the present, always to welcome new experiences and people, and to be free of all prejudices, regrets and single-minded ideals.

During my remaining days in Sucre I would also make a satisfying discovery of a more concrete kind. I would do so in Bolivia's newly refurbished National Library.

Seated almost all alone in the main reading room, attended by a staff of ten, I found what I had unsuccessfully hunted for in Potosí, and what I felt I needed to find before leaving Bolivia – a reference to my grandfather. I had asked to see a complete set of the Cochabamba

daily *El Comercio* for the years 1913-14, and noticed in one of the earliest issues a small column listing all the arriving and departing visitors
to the town. For over an hour I scoured through brittle, discoloured
pages only to come across the name of D. M. Jacobs, putative father
of 'Jacobs the Engineer'. Once again, I thought, my grandfather had
proved himself to be a person of such little importance as to be not
even worth recording in a column of this humble sort.

But then I reached the issue dated 23 July 1913. And there he was,
B. L. Jacobs, staying at the Hotel Unión and on his way to Changolla
camp. It was hardly a document of much significance, but sufficiently
emotive for my skin to break out in goose pimples, and for my whole
being to quiver with satisfaction and a sense of family belonging. I
wanted all the library staff to gather around me so that I could show
them my grandfather's name. But this impulse was restrained after I
had looked more closely at the column to see who was with him at
the time. Two of the names were known to me from his letters – his
Irish friend Samuels and the head of F.C.A.B.'s Bolivian operations,
H. S. Brown. But there were also three other names which sounded
familiar, though at first I did not remember why.

Then a sad realization impinged on my lingering, ambrosia-
induced elation. I knew all of a sudden where I had seen before the
names J. Bethune, F. T. Edmonds and J. A. MacRae: on the commemorative panel in Antofagasta's railway museum. I thought of these
three men, perhaps seated with Bethel at one of the cafés of
Cochabamba's main square, listening to the 'top-hole' military band
that played there on Sunday afternoons. And then I remembered them
as gilded letters on a mahogany board, three of a long list of Bethel's
colleagues who had gone back to Europe to die in what my grandfather would describe to Sophie as 'the war to end all wars'.

Jorge, Marbel and Oswald held me in long embraces as I prepared to
set off once more on my slow return journey towards Antofagasta.
This time I knew it would be ages before I next saw them, if indeed
I ever saw them again at all.

With these thoughts on my mind, I got out of the shared taxi that
had taken me back to Potosí and almost immediately bumped into my
engineer friend Ricardo. Fate, having done so much to postpone

my grandfather's happiness, appeared to be doing everything it could to ensure mine.

'Meechell,' said Ricardo when he learnt that I was on my way back to Uyuni, 'why don't you use your influence with Bolivian Railways to travel there by freight train?'

I thanked him for this suggestion, and said I would do anything to avoid having to do the trip again by bus. However, I had been told by Eduardo MacLean, head of Bolivian Railways, that a journey by train from Potosí would be impossible.

'Meechell,' responded Ricardo, 'you still have not learnt. In Bolivia nothing is impossible.' With his usual confidence he assured me that he would have something sorted out for the following morning.

Ricardo's powers were evidently limitless. Within an hour of our fortuitous reunion at Potosí, this comical womanizer had proved himself again to be not only my guardian angel but also a man who could achieve anything. Though he admitted straight away that he had not got me onto a freight train, he claimed that he had arranged for me 'a much more comfortable form of transport' – one of the 'inspection cabs' used by today's engineers.

'It'll give us much more liberty, we'll be able to get off whenever we want.' Ricardo was apparently coming along himself and clearly looking forward to it. 'We'll bring along a bottle of *singani* and have a good time.'

I reported at the ghostly railway station two hours before dawn. The cab, resembling the solitary cabin of an old-fashioned cable car, appeared phantom-like from out of the darkness and shunted towards me. 'Meester Meechell!' exclaimed a familiar voice that turned out to be that of Ricardo's faithful assistant Jesús, who slapped my hand and said how pleased he was that we were all going to be together again. Ricardo himself was waiting for me inside, together with a benign-looking old driver who told me he had brought with him a tape of his favourite musician, Elton John.

To the sounds of 'Candle in the Wind' we were off, heading down a railway line that had once symbolized Bolivia's future, but whose main purpose today, it seemed, was to transport the private mineral wealth of ex-president Goni. Dawn broke at the sinisterly ugly mining town of Agua de Castilla, after which we disappeared down a narrow gorge where the sun never reached. Buffeted by freezing winds once we were again out in barren open landscape, we continued gradually, unnoticeably, to ascend. Paradoxically, the higher we climbed the flatter became the terrain, so that when we reached the Pass of El Condor, the highest railway pass in the world, we found ourselves in the midst of vast level tundra stretching featurelessly towards a faraway snow-capped range.

The same worn Elton John tape, barely audible above the noise of the engine, and endlessly replayed, was not enough to distract us from the cheerlessness of the environment. When we joined the main line from Oruro to Uyuni at Río Mulatto Ricardo decided to do something about this. Leaving the cab at a bridge we walked along a river in the early afternoon sun. After a quarter of an hour we arrived at a spot where water bubbled lethargically from a tiny hole in the ground, beside which someone had thoughtfully left a plastic cup. 'The mineral water here is delicious,' commented Ricardo, 'but it needs some improvement.' He asked Jesús to pass the *singani*, and mixed it in the cup with the water, some sugar, and the juice from a lemon.

'A *singani* spritzer,' he smiled, revealing again his Bolivian ingenuity at devising simple treats.

We arrived at Uyuni at dusk, after a day remarkably quiet and uneventful by Ricardo's standards. He would do his best that night to animate our last hours together, keeping a secret cache of beer under our restaurant table, flirting with a woman who ran a café underneath the town's bandstand, taking me on to a seedy bar lit by a solitary construction lamp, and persuading the woman at the Andean Jewel Hotel to sell us another bottle of *singani* at two in the morning. But the repeated toasts to my speedy return to Bolivia put me finally into a deep sleep, from which I would groggily emerge several hours later in my hotel bed, unsure exactly as to where I was or how or when I had got there.

Ricardo and Jesús would already be well on their way back to Potosí, I thought sadly as I walked down to the lobby to wait for the Land-Rover that would take me on the three-day tourist excursion across the Salar de Uyuni and down into Chile. It would be strange, I reflected, to follow again a well-worn tourist trail, cocooned from all the difficulties and dangers of travelling, and in the company of other foreigners. Probably I would miss the adventures I had had with Ricardo and others; but at least I would be sure of leaving Bolivia unharmed and alive.

'You're going with Chica Tours!' exclaimed the hotel's shocked owner after I had been waiting around in the lobby for over an hour and a half. 'I shall be praying for you.'

As at San Pedro de Atacama, to which I was returning, there had been an enormous choice of tour agencies at Uyuni. Though I still carried with me the details of the small, pathetic but dignified Bolivian agency which had attracted my attention at San Pedro, I had eventually thrown in my lot with what a guidebook described as the 'oldest, largest and most reliable of the agencies specializing in the Salar'.

'Oh, if only you had asked for my advice beforehand,' continued my friend at the hotel, 'I could have told you all about Chica Tours. We've had clients in tears after having been with them. They're thieves, they're swindlers; they couldn't care less about the people they're working for. It's a miracle that no one yet has died on one of their trips. Their vehicles are old and always breaking down. They have young, inexperienced drivers who don't know the terrain well. The food they provide has caused serious cases of poisoning. But there's something else about them I could never forgive.' She now lowered her voice even though there was no one else in the lobby. 'They have a thriving trade in drugs. Their poor, unsuspecting clients are travelling in vehicles that are stuffed with cocaine. You could be signing up for a three-day tour and spend the next ten years in jail.'

She tried hard to get me onto another tour going to San Pedro; but all of them had left some time before; and in any case I had already paid over my money. In the meantime the Land-Rover belonging to Chica Tours finally turned up, suspiciously empty save for the driver and a representative of the agency. The representative apologized for their late arrival. They had had some cancellations that day, he said, and had been unable to find at the last moment any replacement passengers. But because they were a company that 'honoured its obligations', they were prepared to make a loss of money and take me on my own, 'as a special favour'. Then he left me alone with the driver.

Relieved simply to be getting on my way, I discounted as best I could all the talk about Chica Tours. Mario the driver, a slight, cheerfully smiling young man, did not seem the type of person to be in league with the Devil. Nor did his agency seem superficially any different from the many others I had come in contact with in the course of the journey.

Within half an hour of leaving Uyuni we had caught up with the rival Land Rovers, all of which had assembled at the entrance to the Salar so that their cramped occupants could stretch their legs and haggle over the price of miniature llamas made from salt. From then onwards we would all stick closely together, regrouping shortly afterwards at a hotel built of salt, and then again at an island bristling with cacti and trail signs. And so we continued, from one strange place to another, stopping in exactly the same spots in the course of a slow, halting journey that would take us the whole length of the world's largest salt flat, and then into a natural park full of volcanoes, geysers, wind-crafted sculptures in stone, and eerily coloured lagoons striped pink with rows of flamingos.

On a few occasions Mario was able to pull away from all the other vehicles and be the first to reach these beauty spots so that I could take in their unworldly silence before this was shattered by cries of 'Wow!', 'Intense!', 'Wicked!', '*Wunderbar!*', 'Struth!', '*Fantástico!*', 'Fucking hell, man!'. Having the luxury of a whole Land-Rover at my disposal made me perhaps more sneering than I might otherwise have been towards the other travellers, whose youth, jollity and intimate camaraderie I nonetheless began to envy every time I returned alone to my car. I was also becoming ever more self-conscious, especially after a giggling young Australian woman had been dared by her comrades to sidle up to me and find out who I was.

'Excuse me,' she said as I sat alone, eating the second day's picnic, 'we've all been wondering why you're the only person travelling on your own. We think you must either be very rich or very famous. You're not by any chance Sean Connery?'

A couple of shy Aymaran women took pity on me that night. We had reached a lonely hamlet whose dozen or so inhabitants survived by putting up backpackers in bleak adobe halls. The two women, amazed that I was not only Mario's one and only passenger but also the sole occupant of a large, unheated dormitory where temperatures would soon be falling to twenty below zero, invited me into their simple house, where Mario himself always stayed. They prepared a warming llama stew for me, and gave me alpaca blankets to cover myself as I curled up next to a dying stove.

I was troubled that night, my last for the time being in Bolivia, by violent dreams. These were curiously premonitory of what I would witness on my eventual return to this country one and a half years later, when much of what I had nervously envisaged as happening on my first visit finally did: a country paralyzed by roadblocks; yet another president forced to resign; drunken *campesinos* attacking the bus I was in; waiting in Sucre as thousands of miners descended on the town wielding dynamite; tear gas seeping into my room; the repeated sounds of firecrackers, explosions and breaking glass; a miner killed almost before my eyes; a bloody civil war avoided at the last minute almost by a miracle.

Mario tapped me on my shoulders at four in the morning, and said it was time to get going to 'the Gates of Hell'. We were giving a lift to one of the villagers, a stocky Aymara with an almost Mongolian face, broad-featured, calm and enigmatic. He did not say a single word as we drove in our convoy towards Bolivia's most famous geysers, where Mario stood smiling in the twilight in front of bubbling mud, hissing water, and great clouds of smoke. This, he said, was the door where the Devil entered his kingdom.

The Aymara still did not speak, nor did he smile, nor did he pay any attention at breakfast to all the leering talk from Mario and the other drivers about gorgeous young backpackers who were 'gagging for it'. Two hours later, when our vehicle had succeeded at last in making a major advance on all the others, and we had got out to look undisturbed at the massive cone of Licancapur rising above an emerald-green lake, the Aymara's mouth moved as if finally on the point of articulating some words.

He waited until Mario had gone off to do his 'morning business' before offering me his hand and introducing himself with his full and complex Indian name. Amazed by his sudden recovery of speech, I stared into eyes that appeared to me now to be full of goodness and wisdom. In a deep and measured tone he started telling me about Licancapur, the volcano whose shape I had got to know so well from the Chilean side. He said that it was 'a sacred mountain' and that he had once climbed to its summit and found Inca ruins there. But then he heard Mario returning.

'Be careful,' he whispered, suddenly changing the subject, 'you are with evil people.'

We continued driving, and were soon approaching the frontier, carrying, I now knew almost for certain, cocaine or worse. The Aymara asked to be dropped off a couple of kilometres away from the tiny Bolivian frontier settlement. Explaining to me that it would be best if he were not seen travelling in Mario's car, he said goodbye, and walked away sad and solemn into the distance, as if he were the last of a noble race.

I was trembling when I crossed the frontier. I had been transferred into another car, and was worried that something had been slipped into my luggage during the process. The police unpacked everything I had in my bags before finally waving me on and giving me the chance to calm down. A couple of weeks later I would read a newspaper article about a group of backpackers who had been thrown into prison while travelling in a cocaine-filled Land-Rover belonging to Chica Tours. The tour company would succeed in exonerating not only their clients but also themselves. There clearly existed a web of corruption that extended into the highest places.

I found it difficult at first to adjust to being back in Chile. The switch at the frontier from a dust track to a brand new asphalt road with gleaming white markers signalled an all too abrupt transition from a precarious and unstable world to one of Californian blandness. San Pedro this time proved unbearable – phoney, impersonal, overpriced, and more tainted than ever by tourism, the spoilt middle classes, people who were too busy to see you, and self-regarding camera crews engaged in fashion shoots. After a weekend of trying to relax at a curious outlying swimming pool made from railway scrap, I was pleased to be on my way once more to the dusty ugliness of Antofagasta.

Halfway there, at a time of day when the Atacama's heat and haze were almost unbearable, I unwisely chose to leave the comfort of the air-conditioned bus. I had had a sudden morbid impulse to visit the former nitrate town and concentration camp of Chacabuco. The remembered image of its tall black chimney, as seen at nightfall from the Calama train, had come to mirror the darkness of my thoughts as I tried again to focus on my grandfather's return to a Europe now shadowed by death.

I was dropped near the point where the Pan-American Highway leaves the Calama road to branch northwards towards Iquique. In the middle of these scorched crossroads a madman was shouting and screaming. I attempted to give him the slip but he ran laughing in my direction, and grabbed me by the shoulders. He was selling bottles of Coca-Cola, so I bought one to keep him happy. Sweating and puffing from the weight of my luggage, I took the Iquique turning, and was soon all alone in the arid and empty midday landscape.

Chacabuco was further away than I had thought; and the few vehicles that passed ignored me as I tried to hitch a lift. The ghost town's tall chimney seemed never to get any nearer, and even vanished for ten worrying minutes after I had left the main road to walk the remaining two kilometres on a rough, difficult-to-follow track with forks leading nowhere.

There was a man living in the town I had thought to be uninhabited. He walked out of a small adobe building to see me arrive, worn out, disorientated and undignified. He himself was a lithe, moustachioed old man with the look of someone accustomed to pondering the meaning of the world. He beckoned into his house, where he sold me a ticket to the site, of which he was apparently the guardian and official guide. While he was out of the room looking for some change, I read a magazine article about him that had been pinned to a wall. His name was Ricardo Salvador. He was seventy-five years old, and had been living on his own in Chacabuco for the past twelve years. More bizarrely, he had earlier been a prisoner under Pinochet at this same place.

Later, after we had begun talking together, he told me that he was merely doing what in effect I myself had been engaged in ever since taking up my grandfather's story – 'confronting the ghosts of the past'. I had anticipated from him horrific tales about his years of incarceration in a place that had inspired other prisoners to write books with titles such as *Journey to Hell*. But he had clearly come to terms with what had happened to him here, for he was able to talk about this period with calm objectivity, refusing to sensationalize or even to criticize his captors other than those who had later defended their actions on the grounds that they were only following orders ('they were cowards pure and simple,' he declared).

Ricardo led me into a large main square whose dying trees and desiccated flower beds set the tone for the dust-shrouded architecture. At its central bandstand he left me to guide myself around the rest of the ghost town, saying that he had 'important gardening' to do. On his advice I went straightaway to the nitrate-processing plant, which he had rightly described to me as 'an immense cathedral in the desert', and then finished my tour at the similarly grand theatre. Here, as I walked up a half-broken staircase, I heard some voices coming from the auditorium. There were three people talking to Ricardo, who invited me to come over and meet them.

'They have a family history that might interest you,' he said.

A short, elderly woman with yellow-rinsed hair introduced herself to me as 'Elsa', a name which, she said, had been suggested to her father by an English engineer. She had been born in Chacabuco in 1935, five years before this town of 7,000 inhabitants had been abandoned. She had not been back until that day, bringing with her a daughter-in-law, who wore heavy make-up, and a middle-aged son with tiny shorts, a huge belly, and a string vest revealing gorilla-like arms.

Elsa had delayed her return to Chacabuco for so long because of the place's 'terrible memories' for her. She remembered the sadness of her family on hearing in 1940 that everyone in the town was going to lose their houses and their jobs; and she even remembered the day when the Second World War had been declared, and the 'terrible fights' that had broken out between English and German workers who had once been friends.

But the memory that had most haunted her over the years was the death here of her seven-year-old brother.

'I was only three at the time, but I can never forget the moment when he died. It was my first memory of life, though of course it was not until much later that I would find out what exactly had happened, and to take it all in. My brother had drunk some wine he had found lying around in the kitchen; and it had disagreed with him. He would have recovered quickly in hospital had not the nurse given him an injection totally unsuitable for someone who had just drunk alcohol. It was the nurse who killed him. And it all happened so quickly. I was by his bed, with everyone thinking he was alright, when his body made a sudden jerk, and his eyes turned towards mine. That's really what I remember, his staring eyes, staring into mine as if he had something to tell me. I still dream about them.'

'My mother is a bit of fantasist,' jeered her son, who then offered to give me a lift into Antofagasta if I didn't mind waiting for a short while. 'My mother wants to visit the cemetery here. She's got it into her head that she's going to find the tomb of her brother.' Ricardo Salvador looked at me in a way that confirmed the absurdity of this quest. He nonetheless gave us instructions as to how to get to the cemetery.

We went there by car, and soon started driving in futile circles until finally we found the track we assumed to be the right one. It went over a dip, and started descending towards the distant railway line and what I thought at first to be a rubbish dump.

'That must be it!' shouted the daughter-in-law, causing her husband to chortle, and his mother to twitch in her seat with excitement.

It was like seeing a huge mound of skulls from a massacre. A jagged chaos of metal and wooden crosses jutted from sandy, stony ground littered with rusting coils and other wind-blown detritus. The mother, undeterred, went out of the car to look for her brother.

'You're joking, aren't you?' shouted the exasperated son. 'And in this heat!'

But he dutifully followed her into a cemetery where victims of old age, disease, medical incompetence, industrial accidents, and the actions of cowardly guards obeying the orders of Pinochet's henchmen lay in anonymous confusion, the names having all been made illegible by the unforgiving desert conditions. 'There's not a single fucking inscription,' I overheard the man muttering as his mother continued the search all the same, her face streaked with tears, sweat and melting mascara.

'I told you you'd be wasting your time,' he grunted smugly once we had driven away from Chacabuco, across the railway line, past the screaming man selling Coca-Cola, and onto a main road that appeared to be heading towards infinity.

The sounds of 'Bing Ben' welcomed me back to the centre of Antofagasta, where I was glad to get away from the bickering of Elsa's family, and to find a salubrious hotel which shared its premises with an American-style ice cream parlour glittering in Formica. I revived myself with a Knickerbocker Glory, and then announced to the F.C.A.B. the safe return from Bolivia of 'Don Michael Jacobs'. The news caused little sensation. Miguel Sepúlveda, the company's director, was predictably as busy as ever; but he offered to put aside a couple of hours for me at the end of the week so as to bring me together with the writer Hernán Rivera, as he had promised.

I spent the intervening time wildly speculating about my grandfather's final days in South America. I had virtually nothing to go on, other than a document in the F.C.A.B.'s London archives mentioning his resignation from the company on 18 July (when he had been granted a bonus of £150 and the 'difference between the cost of a first- and second-class passage to England'). All I had was an intuition that an imminent revelation awaited me at one of the few surviving local institutions once favoured by the English engineers – the Masonic Lodge. I went there as soon as I could.

A meeting was about to begin; and a steady stream of aged Masons drifted through the grand and sombre vestibule where I had been told to wait. These gentlemen shook my hand in turn and assumed I was a visiting foreign member of the order. Eventually I met the secretary of the Lodge, who told me that the person I should really talk to about my grandfather was their archivist 'Don Jorge Lyons, whom I believe you already know'. Unfortunately, as it happened, Don Jorge was currently in hospital recovering from an operation, and was thus no longer in a position to help me about anything.

'But just remind me,' added the secretary, 'what did you say your grandfather was called?' I told him again and was overheard by a man next to us, who asked if I was Michael Jacobs, the friend of his son from Sucre who was married to a Bolivian woman and had recently been made a Mason himself.

'But of course I know who your grandfather was,' interrupted the secretary. 'He was that American engineer who settled in Cochabamba. His son Miguel was also an engineer. He used to drop by and see us whenever he was in Antofagasta.'

I made a quick getaway before the meeting began, anxious that I was falling ever further into a supernatural trap intended to ensnare me in the Masonic Order. Either that or I was losing my reason. I decided to spend the next days anchoring myself to firm facts at Antofagasta's public library.

With a microfiche reader in front of me, and a spool dated 'June to August 1914', I reeled through the pages of the *Mercurio de Antofagasta*, scanning at first the purely local items – accounts of petty crime and minor earth tremors, timetables of all the trains and boats, a report about an aviator planning to 'loop the loop', details of all that was being shown at the Ciné Colon – until I was back at last in my grandfather's Antofagasta, saying goodbye to friends at the English Club (with its newly installed billiards table), playing some final rounds of tennis (at a court recently opened by J. R. Mollett), and even fitting in a visit to the cinema to watch the 'renowned Parisian artiste Gabrielle Robinne' acting in a film whose title seemed wholly telling of the times – *The Tragic Parade*.

I had reached the third week of July, and had begun noting down the number of times the words 'tragedy' and 'tragic' were appearing in the *Mercurio*'s pages. It seemed as if the whole world had turned into a sensational melodrama comparable to the serialized instalments of *Tragic Love*, an historical novel which I had been reading with growing absorption as my research into the summer of 1914 wore on. When I managed to tear myself away from this tale, and to switch finally my attention to the paper's reporting of events beyond Antofagasta, I did so only to be confronted with articles headed, 'the Tragedy of Princess Dalmira' (a Uruguayan princess shot dead by the husband who then shot himself'), 'the Tragedy of Peru' (a country brought to the brink of chaos by rebellious natives), 'the Tragedy of Bolivia' (a tale of financial mismanagement, plummeting tin prices, and a corrupt and personality-obsessed president), and, of course, 'the Tragedy of Sarajevo', an on-going saga promising to have as many dramatic ramifications as *Tragic Love*, and supplanting in coverage the once almost daily bulletins about the suffragettes.

As my exhausted hand kept turning the spool of the microfiche reader, and the moment was nearing when the lieutenant hero of *Tragic Love* would be returning from battle to be reunited with his errant mistress, I had to adjust the screen to fit front page headlines that were becoming progressively bigger. History was unfolding at terrifying speed, and events taking place on the other side of the world would soon have major repercussions in Antofagasta itself.

When, on 30 July, war was declared between Austrian and Serbia, Antofagasta's Austro-Hungarian consul implored all the Slavic citizens in town to remain loyal to the empire. However, a large group of these citizens got together to sign a declaration in the *Mercurio* pledging their support for Serbia. Within days the once harmonious relations which had existed between the citizens of different European nationalities living in Antofagasta were clearly disintegrating. By the end of the first week of August the paper was reporting how men who had happily worked and lived together for years were now 'divided by the enmity that exists between their homelands, for which they are prepared today to return to Europe and give up their lives.'

I removed the spool from the machine, and rubbed eyes that were blurred with tiredness. My grandfather was already well on his way home. He had probably left Antofagasta by around 25 July, and had talked about travelling by train to Buenos Aires and catching a boat from there. I did not know whether he had done this or not, so I could not tell where exactly he was on the day that Britain joined the war. I knew only that he was somewhere at sea, where, as I gazed at the empty screen, I saw him in a state of limbo, not knowing what was really happening back in Europe, but perhaps thinking how innocent he had been to have imagined that 'the course of world events will soon be of no more concern to us, for we, my darling Sophie, shall be together again and blind to everything but our happiness.'

I was in the elegant old dining car of a train travelling to nowhere. A waiter in a waistcoat and bow tie was removing the used silver cutlery and plates stained with gravy from our *filets de boeuf Wellington*. I retired with the three other diners to take our coffee on adjacent armchairs upholstered in plush red velvet.

This was a dining car my grandfather had probably eaten at on numerous occasions as he plied backwards and forwards on the Antofagasta–Bolivia line. But today the carriage stood isolated and immobile in front of a station that was a station no longer. It was used to entertain guests of the F.C.A.B.

Miguel Sepúlveda and his assistant Victor Maldonado relaxed in their armchairs, directing towards their two casually dressed literary guests the patrician smiles of munificent corporate sponsors of the arts. With me was my almost exact contemporary Hernán Rivera, looking like an ageing hippy with his white linen shirt, and thick curly black hair lightly dusted with grey.

He was a figure of legendary popularity. Everyone in Antofagasta seemed to know him, and everyone had stories to tell of his approachability, his common touch, his humanity. He was the writer who had become famous while working as a miner in yet another of the Atacama's now deserted nitrate towns, Pedro Valdivia. If he had been British he might have ended up writing novels of gritty working-class realism; but Hernán Rivera was a product of South America, where Indian legends, Spanish fantasy, and the sheer strangeness of so much of the environment have somehow contrived to make reality inseparable from poetry, whimsy and the supernatural. He wrote always of the nitrate towns, but as he imagined them to have been in my grandfather's time, and transformed further through the filters of magic and a baroque prose style.

I handed over my still unread copy of *The Trains are Heading for Purgatory* for him to sign. He wished me a happy journey to Purgatory, and then scribbled lower down the page how delighted he was to have met someone whose grandfather had travelled on these trains. 'And now,' he said, putting down his pen, and accepting the waiter's offer of another cup of coffee, 'you must tell us more about this grandfather.'

I related briefly some of the more telling details of his story, after which Don Miguel told me with a broad smile that I ought to be careful. 'You might find Hernán stealing your material and turning it into a novel.'

'The key elements are all there,' said Hernán, his eyes glancing towards the Manchester-made clock that hung at the end of the wood-panelled carriage. 'A British engineer is dying in a house in London. He is surprised by his two-year-old grandson who inherits his spirit and becomes the book's narrator. The cynicism and aimlessness of the early twenty-first century confront the idealism and moral certainties of the early twentieth, until all are confused in a South America that is in turn liberating, lonely, corrupt and mysterious. And then of course there are the elements of undying love and spiritual searching, which always go down well with readers.'

'And how would you end the book?' asked the well-read Don Victor. 'With the lovers finally reunited and living happily ever after? Or with the advent of a war that destroys all the values and beliefs of the grandfather's generation?'

Hernán pondered this for a few moments while taking in the porcelain, tulip-shaped lamps that adorned the carriage's ceiling.

'At a carnival ball,' he mused, 'where the grandfather learns at last to dance, and finds that he is dead.'

Epilogue
The Waters of Oblivion

O N T H E R O A D once more, on another bus in the middle of the same unchanging desert, I remembered the last time my father had spoken to me about his parents. I had not heard him talk coherently about anything for months, so had been unnerved when he had asked all of a sudden about his long-dead parents, and about the possibility of finding them in the place he called the 'upper part'. 'I would so love to see them again,' he had said with such surprising clarity that I could hear him saying these words now as I stared, mesmerized, at a tiny cloud of dust racing across the evening sands before disappearing into nothingness.

I was travelling south, searching for final memories of my grandfather in the continent to which he would never return. I was leaving the Chile of unending summer, and heading slowly towards the Chile where the summer barely came. Ahead of me I saw a world of glaciers, witches, fogs and ceaseless rains.

The change to winter began as I sat trying to sleep on the overnight train from Santiago to the town of Tamuco, birthplace of Pablo Neruda, the train driver's son. The moon became hazy, and then disappeared; and I woke up at Tamuco to a light rain spitting against the window. Outside the station a lifeless dawn was rising over scenes of Central European drabness. Stocky peasants, weighed down by giant turnips and potatoes, rode in horse-drawn carts along muddy streets reeking of poverty. The 'Pablo Neruda Railway Museum' did not tempt me, so I continued heading south, by bus and ferry, until I reached the archipelago of Chiloe.

They told me there that the summer was over, and that all I could now expect was the damp low-lying blanket of grey that had set in over a boggy landscape dotted by ugly modern chalets. But then, against all predictions, the sun came out. It was market day, and the harbour of the fishing village where I had spent the night became alive with miniature boats arriving from across the sparkling bay. A fisherman called Luis offered to take me back with him that afternoon to his home on La Lligua. He said that his was a 'virgin island', a place with 'no cars, no electricity, no running water, no crime, no fights'.

Shortly after midday, with the colours almost too bright to be of the real world, we sailed towards a hilly island draped in woods of emerald green. My grandfather, as he tried imagining his happiness on being once more with Sophie, had fantasized about scenes such as these. For the summer of his return, he had dreamt of taking her to 'some isolated seaside cottage where we could be on our own and go for long rambles above the cliffs.' For the more distant future he had visions of the two of them lying together on a boat 'somewhere out in the blue Pacific'.

We landed at a hamlet which resembled a Samuel Palmer painting of Shoreham Vale. Behind the wooden church a steep path climbed between hedgerows to Luis's farm at the top of the island, where I ate freshly caught salmon, and drank cider made in an old wooden press. Gradually, as I gained Luis's confidence, he started to tell me about the spirits of the dead.

They took the form of birds, he said, and there was a rare type of crow special to the area which harboured only the spirits of evil people. His father had known an old farmer from the mainland whose dead neighbour, an evil man, had come to haunt him in the guise of this bird. The farmer had taken out his gun and shot his 'resurrected neighbour', was cursed for doing so, and had soon afterwards lost his mind.

'But the spirits on La Lligua are all benign,' Luis reassured me, as we walked along an overgrown woodland path in the hour before sunset. Pushing through brambles to reach a grassy clearing at the island's perilous edge, we looked across the purple waters of the sea as they stretched without a wave towards a reddish horizon faintly etched with the white serrated profile of mountains and glaciers. 'My dead grandfather,' continued Luis, 'came back to visit us as a gull. Perhaps that's him up there.' A solitary bird hovered in circles high above us, taking in our earthly paradise before heading south, towards the Gulf of Sorrows.

★

I had come to Chiloe while waiting for the weekly ferry that would take me from nearby Puerto Montt to the southern tip of Patagonia. I was longing for a few days at sea, if only because I had reached a stage in my grandfather's story when I kept picturing him on the deck of a ship, searching in the water for 'feelings of calm and peace and repose', and perhaps for memories of January 1911, when he too had sailed through Patagonia's glacier-lined fjords, towards a future that was still innocent and uncomplicated.

My ship, the *Magallanes*, was scheduled to leave at five in the afternoon, and to arrive four days later at Puerto Natales, on the Sound of Last Hope. Its passengers, mainly young and foreign, and on the last stage of the backpacker's trail from Quito, assembled shortly after departure to be told by a smiling hostess about the journey's scenic high points, the activities and lectures planned, the 'Happy Sours' (two *pisco* sours for the price of one), and the possibility of expulsion from the boat in the case of 'unacceptable drunkenness'. I had no idea where the captain intended to leave any passengers misbehaving in this way. Over the next four days we would be passing only one place that was inhabited.

To the ominous drone of the engines, our Ship of Fools pursued its way south, between forested islands, alongside waterfalls, within sight of glaciers, past an abandoned Greek ship from the 1930s, through narrow channels bordered by rocks, and into the notorious Gulf of Sorrows, scourge of mariners. Dark clouds became our constant companions, dispersing slightly every so often to create rainbows and spectacular dawns, but then returning with increasing frequency to release violent rains that had the passengers going back into the lounge to read, play cards, exchange travel notes, and – as all this enforced intimacy began having its effect – talk about their lives, hopes and relationships.

I tried working out which of these people my grandfather would have thought 'interesting'; but I suspect they would not have included the prim young American woman in search of a boyfriend, nor the arrogant Old Wykehamist hoping to get disgracefully (though not 'unacceptably') 'sloshed', nor the brazen New Zealander with endless tales of 'fantastic sex', nor the bearded New Yorker wanting to give up his 'prestigious management' job and head out across the world on a Harley Davidson.

Bethel would probably have found something in common with Des, a deceptively serious-looking person who, alone of those on board, did not have a backpack. Des had come straight from a conference at Santiago on copyright laws in publishing, and was clearly not pleased to see my pirated copy of *The Trains are Headed to Purgatory*. A philosopher by training, he spent his time on the ship ignoring everybody else as much as he could, and giving token glances at the scenery before returning to the pages of a weighty book that I was keen to look at myself: it was about Gallipoli. On a night when the ship was rocking and rolling in the Bay of Sorrows, and most of the passengers had retired sick to their bunks, I managed to tear Des away from it, and to explain to him why its subject so interested me. My grandfather had fought there, I told him. Des took off his reading glasses, asked if I wanted a beer, and said he would like to hear the whole story 'from the beginning'.

The ship had sailed into Liverpool on the penultimate Sunday of August, three weeks after Britain had entered the war. Bethel, worn out by nerves, the journey, and the after-effects of malaria, prepared to go down on to the quay. He was half-expecting to see Sophie, or, at the very least, have news that she was on her way to meet him. But when he walked down the gangway, he found only his sister Louise waiting for him. Louise was obliged reluctantly to tell him that Sophie had left England and gone back to Dublin.

'I am back and you are not here,' he wrote the next day from Hull, 'not yet accessible! There is little else that fills my mind. I wonder if you can picture or imagine into what depths of bitter disappointment I am plunged.' In eight pages of desperate, self-pitying and uncharacteristically repetitive prose, he asked Sophie if she realized what it meant 'to have all the hopes I have cherished these last three years and still bright but a month ago crumble and fall like this.' To engage further her sympathies he ridiculously compared himself to a prisoner of the Spanish Inquisition who is given false hopes of freedom before being locked up again forever.

He spoke romantically of destroyed illusions while perhaps suffering more than anything from feelings of anticlimax. After all his adventures in the world of the sublime he was back in a Hull that must have appeared dreary and predictable. His mental tribulations in South America had in retrospect an element of drama and glamour which made them preferable to what he now faced: a never-ending greyness. Nothing excited him any more, least all the prospect of having to go to London shortly to collect his salary arrears from the company, and to look for another job. The war had made his chances of finding employment extremely slim; and the idea of being in London without Sophie was 'totally unbearable'. He thought that if he went there on his own to a concert he would certainly 'break down, not only through the recollection of your own beautiful voice but through a sheer sense of loneliness.'

Four days later, after Sophie had replied to this letter with an invitation on her mother's behalf to come and stay with them in Dublin, Bethel wrote back demanding total emotional honesty on her part: if she did not feel the same way about him as he did about her, it was better that they did not see each other again. He went to Dublin all the same and, as he would later apologetically admit, behaved there like a 'sighing lover' and 'gloomy old stodge'.

What he so urgently wanted was to be alone with Sophie; and this was rarely possible while he was a guest in her parents' house. On the few occasions they managed to have a proper talk together, Sophie confided that her parents, like his, were concerned about the medical wisdom of marriage between first cousins. The disgruntled Bethel told her soon afterwards of a plan that he had conceived out of a mixture of patriotism, despair and possible emotional blackmail: he intended to volunteer for the Engineering Corps of the British Army.

As a means of getting Sophie to confess her undying love for him, the plan worked. On 12 September he was writing to her from Hull to say that he was in a much 'chirpier mood', and how wrong he had been ever to have doubted her love. He also said he had been to a doctor, who had pronounced him to be generally fit but in need of rest so as to make a full recovery from malaria and be accepted for army training. More encouragingly, the doctor had discounted any idea that children born to first cousins ran a far greater risk than others of inheriting genetic defects.

On this man's advice Bethel took a holiday, and went to a cottage 'with gorgeous cliff and cove' near Tintagel in Cornwall. This was exactly the sort of place he had had in mind for his return from South America; but instead of going there with Sophie, he had to content himself with Louise. The beauty of the weather in the first few days helped him to maintain his recovered happiness, which, as ever, was 'crying out' only for Sophie's presence to make perfect.

To begin with he had every intention of 'resisting reading newspapers' and not troubling his mind with thoughts about the war. But the war was impossible to avoid. It was turning the world 'topsy-turvy', and having effects that were infiltrating even his rural retreat, and making it impossible to think too far into the future. 'I find it as difficult to think normally about anything, as one would to play the Moonlight Sonata in the middle of some great steelworks.'

He stayed in Cornwall until around the middle of October, by which time his malaria had 'pretty much left' him. By 22 October he was in Louise's Chelsea apartment in London, and had been accepted into the 'Engineer's Societies Battalion'. Two days later he was reporting for duty at 'Oxney Bottom Camp', near Dover.

Bethel's enrolment in His Majesty's Service involved numerous pages of justification to Sophie, who was not only the daughter of the former honorary Austro-Hungarian consul to Dublin, but also by now a fervent sympathizer of the Irish Republican Army. On the subject of Ireland's independence, Bethel fortunately revealed himself a more tolerant person than he had been while discussing the suffragettes. In fact he was largely in agreement with Sophie on this issue, and saw no contradiction between his support for a free Ireland and his touchingly innocent faith in the British Empire. 'I think that if Britain can pride itself on the principles by which she claims to have founded her world Empire, if it is really based on the "twin principles of liberty and diversity", she cannot logically resist Ireland's claim to autonomy.'

As for going to fight against Germany, Bethel said that though he, like Sophie, was 'naturally a very peacefully disposed individual', and opposed to 'anything of an aggressive nature', he was 'absolutely convinced of the necessity and duty of us to be fighting, not merely for the safety of our country, but because I believe this really will be the last great war, and that smaller and weaker states will henceforth be free from the menace of any great Power.'

Bethel embarked on his career in the army with much the same optimistic and idealistic spirit as he had shown when he had set off to South America. Camp life at Oxney Bottom and other places in southern England would also prove to have much in common with the life he had led in Chile and Bolivia, and would even reunite him with at least two people with whom he had worked in those countries.

'Curiously,' he wrote to Sophie on 26 October, 'one of the lieu-tenants in my Company is a man who was with the Antofagasta railways and whom I know quite well. He was an awful tough and hard case out there.'

Towards the end of the following month, he announced to her that he was about to be joined at another camp by one of his assistants on 'the right of way surveys' he had carried out on the Cochabamba line. 'As you observe,' he noted on 14 December, when writing to her in pouring rain after only three hours of sleep, 'I might almost be in Bolivia.'

But Bethel's time in Bolivia soon seemed an uninterrupted idyll in comparison to what he now had to put up with. Whereas then he had had 'a tent to myself and camp bed and other furniture to say nothing of servants', he found here that 'we are packed like sardines in a tiny tent', not provided with an overcoat, and 'having to make do with only two blankets despite it being devilishly chilly at night'.

'I never thought three months ago,' he later reflected, 'that I should ever find myself working all day with a pick and shovel, or having to clean my own boots, and sew my own buttons, etc.'

Nostalgia for his recent past soon took on a much broader dimen-sion. 'I find myself,' he observed in January from a camp at Walmer, 'weakly and foolishly regretting my lost freedom. As you know I loved the freedom that I enjoyed in South America and wrote to you more than once that I wanted to return there with you rather than remain in England.' What he remembered most was 'the wildness and gran-deur and yet withal the peace of those great mountains and one's nearness to nature'.

Camp life in wartime England had no such scenic distractions, and was merely making him a more exacting critic than ever. He said that England was 'bungling through this war business', and had no right to pat itself on the back for its military prowess. He was shocked by the inadequacy of the training he was receiving, the incompetence of

his officers, and the way that even the best-travelled of his fellow soldiers had remained as insular as everybody else, and completely
'unaffected and unaltered by their experiences' ('It may be,' he commented, 'that they have the gift of "forgetting" better than I have').
After weeks of being in a camp, the one 'interesting point' he seems
to have learnt (from a 'poorly delivered talk' of otherwise 'little interest') was 'the fact that today we are faced with entirely new conditions of warfare.'

In the meantime, news of how the war was progressing overseas
was sufficiently grim to break even the most optimistic spirits. The
accounts that Bethel was hearing at first and second hand 'of terrible scenes and atrocities', had made him doubt the existence of a
'God of love and mercy and justice', and were reinforcing the fatal-
ism that he had developed as a way of dealing with his own personal
situation. 'One's destiny,' he mused to Sophie at the end of 1914,
'must be ruled largely by inexorable Fate, over which one has no
control . . . And each one of us must work out his own salvation as
best he can.'

Bethel's pessimism continued to grow during January and February
1915. Though at no stage during his time in South America did he
ever stop to consider the possible negative effects of Western technol-
ogy, he began to do so now. After commenting on 'what a waste of
human energy and intellect this war is', he concluded that 'it is engineering science that is making it so dreadful.' He despaired at the
thought of all the appliances that had been devised by engineers for
the 'sole purpose of destroying our fellow man, and laying waste to
the country'.

By late February he was not even confident any more that 'this war
will be the last great war . . . Despite thousands of instants of personal
devotion, self-sacrifice, patience and other virtues, no clear step
forward in the progress of the human race seems to be foreshadowed
by this titanic struggle.'

Unlike Rupert Brooke, he had lost any notions he might once have
had of the glamour of being killed while fighting for Britain. 'I think
that when my time comes, as it must some day, I would forego all the
vaunted glory of death in the field of battle for a last gaze on some
glorious and untroubled view.'

The time was approaching at last for his battalion to be sent to the front. The original rumours were that they would be going to France, and would not be doing so until the late spring at the earliest; but it seemed now as if this date was being put forward to early March, and that their destination was Egypt.

All Bethel now asked for was to see Sophie again before heading off to ponder further the 'riddle of human destiny'. Since coming back from South America he had only been with her during those unsatisfactory few days in Dublin. War and the possibility of being killed made it more imperative now than ever that they should be together again, but away this time from their interfering families. He had also been sufficiently emboldened by circumstances to bring up a subject hitherto untouched in their correspondence. A full 'sharing of feelings', he wrote, as he begged her to come and spend a weekend with him in London, 'is really impossible until there is also complete possession and the consummation of physical love.'

However, new obstacles soon presented themselves. German sub-marines in the Irish Channel made the crossing from Dublin a dangerous one; and Bethel was not keen for Sophie to take any risks. Though Sophie herself was quite prepared to do so, the letter in which she announced her firm intention of coming to London was delayed in the post. By the time it arrived Bethel had already spent his few days of leave, and was back in camp at Walmer. 'I take it for granted,' he sighed, 'that the time will come when we look back at this long period of waiting and disappointment as a sort of bad dream.'

In his last letter before departing for Egypt, Bethel did all that he could to put Sophie's mind at rest. The war, he said, would be over in twelve months at the most ('not a long time'), and his life was unlikely to be in any danger. 'You mustn't feel anxious about me, dearest, I don't think they'll give our unit very ticklish work to do, and anyhow I don't think the Turks will prove very troublesome in Egypt.'

The next surviving letter from Bethel was sent nearly a year later from an unspecific location in what he called 'Mesopotamia'. In the intervening period he taken part in the militarily inept Dardanelles campaign, which had just reached its indecisive conclusion after the un-troublesome Turks had succeeded in killing 213,800 British and Commonwealth troops. But the sole troubles to which Bethel referred in his letter were ones Sophie had been having with her throat, and which were now fortunately cleared. The only other news he had to report was the safe arrival of a package containing 'asparagus, cake, chocolate, writing pad, paper and a book of verse'.

Bethel, in later life, would never speak in any detail about his months in Gallipoli; and the fate of the many letters he must surely have written from there is an irresolvable mystery. The one time during the war he wrote in passing about the 'Gallipoli show' was to urge Sophie to read a book by a 'French medical officer' entitled *Uncensored Letters from the Dardanelles*. However, he warned her, 'the author does pile on the agony; one would think that they lived under a continuous rain of shells.' Bethel added that from his own experiences of the French camp this was not the case at all.

Military censorship perhaps partially dictated the defensive tone that Bethel now took towards the war, and the way he played down as much as possible its horrors. Having written so negatively about the war before sailing off to Egypt, he now began soundly berating Sophie from Mesopotamia for describing it as 'senseless'. Later, and perhaps as a way of giving some meaning to all the sufferings he had witnessed, he wrote to express his conviction that 'the dawn of a new era is breaking, and that the generations to come will be happier and will have learnt from this great cataclysm the curse of false patriotism.'

When he penned those words, in February 1917, he was in a hospital in the Eritrean town of Asmara, laid up with a leg wound that he tried to make light of. To continue his convalescence he was shipped off a few days later to Bombay, where he and his fellow wounded soldiers were visited by local celebrities 'who all tried to be very charming but were really a wee bit boring'. By 8 March he was finally in a fit enough state to return to England for a well-deserved leave.

He should have been blissfully happy; but the letter he wrote to Sophie on the voyage back revealed a disturbed state of mind. For several weeks now he had been repeatedly mulling over a piece of news relayed to him shortly after he himself had been injured. His best friend in the battalion, a man called Brydon, had been 'hideously killed' in Mesopotamia while carrying out a 'wiring job'. Brydon, who had previously worked as an engineer in Nigeria, was someone different in character to Bethel. He was not an 'analytical' person, nor was he able to give voice to his inner feelings. 'And yet the knowledge that we had both gone through adventures in strange countries before the war formed the basis of a mutual sympathy.'

On arrival back in England, Bethel was diagnosed as suffering from shell-shock. Sophie came over to visit him at the rest home outside London where he was being treated. And the resolution to seven years of frustrated longings finally came about, though not in the spectacular Hollywood style that such a long build-up might have suggested. The two lovers were married in a simply ceremony performed in the hospital chapel, with only a few close members of the family in attendance. There was no honeymoon, just a slow recovery from traumas and nightmares, and Bethel's eventual return to duty in July 1917.

'And what happened to him then?' asked Des, my fellow passenger on the *Magallanes*, no doubt feeling somewhat cheated by so flat an ending to the lovers' tale.

I wanted to humour him by inventing some melodramatic postscript in which a soldier turns up at the door of a now pregnant Sophie with the news that Captain Bethel Lyon Jacobs, a man greatly loved by all who knew him, and universally respected as an engineer, had been killed in action while valiantly trying to save the life of his former assistant on the Antofagasta railway. But in the end all I said was, 'Nothing very much.'

Bethel would spend much of the rest of the war in France, where he sat down every night with pen and paper to have what he liked to think of as 'a long talk' with 'Mrs B. L. Jacobs', relaying to her all the often trivial occurrences couples tell each other at the end of a working day. Discharged finally in the spring of 1919, he settled down with Sophie to a quiet married life in England, where their first son, my uncle, was born soon afterwards. There was just one last great journey ahead of him.

With their baby only a few months old, Bethel was offered a job building a railway across China's Gobi desert. Sophie, determined to be with him this time, would later tell me stories of the remote corner of China where they set up home. She talked to me of my father's birth at a place miles away from any doctor; of the nanny whose previous position had been 'back-scratcher to the Imperial Dowager'; and of the time when they got back to their isolated desert house to find that all their servants had been decapitated by marauding bandits.

China, my grandfather had then decided, was perhaps not such a suitable place in which to raise a family. Reluctantly Sophie took herself and her children back to England, while Bethel stayed on for a further year, to witness the collapse of one of his bridges after a train had been sent prematurely over it. His letters from this period are the last of his that I possess.

From this point onwards, Bethel begins rapidly to fade in my perception. After his return from China in 1924 he seems never to have been employed again, though he did apply for a job with Spanish Railways which, had he got it, would have made him an employee of Alfred Löwy, the uncle of Franz Kafka. For most of his remaining years he lived at 30 Meadway where, thanks to a posthumous act of generosity on the part of Uncle Charles, he was able to lead the sort of life he might have thought of as the reward for all his ordeals, until this too was disturbed by the Second World War and the onset of Parkinson's. Perhaps he might then have tried to focus his mind once more on what he called 'the ceaseless murmur of the sea', and on a 'rocky shore undefiled by the hand of man, besides which all the history of human passions and endeavours is but of a moment's duration.'

Des was once again buried in his book, and the ship was sailing through a landscape of rocky islands half-hidden by the clouds. Then the boat's siren sounded, and the sky opened for a few moments to expose a group of tin-roofed wooden shacks scattered beneath a distant snowy peak. We had emerged from limbo to arrive at Puerto Eden, an inappropriately named settlement of Keshawagi Indians. As in films of Pacific voyages of old, our ship was instantly surrounded by boats rowed by native islanders inviting us ashore.

A slippery wooden walkway encircled this quagmire of an island, where the rains and the snows never stopped, according to the man who had rowed me there. He also told me that the last two years had been affected by the notorious 'red tide', which had poisoned the fishes that were the island's livelihood, and had driven most of the men down to the ports of the extreme south. The women, it seemed, had been reduced to the ineffectual selling of seashells to the weekly boat-loads of tourists.

On the man's suggestion I went to see the village schoolteacher, Ana Rosa. A plump, lively woman, she said how rare it was that people came to talk to her.

'Tourists arrive, take photos of us as if we were anthropological specimens, and then go away.'

She had become the main spokesman of the Keshawagis and wanted to teach the traditions and language of her people before there was nothing left to teach.

'We'd been surviving in terrible conditions for 500 years. And then outsiders came, exploiting our few resources, and bringing pneumonia, diphtheria, syphilis and all manner of diseases.'

I asked her how many Keshawagi speakers there were still left. 'There are just five of us,' she answered with a melancholy smile, pressing into my hand a piece of paper in which she had written the email address of her school. 'Please keep in touch,' she urged. 'It's so important that people remember us.' I put the paper in my trouser pocket; but then a downpour came when I was being rowed back to the ship, and the water soaked through my clothes, obliterating completely the address of the last teacher of the Keshawagi language.

The ship sailed on through intermittent rains until the journey's end approached, and a last night's party was held at which Bingo was played, and the Old Wykehamist finally achieved his aim of getting senselessly drunk. The passengers, tired and hung-over the following morning, filed down the gangway at Puerto Natales to enjoy the welcoming sight of a giant bay fringed with sunlit white mountains. There were hugs and kisses and a few tears as everyone dispersed, eventually to join the last of the season's tourists heading towards the promised peaks and lakes and 'gorgeous blue' icebergs of the National Park of the Torres del Peine.

My ultimate destination was Punta Arenas, on the Straits of Magellan. It was the last important town before Antarctica, and the first place in Chile my grandfather had seen. To him it was a 'queer little town that seems largely to be composed of the consulates of all nationalities, hotels and small pubs.' He explored the place with his friend Dr Sturdy, and had 'a very good lunch' at the Hotel de France, where they were the guests of the Uruguayan consul. 'Punta Arenas,' he concluded, 'had a fairly attractive appearance from the distance and that was all we could say for it. It must be a terrible place to live in during the winter, when it is frightfully cold.'

I had no clear image of what Punta Arenas would be like today, and had been made none the wiser by Bruce Chatwin's celebrated *In Patagonia*, which had done so much to reinforce notions of the exotic strangeness of this 'uttermost part of the earth' without attempting to give much of a physical sense of the place. I had vague notions of land-scapes as uniformly spectacular as those of the Torres del Peine, and towns of an almost surreal end-of-the-world pathos. The approach to Puerto Arenas from Puerto Natales showed me another side to Patagonia for which I was barely prepared. Under a low sky at dusk, the flat damp expanse that seemed to make up most of this region made me think that I was not really in South America at all but back in Yorkshire, driving beside the Humber.

As I walked in the freezing winds through the streets of Punta Arenas itself, this prosaic sensation of returning to the land of my fore-bears continued to grow. The inappropriately dressed Saturday night revellers, the pompously eclectic late nineteenth-century architecture, and the way the buildings boldly defied the bleak environment to flout the values of an era convinced of its own greatness – all this was uncannily like the place where I had started my journey. I had been to the end of the world, and had found myself in Hull.

In the morning I went straightaway to Punta Arenas's best known attraction, which, typically for Chile, happened to be the cemetery. It had rows of beautifully clipped hedges and cypresses, and a wealth of well-kept tombs and mausoleums dating back to those twenty years in Punta Arenas's history (before the opening of the Panama Canal) when sheep farming and control of the trade routes had created huge fortunes, expanded the town sevenfold, and made it the first place in Chile to have electric lighting.

For an hour or so I paced up and down the cemetery's alleys, obses-sively reading the names, ages and nationalities on all the plaques and headstones. At one point, as I hastily pushed aside a bunch of recently placed flowers, I thought that I had uncovered the true whereabouts of my namesake 'Miguel Jacobs'. In my excitement, however, I had misread 'Michelle' for 'Miguel'. A few minutes later my heart missed another beat. I found the tomb of a Jacobs whose dates seemed from a distance to be those of my grandfather, and who also had the initials B. L.; but, looking closer, the dates were a few years out, and the initials stood for Brendan Leonard. Then, further on, I came across a feature I had never noticed before in any cemetery: the recording of the exact time of death, or 'Hour of Expiry'. The person in question happened to be an Irishwoman who had died at 02.37, the precise moment of my grandmother's death, and the time at which the clock at 30 Meadway had inexplicably stopped.

I had no idea of what I was hoping to find at this concluding stage of my journey. Some message from the dead? Some resolution to the mystery surrounding my elusive Bolivian namesake? The reawakening of my grandfather's spirit? A meeting with the woman with the glass eye? Perhaps I was looking for the sort of supernatural ending only to be encountered in the pages of a South American novel.

As I left the cemetery to walk back to the town centre, I recalled a Spanish expression often used by my grandfather in the letters written after his return to Europe. It was an expression appropriate for someone no longer certain about anything, and which also seemed pertinent to my own mood as I occupied my few remaining hours before flying away from Punta Arenas and from South America: '*Quien sabe*'. 'Who knows?'

Perhaps I owed more to my grandfather than I had ever realized until now. Perhaps his years of longing for a woman who must have seemed, at times, like a figment of his imagination had been transformed in his grandson into a life lived more in daydreams than in reality. Perhaps the epic scale of his love for my grandmother had set standards that would leave me with a permanent sense of yearning that could never be satisfied. *Quien sabe*.

If there was one certain factor other than blood that tied me to Bethel, it was our mutual obsession with Sophie. As I dutifully visited all of Punta Arenas's sights, I began wondering if the ultimate reason for my retracing Bethel's footsteps had been to lead me closer to her. I thought of her now more than ever as a companion beyond the grave, as someone whose extraordinary passion for life had done so much to fuel my own.

So many of the memories I had of her in her last years were expressive of her defiance of mortality: her absolute denial of her age; her refusal to lose her independence; her misguided belief to the very end in her brilliance as a driver; her drinking of champagne on the day she died; and her radiant apparition at the 'hour of expiry' – a memory that would later help me to overcome the chilling sense of finality I would feel at my father's death.

Sophie was now so much on my mind that I was beginning to have the delusions that lovers have, that Bethel had. An old woman with blue-rinsed hair flashed past me as I went off to look for the 'Victorian parsonage' bought by Bruce Chatwin's great-uncle Charlie Milward; and I was sure that this same person was later in the building where I tracked down some of the bones and fossilized turds of the prehistoric 'milodon', the inspiration behind Chatwin's own journey to Patagonia – the creature had fascinated him ever since he had seen a fragment of it in his grandmother's English home.

Everything in Punta Arenas seemed to be conspiring to remind me of Sophie, even the local history museum, which was housed in a building that had had belonged to a family of local worthies reminiscent of my Yorkshire ancestors. The furniture was all English, and the kitchen had old tins of curry powder and Lipton's tea, and a venerable bottle of Lea and Perrin's sauce. On the coffee table in the living room there was a mah-jong set, described in an adjacent panel as 'an ancient Chinese game made popular in the West by British expatriates in Shanghai'. And in the background was a mahogany tea trolley, identical in my imagination to the one I remembered from Sunday afternoons at 30 Meadway.

The image I had retained of Sophie seated behind this trolley was so exceptionally vivid that I almost believed she was in front of me now. I saw her frozen in the act of pouring out a cup of tea, giving me that knowing look she usually did when I came down from the attic. Her wavy hair was streaked with blue, but her expression was unchanged from the days when she had been 'the Innocent from Ireland'.

Sophie was waiting for me at the end of my journey as she had waited for Bethel. I had so much to tell her about the marvels I had seen, and the people I had met; and, if I had not been so inhibited by my Englishness, I might perhaps have added how deeply I still missed her. But all I could mutter were some words I had just read on a tomb: 'Until we meet again!'

Acknowledgements

Following my grandfather's lonely path to South America should by rights have been a profoundly solitary experience. That it was far from being so is a testimony to the many new friends I have made in the course of this book's gestation, and to the unfailing helpfulness of all those whom I have encountered on the way. To begin with I must acknowledge my enormous debt to Antofagasta PLC, in particular to the company's former director, Lord Montgomery of Alamein, and to the present director Philip Adeane, who took a great interest in this project, and provided me with essential contacts in Chile. I am also very grateful to the company's archivist, Andrew Bernard, for looking after me so well in the old Finsbury Circus offices, and for patiently combing all the records in search of references to my grandfather and his colleagues.

In Hull I received much assistance from Geoffrey Boland and the staff of the public reference library, from Arthur G. Credland of the Maritime Museum and from the staff of the Judeo-Christian Society, and above all from the unfailingly friendly and enthusiastic Doug Smelt.

As readers of this book will gather, I was made instantly welcome in Chile by Gonzalo Donoso and his wife Geraldine, whose remarkable kindness and hospitality were particularly appreciated by someone timidly setting out on an ambitious trip. A similar generosity was shown by Gonzalo's father Gonzalo Donoso Yáñez, who introduced me to Chilean culture and tradition in a way I shall never forget, and who was the most attentive of hosts at La Retama de Catapilco.

My writer friend Carlos Franz, grandson of a Swiss engineer working on the Transandino, has been an important source of information about Chile, and was responsible, among other things, for putting me in touch with Alonso Barros and his wife Emmanuelle, who made my first stay at San Pedro de Atacama such a pleasurable one, and gave me much insight into local life and customs. Yenko Morage was an excellent and thorough guide at Antofagasta and Mejillones, while the writer Hernán Rivera Letelier and his novels helped open my eyes to the poetic reality of the region. For such diverse contributions as discussing the mining industry at Chuquicamata, volunteering to find out whether my grandfather was a member of Antofagasta's Masonic lodge, and supplying necessary light relief at Calama, I am grateful respectively to Dr Francisco Javier Rivera Flores, Miguel Gausachs P., and Mathieu Chamagne and Axelle Bochelen. But my special thanks in Chile's 'Great North' must go to the enlightened Miguel Sepúlveda and to all his staff at the F.C.A.B., notably Victor Maldonado, Carmen Bailey, Jorge Zlatar Varas, Jorge Lyons, Fuad A. Yaksic Daud and Rolando Henriquez.

In Chile's south I enjoyed the lively company and conversation of both Juan Eladio Susaeta and the Chiloe-based architect and scholar Edward Rojas. The wise and funny Des Brennan from London travelled with me to the far south of Patagonia, a trip that was facilitated by María Eliana Valenzuela of Navimag, and by the urbane Alfonso Luna Andrades, director of the Antofagasta office of LanChile, who kindly arranged for me to have a free flight back to Santiago from Punta Arenas.

My briefest of visits to Peru was made memorable by Meriel Larkin, the owner and indefatigable restorer of the Lake Titicaca steamer, the *Yavari*, to whom I had been introduced by my old Irish friend John O'Keeffe. I am grateful to her, to her assistant Giselle Guldentops Benavides, and to the ship's pensive captain Carlos Saavedra de Carpio.

The Bolivian part of my journey would have been infinitely less rewarding had it not been for the director of Bolivian railways (F.C.B.), Eduardo MacLean Abaroa, who, among many other kindnesses, put me in touch with the engineering company in charge of Bolivia's railway network, SOCAIRE. The latter's role in my journey proved critical, and I cannot express enough my gratitude to the company's director Carlos Teran Pol, and to staff members Querubino Rivero Arias, Adolfo Rico San Martín, and my great companion in danger Ricardo Rosales Muñoz, without whom I might not still be alive. I must also thank Ricardo's wife Susana Miranda, and their son Mauricio Rosales Miranda, who first fired in me a passion for Bolivia's carnival music.

Among the others in La Paz whose help and friendship I have greatly valued are Denise Arnold, Ian Mare, and Juan de Dios Yapita of the Aymara Institute, and the two radically different 'Paceñas', Macri Bastos and Amparo Kohlberg. In Potosí I benefited greatly from the scholarship of Carlos Serrano, the exceptional amiability of the president of the Club Internacional, Rogier Fr. Subieta C, and from the support of the organization PRAH. The latter's energetic director, Luis Prado Ríos, had every door opened for me in the city, while his assistant Shirley Marcela James cheerfully guided me through many of its monuments.

One of the great joys of researching this book has been discovering the descendents of my grandfather's friends and acquaintances in South America, specifically the Galindos of Cochabamba and the Soux family of Potosí. My meeting in London with Susana Sánchez de Lozada was the catalyst to my getting to know such members of the Galindo family as her mother Julia, her cousins Rosemarie and Pablo Barrientos and her uncle Arturo. Enquiries about the magnificent Hacienda Cayara on the outskirts of Potosí led me to Edgar Soux and Arturo Layton, whose courtesy, wit and knowledge were clearly qualities inherited from their own grandfather, the redoubtable Luis Soux.

The love I developed for Bolivia was finally consolidated in Sucre, the native city of Humberto Barron, co-founder of the exemplary agency Magic of Bolivia, and someone whose boundless optimism and enthusiasm make him a man very much after my own heart: he proved a saviour during my troubled return visit to his country in the winter of 2005. Also in Sucre I greatly benefited from the efficient staff at Bolivia's National Library, and from the knowledge of local writer Felipe Medina Espada. But my exceptionally fond memories of the city are due especially to Jorge and Karina Barrera, Silvia Octavia Pizza Tito and Marbel and Oswald Garrón Gonzales and all their family. The close friendship we established has been a great sustaining force even after my return to Europe.

Back in London I have enjoyed many conversations about South America with Carmen Suárez, Cristina Fuentes, Gina Marsh and Bob Goodwin, and received useful tips from James Read, author of the excellent *Rough Guide to Bolivia*. In Seville, Magdalena Torres Hidalgo, Nicolás Ramírez and Felix Pozo kept me up to date with the activities of the Junta de Andalucía in Chile and Bolivia. While writing this book in my adopted Andalucían village of Frailes, my spirits were constantly maintained by my large circle of local friends, including Manuel Ruiz López ('El Sereno'), Santiago Campos, José Chica, Paqui Machuca, Juan Antonio Díaz, Chris and Ana Stewart, Juan Matias and family, Manolo Caño, the Dornillo society, and Merce García Castillo and all her fellow 'Pajaricos'. Distraction and companionship has also been provided by my Spanish mastiff Chumberry ('Chumba').

This book was first commissioned by Caroline Knox, whose encouragement and advice I have always enormously appreciated. I have also been very lucky with my two subsequent editors at John Murray: Gordon Wise helped greatly to polish the manuscript, while Eleanor Birne brought the book to publication. Invaluable technical assistance was supplied by computer genius Christopher Robin, the son of one of my most diehard supporters, Charles Krumheim. My thanks as well to Cathy Benwell, Caro Westmore, Sam Evans and Roland Philipps; to my loyal editor friend of many years James Hughes; and to my agent David Godwin, and to his assistants Sarah Savitt and Sophie Hoult.

Finally, in a book dealing to a large extent with my roots, my greatest debt of all must be to my own family, including to my newly found relations Arthur and Ruth Walker and Susan Solomons. Jackie Rae, though often far away from me in person, is always by my side in spirit, and helped keep me going during some of my more difficult moments in South America. My patient and understanding uncle Brendan Jacobs has enlightened me with his many memories of his father, as has my mother Mariagrazia. My own late father, after suffering so many frustrations in trying to see Bethel's letters published, would have been delighted to know that his efforts had not been entirely in vain. Without my grandparents, Bethel Jacobs and Sophie (née Solomons), this book would, of course, not have existed. I have dedicated it to their memory, and to my niece and god-daughter Sophie, most ardent of readers.

Select Bibliography

Aramayo Ávila, Césareo, *Ferrocarriles Bolivianos: Pasado, Presente, Futuro*, La Paz, 1959

Aarons, John, and Vita-Finzi, Claudio, *The Useless Land: A Winter in the Atacama*, London, 1960

Allende, Isabel, *My Invented Country: A Memoir*, London, 2003

Anderson, Jon Lee, *Che Guevara: A Revolutionary Life*, London, 1997

Baeriswyl Rada, Dante, *Arquitectura en Punta Arenas: Primeras edificaciones en ladrillo, 1892–1935*, Punta Arenas, 2004

Bayo, Ciro, *El peregrino en Indias*, Madrid, 1912

Beckett, Andy, *Pinochet in Piccadilly: Britain and Chile's Hidden History*, London, 2002

Blakemore, Harold, *British Nitrates and Chilean Politics, 1886–1896*, London, 1974

——*From the Pacific to La Paz: The Antofagasta (Chili) and Bolivia Railway Company 1888–1988*, London, 1990

Bowman, Isaiah, *Desert Trails of Atacama*, New York, 1924

Burton, Anthony, *The Railway Empire*, London, 1994

Carlyon, L. A., *Gallipoli*, London, 2002

Chatwin, Bruce, *In Patagonia*, London, 1977

Collier, Simon, and Sater, William F., *A History of Chile, 1808–1994*, Cambridge, 1996

Coloane, Francisco, *Sus mejores cuentos*, Santiago de Chile, 1997

Credland, Arthur G., *Artists and Craftsmen of Hull and East Yorkshire*, Kingston-upon-Hull, 2000

Darwin, Charles, *Voyage of the Beagle*, London, 1839

Dorfman, Ariel, *Desert Memories: Journeys Through the Chilean North*, Washington, DC, 2004

Fawcett, Brian, *Railways of the Andes*, London, 1963

——*Steam in the Andes*, Truro, 1973

Feinstein, Adam, *Pablo Neruda: A Passion for Life*, London, 2004

Fifer, J. Valerie, *Bolivia: Land, Location and Politics Since 1825*, Cambridge, 1972

Finestein, Israel, *Scenes and Personalities in Anglo-Irish Jewry, 1800–2000*, London, 2002

Geddes, Charles F., *Patiño: The Tin King*, London, 1972

Galindo Granchant, Eduardo, *Crónicas de un soldado cuando nos enfrentamos al Che*, Cochabamba, 2001

Gillet, Edward, and Macmahon, Kenneth A., *A History of Hull*, Kingston-upon-Hull, 1980

Goodall, D. (ed.), *Aspects of Hull's History*, Kingston-upon-Hull, 2003

Granado, Alberto, *Travelling with Che Guevara: The Making of a Revolutionary*, London, 2003

Guevara, Ernesto Che, *The Motorcycle Diaries*, London, 2004

Guevara, Ernesto Che and Waters, Mary-Alice, *The Bolivian Diary of Ernesto Che Guevara*, New York, 1994

Guise, A. V. L., *Six Years in Bolivia: The Adventures of a Mining Engineer*, London, 1922

Hemming, John, *The Conquest of the Incas*, London, 1983

Horne, Alistair, *Small Earthquake in Chile*, London, 1972 (rev. 1990)

Jordison, Sam, and Kieran, Dan, *The Idler Book of Crap Towns: The 50 Worst Places to Live in the UK*, London, 2003

Junta de Andalucía, *Potosí, Bolivia: Guía de Arquitectura*, Seville, 2004

Kamen, Henry, *Spain's Road to Empire: The Making of a World Power, 1492–1763*, London, 2002

Keogh, Dermot, *Jews in Twentieth-Century Ireland: Refugees, Anti-Semitism and the Holocaust*, Cork, 1998

Klein, Herbert S., *Parties and Political Change in Bolivia, 1880–1952*, Cambridge, 1969

——*Bolivia, The Evolution of a Multi-Ethnic Society*, Oxford, 1992

Koebbel, W. H., *Modern Chile*, London, 1913

Lamb, Simon, *Devil in the Mountain: A Search for the Origin of the Andes*, Princeton, 2004

Long, W. Rodney, *Railways of South America, Part III*, Washington, 1930

Lora, Guillermo, *A History of the Bolivian Labour Movement*, Cambridge, 1977

Mair, Craig, *The Life and Adventures of a Victorian Railway Engineer*, Stevenage, 1981

Maitland, Francis, *Chile: Its Land and People*, London, 1914

Mesa, José de, and Gisbert, Teresa, *Monumentos de Bolivia*, La Paz, 2002

Mesa, José de; Gisbert, Teresa, and Mesa Gisbert, Carlos D., *Historia de Bolivia*, La Paz, 2003

Mörner, Magnus, *The Andean Past: Land, Societies and Conflicts*, New York, 1985

Mouat, Francisco, *El empapado Riquelme*, Santiago de Chile, 2001

Neruda, Pablo, *Selected Poems* (Nathaniel Tarn ed.), London, 1970

——*Memoirs,* London, 1977

Prescott, William, *History of the Conquest of Peru*, New York, 1847

Read, James, *The Rough Guide to Bolivia*, London, 2002

Rivera Letelier, Hernán, *La Reina Isabel cantaba rancheras*, Santiago de Chile, 1994

——*Fatamorgana de amor con banda de música*, Santiago de Chile, 1998

——*Los trenes se van al Purgatorio*, Santiago de Chile, 2000

Rosen, Lionel, *A Short History of the Jewish Community in Hull*, Kingston-upon-Hull, 1956

Sheahan, J. J., *History of the Town and Port of Kingston-upon-Hull* (2nd edn), Beverley, 1866

Spitzer, Leo, *Hotel Bolivia: The Culture of Memory in a Refuge from Nazism*, New York, 1998

Swinglehurst, Edward, *Silver Mines and Incidents of Travel*, Kendal, 1893

Thomson, Ian, *Red Norte: The Story of State-owned Railways in Northern Chile*, Birmingham, 1997

Thomson, Ian, and Angerstein, Dietrich, *Historia del ferrocarril en Chile*, Santiago de Chile, 2000

Titus, A., *Monografía de los ferrocarriles particulares de Chile*, Valparaíso, 1910

Turistel, *La guía turística de Chile: Norte*, Santiago de Chile, 2004

Turistel, *La guía turística de Chile: Sur*, Santiago de Chile, 2004

Tschiffely, Aimé, *Tschiffely's Ride*, London, 1933

Universidad José Santos Ossa, *Geografía poética de la region de Antofagasta*, Antofagasta, 2003

Vázquez de Acuña, Isidoro, *Santería de Chiloé*, Santiago de Chile, 1995

Vicuña Urrutia, Manuel, *La imagen del desierto de Atacama, (XVI–XIX): Del espacio de la dissuasion al territorio de los desafíos*, Santiago de Chile, 1995

Walle, Paul, *La Bolivie et ses mines*, Paris, 1913

Williamson, Edwin, *The Penguin History of Latin America*, London, 1992

Wilson, Jason, *Traveller's Literary Companion to South and Central America*, Brighton, 1993